CONSTITUTIONAL FOUNDINGS IN SOUTH ASIA

This volume addresses the idea of origins, how things are formed, and how they relate to their present and future in terms of 'constitution-making' which is a continuous process in South Asian states. It examines the drafting, nature, core values and roles of the first modern constitutions during the founding of the eight modern nation-states in South Asia.

The book looks at the constitutions of Afghanistan, Bangladesh, Bhutan, India, Maldives, Nepal, Pakistan and Sri Lanka. It provides an explanatory description of the process and substantive inputs in the making of the first constitutions of these nations; it sets out to analyse the internal and external (including intra-regional) forces surrounding the making of these constitutions; and it sets out theoretical constructions of models to conceptualise the nature and role of the first constitutions (including constituent documents) in the founding of the modern nation-states and their subsequent impact on state-building in the region.

Constitutionalism in Asia series

NUS National University of Singapore | Centre for Asian Legal Studies Faculty of Law

Constitutional Foundings in South Asia

Edited by
Kevin YL Tan
and
Ridwanul Hoque

•HART•
OXFORD • LONDON • NEW YORK • NEW DELHI • SYDNEY

HART PUBLISHING

Bloomsbury Publishing Plc

Kemp House, Chawley Park, Cumnor Hill, Oxford, OX2 9PH, UK

1385 Broadway, New York, NY 10018, USA

HART PUBLISHING, the Hart/Stag logo, BLOOMSBURY and the Diana logo are trademarks of Bloomsbury Publishing Plc

First published in Great Britain 2021

A catalogue record for this book is available from the British Library.

Library of Congress Cataloging-in-Publication data

Names: Tan, Kevin, editor. | Hoque, Ridwanul, editor.

Title: Constitutional foundings in South Asia / edited by Kevin YL Tan and Ridwanul Hoque.

Description: Oxford, UK ; New York, NY : Hart Publishing, an imprint of Bloomsbury Publishing, 2021. | Series: Constitutionalism in Asia series | Includes bibliographical references and index.

Identifiers: LCCN 2020038526 (print) | LCCN 2020038527 (ebook) | ISBN 9781509930258 (hardback) | ISBN 9781509944033 (paperback) | ISBN 9781509930265 (Epub) | ISBN 9781509930272 (pdf)

Subjects: LCSH: Constitutional law—South Asia—History.

Classification: LCC KNC524 .C654 2021 (print) | LCC KNC524 (ebook) | DDC 342.54—dc23

LC record available at https://lccn.loc.gov/2020038526

LC ebook record available at https://lccn.loc.gov/2020038527

ISBN: HB: 978-1-50993-025-8
ePDF: 978-1-50993-027-2
ePub: 978-1-50993-026-5

Typeset by Compuscript Ltd, Shannon

Contents

List of Contributors

Kevin YL TAN is one of Singapore's leading constitutional law scholars and its foremost legal historian. He graduated from the Faculty of Law of the National University of Singapore with an LLB (Hons) and obtained his LLM and JSD from the Yale Law School. He specialises in constitutional and administrative law, the Singapore legal system, law and society, legal history and human rights. He is the author and editor of over 50 books on the law, history and politics of Singapore, including *Constitutionalism in Asia* (Hart, 2014); *The Singapore Constitution: A Contextual Analysis* (Hart, 2015); and *Constitutional Foundings in Southeast Asia* (Hart, 2019). He is currently Adjunct Professor at the Faculty of Law, National University of Singapore and Professor at the S Rajaratnam School of International Studies, Nanyang Technological University. He is also Editor-in-Chief of the *Asian Journal of Comparative Law* and Consulting Editor of the *Asian Yearbook of International Law*.

Ridwanul HOQUE is a Professor of Law at the University of Dhaka and a University Fellow at Northern Institute, Charles Darwin University, Australia. He had earlier taught at the University of Chittagong in Bangladesh. He has studied law at the Universities of Chittagong, Cambridge, and London and has held visiting positions at Cornell Law School, Melbourne Law School, La Trobe University, and National Law University, Delhi. Professor Hoque has been recently awarded IASH-Alwaleed Research Fellowship at Edinburgh University for January–March 2021, to do research on mass denationalisation. A leading scholar of the Bangladeshi constitutional law, he specialises in South Asian and comparative constitutional law. As a foreign law expert, he has written over a dozen expert reports for the UK, US, and Australian courts on various issues including citizenship and torts. He has an extensive experience of consultancy in the areas of children's rights, labour migration, and human trafficking. He is the author of *Judicial Activism in Bangladesh: A Golden Mean Approach* (Cambridge Scholars, UK, 2011).

CONTRIBUTORS

AFGHANISTAN—**Ebrahim AFSAH** is a Professor of Islamic law at the Department of European, International and Comparative Law at the Faculty of Law of the University of Vienna. He is currently on leave as an Associate Professor of Public International Law at the Faculty of Law of the University of

Copenhagen, and a Visiting Professor of International Relations at the University of Brest, France. He has been trained at the Universities of London, Dublin and Harvard, and the Max Planck Institute for International Law in Heidelberg. Prior to his academic posts, he worked for many years on state-building and legal and administrative reform, especially in Afghanistan. In recent years, he has won fellowships to the European University Institute in Florence (Fernand Braudel), the Norwegian Academy of Science (Nordic Civil Wars), Harvard Law School (Islamic Legal Studies Program) and the National University of Singapore (Centre for Asian Legal Studies). He is a keen photographer and lives with a dog called Yoda.

BANGLADESH—**Ridwanul HOQUE.**

BHUTAN—**Winnie BOTHE** is an independent scholar. She was educated in Denmark where she attended Aarhus University and obtained her PhD from the University of Copenhagen for her thesis – *Forming Local Citizens in Bhutan: The Traditionalization of Participation – Empowerment, Domination or Subjugation?* She was formerly a post-doctoral fellow at the University of Lund. Winnie is the author of 'The Monarch's Gift: Critical Notes on the Bhutanese Constitutional Process' (2012) 40 *European Bulletin of Himalayan Research* 27–59; and 'In the Name of King, Country, and the People on the Westminster Model and Bhutan's Constitutional Transition' (2015) 22(7) *Democratization* 1338–1361.

MALDIVES—**Shamsul FALAAH** is an expert on Maldivian constitutional law and a researcher on Islamic constitutionalism. He obtained his PhD from the University of Auckland, New Zealand. He also holds an LLM in International Human Rights and Humanitarian Law from the European University Viadrina, Germany, and an LLB with emphasis on Islamic Shari'ah from the Maldives College of Higher Education (the Maldives National University). Dr Falaah has taught modern Perspectives of Islamic Law at the Faculty of Law, University of Auckland, and Human Rights Law and General Principles of Law at the Maldives National University. He had also taught at the Islamic University of Maldives. He has published in the areas of theocratic constitutionalism, Islamic constitutionalism, and human rights adjudication. Dr Falaah is an Advocate of the Supreme Court of the Maldives. He also served in the Maldivian Government as the Legal Affairs Secretary at the President's Office, a Commissioner of the Judicial Service Commission, the Legal Adviser to the Defence Minister, and as a draftsman of several Bills pertaining to human rights and the defence sector.

NEPAL—**Bipin ADHIKARI** is an expert on Nepalese constitutional law and is currently the Dean of Kathmandu University School of Law. Bipin has a keen interest in the legal aspects of the Belt and Road Initiative (BRI) programme and its implications for Nepal. He holds a Master of Comparative Law (MCL) and a PhD from the University of Delhi. He also studied for a course on financial law at Lancaster University, UK. Dr Adhikari has a legal career of more than 30 years. Before moving into academia, he worked as a constitutional jurisconsult while leading the *Nepal Consulting Lawyers, Inc.* He was also the chair of the *Nepal Constitution Foundation*, a foremost not-for-profit thinktank in the area of constitutional law and public policy. Notably, he was involved with legal reform and institution-building initiatives in Nepal.

INDIA—**Arun K. THIRUVENGADAM** is a Professor of Law at the School of Policy and Governance, Azim Premji University, Bangalore, India. He holds graduate degrees in law from the National Law School of India University, Bangalore and the New York University School of Law. He served as a law clerk to Chief Justice A.M. Ahmadi at the Supreme Court of India between 1995–97, before working as a litigator in the Delhi High Court and the Indian Supreme Court. In his academic career, he has focused his teaching and research on Indian and comparative public law, regulatory law, and law and development. He holds current visiting teaching appointments at the University of Zurich (Switzerland), the Central European University (Hungary), and the City University School of Law (Hong Kong). He has previously taught or delivered lectures at the National University of Singapore and the Universities of Toronto (Canada), Trento (Italy), and Melbourne (Australia). He is the author of *The Constitution of India: A Contextual Analysis* (Hart, 2017) and has co-edited three other volumes. He serves as co-General Editor of the *Indian Law Review* and is also an editor of the *Asian Journal of Comparative Law* and *World Comparative Law*.

PAKISTAN—**Sadaf AZIZ** is a founding member of the Shaikh Ahmad Hassan School of Law in Lahore, Pakistan. She is the author of *The Constitution of Pakistan: A Contextual Analysis* (Hart, 2018), and works broadly in the areas of comparative constitutionalism, legal pluralism and postcolonial legality. She gained her doctorate from Melbourne University School of Law and has been a Visiting Fellow at the University of Cambridge, University of Michigan, and New York University.

Moeen CHEEMA is a Senior Lecturer at the ANU College of Law, Australia. He has extensive experience of research, teaching and consultancy in the fields of comparative public law, the criminal justice system and legal developments in Pakistan. Moeen's research is interdisciplinary and draws on critical approaches to law. He is especially interested in constitutional politics and judicial review, intersection of the state and Islamic law, and post-conflict state-building.

SRI LANKA—**Roshan de SILVA-WIJEYERATNE** is currently a member of both the Edinburgh Centre for Constitutional Law, University of Edinburgh and the Centre on Human Rights in Conflict, University of East London. In 2019 he was appointed to the Executive Board of the Commonwealth Legal Education Association. He graduated in law from the School of Oriental and African Studies (SOAS) of the University of London in 1990 and completed his doctorate at the University of Kent. He has taught at universities in the UK and Australia. He is currently an Adjunct Lecturer at Griffith Law School, Griffith University, Australia. He has published extensively on Ceylonese/Sri Lankan constitutional history. He is currently working on a co-authored book on the rule of colonial legal difference in the British Empire and on the nineteenth century Australian colonial legal history.

1

South Asian Constitutional Foundings: Beyond History

KEVIN YL TAN AND RIDWANUL HOQUE

INTRODUCTION

WHILE THERE HAS been heightened interest and growth in Asian constitutional scholarship in recent years, the constitutional history of many parts of Asia remains largely understudied.[1] And save for India, scholarship on the constitutional history of South Asia has been even more scant, although recently there has been considerable comparative constitutional law scholarship centred on South Asia.[2] With a few exceptions, scholars of constitutions in South Asia have tended to focus on contemporary issues rather than on historical ones. Yet, contemporary constitutional law and practice is invariably informed and influenced by its historical experience. At the same time, there has been much cross-fertilisation and borrowing of constitutional ideas within the region.

This book attempts to fill this gap in scholarship by having individual contributors focus on the act of constitution-making, and in particular, the nature and role of the first modern constitutions in the eight SAARC (South

[1] A notable exception, in line with the aims and objectives of this volume, is the 2019 book on comparative constitutional foundings in Southeast Asia: KYL Tan and NS Bui (eds), *Constitutional Foundings in Southeast Asia* (Oxford, Hart Publishing, 2019). See earlier works (modest attempts): KYL Tan, 'The Making and Remaking of Constitutions in Southeast Asia: An Overview' (2002) 6 *Singapore Journal of International & Comparative Law* 1–41; and WC Chang, L-ann Thio, KYL Tan and JR Yeh (eds), *Constitutionalism in Asia: Cases and Materials* (Oxford, Hart Publishing, 2015), ch 1 'Constitution-Making and State Building'; J Blount and T Ginsburg, 'Participation in Constitutional Design: Asian Exceptionalism', in R Dixon and T Ginsburg (eds), *Comparative Constitutional Law* (Cheltenham, Edward Elgar, 2014).

[2] For a historical account of constitutional law scholarship in South Asia, see S Khilnani, A Thiruvengadam and V Raghavan, 'Introduction: Reviving South Asian Comparative Constitutionalism', in S Khilnani et al (eds), *Comparative Constitutionalism in South Asia* (New Delhi, Oxford University Press, 2013) 1–9.

Asian Association for Regional Cooperation) nations.[3] Of the eight South Asian states, Bhutan and Nepal have arguably never been colonised and thus did not experience the typical and prevalent form of constitutional foundings that transitioned colonies to nation-states. Interestingly, Bangladesh is the only country in the region to achieve independence from another South Asian nation, Pakistan. Similar to Singapore in Southeast Asia, Bangladesh became independent twice, once from the British colonial rule in 1947 and then from Pakistan in 1971. Somewhat similar to Bangladesh, but in a less dramatic way, Sri Lanka obtained its independence twice from the British, first in 1948 as an independent dominion and then in 1972 as a sovereign Republic.[4] The Maldives, on the other hand, drafted its first constitution in 1932 but did not achieve full independence until 1965; and its first democratic Constitution was only adopted in 2008. Interestingly, Bhutan adopted its first-ever Constitution only in 2008 even though the country has existed as a sovereign state for several centuries. There are similarly complicated histories of constitutional foundings in the other South Asian states too. The independence of British India and its break up into two, and later, three separate states is probably one of the most intriguing and complex. Afghanistan, Pakistan, and Nepal have had multiple constitutions, and they present interesting scenarios for the making of founding constitutions in 'divided societies'.[5] Nationalistic divisions in society was also a primordial factor that influenced the making of Ceylon's founding Constitution of 1948.

Given this interesting diversity in the history of constitutional foundings in South Asia, we take as the 'first constitutions' those which were drafted during the transition from colony to independent sovereign state or, in some cases, where the constitution was adopted as an instrument of democratic or sovereign transition. Thus, the constitutions covered in this volume include those of

[3] Since the geographical scope of South Asia is not undisputed, South Asia in this book is taken to mean the current eight Member States of SAARC. The organisation was established in 1985 pursuant to a Charter drawn by the seven founding states in Dhaka. Afghanistan joined SAARC in April 2007 following its compliance with the SAARC condition of transition to democracy. SAARC's objectives, among others, are to promote the welfare of the peoples of South Asia and to improve their quality of life, and to accelerate economic growth, social progress and cultural development in the region. For an introduction to geographical and socio-economic history of South Asia, see BH Farmer, *An introduction to South Asia,* 2nd revised edn (London, Routledge, 1993). On India, Pakistan, and Bangladesh (the so-called 'Indian Sub-continent'), see R MacDermott et al (eds), *Sources of Indian Tradition: Modern India, Pakistan and Bangladesh,* 3rd edn (New York, Columbia University Press, 2014).

[4] On juridical evidences that Ceylon in 1948–1972 'was less than a sovereign' nation, see R Abeyratne, 'Uncertain Sovereignty: Ceylon as a Dominion, 1948–1972' (2020) *International Journal of Constitutional Law* (forthcoming).

[5] See, generally, H Lerner, *Making Constitutions in Deeply Divided Societies* (Cambridge, Cambridge University Press, 2011); B O'Leary, 'Making Constitutions in Deeply Divided Places', in David Landau and H Lerner (eds), *Comparative Constitution Making* (Cheltenham, Edward Elgar, 2019) ch 9; and S Choudhry (ed), *Constitutional Design for Ethnically Divided Societies* (Oxford, Oxford University Press, 2008).

Afghanistan (1964), Bangladesh (1972), Bhutan (2008), India (1949), Maldives (1932 & 1968), Nepal (1948 & 1951), Pakistan (1956), and Sri Lanka (1948).

This volume is part of a three-part interdisciplinary project traversing constitutional history and comparative constitutional law.[6] It draws on the scholarship of constitutional law to understand the process and substance of constitution-making while integrating knowledge in cognate disciplines such as historical studies and political science. The wider objective of such integration and interdisciplinarity is to better appreciate the factors of constitution-making and the relationship between the founding constitutions and state-building as well as the impact of the foundings on the subsequent constitutional developments. The book is also contextual in its overall approach which has a strong comparative underpinning. The term 'comparative' is not used in any normative or methodological sense[7] but rather to identify commonalities and differences in constitutional responses to the challenge of founding new nation-states.

For each country, we asked contributors to offer three things. First, to provide an *exploratory description of the process and substance* in making the first modern constitution in their respective countries of study. In particular, we asked each country expert to answer to these questions:

(a) How was the constitution-making body constituted and who were in that body?
(b) How was the Constitution drafted?
(c) What were the fundamental constitutional questions that the drafters considered?
(d) How were these questions debated in the constitution-making body and, if at all, among the public? and
(e) How was the Constitution approved?

Second, we asked our contributors to provide an *explanatory analysis of the internal and external factors* involved in the making of their respective founding constitutions. Internal factors would include a polity's political-legal tradition, colonial past, revolution, socio-economic condition, political/civil/ethnic conflicts, social division, ideology, and local intellectual environment/movements. External factors, on the other hand, would include the influence of foreign constitutional experiences and ideas or/and international bodies or experts and how these externalities interacted with the internal factors at the time of constitutional founding.

[6] The first product of this project is KYL Tan and NS Bui (eds), *Constitutional Foundings in Southeast Asia* (Oxford, Hart Publishing, 2019). A third part, covering the states of Northeast Asia is currently in progress.

[7] On the theory and practice of constitution-making in a comparative setting, see Landau and Lerner (eds), *Comparative Constitution Making* (n 5).

Third, we asked the contributors to offer *some reflections on the role of the first constitutions* in the founding of their respective modern nation-states and the subsequent state-building processes. They were also asked to specifically address the following questions:

(a) How did the Constitution impact the founding of state-institutions – the legislature, the executive government, courts, and others?
(b) Did the founding Constitution influence the subsequent constitutional developments and practices?
(c) Does the founding Constitution still influence contemporary constitutional design and structural reform plans, and, if yes, how?

Contributors presented their chapters in a two-day workshop that was held in Singapore by the Centre for Asian Legal Studies at the National University of Singapore Faculty of Law on 22–23 March 2019. Following the workshop, the country experts were invited to revise their papers in light of the comments received and, of course, the above analytical framework.

In this introductory chapter we propose to address some common themes in the South Asian constitutional foundings rather than summarise the country studies in the traditional way. References to summaries and conclusions of various chapters will only be made to locate the respective country's experience in founding its constitution within the general study of constitutional history. Our principal proposition is that constitutional history is important for us to understand how the constitutional law and principles of constitutionalism of any particular country operate in practice.

Knowingly or unknowingly, we constantly make references to our intellectual and political history as sources of legitimacy and for guidance on contemporary constitutional issues. A constitutional historical check, especially in light of comparative constitutional developments in the constitutional neighbourhood or elsewhere, is both instructive for charting out possible constitutional reform and preventing potential derelictions from the founding mandates. The present volume looks beyond what courts do with the governing constitutions (juris-centric originalism) and how they interpret them in light of comparative/western liberal constitutionalism. The inquiry into the constitutional foundings of South Asian states requires us to consider a range of historical issues from a three-pronged analytical framework:

- What was the intellectual and political history of making and founding the first constitutions?
- What were the historical internal and external factors that influenced the processes and substances of foundational constitution-making?
- What is the possible impact of the founding constitutional values on the subsequent and contemporary constitutional trajectories in South Asia?

In developing the above framework of analysis, we have relied upon a successful previous project, which culminated in a companion volume titled *Constitutional Foundings in Southeast Asia*.[8] The structure of this introductory chapter fits into the above analytical framework.

I. WHY THIS BOOK?

As indicated above, the scholarship on the constitutional history of the South Asian region has been sparse and, where in-roads have been made, have generally been locally focused. There have hardly been any works looking at developments of the region as a whole, with perhaps the exception of Harshan Kumarisingham's *Constitution-making in Asia*,[9] which examines the process of constitutional formation and state-building in certain decolonised Asian states and the influence of the British on constitution-making. However, the only four South Asian countries covered in that edited volume were India, Nepal, Pakistan, and Sri Lanka and it focused specifically on the said theme.[10] In any case, it was not that book's purpose to provide an in-depth discussion of the constitutional histories of these states or how their constitutions subsequently developed. Significantly, that volume did not – like so many others – include case studies of the 'Cinderella states' in the region: Afghanistan, Bangladesh, Bhutan, and the Maldives.

Comparative constitutional studies of the South Asian states have traditionally focused on developments in just three states: India, Pakistan, and Sri Lanka. Such comparative studies have also often been thematic,[11] covering subjects such as public interest litigation,[12] secularism,[13] inclusive constitutionalism,[14]

[8] KYL Tan and NS Bui (eds), *Constitutional Foundings in Southeast Asia* (Oxford, Hart Publishing, 2019).

[9] H Kumarasingham (ed), *Constitution-Making in Asia: Decolonisation and State-Building in the Aftermath of the British Empire* (London, Routledge, 2016).

[10] The chapters on Nepal and Sri Lanka presented analyses of Sir Ivor Jennings' influence on their respective constitutions and constitutionalism, while the chapter on Pakistan focused on centralisation in the Pakistani constitutional order.

[11] See, eg, H Kumarasingham, *Political Legacy of the British Empire: Power and the Parliamentary System in Post-Colonial India and Sri Lanka* (London, IB Tauris, 2013).

[12] See, eg, S Hossain, S Malik and B Musa (eds), *Public Interest Litigation in South Asia: Rights in Search of Remedies* (Dhaka, University Press Limited, 1997); and AK Thiruvengadam, 'In Pursuit of the Common Illumination of Our House: Trans-judicial Influence and the Origins of PIL Jurisprudence in South Asia' (2008) 2 *Indian Journal of Constitutional Law* 67–103.

[13] GJ Jacobsohn and S Shankar, 'Constitutional Borrowing in South Asia: India, Sri Lanka, and Secular Constitutional Identity', in Khilnani et al (eds), *Comparative Constitutionalism*, (n 2).

[14] M Guruswamy, 'Constitution Crafting in South Asia: Lessons on Accommodation and Alienation', in Landau and Lerner (eds), *Comparative Constitution Making*, (n 5) ch 22 (studying accommodation and alienation of religious, ethnic, and linguistic minorities in India, Pakistan, and Nepal).

the doctrine of unconstitutional constitutional amendment (the so-called basic-structure doctrine),[15] or the failure of constituent assemblies.[16] And where constitutional history is concerned, scholarly attention has, again, focused on India, Pakistan, and Sri Lanka – the 'usual three'. While there are several works on the constitutional histories of these three countries,[17] the stories of their constitutional foundings remain under-studied. None of these country-specific works have cast constitutional foundings against the backdrop of other similar constitutional trajectories in the region. A more granular account of constitutional foundings in these states still needs to be written. In so far as the constitutional history of the other five SAARC countries – Afghanistan, Bangladesh, Bhutan, the Maldives and Nepal – is concerned, there is virtually no literature except for some work on Bangladesh and, of more recent vintage, a growing scholarship on Nepal.[18]

This book thus offers the first scholarly examination of the first South Asian constitutions and their impact on the founding and contemporary governance of the eight SAARC states. We are particularly pleased to be able to include in this volume studies of the constitutional foundings of Afghanistan, Bhutan, and the Maldives since these states are often left out in studies of the region. Given how difficult it is in most cases to identify what or which is the first or foundational Constitution, we left it to our contributors to theorise this idea of a foundational constitution in the context of their respective local (or regional) specificities and evolving constitutional history.

Our hypothesis is that the making of a state's first modern constitution constitutes a major component of state-building and identity-making. This is what we call the 'constitutional founding'. This is not the same as

[15] See, eg, R Hoque, 'Implicit Unamendability in South Asia: The Core of the Case for the Basic-structure Doctrine' (2018) 3 *Indian Journal of Constitutional and Administrative Law* 23–34 (studying Bangladesh, India, and Pakistan); and GJ Jacobsohn (2006), 'An Unconstitutional Constitution: A Comparative Perspective' (2006) 4(3) *International Journal of Constitutional Law* 460–487. An important, comparative-focused event on the migration of the Indian basic structure doctrine was held in Jindal Global Law School, India, on 20–21 March 2019. Another interesting project on Politics of Unconstitutional Constitutional Amendment in Asia, covering India, Bangladesh, Pakistan, and Nepal from South Asia, by Rehan Abeyratne and Bui Son at the Chinese University of Hong Kong is forthcoming in 2021.

[16] M Malagodi, 'Constituent Assembly failure in Pakistan and Nepal', in J Elster, R Gargarella, V Naresh and BE Rasch (eds), *Constituent Assemblies* (Cambridge, Cambridge University Press, 2018) 79–108.

[17] Earlier volumes have been published on two of the eight South Asian states, namely India and Pakistan in the *Constitutional Systems of the World* series. See AK Thiruvengadam, *The Constitution of India: A Contextual Analysis* (Oxford, Hart Publishing, 2017); and S Aziz, *The Constitution of Pakistan: A Contextual Analysis* (Oxford, Hart Publishing, 2018). On Sri Lanka's independence Constitution of 1972, see AJ Wilson, *The Gaullist System in Asia: The Constitution of Ceylon* (London, Macmillan, 1980); and A Welikala (ed), *The Sri Lankan Republic at 40: Reflections on Constitutional History, Theory and Practice*, 2 vols (Colombo, Centre for Policy Alternatives, 2012).

[18] In addition to the chapter on Nepal in this volume, see M Malagodi, 'Constitutional Developments in a Himalayan Kingdom: The Experience of Nepal', in Khilnani et al (eds), *Comparative Constitutionalism*, (n 2) 87–115.

constitutional foundationalism,[19] nor does it refer to the founding moments in constitutionalism,[20] nor to theories of constitutional constructivism.[21] While founding constitutions are drawn up during founding moments when the state breaks its 'ties with the *ancien régime*' to 'lay the foundation for the establishment of a new constitutional order',[22] this is not always the case. In our study, states like the Maldives, India, Pakistan and Bangladesh experienced several founding moments before they became independent. This was also the case for Nepal. For the same reason, our concept of founding constitutions is not necessarily revolutionary either. Constitution-making processes need to be understood against the backdrop of the multiple and competing factors and forces busily swirling amidst the founders.

This book is built on two key assumptions. First, that while first constitutions play a critical role in creating a new political order, they are not necessarily nor always a clean break from the past. Legal and political change ebb and flow through changes and continuities in the constitutional trajectories of all states and while a constitutional founding is invariably informed by the pre-existing and prevailing political and legal culture and practice, it also impacts subsequent constitutional developments. Second, these first constitutions did not necessarily create constitutionalist systems nor participatory governance. Instead, we argue that the constitution's *primary role* was to lay down the foundational framework for the modern nation-state, rather than limit state power and protect individual rights. To be sure, the creation of a new political order as a component of this founding would incorporate modern constitutional ideas and institutions but this order is not necessarily that of a liberal constitutional democracy. As the following chapters will demonstrate, this has been the case with the first constitutions of the Maldives and Nepal. This particular role of the founding Constitution also helps explain why Pakistan's 1956 Constitution was short-lived and ultimately failed, and why Bangladesh's 1972 Constitution was helpless in preventing a major constitutional breakdown in 1975 when the country transited to a one-party system.

Beyond a chronological retelling of foundational stories, we hope this volume will help enrich the existing literature in three ways. First, to address the dearth of knowledge on comparative constitutional history in South Asia. Second, to help further our understanding of contemporary constitutional practices and to anticipate possible developmental trajectories in light of the foundational values embedded in these founding constitutions. Third, to develop plausible theoretical frameworks to help us better understand constitutional history in South Asia. We hope that this book will not only pique the interest of those who study

[19] B Ackerman, *The Future of Liberal Revolution* (New Haven, Yale University Press, 1992).

[20] R Albert, M Guruswamy and N Basnyat (eds), *Founding Moments in Constitutionalism* (Oxford, Hart Publishing, 2019).

[21] R Teitel, *Transitional Justice* (New York, Oxford University Press, 2000).

[22] Albert et al (eds), *Founding Moments* (n 20).

South Asian constitutionalism but will also help comparative constitutional scholars gain informed perspectives of the South Asian founding constitutions.[23]

II. CONSTITUTIONAL HISTORY MATTERS

A. Constitutional Foundings

The end of the First World War ushered in what scholars describe as the first wave of constitution-making across the world.[24] The Second wave of constitution-making was in the aftermath of decolonisation in the 1960s to early 70s.[25] Generally, constitutions are made in the wake of crises, wars, revolutions, or certain exceptional circumstances such as decolonisation.[26] Among our case studies, Bhutan stands out from the rest since its democratic Constitution was written during peacetime at the behest of the King determined to surrender his formal powers even though the Bhutanese public were as yet not ready for such a drastic change. Not all constitutions laid foundations.

In South Asia, as elsewhere, states have both foundational and transitional constitutions, both of which are informed by their constitutional pasts and seek to address the concerns of the future. Yet, a founding constitution may lay the foundations of the state by adopting certain core, enduring and unassailable values. In some cases, the founding constitution may even be drafted by a foreign sovereign or colonial power, but the key determinant of a 'founding' remains the constituent people.[27] As Dupre and Yeh succinctly put it, 'sovereignty, people and constitution-making' become mutually constituted at a single moment – the founding moment of a nation – that 'gives the constitution a normative priority over later actions'.[28] This is referred to as the 'constitutional moment', when the

[23] It should be noted that currently western comparative law scholars have shown interest in studies of Indian or Sri Lankan constitutions. See, eg, SG Calabresi, 'Comparison of the Founding and Basic Structures of the Constitutions of India and of the United States' (2018) 2 *Indian Journal of Constitutional & Administrative Law* 83–106 (comparing, briefly, the foundings of the Indian and the US constitutions).

[24] See J Elster, 'Forces and Mechanisms in the Constitution-making Process' (1995) 45 *Duke Law Journal* 364–396, 368–69.

[25] For a theoretical understanding of post-British Commonwealth constitutional history, see generally H Kumarasingham, 'Written Differently: A Survey of Commonwealth Constitutional History in the Age of Decolonisation' (2018) 46(5) *The Journal of Imperial and Commonwealth History* 874–908.

[26] Elster 'Forces and Mechanisms in the Constitution-making Process' (n 24). See also A Sajo, *Limiting Government: An Introduction to Constitutionalism* (Budapest, Central European University Press, 1999).

[27] A prime example of this is the Australian Constitution enacted by the British Parliament even before the country's full independence. T Fleiner and C Saunders, 'Constitutions Embedded in Different Legal Systems', in M Tushnet, T Fleiner, and C Saunders (eds), *Routledge Handbook of Constitutional Law*, paperback edn (London, Routledge, 2015) 23.

[28] C Dupre and JR Yeh, 'Constitutions and Legitimacy Over Time', in M Tushnet et al, ibid, 45–57, 51 & 52.

'long-existing' values of a nation are entrenched or formulated 'as the guiding framework for future generations'.[29] In this sense, their concept of 'constitutional moment' is similar to our concept of a 'constitutional founding'.

Founding constitutions are frameworks for governance that gives a nation its social, political, and normative foundations.[30] As we noted previously, those foundings may not necessarily be liberal nor democratic. Depending on a state's politico-constitutional history, these foundational values or events may even occur before its emergence as a nation-state. In South Asia, this happened in the case of the Maldives, India, Pakistan and Bangladesh. For India and Pakistan, the Indian Independence Act of 1935 – which sought to introduce the democratic practices demanded by these colonies – acted as a transitional founding document. Likewise, Bangladesh's 1972 constitutional founding was informed by and based on the higher values of democracy and the rule of law that drove many of its pre-independence popular movements.

Karl Llewellyn argued that constitutions function to organise (constitute), permit, and limit government.[31] Beyond being fundamental legal documents, he saw constitutions as institutions embedding ways of living and doing.[32] Thus, the first task of a foundational constitution is to establish the state and provide a normative framework for its future governance. It is in this foundational and normative sense that first constitutions have a necessary connection with both a nation's past and future. Cicero (106–43 BC), the Roman statesman and lawyer-philosopher, for example, saw the constitution as an initiator of 'the foundation of a republic', asserting that such a constitution cannot emanate from the act of a single man 'but from that of many men acting through centuries and ages rather than within a single generation'.[33] As we shall see, the Indian and the Bangladeshi founding constitutions were products of these nations' respective past constitutional struggles and were essentially transformative, and sought to reshape their exploited masses into societies based on social justice.[34] On a similar note, the Constitution of Bhutan 'is the culmination of more than a century

[29] ibid.

[30] See DJ Galligan and M Versteeg (eds), *Social and Political Foundations of Constitutions* (Cambridge, Cambridge University Press, 2014).

[31] KN Llewellyn, 'The Constitution as an Institution' (1934) 14(1) *Oregon Law Review* 108–30, 116 &117.

[32] KN Llewellyn, 'The Constitution as an Institution', (1934) 34 *Columbia Law Review* 1–40, 16.

[33] Y Hasebe and C Pinelli, 'Constitutions', in Tushnet et al (n 27) 9–19, 10, citing Cicero, *De Re Publica*, vol. II, 1).

[34] See ch 2 on India (especially under the subheading – 'Broad Goals and Incidental Features') and ch 4 on Bangladesh (especially under the subheading – 'Socialism'). On transformative constitutionalism see, among others, P Langa, 'Transformative Constitutionalism' (2006) 17 *Stellenbosch Law Review* 351–360; M Hailbronner, 'Transformative Constitutionalism: Not Only in the Global South' (2017) 65(3) *American Journal of Comparative Law* 527–565 ('transformative constitutions differ from traditional liberal constitutions by conceptualising the constitution as a comprehensive order for a more just and equal society').

of the democratic culture and traditions' that existed since Bhutan's founding as a nation-state in 1907.[35]

B. Conditions and Functions of Constitutional Foundings

'Constitutional foundationalism' – which pivots on the 'founding moment' – was originally 'an eighteenth-century Western European notion'[36] that offers three broad propositions: (a) a constitutional founding moment is a radical break with the past or the '*ancien régime';* (b) the founding moment is the culmination of a liberal revolution; and (c) the making of a founding constitution is fundamental to the creation of a new democratic constitutional order.[37] A contemporary proponent of this theory is Bruce Ackerman, who argues that a 'constitutional moment' occurs when significant and transformative constitutional change is effected through a process outside the established formal channels by which constitutional change is mandated. Such a moment can come about through the courts, constitutional politics or transformative political movements. They are, in Ackerman's view, instances of 'higher lawmaking'.[38]

South Asian experiences of constitutional foundings depart from these constitutional foundationalist claims in several ways. Almost certainly, foundational constitution-making in South Asia was not solely the result of a liberal revolution. Decolonisation or the aspiration for self-autonomy in the region resulted in various different conditions that impacted the foundational moments: *revolution* (or better the revolutionary act of 1947 leading to 'Partition' of British India) in the case of India and Pakistan; *negotiations with the imperial and evolution* in the case of Sri Lanka (the 1948 Dominion Constitution); *royal determination with the aid of ostensibly public engagement* in the case of Bhutan

[35] LS Tobgye, *The Constitution of Bhutan: Principles and Philosophies* (Thimphu, The Supreme Court of Bhutan, 2015) 3.

[36] MS Khan, 'What's in a Founding? Founding Moments and Pakistan's "Permanent Constitution" of 1973', in Albert et al (eds), *Founding Moments,* (n 20) 201.

[37] B Ackerman, *We the People, Volume 1: Foundations* (Cambridge, MA, Harvard University Press, 1991); *The Future of Liberal Revolution* (New Haven, Yale University Press, 1992). See also, H Arendt, *On Revolution* (London, Penguin, 1977). For critical discussions, see GJ Jacobsohn, 'Theorizing the Constitutional Revolution' (2014) 2 *Journal of Law and Courts* 1–32. On theories of constitution-making with critical reflections on Ackerman's and Arendt's concepts, see Arato 'Forms of Constitution Making and Theories of Democracy', (n 41).

[38] M Mate, 'Two Paths to Judicial Power: The Basic Structure Doctrine and the Public Interest Litigation in a Comparative Perspective' (2010) 12 *San Diego International Law Journal* 175–222, 210, citing Ackerman, *We the People,* (n 37) 3, 8–16, 33–57. For a critical view of Ackerman's higher lawmaking through public engagement and deliberations, see S Choudhry, 'Ackerman's Higher Lawmaking in Comparative Constitutional Context' (2008) 6(8) *International J of Constitutional Law* 193–230. For a further critique of his constitutional moments, see MJ Klarman, 'Constitutional Fact/Constitutional Fiction: A Critique of Bruce Ackerman's Theory of Constitutional Moments' (1992) 44 *Stanford Law Review* 759–797.

(the Constitution as a 'Royal vision');[39] *revolution and violent dismemberment* in the case of Bangladesh and, to a lesser extent, in Nepal; *internal political arrangements softly inspired by external forces and also the monarchy-dictated*[40] in the case of the Maldives' first founding Constitution of 1932; and the *executive-driven legal founding*[41] as in the case of Afghanistan's 1964 Constitution.

Even where constitution-making is the culmination of a revolution, that revolution is in some cases not necessarily a liberal one. Nepal provides a curious example of this. The 1950–1951 popular revolution against the oppressive Rana regime and subsequent demands for constitutional democracy resulted in the three inchoate founding Constitutions of 1948, 1951, and 1959; all instruments promulgated by the King. They provided for a peculiar type of parliamentary democracy[42] by shifting autocratic power from the Ranas (who instituted a system of hereditary Prime Ministers) to the King, thus legitimising and consolidating the King's autocratic power. Indeed, in some South Asian states, state-formation was not followed by the codification of values and achievements of liberal revolutions and, as such, did not offer a framework for the creation of a democratic constitutional order. Among these were the Maldives, Nepal, and Afghanistan, whose founding Constitutions were executive-or-monarchy-driven and aimed at consolidating authoritarian power.

A related observation is that foundational constitution-making in South Asia is not necessarily a radical repudiation of the past but a continuity instead. For example, Maldives retained its authoritarian monarchy in its Constitutions of 1932 and 1968 while Bhutan's 2008 Constitution was said to be based on pre-existing democratic practices and behaviour.[43] Pakistan carried over its 'authoritarian legacies' in its 1956 Constitution which was modelled on the Government of India Act 1935.[44] At the same time, its traditional communitarian and religious values succeeded in entrenching Islam as its state religion and transformed it into an Islamic Republic, thus obliterating the historical-revolutionary promises of a secular founding. Almost all South Asian founding constitutions were not designed to limit government power in favour of individual liberty. The tension between individual liberty and the collective need for a

[39] Bhutan's constitution-making took a long 7 years from 2001 to 2008 and was largely participatory, yet the framers were overwhelmingly instructed by 'guidance' from the King. See Tobgye, *The Constitution of Bhutan*, (n 35) and ch 7 on Bhutan in this volume.

[40] As ch 8 on the Maldives explains, these forces were the 1931 Donoughmore Constitution of Ceylon and the Constitution of Egypt.

[41] Andrew Arato gave a typology of five types of constitution-making by: (a) constitutional convention; (b) sovereign constituent assembly; (c) normal legislature; (d) executive; and (e) evolutionary process such as in the UK. See A Arato, 'Forms of Constitution Making and Theories of Democracy' (1995) 17 *Cardozo Law Review* 191–232, 198–199, 207.

[42] In case of the 1948 instrument, for example, the members of the upper house and a majority of the lower house were to be selected by the Prime Minister. See ch 6 on Nepal in this volume.

[43] Tobgye, *The Constitution of Bhutan*, (n 35).

[44] See ch 3 on Pakistan.

transformative and equal society manifests itself in the Bangladeshi, Indian and Pakistani constitutions which include fundamental rights and judicially non-justiciable fundamental state policy principles of social justice.

We run the risk of reductionism in attempting to make generalisations about the roles and functions of foundational constitution-making in South Asia given the diverse and complex histories of its constituent states. This is especially so when independence was won in different ways by different states. And while new constitutions signal new beginnings and represent a break of some sort from the past,[45] we also know that such constitutions also contain nationalistic ideas and traditional values that were included to unify the nascent State.

III. FACTORS IMPACTING CONSTITUTIONAL FOUNDINGS

A. Internal Factors

As highlighted earlier, all the states in South Asia except for Bhutan and Nepal had once been British colonies or protectorates. The British decolonisation process in Asia began with Burma and India in 1947. The decolonisation and break-up of British India and the process of its constitution-making was one of the most significant and influential in the Empire. In many ways, the drafting of the Indian Constitution became an idealised template which others sought to emulate. None of the states in South Asia had to fight a nasty war to rid themselves of the British. Decolonisation and the grant of statehood was orchestrated in a way that would allow the British to withdraw in a dignified manner while putting in place a functional constitutional system that would guarantee equality to all and protection for minorities.

The constitutional template had, in the cases of India and Pakistan, already been forged more than a decade earlier with the passage of the Government of India Act 1935. The structure of government was the Westminster-export model with a bicameral legislature, a ceremonial head of state, and judicial review powers vesting in a Supreme Court. What remained to be worked out were details on state-federal relations and guarantees and protection for minorities. The British were also anxious that sovereignty and power be transferred to those whom they trusted – typically Anglicised local intellectuals like Nehru and Jinnah – with the hope of keeping the new states within the British Commonwealth. And to help their chosen successors along, constitutional

[45] Tan and Bui (eds), *Constitutional Foundings*, (n 8) 7. An example of this is Pakistan's 1973 Constitution which a commentator has recently considered to be giving a 'founding moment'. Although we distinguish our approach to constitutional foundings from 'founding moments', Pakistan's 1973 Constitution can logically be seen as a founding. See Khan, What's in a Founding? (n 36).

advisors like Sir Ivor Jennings were pressed into action to advise, and in some cases help draft the Constitutions.

B. Local Politics

Another influential factor was internal or local politics, in particular the rise and actions of popular movements and internecine political struggles among key local political actors. These factors tend to overlap since popular movements often arise from various political struggles – such as the battle for Muslim representative equality – in the case of Pakistan – or the struggle for a separate Bengali identity – in the case of Bangladesh. The jockeying for power by key political actors also resulted in parliamentary politics being displaced by authoritarian rulers or aggregation of power in a strong central executive as we have seen in the cases of Afghanistan and Pakistan. And where a major faction gains power, changes can be made to the constitutional order to privilege the majority – as in the case of Sri Lanka. In the Maldives, referenda were held for the establishment of both 'republicanism' (1952) and monarchy (1954) but this only resulted in a failed Republican Constitution (1952), three revolts against the British, and a short-lived 'runaway' state. It was clear that 'the main driving forces' behind the Maldives' 1968 independence Constitution 'were the political infighting' between the new elites.[46]

C. Socio-Economic Conditions

Prevailing difficult socio-economic conditions and attempts at resolving them have also impacted the constitution-making process in the South Asian states. Conditions include the diversity of ethnicities, language, intellectual environment, religion, and traditional values. Socio-economic conditions that gave birth to independence movements or struggles for democratic constitutions permeated almost all South Asian founding constitutions. For example, the excessive and discriminatory economic disparity between the two wings of Pakistan was a key reason leading to Pakistan's dismemberment in 1971.[47] On the other hand, religion played a major part in the making of the founding constitutions of Pakistan, Afghanistan, Ceylon and the Maldives whereas traditional values or ethnicism are notable factors surrounding the developments of the first constitutions of Nepal and Bangladesh ('Bengali nationalism').

[46] See ch 8 on the Maldives.

[47] See R Sobhan, *From Two Economies to Two Nations: My Journey to Bangladesh* (Dhaka, The Daily Star Books, 2015); and A Sengupta, 'Regional Disparity and Economic Development of Pakistan' (1971) 6(45) *Economic and Political Quarterly* 2279–86.

D. External Factors

i. The Role of Experts

All South Asian founding Constitutions were influenced by external forces and factors, including the use of foreign constitutional advisors, foreign constitutional texts or movements, foreign governments, and the deliberate reference to international law and human rights instruments. The ubiquitous British jurist Sir Ivor Jennings, for example, influenced the writing and design of the Constitutions of Sri Lanka (1948 Constitution), Nepal (1959 Constitution),[48] and the Maldives (1952 Constitution)[49] and advised policymakers in Pakistan that the Westminster model of parliamentary democracy might not be suitable, following the arbitrary dissolution of the Constituent Assembly in 1954.[50] While drafting the Constitution, India retained the services and good counsel of Sir Benegal Narsing (BN) Rau, an Indian constitutionalist, who had 'considerable exposure' to comparative constitution-making and who was familiar with the constitution-making experiences in the US, Canada, and South Africa. Rau even made a study tour for the purposes of his own learning.[51] So, even though India's founding Constitution could be said to be autochthonous, we also see active 'engagement' with external traditions and practices. Nepal's first Constitution of 1947 was drafted with the technical expert support of two Indian lawyers, and in Bhutan, it was the well-known Indian lawyer KK Venugopal who provided expert advice.

ii. Constitutional Inspirations and Borrowings

Constitutional foundings in South Asia were not purely the products of self-engagement detached from lessons and developments elsewhere. Bangladesh,[52] for example, drew on international legal and constitutional norms and ideals in what might be termed transnational[53] or cosmopolitan borrowing.[54] Inspired by

[48] See Kumarasingham (ed), *Constitution-Making in Asia*, (n 9).

[49] Note that this Constitution has not been treated as a founding one. Jennings' contributions are considered deficient in a democratic character of that Constitution. See ch 8 on the Maldives.

[50] See for details H Kumarasingham, 'Transnational Actor on a Dramatic Stage – Sir Ivor Jennings and the Manipulation of Westminster Style Democracy: The Case of Pakistan' (2017) 2 *UC Irvine Journal of International, Transnational, and Comparative Law* 33–56.

[51] See ch 2 on India (Mr Rau was involved in the making of the Government of India Act 1935 and the 1947 Constitution of Burma); and Thiruvengadam, *The Constitution of India*, (n 17) 32.

[52] Bangladesh's reliance on the international community, in the context of the country's independence from Pakistan, has a resemblance with the similar case of East Timor in Southeast Asia.

[53] See JR Yeh and WC Chang, 'The Emergence of Transnational Constitutionalism: Its Features, Challenges and Solutions' (2008) 27 *Penn State International Law Review* 89–124.

[54] S Choudhury, 'Postcolonial Proportionality: *Johar*, Transformative Constitutionalism and Same Sex Rights in India', in P Dann, M Riegner and M Bönnemann (eds), *The Global South and Comparative Constitutional Law* (Oxford, Oxford University Press, 2020).

the Egyptian Constitution, the Maldives's first Constitution of 1932 entrenched constitutional rights that were later to be found in the 1948 Universal Declaration of Human Rights. Other founding constitutions, such as those of India and Pakistan, were cosmopolitan in their appeal to and reliance on international law principles, especially with regard to constitutional rights.[55]

In some cases, constitution-making was influenced by ideas, values, and institutions of the former colonial powers. The classic example comes from India, Pakistan, and Sri Lanka with regard to, at the least, the internalisation of the Westminster model of democracy.[56] In the cases of Bhutan and Nepal, foundational constitution-making was free from colonial domination, yet constitution-makers drew inspirations from different constitutional models, particularly the British system of constitutional democratic monarchy as well as from India.

Interestingly enough, there were intra-regional external influences too with India being a predominant inspiration. Everything from the process of establishing a constituent assembly as a separate and distinct body with plenary powers to create a constitution, to the use of Directive Principles of State to embed unenforceable social-economic rights, and special lists of protected minorities and disadvantaged groups were deemed worthy of emulation. The creation and design of both Pakistan's and Bangladesh's founding constitutions were greatly inspired by the Indian example. And both these states followed the 'Indian model' of entrenching fundamental human rights and making social rights non-justiciable.[57] The Maldives' 1932 Constitution was influenced by Ceylon's 1931 Constitution. This type of organic borrowing had as its object the modernisation of the domestic constitutional order.

As one of us has previously observed, '[c]ountries may incorporate foreign experiences into their Constitutions to socialise themselves to the "civilized world" to gain more international recognition'.[58] This was clearly the case when Bangladesh committed to be bound by its international law obligations and the United Nations Charter. Since all the South Asian first constitutions – except that of Bhutan – were adopted before the globalisation process, the incentive to adopt transnational constitutional values to compete for foreign investments was not an obvious motivation.[59] It is worth noting that reactions to, or rationale

[55] For cross-learning during the framing of foundational constitutions, see the respective country chapters in this volume. In this regard, the case of the Maldives' first Constitution is quite interesting. See (n 40).

[56] A Harding, 'The "Westminster Model" Constitution Overseas: Transplantation, Adaptation and Development in Commonwealth States' (2004) 4(2) *Oxford University Commonwealth Law Journal* 143–166.

[57] Harding, ibid 82. While Sri Lanka also did this, the Indian founding influence was rather a clear case for Sri Lankan's subsequent Constitution of 1972.

[58] Tan and Bui, *Constitutional Foundings*, (n 8) 8.

[59] This tendency is indeed associated with economic globalisation. See B Goderis and M Versteeg, 'Global Diffusion of Constitutional Rights' (2014) 39 *International Review of Law & Economics* 1–19.

for, external influences/borrowing during foundational constitution-making were not always positive; nor were they always an easy option. Resistance is common in transnational constitutional interactions whether it be because of strident nationalism, concerns about sovereignty, or the fear of western hegemony or constitutional imperialism.[60] Several states – such as Nepal, Bhutan and even Pakistan – went so far as to consciously and deliberately reject foreign or western constitutional ideas as unsuitable to their local conditions. Interestingly, most instances of such resistance is often a thinly-disguised manoeuvre by selfish sectoral and other interests that often led to the perpetuation of executive dominance.

IV. THE LEGACIES OF CONSTITUTIONAL FOUNDINGS

The study of constitutional foundings offers us a framework and a dynamic perspective with which to understand constitutions and their development in context. It does not attempt to posit a particular theoretical or dialectical model of constitutionalism at work. That is why studies of this sort, being necessarily grounded in the local – yet sometimes transcending and borrowing from the foreign – tend to be granular and particularistic. Yet, human reaction to politics and constitutional arrangements appear quite similar wherever we go. Our pasts continue to shape our present and sometimes guide our futures. Thus, founding constitutional legacies continue to provide the ideas, forces, and inspirations for constitutional debates and mobilisation many years after their promulgation.

Consider the cases of Pakistan and Bangladesh, for example. The anti-autocracy movements in Pakistan in the late-1960s and in Bangladesh in the late-1980s were largely informed and boosted by the founding values of parliamentary democracy in their 1956 and 1972 foundings respectively. Founding constitutions also impact subsequent constitutional design or 'constitutional restoration'. In Pakistan, the aborted constitutional foundings of 1956, especially those involving democratic principles, 'formed the bedrock' of the subsequent constitutional design of the 1973 Constitution.[61] And in Bangladesh, the founding principle of participatory parliamentary democracy was restored in 1991, after its long absence from 1975 to 1990. Likewise, two other founding values – 'secularism' and 'Bengali nationalism' – were also restored, albeit in compromised form.[62]

[60] VC Jackson, 'Constitutional Comparisons, Convergence, Resistance, Engagement' (2005) 119 *Harvard Law Review* 113–14; and KL Scheppele, 'Aspirational and Aversive Constitutionalism: The Case for Studying Cross-Constitutional Influence Through Negative Models' (2003) 1 *International Journal of Constitutional Law* 296–324. For a recent account, see R Hirschl, 'Opting Out of "Global Constitutionalism"' (2018) 12 *Law & Ethics of Human Rights* 1–36.

[61] See ch 3 on Pakistan.

[62] On this, now see arts 6 and 9 (nationalism), and 12 (secularism) and 2A (Islam as State religion) of the Bangladeshi Constitution as were amended by the Fifteenth Amendment in 2011.

When it comes to the questions of constitutional past and the imagination of the constitutional future, the attachment to the founding constitutional legacies is inescapable. As Schepelle observed, '[c]onstitutions in their moments of creation cannot be inspired solely by imagined futures' but crucially 'encode imagined pasts' for 'constitution drafters ultimately understand and react most of all to what they take to be the crucial histories of their own countries'.[63] As Chief Justice Sognam Tobgye, Chairman of Bhutan's Constitution Drafting Committee, observed, a 'Constitution is neither abandonment of the past nor resistance to change. It must respect and build on the past shaped by history and hence … be preservative to maintain certain existing practices'.[64] Whether it be in constitutional debates or popular mobilisations or constitutional design, constitutional histories – whether progressive or repressive – are often invoked as justifications for constitutional reform, stasis, or avoidance. In the case of Bangladesh, for example, its founding Constitution and constituent instruments sought to adopt and entrench parliamentary democracy and secular constitutionalism on the basis of the nation's struggle for democracy and its experience of the harm of religious constitutionalism in Pakistan. And in the Maldives, the 1932 Constitution proudly declared the sovereignty of the people and the principle of constitutional supremacy, and thus discarded the long-standing tradition of monarchical sovereignty.

As has been previously observed, a reference 'back to the founding constitutional legacies may also be instrumental in gaining more legitimacy and social support for new constitutional designs as societies often prefer continuity to change'.[65] And this kind of historicising may occur even when past constitutional experiences prove flawed. Pakistan's 1956 Constitution, for example, shied away from the founding promise of secularism based on a reference to the so-called two nation theory that partitioned British India along a Hindu-Muslim divide. Bangladesh, on the other hand, made it a point to restore this same founding principle in 2011 but without discarding Islam as the state religion. And it did so as a compromise, providing yet another example of how attempts were made to correct actual or perceived founding constitutional mistakes or flaws. In such situations, constitutional actors do not simply hark back to the founding values but recalibrate them for the sake of constitutional continuity in a changed political reality. Thus, constitutional pasts that are linked to a nation's foundings often provide a meaningful anchor when states grapple with the needs of the constitutional present and provide a glimpse and hope of the constitutional future.

[63] KL Scheppele, 'A Constitution Between Past and Future' (2008) 49 *William & Mary Law Review* 1379–1407.
[64] Tobgye, *The Constitution of Bhutan*, (n 35) 9.
[65] Tan and Bui, *Constitutional Foundings*, (n 8) 10.

V. A NOTE OF ACKNOWLEDGEMENT

We end with a word of acknowledgement. We would like to thank the Centre for Asian Legal Studies (CALS) at the Faculty of Law, National University of Singapore, for supporting this project and to the contributors and commentators who generously contributed to the workshop and to this volume. Finally, we thank Hart Publishing for its unwavering support of the constitutional foundings series of books.

2

India's Constitutional Founding: An Enduring but Mixed Legacy

ARUN K THIRUVENGADAM*

INTRODUCTION

> The birth of modern India marked the historical node at which democracy, constitutionalism and modernity occurred simultaneously. The Indian revolution combined a set of concerns that had proceeded at separate rates in the West ... The global challenge for constitutionalism since the mid-twentieth century has been to construct democracy in settings where its imagined ingredients are seen as absent – under conditions where the people as free citizens must be created rather than assumed.[1]

INDIA'S CONSTITUTIONAL EXPERIENCE is relatively rare in South Asia and in the postcolonial world generally, in that it is still governed under its 1950 independence Constitution. That founding Constitution has continuously been in operation across seven decades except for a brief period of internal emergency (1975–1977) when it was formally suspended by Prime Minister Indira Gandhi's government. This accomplishment needs to be measured against another unequivocal fact: the Indian Constitution has been amended more than a hundred times,[2] amounting to an average of more than an amendment in each year of its existence. While many of these amendments have been for technical, trivial issues, several amendments have vitally reworked the original constitutional design, adding some question marks to the claim of a single document having shaped the nature of its constitutional polity over time. The infamous 42nd Amendment, for instance, made consequential changes to nearly 50 separate provisions. Thus, even as the focus of this chapter is on the original

*This chapter draws heavily upon my previous work, which has been adapted and expanded to meet the needs of this project. See generally, AK Thiruvengadam, *The Constitution of India: A Contextual Analysis* (Oxford, Hart Publishing, 2017).

[1] M Khosla, *India's Founding Moment: The Constitution of a Most Surprising Democracy* (Cambridge, MA, Harvard University Press, 2020) 24 & 156.

[2] As of January 2020, the count stands at 103 times.

1950 Constitution, it is important to recognise that there have been multiple crucial shifts from the founding vision over the intervening years.

Across this period, India transited from a state-led redistributive model of economic development to one based on policies of economic liberalisation and openness to the global economy, a process that has inevitably entailed massive changes to the economy's regulatory framework. As India's population grew four-fold between 1947 and 2020, its state apparatus has had to grow and adapt to the needs of modern administrative realities. Across this same period, India has transitioned from a more ardently secular state of the Nehruvian model (under its first and longest-serving Prime Minister) to one that is far more accommodative of the needs of the majoritarian Hindu population under Narendra Modi (India's latest and 14th Prime Minister). The changes across political, sociological and ecological terrains have also been radical. Yet, through it all, the country has been governed under a seemingly continuous constitutional vision, for which the framers of the Indian Constitution are credited for their statesmanship and prescience. Such credit may well be justified, but there are many other reasons why the independence Constitution has endured. A less romantic view was offered by the editor of a work that sought to assess India's success as a democracy on its 50th anniversary: the Indian democratic experiment succeeded and lasted this long because it gave each of the varied stakeholders enough hope to continue to be in the game rather than out of it.[3] This is hardly a ringing endorsement of the viability of the Indian model and seems contingent on fairly tenuous premises.

Over the last 70 years, the Indian Constitution has almost continuously made its presence felt. While it has often been violated, criticised and attacked, it is no mere paper document; it has had a visible, living effect on the law, politics, governance, and social and economic life of India. In some respects, the Indian constitutional experience is comparable to that of the United States, which is perhaps natural given that the framers of the Indian Constitution consciously strove to emulate specific aspects of that constitutional order. Alexis de Tocqueville had famously noted that in the US constitutional experience, most political questions raised were changed into judicial ones. Scholars writing about the Indian Constitution have extended Tocqueville's insight in asserting that in India, 'a vast range of political, administrative and judicial matters have become constitutional questions' that are routinely brought before the courts and resolved by them. This has resulted in a 'pervasive institutionalization of legal disputation against State power' that may have reached unparalleled levels in the Indian constitutional system.[4]

[3] A Kohli, *The Success of India's Democracy* (Cambridge, Cambridge University Press, 2001) 23.

[4] S Choudhry, M Khosla and PB Mehta (eds), *The Oxford Handbook of the Indian Constitution* (New Delhi, Oxford University Press, 2015) 6–7 [hereinafter '*Oxford Handbook*'].

This chapter seeks to build its argument by engaging with the 'two hypotheses' advanced by the editors in their concept note. The first of these hypotheses is stated as follows: 'Constitutional founding is invariably informed by pre-existing political and legal culture and practice and informs subsequent constitutional trajectories.' As the chapter will show, this first hypothesis is amply borne out by the Indian constitution-making experience. The Constitution of India did not make a clean break from its past, but did in fact build on many continuities from the pre-modern era and the colonial period. This has led to a consistent line of critique in Indian constitutional discourse, of 'colonial continuities' which is used as a pejorative term.[5] The bulk of this chapter seeks to make good on this descriptive claim, by showing in some detail how the making of the Constitution of India between 1947 and 1950 was a continuation of efforts begun nearly a century ago, and built upon the work of both colonial draftspersons, as well as many efforts by nationalist and non-nationalist Indian constitutional thinkers.

The chapter engages with the 'second hypothesis' by pushing back against the claim of the editors in part. In the concept note, the editors assert their second hypothesis in this formulation:

> [W]e do not insist that written constitutions are necessarily constructive to the creation of liberal constitutionalism. Instead, we argue that the first constitution's primary role is to lay down the foundational framework for South Asian modern nation states rather than to limit the state power and protect individual rights. To be sure, the creation of a new political order as a component of this founding may incorporate modern constitutional ideas and institutions. However, this order is not necessarily a liberal constitutional democracy.

I will argue that at least with respect to India, this claim is problematic. While it is difficult to discern a single clear line of motivation with respect to the making of the Indian Constitution – given the multiplicity of actors and agendas involved – some broad claims can be made. The editors are certainly correct in noting that many of the framers of the Indian Constitution were keen to 'lay down the foundational framework' for a modern nation state in India. This is evident in the deep desire to foster national unity in a region which had not conceived of itself as a single nation state before the advent of the British. The ideal of a modern nation state is also evident in the government's zeal to improve the socio-economic condition of the people of India and with the determined focus on securing 'development' for the masses. At the same time, however, the long-standing mobilisation of the Indian people against the brutalities of the colonial period had given rise to a genuine commitment to freedom and rights among the framers and the people of India. These new citizens (who had only been 'subjects' during the colonial era) were wary of a totalitarian state and made

[5] A Burra, 'Arguments from Colonial Continuity: The Constitutionality of the First Amendment, 1951' (7 Dec 2008), available at SSRN: https://ssrn.com/abstract=2052659 or http://dx.doi.org/10.2139/ssrn.2052659.

clear their preference for a culture of rights that could not be dismissed easily in the pursuit of a 'social revolution'. Many of the framers were committed to both 'development' and 'freedom' that they sought to pursue simultaneously. So, any attempt to advance 'development' before 'democracy' – as happened in many parts of South East Asia for instance – would not have succeeded in India. Indeed, scholars have argued that the 'developmental state' model was doomed from India's inception precisely because of the constitutional commitment to a federal state, to bills of rights, and to a strong and independent judiciary which would often frustrate the ideologies and actions of legislators and technocrats in the bureaucracy.[6] The tension between these competing goals led to many institutional struggles across post-independent India's history and continue to mark its current legal and political discourse.

The framers of India's Constitution did, therefore, intend to inject elements of liberal, indeed progressive, constitutional democracy and, according to many commentators,[7] succeeded in part in entrenching some of those elements into Indian constitutional culture. Many of the framing generation had studied examples of the evolution of the nation state in Europe, but at least in India, the dominant voices in the Constituent Assembly sought to avoid the homogenising effects of nation-building, in part because of their understanding that the multiple pluralities of the Indian subcontinent would not be amenable to the historical experiences of nation states in Europe, and also because of the devastating effects of such attempts that resulted in Partition in their immediate lifetimes.

Thus, the resulting constitutional compact has many elements of liberalism, but it is a peculiar combination of liberal and non-liberal ideas and amalgamations. India's Constitution departs from standard liberal theoretical models in insisting that democracy can be embedded in a populace marked by widespread poverty and illiteracy. To give some sense of how these were reflected in measurable indices, consider some basic facts. In 1951, the average life expectancy in India was 32 years, infant mortality rates were at 180 per thousand, and the female literacy rate was 9 per cent. A significant departure from liberal theory is the choice of enabling a system of personal laws that codify customary and religious systems of law within a broader legal system that promises equality to all. A further deviation was the promise of group rights to cultural and religious minorities as well as other forms of pluralism that sit uneasily with conventional liberal thought. At the same time, it entrenches many elements of liberal theory and ideas drawn from the template of liberalism.

[6] RJ Herring, 'India's failed Developmental State', in MW Cummings (ed), *The Developmental State* (Ithaca, Cornell University Press, 1999) 306–334.

[7] The most famous of these accounts is still by G Austin, *The Indian Constitution: Cornerstone of a nation* (Oxford University Press, Oxford, 1966). A more recent work which emphasises the liberal heritage of the Indian Constitution is Khosla, *India's Founding Moment* (n 1).

To provide a further sense of the factual context, consider the following statistics. At the time of Independence in 1947,

> … 20 per cent of India's Hindu-majority population were Muslim, while other religious minorities included Christian (2.5 per cent), Sikhs (almost 2 per cent), and Buddhists, Jains and Parsis (together comprising about 2.5 per cent). Although they made up just 12 per cent of the national population after Independence, India's Muslims constituted the world's third largest Muslim community (after Indonesia and Pakistan). In addition, India is one of the world's most ethnically and linguistically diverse countries. At Independence, India was home to nearly twenty major languages, each of which was spoken to by at least one million people. The total number of less represented languages and dialects exceeded 1,600. Hindi was spoken by no more than 40 per cent of the population. In addition to this vast religious, cultural and linguistic diversity, the Indian framers faced the challenge of incorporating under the Constitution the 562 Princely States, which for the most part had their own monarchic traditions.[8]

Given these trying circumstances and formidable challenges, the endurance of the Constitution has attracted praise and astonishment. To ensure that the Constitution would garner a modicum of consensus across the various streams of Indian society represented in the Constituent Assembly, the framers had to make a number of compromises. This resulted in the incorporation of a series of contradictory impulses, and a range of features which were decidedly illiberal and unconducive to the principles of freedom and egalitarianism that motivated other parts of the Constitution. This is integral to the very nature of constitution-making, which is almost always an admixture of high minded values as well as often shameful compromises to bring on board powerful sections determined to preserve the status quo. So, while the Constitution of India has endured, its operation has also seen the playing out of decidedly illiberal values, including when people at the helm were genuinely committed to its values. When those at the helm, like Prime Minister Indira Gandhi, India's second longest-serving Prime Minister, saw the Constitution as an instrument to be bent to their will, the conduct of government strayed from liberal and progressive ends, and illiberalism flourished.

The present moment is another such time. In the period since 2014, the constitutional vision of the framers has faced a different level of challenges under the government of Prime Minister Modi. During these six years, India has embraced policies that can at best be described as 'non-liberal' and especially since May 2019 when Prime Minister Modi was re-elected, those that are even deeply 'illiberal' and authoritarian. In the contemporary moment, the constitutional battles within India seem to be between forces of constitutionalism and those who favour authoritarianism of a Hindu majoritarian stripe. It may be

[8] H Lerner, 'The Indian Founding: A Comparative Perspective' in *Oxford Handbook*, (n 4) 55.

too early to predict which side will prevail, but at the time of writing, there is evidence of the strength in both forces within the Indian polity.

Liberalism and constitutionalism are under threat in many parts of the world, including in South Asia, but the Indian constitutional model provides many tools and avenues for those seeking to oppose the forces of authoritarianism. This complex dynamic needs to be recognised in order to better understand the tangled ways of Indian constitutionalism.

I will seek to make good my claims in respect of the two hypotheses across this chapter. In what follows, I focus first on the descriptive aspects of the founding of India's independence Constitution. For this, the focus, in section I of the chapter, is on the pre-modern period till the advent of Europeans in the Indian subcontinent, and then on to the nine decades of formal colonial rule (from 1858 to 1947). The second section of the chapter turns to the making of the Indian Constitution between 1947 and 1950. This is followed by a brief concluding section which covers the post-independence journey of the Indian constitutional order in broad sweep.

I. CONSTITUTIONAL DEVELOPMENTS IN PRE-MODERN INDIA AND DURING THE COLONIAL PERIOD (1550–1947)

India has a long civilisational history dating back to ancient times. Historians have noted how the many kingdoms and dynasties that ruled over parts of the Indian subcontinent from 500 BC onwards experimented with and implemented many innovative features of law and governance.[9] Some aspects of the older legal traditions survive, especially in the realm of religious laws, and have influenced the nature of multiculturalism in Indian constitutionalism in significant ways. These ancient traditions of law and governance are often invoked in contemporary political and constitutional discourse and accounting for them is important to understand contemporary constitutional discourse. However, all of these measures were engineered while staying broadly within the structural framework of monarchical and dynastic systems, which, despite their many variations, did not impose constitutional limits upon the authority of the ultimate power holder. Nevertheless, some scholars have sought to argue that ideas similar to modern notions of constitutionalism existed in India from very early times.[10]

I am of the view that while law and governance in India have a long pedigree, and one can find many innovative forms of legal thinking in ancient and medieval

[9] See generally, PV Kane, *History of Dharmasastra: Ancient and Medieval Religious and Civil Law*, 2nd edn (Pune, Bhandarkar Oriental Research Institute, 1968–1975); J Keay, *India: A History* (New York, Gloria Press, 2000).

[10] See, eg, MR Jois, *Legal and Constitutional History of India* (New Delhi, Universal Law Publishing, 2012, 1984). For a contrary view, see AK Thiruvengadam, 'Excavating Constitutional Antecedents in Asia: An Essay on the Potential and Perils' (2013) 88(1) *Chicago-Kent Law Review* 45–61.

India, constitutionalism in India, as in other parts of Asia and Africa, is a modern project, whose origins can be traced to much more recent times. This section thus focuses on the colonial period, particularly since 1857, when, in the aftermath of an event that the British colonial regime referred to as the Mutiny and the nationalist movement would term the First War of Independence, the British Government formally took charge of the East India Company. Soon thereafter, the demand for forms of constitutional government was increasingly articulated by leaders of the nascent Indian nationalist movement starting from the late nineteenth century. In response to such demands, the colonial authorities ceded constitutional powers to the representatives of the people of the Indian subcontinent gradually over a period of half a century, culminating in the independence of the new nations of South Asia through the Indian Independence Act of 1947. There is a rich body of work that documents this complex narrative.[11] My goal is to sketch the broad contours of that narrative, with a focus on specific parts that are relevant for the purposes of the argument and analysis of this chapter.

Specifically, this section seeks to track two parallel lines of development – the gradual ceding of constitutional powers by the colonial government from 1861 onwards, and the increasingly sophisticated constitutional demands raised by the nationalist movement (represented principally by the Indian National Congress which was formed in 1885). A focus on both tracks is essential for understanding the complex ways in which the crafting of the Constitution of India of 1950 sought, simultaneously, to achieve two seemingly contradictory objectives: the adaptation of colonial structures of governance that were premised on efficiency in achieving imperial, exploitative goals, with the insertion of new instruments and institutions to usher in an egalitarian and democratic spirit within the new constitutional order. While seeking to provide a chronological account that spans three and a half centuries, my goal will be to focus on key moments that help set out the overall narrative, in order not to overwhelm the reader with historical detail.

Descriptively, this section begins with a short section on the entry of the East India Company into India towards the end of the Mughal empire, and the legal rules and systems it established to initially supplement and eventually supplant the system that existed in India during the Mughal era. This is followed by a focus on the reforms brought about in the post-1857 era when the British Government formally took charge of the Indian colony. The next part of the section focuses on the significant period of about 90 years during which many constitutional ideas and reforms were discussed and introduced focusing on the perspective of the colonial authorities. Thereafter, the focus shifts in particular on the early attempts at constitution-making by the Indian nationalists, which is dealt with in section II of this chapter.

[11] See generally, WAJ Archibald, *Outlines of Indian Constitutional History* (London, Curzon, 1926); AB Keith, *A Constitutional History of India* 1600–1935 (Delhi, Pacific Publication, 1937); and MP Singh, *Outlines of Indian Legal and Constitutional History*, 8th edn (New Delhi, Universal Law Publishing, 2006).

A. The Mughals and the East India Company (1550–1857)

The Mughals were the last of the great empires to control large portions of the territory of modern-day India before the advent of colonial rule. The Mughal empire was at its zenith from the middle of the sixteenth century till the early part of the eighteenth century, shortly before the death of Emperor Aurangzeb in 1707. Although it covered a vast territory across present-day India, the Mughal Empire was primarily concerned with issues of commerce, trade and taxation. Ideas of constitutional governance, as understood in the contemporary, modern sense, were not well developed in any of the pre-colonial regimes in India. As in many other parts of Asia and Africa, such ideas were often developed by leaders of anti-colonial movements whose introduction to ideas of nationalism, liberalism and constitutional democracy emerged through their exposure – either through education or through texts – to discourses in the metropolitan centres of colonial rule.

The Portuguese were the first Europeans to arrive in India in 1510, followed successively by the French, the Dutch and the British. By the early part of the seventeenth century, several European trading posts had been established in India. By the time the Mughal Empire went into active decline around the middle of the eighteenth century, the struggle for control over trade between the European powers was largely between the British and French as other European powers had been marginalised. Eventually, the British became the dominant European power in the Indian subcontinent.

The British presence in India was established through the East India Company, which had been created by a charter of the British Parliament in 1600 as a mercantile body that was to possess a trading monopoly in the East. Soon after its creation, the East India Company was able to obtain a toe-hold in India during the reign of the Mughal Emperor Jahangir and initially focused on expanding its commercial and mercantile activities in India. The East India Company was initially granted certain limited powers of a legislative character, including the power to impose penalties, to enable it to perform its commercial functions.[12] As the Company's operations expanded, it demanded and obtained greater legislative, executive and ultimately, judicial powers. The initial laws issued by the Company sought to establish courts and other institutions of English/Continental law in several of the territories under their control. This led later to the codification of criminal, civil and 'personal' laws of various Indian religious communities. Over time, the Company officials obtained powers similar to legislators for India, but continued to deny the responsibilities that came with exercising effective state authority in India.[13]

[12] Keith, *A Constitutional History*, (n 11) 5–6.

[13] See generally, R Mukherji, *The Rise and Fall of the East India Company: A Sociological Appraisal* (New York, Monthly Review Press, 1974); CH Philips, *The East India Company, 1784–1834* (Manchester, Manchester University Press, 1961); and T Roy, *The East India Company: The World's Most Powerful Corporation* (London, Penguin Books, 2012).

For nearly a century before its formal control over India ended, from about the middle of the eighteenth century till the middle of the nineteenth century, the Company conducted itself as a proxy for the British Government. The foundation of the colonial legal order was established in India during this period. The Company followed a practice of governing the Indian colony through a Governor General and his Legislative Council at the central level, and through a Governor and his Legislative Council at the level of the provinces. Appointments to these offices were based on nominations which in turn depended on the judgment of the Company and its supervising governmental authorities.

By the late eighteenth century, the East India Company adopted the coercive, administrative and financial processes typical of contemporaneous empires, and gradually took on more of the functions of sovereignty, such as collecting revenue, making treaties or fighting wars with regional potentates and exercising juridical authority.[14] This was accompanied by high levels of corruption, acts of despotism, and a growing perception that the officials of the Company were exploitative and immoral in their extractive zeal. This led to demands, primarily from within Britain, that the British Parliament intervene to remedy the situation which in turn led to legislative acts to regulate the functioning of the East India Company. In response, the British Parliament enacted the Regulating Act of 1773 to overhaul the management and operations of the East India Company. A decade later, to rebut the perception that the Regulating Act was not effective in its mission, the East India Company Act of 1784 sought to further these reforms by establishing a Board of Control and by strengthening the British Government's regulatory powers over the Company. The clamour against company misrule also resulted in the impeachment of the former Governor-General, Warren Hastings which, while ultimately unsuccessful, ignited a heated domestic debate championed by figures such as Edmund Burke on empire, liberalism and its consequences for ideas of British governance and democracy.

B. The British Raj and Colonial Forms of Constitutional Government (1858–1947): A Bird's Eye View

> It was the aim of the greatest among the early British administrators in India to train the peoples of India to govern and protect themselves … rather than to establish the rule of a British bureaucracy.
>
> Arthur Berridale Keith[15]

This statement captures, in overarching terms, the view of a section of the British colonial administrators about the overall objective of colonial government in

[14] J Burbank and F Cooper (eds), *Empires in World History* (Princeton, Princeton University Press, 2010) 170–178 & 240–245.

[15] Keith, *A Constitutional History*, (n 11) 1.

India during the period of direct British rule. This 'pedagogical' self-perception of the colonial role was severely contested by the growing nationalist movement and, in the next section, we will see how it led the nationalists to evolve constitutional documents that set out a competing vision for constitutionalism in India. At the same time, each constitutional development initiated by the colonial authorities across this period was at least in part a response to the nationalist movement's criticism of the previous initiative. In what follows, due to constraints of space, I focus on significant legislative instruments enacted by the British Parliament during this period, rather than other events that were also salient. This survey of laws enables one to appreciate how the colonial forms of constitutional government evolved over this nine-decade period.

The Great Indian Mutiny of 1857 – or the First War of Independence as it came to be called by the nationalists – was the death-knell of East India Company rule, which had already been facing criticism in Britain for over a century. Through the enactment of the Government of India Act 1858 by the British Parliament, the task of governing India was formally transferred to the British Crown, acting through the Secretary of State. The colony of British India – comprising the territory of present-day India, Pakistan and Bangladesh – was formally ruled by the British Government for 90 years (from 1857 to 1947), a period often referred to as the period of the 'British Raj'. One major change to the structure of the Governor-General's Legislative Council from the time of Company rule was that under the new regime, an Executive Council was set up to aid the newly-created office of Viceroy (which replaced the office of the Governor-General of India).

i. Early Constitutional Developments in The Indian Councils Acts

Despite the formal change, little of substance changed on the ground, at least initially. The Indian Councils Act of 1861 made a few technical changes to the governmental superstructure that had been used by the East India Company to govern India, without addressing the increasing demand for representation in the Councils by Indians. The demand for real change became more pressing after the formation of the Indian National Congress in 1885. This event represented the growing clout of the emerging Indian middle class, which was still small in numerical terms but whose growth was a consequence of the introduction of schools, the press and associational forms facilitated by the policies of the East India Company. Initially, the Congress was dominated by a moderate wing, led by Gopal Krishna Gokhale, who chose the path of negotiating with the colonial authorities through the route of petitions to seek incremental reforms, while engaging in social service alongside.

The Indian Councils Act of 1892 sought to respond to the nationalists' demand for greater representation for Indians in the Legislative Councils, by making some minor administrative changes. However, the worsening economic and political situation, caused by famine, the spread of bubonic plague and the growing popularity of Bal Gangadhar Tilak (the leader of the extremist wing of the Congress) led to the perception that these were feeble attempts to assuage a rising tidal wave of demands for reform. These rising demands were not satisfied by the next legislative measure – the Indian Councils Act of 1909 – which increased the representative capacity of the Legislative Councils, extended their powers and also recommended that Indians be appointed within the Governor General's Council. However, like its predecessor enactments, it effectively left control in the hands of the executive with little restraint on its powers. It therefore lacked credibility as a serious initiative towards constitutional reform. Keith approvingly notes that the authors of this particular reform 'absolutely disclaimed the idea of introducing responsible government or parliamentary institutions within India'.[16] They did, however, seek to 'consult' Indians in matters affecting their interests. The overall approach of British administrators (and scholars such as Keith who recorded their efforts) was to oppose the introduction of representative politics of the British type in India, convinced as they were alongside leading British liberals like JS Mill, that Indians were not ready for full liberal democratic politics because of the stage of their civilisation.

To understand why there was a mismatch between the approaches of the colonial administrators and the growing nationalist movement, it is important to recall that the Indian nationalists were closely following developments across the globe, and especially in other British colonies. The granting of dominion status, with concomitant concessions to autonomy and self-rule, to Canada in 1867, Australia in 1901, and South Africa in 1910, emboldened the nationalists to press for similar concessions for Indians. However, the British were not willing to concede such a status to India for a long time to come. Among the first to understand this was Mohandas Gandhi, who had struggled unsuccessfully in South Africa through much of the 1890s and the 1900s to seek parity with the white settler population for his fellow Indians in South Africa.[17] Upon his return to India in 1915, Gandhi began a process of self-discovery and re-examination of his beliefs in relation to his approach towards British colonial authorities. By 1919, he concluded that the British would never treat Indians on par with the white settler colonies and that a different approach would be required.

ii. The Government of India Acts of 1909 and 1919

To return to the chronology of colonial concessions to constitutional governance for Indians, Keith notes that the reforms of 1909–1912 were 'clearly unlikely' to satisfy the demands of the extremist wing of the Congress party led by Bal Gangadhar Tilak, and 'in fact went but a small way to conciliate the moderates'[18] led by Gopal Krishna Gokhale, who had become a mentor to Mohandas Gandhi.

[16] ibid, 258.
[17] For details, see generally, R Guha, *Gandhi before India* (New Delhi, Penguin, 2013).
[18] ibid, 264.

The First World War and the stellar role played by Indian soldiers in the important theatres of the war,[19] made it imperative that the colonial government be seen to be responsive to the growing demand of Indians for representative government.

It was against this context that the Government of India Act 1919 was enacted in December 1919, which promised some significant changes 'with a view of the progressive realisation of responsible government in India'.[20] In its details, the Act sought to fulfil its promises by emphasising greater autonomy to the provinces, and by making changes to the powers of the Secretary of State and his Council, and those of the Central and provincial governments. The Act introduced a system of 'dyarchy' in the provinces whereby for some subjects in a 'transferred list', authority to legislate would be subject to scrutiny and accountability by the Provincial Council. These reforms were truly significant in that they held the prospect of enabling Indians to exercise real legislative power, especially at the provincial level. But, the Act offset the impact of these changes by providing a very restricted franchise, by making very small budgets available to provincial legislatures, and by including rural and special interest seats that were perceived as amenable to control by the colonial authorities. The reforms sought to be ushered in by the Act of 1919 were diluted by the near simultaneous enactment of the draconian Rowlatt Act 1919 and the brutal massacre ordered by General Dwyer at the Jallianwala Bagh, which definitively turned public opinion against the colonial authorities. Although the Government of India Act 1919 did not have a great impact in practice, its innovations were later discussed for inclusion in the text of the Constitution of independent India, and for this reason, it remains a significant constitutional landmark, apart from it being an improvement over its predecessor enactments.

By 1920, Mohandas Gandhi had emerged as the undisputed leader of the Congress Party. Although he started as Gokhale's protégé, his experience of following 'moderate' politics in South Africa appears to have convinced him of the limitations of such an approach. After his return to India in 1915, Gandhi began to initiate campaigns that had seeds in the experiments that he had begun while in South Africa. These campaigns – built on the strategies of *satyagraha* (Striving for Truth) and *ahimsa* (Non-violence) – in turn converted the Indian National Congress from an elite group of middle-class intellectuals to a mass movement with deep roots across the Indian subcontinent. In the aftermath of the Jallianwala Bagh massacre, Gandhi started a non-cooperation movement which found support across the whole of British India and signalled the emergence of a new kind of anti-colonial movement.[21]

[19] See generally, S Sen, *For King and Another Country* (New Delhi, Bloomsbury, 2016).

[20] This quote is taken from the statement of the newly appointed Secretary of State, Edwin Montague, who took office in June 1917. Montague, together with Lord Chelmsford, the erstwhile Viceroy of India, authored the Montague-Chelmsford report which formed the basis of the Government of India Act of 1919.

[21] For details, see generally, R Guha, *Gandhi: The Years that Changed the World* (New Delhi, Penguin, 2018).

iii. The Government of India Act of 1935 and the Indian Independence Act of 1947

The next significant law to be passed by the British Parliament to regulate constitutional development in India was the Government of India Act 1935. This law made some pivotal changes and introduced many elements, especially in relation to its federal provisions, that were ultimately retained in the Constitution of India. The Act of 1935 introduced direct elections and expanded the franchise, enabling several million Indians to exercise voting rights. It also established the Federal Court in India, which became an important judicial institution, and was both the predecessor and a role model of sorts for the Supreme Court that was eventually established by the Constitution of India. Indeed, one respected scholar has asserted that as much as 75 per cent of the Government of India Act 1935 was to find place in the new Constitution of independent India.[22] However, we should not assume that the 1935 Act actively sought to secure 'responsible government' for Indians. While it had several notable features, the 1935 Act was apace with other colonial constitutional documents in empowering the colonial executive with supreme powers, including the power to take back any of those conferred upon bodies where Indians were allowed to exercise legislative and executive power. The 1935 Act abolished the system of dyarchy introduced by the 1919 Act, which was both unpopular and impractical. It went further than any other colonial statute in empowering provincial governments but, as mentioned earlier, also enabled the colonial executive to step in and retrieve powers, should it perceive any threat. This was viewed as paternalistic and thus an incurable flaw by the nationalist movement. As we will see in the next section, the nationalist movement had, by this time, experimented with several constitutional documents and had presented them to the colonial authorities. What is striking about the 1935 Act is how completely it ignored the demands of the nationalist movement on many fronts, including their demand for a bill of rights, and how it represented a step back even from the 1919 Act. It is important to recall that the 1935 Act was the result of a compromise between those who sought to advance responsible government in India and those who were completely opposed to it. Since the law was enacted by a Conservative Government, it is perhaps no surprise that those opposed to granting any meaningful concessions to the Indian nationalist movement won out.

As it happened, the federal provisions of the 1935 Act never came into effect. The Act of 1935 came into force in relation to the provinces only in 1937.

[22] SC Kashyap, *Our Constitution: An Introduction to India's Constitution and Constitutional Law* (New Delhi, National Book Trust, 2004) 4–5. See also, A Elangovan, 'Provincial Autonomy, Sir Benegal Narsing Rau, and an Improbable Imagination of Constitutionalism in India, 1935–38' (2016) 36(1) *Comparative Studies of South Asia, Africa and the Middle East* 66–82 (noting that the continuity can also be explained by the fact that Sir BN Rau was an important contributory draftsperson of both constitutional documents).

In elections held in 1937, Congress governments were elected in 8 out of 11 provinces. For the next two years, until 1939 when the Indian National Congress decided that its provincial governments would resign en masse to protest against the British Government's unilateral decision that British India join the Allied cause in the Second World War, the Congress had, for the first time, the direct experience of governance. This was to prove crucial for many reasons, and also explained why, despite their awareness of the flaws of the 1935 Act, Congress was willing to retain elements of the 1935 scheme in the Constitution of independent India.

As noted above, the start of the Second World War in 1939 affected the implementation of the 1935 Act. As in the case of the First World War, Indian soldiers were used extensively in the major theatres of the War, and India's involvement in the war, once again, led to demands for the grant of independence in exchange for loyalty to the Allied cause.[23] These efforts did not yield much result due to opposition from Conservative politicians in England.

After the Second War ended in 1945, a Labour Government under Clement Atlee was elected. Atlee's Government brought about radical reforms within the UK and presided over the start of the decolonisation of the British Empire in South Asia. Atlee's Government took a realistic view of the following factors in reaching its decision to exit from the colonies: the state of the UK's poor finances in the post-War era; the international pressure that the UK was facing for the hypocrisy between its rhetoric against the Axis powers and its own oppressive conduct in its colonies; and the lack of confidence expressed by imperial generals about the ability of the Indian army to remain impervious to the call of nationalism.

The Indian Independence Act of 1947 was the principal legal instrument by which the new nations of Pakistan and India came into being in August 1947. Its effect was to formally bring to an end to 182 years of British rule in India, confer dominion status upon the new nations of Pakistan and India from 15 August 1947, and to provide for legal and administrative continuity until the new constitutional orders in both nations emerged. In India, the process of creating a new constitution began formally on 9 December 1946, when the Constituent Assembly held its first sitting. The next section of this chapter will delve into the details about the body and its processes. However, since this factor is underemphasised in the current literature, it is important to acknowledge that the intellectual groundwork for the process of crafting a new constitution for independent India was a process that began at least half a century before the first sitting of the newly-constituted Constituent Assembly.

[23] See generally, S Raghavan, *India's War: The Making of Modern South Asia, 1939–45* (New Delhi, Allen Lane, 2016) and R Karnad, *Farthest Field: An Indian Story of the Second World War* (New Delhi, Fourth Estate, 2016).

C. The Nationalist Movement and the Build-up of Attempts at Constitution-Making (1885–1947): A Worm's Eye View

As noted in the previous section, the Indian National Congress went through a process of change and evolution since its founding in 1885. At first, it was a small organisation formed of middle- and upper-class Indians and was derisively referred to as a 'debating club'. By 1920, under Gandhi's charismatic leadership, it had been transformed into a mass movement that grew in numbers and popularity almost continuously until India gained independence in 1947. In the previous section, we noted how the Congress resisted and opposed the incremental and often painfully slow concessions made by the British colonial regime towards providing autonomy and self-governance to Indians. However, the Congress was not just an oppositional force; it was equally a constructive force, and was simultaneously involved in creating a new vision for the independent country that India would eventually become. This nation and constitution-building aspect of the Congress' working has been relatively neglected in contrast to the large body of work that has studied its resistance to colonial constitutional statutes by demanding greater autonomy as a means towards *Swaraj* or self-rule. This section focuses on the constitutional documents that were drafted by the Congress from fairly early on in its history. The focus will be on the evolution of this constitutional vision as the Congress' own sense of what the independent Indian nation would represent and symbolise changed over time.

i. The Earliest Attempts at Constitution-Making (1885–1895)

An early example of the first phase of the Congress is to be found in two resolutions passed by the 1889 session of the Indian National Congress held in Bombay. These resolutions, passed within five years of its inception, saw Congress seeking more representation for Indians in the Legislative Councils.[24] However, soon thereafter in 1895, came the Constitution of India Bill. While its author remains unverified, the document states that it had been prepared after a study of the constitutions of the US and Brazil, and contained provisions relating to the Government of India which were housed in separate chapters detailing provisions relating to the legislature, executive and judiciary.[25] The Bill also contained a set of rights provisions which primarily sought guarantees of civil and political rights. This was, from the point of British constitutional tradition, a radical demand, since British constitutional culture, even today, is very sceptical about constitutionalised bills of rights. The Bill further sought to catalogue the issues that could potentially form the subject of legislation (an early form of the List system that would be used in the final Constitution to classify subject

[24] The full text of the two resolutions are reproduced in BS Rao, *The Framing of India's Constitution*, vol 1 (New Delhi, Universal Law Publishing, 1967) 3–4.

[25] The full text of the Constitution of India Bill is set out at Rao, ibid, 5–14.

matter competence between the central and state legislatures) and also made a bold attempt to catalogue the departments within the executive (equivalent to Ministers in our time). Consisting of 111 provisions, this Bill represented an early yet sophisticated attempt at drafting a Constitution for independent India. What is striking is that this document – conceived more than half a century before the eventual Constitution for independent India was drafted and adopted – anticipates many of the institutional issues that would come to dominate the imagination of the framers of the independence Constitution.

ii. Evolution of Constitution-Making Efforts: The Commonwealth of India Bill, 1925 and the Motilal Nehru Report, 1928

As Congress continued to grow and internal debates became more sophisticated, more resolutions, declarations and models continued to emerge. In 1918, at another annual session held in Bombay, Congress issued a Declaration of Rights that sought a statute from the British Parliament recognising a series of rights for Indians that were on a par with British citizens. In the early 1920s, under the leadership of Annie Besant and the respected lawyer, Tej Bahadur Sapru, the Commonwealth of India Bill was drafted by a Convention consisting of 255 persons endorsed by Congress and introduced in the British House of Commons in 1925 but this went nowhere with Labour's loss of office in 1924. Nevertheless, the contents of the Bill are noteworthy also because they influenced models of constitutions that emerged in its wake. The Commonwealth of India Bill conceived of the right to local self-government and envisaged five levels of government across the village, taluk, district, province and central level.[26] It guaranteed a set of rights which went beyond the classic civil and political rights (including the right to liberty, property, freedom of conscience and free expression) to social rights (specifically the right to free elementary education).

Shortly afterwards, at the Madras session of the Congress in 1927, it was resolved that a Swaraj Constitution would be drafted for India. This eventually led to the creation of a committee led by the senior Congress leader, Motilal Nehru, and consisting of others such as Tej Bahadur Sapru. The Nehru Report, as it came to be known, drafted a constitution that was based on the principle of Dominion status for India (seeking parity with the colonies of Canada, Australia, New Zealand, South Africa and the Irish Free State), and devised a responsible government of the parliamentary model. As Niraja Jayal has argued, the Constitution drafted by the Nehru Report was 'a rather exceptional document' as it envisioned many novel aspects.[27] It contained an extensive provision on rights, which directly inspired many provisions in the Fundamental Liberties chapter (Part III) of the eventual Constitution while some others inspired

[26] For the full text of the Bill, see Rao, ibid, 43–50.

[27] NG Jayal, *Citizenship and its Discontents* (Cambridge, MA, Harvard University Press, 2013) 138–139.

provisions in the chapter on Directive Principles of State Policy (Part IV). The Nehru Report had more elaborate provisions on the structure and form of the three wings of government than any previous constitution-making effort, and also sought to tackle the thorny issue of communal representation explicitly.

iii. Alternative Conceptions of the Constitution and the Sapru Committee Report (1945)

In the period after the Nehru Report was published in 1928, Congress continued to demand greater autonomy from the colonial regime while also investing in developing its own constructive vision of what a constitution for independent India should consist of. Once the Second World War began, followed by the 'Quit India' movement launched by Congress in 1942, attempts at constitution-making with the view to influencing the new Constitution became even more urgent. Before turning to Congress's efforts, it is worth noting that three attempts by non-Congress individuals and groups sought to provide alternative conceptions of the new Constitution. These include: MN Roy's *Constitution of India: A Draft* (1946), SN Agarwal's *Gandhian Constitution for free India* (1946), and the Socialist Party's *Draft Constitution of Indian Republic* (1948).[28] Roy, a former Communist, authored a radical and populist Constitution which contained many guarantees of social rights. Agarwal's Constitution drew from Gandhian ideas of village-based, decentralised governance. The Socialist Party's Constitution conspicuously left out the right to property. These alternative conceptions are worth emphasising to draw attention to the fact that while the Indian National Congress enjoyed great popular support, it had to contend with many other streams of opinion and thought which often clashed with its own ideas, and which were difficult to build consensus upon given the wide range of interests and ideologies represented within the Congress itself. Recalling these facts is necessary to appreciate the importance of the inclusive style of decision-making followed in the Constituent Assembly.

In December 1945, a committee under the leadership of Tej Bahadur Sapru and consisting of members including N Gopalaswami Ayyangar (who would play a pivotal role within the Constituent Assembly) was constituted to deal with the growing problem of communalism and the significant issue of minority rights. The Sapru Committee Report placed considerable emphasis on minority protection and the rights of minorities, and became an influential model for these provisions in the eventual Constitution of India.[29]

[28] Jayal, ibid, 143.

[29] This voluminous report also saw several notes of dissent drafted by some of its members. The full text of the Report, being too large to be included in its entirety in the B Shiva Rao papers, is available online at: https://ia801407.us.archive.org/19/items/saprucommittee035520mbp/saprucommittee035520mbp.pdf.

II. CRAFTING A CONSTITUTION FOR INDEPENDENT INDIA: THE WORK OF THE CONSTITUENT ASSEMBLY (1946–1949)

A. Background and Origin of the Constituent Assembly

The work of India's Constituent Assembly has been described in laudatory, even heroic, terms.[30] It has also been the subject of strong criticism, both contemporaneous and recent.[31] Regardless of whether one thinks of it as broadly positive or not, the result of the framers' efforts have been markedly influential across the post-colonial world, and its provisions came to be emulated by many other constitutions. This section focuses on the origins of the Constituent Assembly, its processes and the main themes that it dealt with.

As noted in the previous section, many Indians – and not just the leaders of the nationalist movement – had focused on the nature and type of constitution that independent India should be governed by for a considerable period of time before independence was actually achieved. The Indian National Congress' previous efforts at constitution-making were marked by robust debate among several contending positions and had reached an advanced stage of deliberation whereby consensus was reached on some broad issues such as the need for a strong bill of rights, agreement that a parliamentary system would work best for India's many needs, and the need for a federal system which would guard against fissiparous tendencies while allowing India's diversity to flourish.

It is important to consider the backdrop against which the Constituent Assembly was established in December 1946. After the Second War and the election of Prime Minister Atlee's Labour Government, Great Britain was finally willing to grant independence to India, albeit on its own terms. By the mid-1940s, the differences between the Indian National Congress and the Muslim League had become unbridgeable in part because Mohammed Ali Jinnah, the leader of the Muslim League, who had been a prominent and important member of the Congress during its crucial foundational period, was deeply sceptical that the Congress would successfully represent India's diversity beyond its own constituency, the dominant sections of the Hindu population. In 1945, Jinnah had expressed scepticism about the idea of a single Constituent Assembly,

[30] The most prominent of these adulatory accounts is still by G Austin, *The Indian Constitution: Cornerstone of a Nation*, 2nd edn (New Delhi, Oxford University Press, 1999). Austin's account of the making of the Indian Constitution is regarded as authoritative, five decades on, but is written in stirring, adulatory tones which, even as it seeks to critique several aspects of the working of the framers, has a consistently positive appraisal of the process and the results reached.

[31] See generally, S Chaube, *Constituent Assembly of India: Springboard of Revolution*, 2nd edn (New Delhi, Manohar Publishers, 2000). A recent work which is scathing in its criticism of the overall 'imperial' approach of the Constituent Assembly is by M Mukherjee, *India in the Shadows of Empire* (Oxford, Oxford University Press, 2010); see also, P Anderson, *The Indian Ideology*, 2nd edn (New Delhi, Three Essays Collective, 2015) 103–134.

demanding two separate Assemblies for the new nations of India and Pakistan. For its part, Congress, which had the backing of many Muslims, regarded Jinnah as unfairly attacking its secular character, and exploiting long-simmering communal tensions to build his 'two-nation' theory. The primary reason for Partition was undoubtedly the fact that these two significant political groupings could not come to an agreement on the future of colonial India. Their differences notwithstanding, there were several rounds of negotiations between the Congress and the Muslim League to begin the process of constitution-making even as such tensions persisted.

In May 1946, the Cabinet Mission, which had been established by the Atlee Government to effect the transfer of power from the British to the Indians, delivered its report. Although both Congress and the Muslim League had reservations, both formally accepted the plan, after which elections for the Constituent Assembly of India were held in July 1946. Congress had long demanded a Constituent Assembly elected on the basis of universal adult suffrage. It, however, gave in to the Cabinet Mission proposal that the Constituent Assembly be indirectly elected, through the existing provincial legislatures, because it recognised that holding general elections on the basis of universal franchise would delay the important task of convening the Constituent Assembly. The decision of the Congress to constitute a Constituent Assembly on such a limited franchise was criticised at the time and has attracted perennial criticism by scholars and commentators since. We will examine some of the issues involved in a later section.

The three major groups with representation within the Assembly were Congress, the Muslim League and the representatives of the 562 Princely States. Of the 389 seats in the Constituent Assembly, 93 were accorded to the representatives of the Princely States, while Congress (208) and the Muslim League (73) emerged as the dominant political parties. The first session of the Constituent Assembly was held on 6 December 1946, but given the tense atmosphere, not much business was transacted. On 13 December 1946, Nehru moved the 'Objectives Resolution' which set out the broad objectives and contours of the constitution-making process. The Constituent Assembly also started identifying the various working committees that would do the major work of drafting portions of the eventual Constitution, but discussions did not begin in earnest until after independence. The Muslim League participated only half-heartedly in the Assembly's initial sessions; even this stopped after Jinnah instructed its members to boycott the Assembly in July 1947. The second and third sessions of the Constituent Assembly were held in January and April 1947, but the prospect of Partition ensured that substantive deliberations on important issues were minimal. Once the Indian Independence Act of 1947 came into force on 15 August 1947, the Constituent Assembly was formally granted legal recognition, enabling it to move much faster towards its goal. It did so, however, without the presence of members of the Muslim League or the Princely States. This too has affected the perception of its credibility and legitimacy.

B. The Ambient Atmosphere of Constitution-Making

The immediate effect of the Indian Independence Act 1947 was to make the Constituent Assembly also the Dominion Parliament. Members of the Assembly were simultaneously converted into parliamentarians and they spent half of their time dealing with the day-to-day matters of government. Being seized with immediate problems inevitably affected their long-term constitutional vision, especially on crucial issues such as the powers that the executive and Parliament should have to restrict the rights of citizens. Awareness of the broader context at the time will help us situate their decisions better.

From 1946 to 1950, the Indian subcontinent was, to put it mildly, in a state of turmoil. Although the Atlee Government was praised for its decision to free India and its other South Asian colonies, this decision was made in an overly hasty manner, which made the by-then inevitable partition of the Indian subcontinent into the Muslim-dominated Pakistan and the Hindu-dominated India more messy and violent than it had to be. The British Government had originally announced in February 1947 that it would quit India by June 1948. However, in June 1947, the newly appointed viceroy, Lord Mountbatten, announced that Partition would come into effect not after a year, but in two months. This led to a sense of panic that historians – both British and Indian – believe exacerbated the problems involved. The subcontinent had been roiled by communal riots since August 1946. After starting in the eastern city of Calcutta, the riots had spread westwards through the states of Bihar, and to the capital in Delhi. By 1 November 1946, the death toll across India had reached 5,000. Once Partition was effected in August 1947, the subcontinent bore witness to 'the greatest mass migration in history': between 10 and 15 million people emigrated in response to the physical dismembering that led to the creation of the new state of Pakistan out of parts of the eastern and western perimeters of British India. Both new nations had to scramble to prevent mass carnage. In the latter, they were only partly successful: erstwhile estimates of the killings put the number of deaths at one million, while more recent historians believe that the death toll reached two million. On 30 January 1948, after he had made valiant efforts to quell the communal killings, Gandhi was assassinated in Delhi by a Hindu fundamentalist who later blamed him for causing the partition of India by conceding to Muslim demands.

There were other monumental problems. It is often forgotten that British India was not a cohesive political entity. The British governed a large portion of their territory in India indirectly, large pockets of which were constituted by the 562 assorted chiefdoms and states known as the 'princely states'. The new governments of India and Pakistan had to negotiate with each of these rulers to persuade them to join their territories or face the prospect of 'balkanization' of the sub-continent. While most rulers eventually agreed to join the new states, some rulers held out: Junagadh (in western India), Hyderabad (in southern India) and Kashmir (in northern India, with a shared border with

Pakistan). While the ruler of Junagadh eventually agreed in November 1947, the Indian Government had to send in its military to overwhelm the defiant ruler of Hyderabad in September 1948. Kashmir would prove to be a much harder case. It has been a continuing source of strife between India and Pakistan and has resulted in armed skirmishes on several occasions, including for many long months from 1947 to 1948. The terms under which Kashmir joined India have led to continuing legal uncertainty, and social and political strife nearly continuously to the present time.[32]

In the immediate aftermath of Partition, many of the major Indian cities were flooded with refugees: the numbers ranged from half a million each in Delhi and Bombay, to 1.7 million in Calcutta. In all, an estimated eight million refugees entered India. What made the problem worse was the serious shortage of food supply, coupled with an inflationary crisis across the nation. These were only some of manifestations of the grave economic problems that the British Empire bequeathed to the subcontinent. Exploitative economic policies over two centuries resulted in a huge mass of the population being left in the grip of poverty, illiteracy and severe forms of underdevelopment. To address these issues, Nehru's government was determined to carve out space for a strong, centralised government in the Constitution to undertake the massive social development programmes that were urgently needed.

Those broader problems were made more acute because of the effects of the Partition, the influx of refugees and the continuing spectre of communal and other forms of violence. The communist parties in India, which enjoyed popular support in the Telangana region of Hyderabad state and in parts of Bengal, had, in February 1948, proclaimed the start of a general revolution in India and advocated forms of violence against the Indian state. The Indian Government responded with propaganda and repression, causing their support to dwindle temporarily. The government also turned its instruments of force upon members of the Hindu fundamentalist groups in the wake of Gandhi's assassination, banning the Rashtriya Swayamsevak Sangh (RSS) and arresting several of its cadres. Having to deal with the threat posed by the RSS and the communists gave many of the leaders of free India an appreciation of the police powers enjoyed by the colonial state, and this appreciation is also reflected in their attitude towards restrictions on fundamental liberties that were then under discussion in the Assembly. These factual circumstances resulted in substantive and structural responses and solutions from the framers that influenced the

[32] In August 2019, the Modi government sought to address the issue of Kashmir by abrogating the provision which gave special status to Kashmir and downgrading it from a state to a Union Territory. Kashmir has been in a state of lockdown since then, and while the civil liberties of the residents of Kashmir have attracted international attention, there have been constitutional challenges to these actions which are now pending before the Supreme Court, having been stalled for inexplicable reasons. At the time of writing, therefore, the legal uncertainty around the status of Kashmir continues.

broader constitutional vision and specific institutional arrangements in the new and independent India.

C. Processes, Modes of Functioning, and Stages of Constitution-Making in the Constituent Assembly

The Constituent Assembly of India was in existence for two years, 11 months and 18 days, between its first session on 6 December 1946 and its final session on 26 November 1949 when the final draft of the Constitution was adopted. A great deal of attention was paid to the processes and procedures that would be followed in order to make the 389-member body function efficiently and democratically. For this purpose, the Assembly had engaged the services of Sir BN Rau, who had recently retired from the judicial side of the Indian Civil Service and had considerable exposure to comparative trends in constitution-making, having been involved in the making of the Government of India Act 1935 and the Constitution of Burma of 1947. The level of preparation and planning is evident from a note prepared by him in September 1946 which contained comprehensive notes on the modes of voting, whether sessions should be open or held *in camera*, how the Chairman should be chosen, the language to be used, and cited precedents from the constitution-making exercises in the US, Canada, and South Africa.[33] The Assembly had access to a well-staffed Secretariat which was paid for out of central revenues and was thus able to attract high-calibre officials.[34]

The Assembly constituted itself into several committees (more than 15 in total) to complete its work. Of these, eight handled the major issues: Rules, Steering, Advisory, Drafting, Union Subjects, Union Constitution, Provincial Constitution and States. These eight committees had approximately 36 members in all. Granville Austin notes that some of the members of the Assembly were more equal than others because of their stature as leaders of the nationalist struggle and their role in government. Austin refers to four of these – Jawaharlal Nehru, Vallabhbhai Patel, Abul Kalam Azad and Rajendra Prasad – as the 'oligarchy' who wielded enormous authority within the Assembly while also holding important positions in the Dominion Government. Another prominent member of the Assembly was BR Ambedkar who was appointed, at Gandhi's insistence, as the Chairperson of the Drafting Committee. Dr Ambedkar was the undisputed leader of the former Untouchables and his appointment was an important symbolic reminder of the diversity within India. Other influential Assembly members, representing a range of regional, linguistic, religious and

[33] 'A Note on points of procedure- Sep 2, 1946', available in Rao, *The Framing of India's Constitution*, (n 24) 405–418.

[34] 'Setting up the Constituent Assembly Secretariat: Correspondence and Notes', available in Rao, ibid, (n 24) 360–372.

intellectual strands included KT Shah, KM Munshi, Syama Prasad Mookherjee, Purushottamdas Tandon, Rafi Ahmed Kidwai, Bakshi Tek Chand and AK Aiyar. Significantly, the Assembly had 15 women representatives with Hansa Mehta playing a significant role in the Fundamental Rights Sub-Committee, and Begum Aizaz Rasul being a consistent and vocal voice on the floor of the Assembly across a range of issues. As several commentators noted, the Congress took several concrete measures to ensure that the constituents of the Assembly represented as far as practicable, the range of interests present in Indian society particularly after Partition when the departure of the Muslim League members left it with an overwhelming dominance in the Assembly. Whether its efforts resulted in full and complete representation for all sections of Indian society remains a matter of controversy.

The Assembly completed its functioning in five stages:[35]

(1) The Working Committees for specific subject areas met, debated and deliberated, and prepared reports often requiring several revisions. This process lasted from December 1946 until August 1947.

(2) Sir BN Rau, the Constitutional Advisor, considered these reports and prepared a first draft of the Constitution in collaboration with the Assembly Secretariat between August–October 1947. This preparatory work included a tour to the US, Ireland and the UK where he met Presidents Truman and De Valera, and prominent judges in each country.

(3) The Drafting Committee, led by Dr BR Ambedkar, scrutinised the draft Constitution prepared by Sir BN Rau, and produced its own revised draft through daily meetings between 27 October 1947 and February 1948. This revised draft was then made public, inviting comments, suggestions and criticisms. The phase of gathering public responses and responding to them lasted from February to November 1948.

(4) In November 1948, Dr Ambedkar introduced the draft Constitution on the floor of the Constituent Assembly, following which a clause-by-clause deliberation was conducted over an eleven-month period between 15 November 1948 and 17 October 1949. Following this, the Drafting Committee met again to revise the draft Constitution, incorporating all the amendments that had been accepted and giving final shape to the Constitution.

(5) In November 1949, Dr Ambedkar presented the final draft of the Constitution before the Assembly. Amendments were considered by the Assembly between 14 and 16 November and on 26 November 1949, the Assembly adopted the final draft of the Constitution.

Two months later, the Constitution of India was formally enforced on 26 January 1950. In its original form, it contained 395 articles (divided into 22 parts) and 8 schedules and was one of the world's longest constitutions.

[35] 'Progress of the Constitution through the Assembly' in Rao, ibid, (n 24) 107–118.

This description of the working and methods of the Constituent Assembly allow us to note some striking features of its processes. Vatsal Naresh has recently argued that the astute processual strategies followed by the framers ensured that the Assembly's deliberations remained broadly untouched by the surrounding tumult and the 'hot passions' they inevitably generated.[36] The strategies he focuses upon include time delays at every stage of the constitution-making process, as well as conditions of separated responsibilities between the interim government and the assembly as well as between legislative and constitution-writing tasks within the Assembly. However, Naresh argues, the Assembly members were in fact influenced by 'cold passions' such as fear, anger and contempt in rejecting political safeguards for minorities (an issue that we return to in the next section).

Significantly, the Constitution of India was never ratified by the Indian people. This fact is also marshalled by critics of the Constitution who add this to the flawed democratic origins and legitimacy of the constitution of the Assembly. However, it is clear that the Assembly enjoyed wide support during its existence. In the first general elections, held in 1951–52, within two years of the adoption of the Constitution, the Nehru Government won a massive mandate, securing 364 of the 489 seats in the Lower House of Parliament. This was interpreted by many as a strong endorsement of the nationalist Congress government and also of the Constitution that was largely a product of the vision of the nationalist project.

D. A Survey of Important Provisions and Themes in the Text

This section provides a selective summary of some important features of the Constitution as a whole. Many important features have been omitted because of constraints of space. In summarising what was ultimately enshrined in the text and structure of the Constitution, this section also describes alternatives considered and debated, but eventually discarded. For some other provisions, the various considerations that were at play are concisely examined.

i. Separation of Powers and the Nature of the Executive

The Constitution of India established a modified version of the British Westminster form of parliamentary democracy in India. It divides power between the three classic wings of government by creating, at the federal/central level, a bicameral Parliament, a powerful Executive with an elected Prime Minister being the engine but with an indirectly-elected President also being

[36] V Naresh, 'Pride and Prejudice in Austin's Cornerstone' in U Bhatia (ed), *The Indian Constituent Assembly: Deliberations on Democracy* (New Delhi, Routledge, 2018) 58–82, 65.

given an important role, and a unitary Judiciary. Within this parliamentary form of government, the Executive is part of the Legislature and responsible to it. The Union Parliament consists of two Houses. The Lower House of Parliament consists of 543 representatives, each of whom is chosen through direct elections. The Upper House of Parliament consists of members elected on a rotational basis every two years. While the Upper House represents the States, they do not have equal representation and the seats are allocated on the basis specified in the Fourth Schedule to the Constitution. The President appoints the Prime Minister, and the Prime Minister and her Council of Ministers is responsible to the Lower House of Parliament. At the State/Provincial level, the arrangement is similar with an unelected Governor, appointed by the President, as the head of government, with a Council of Ministers headed by a Chief Minister to advise her. Most States have a unicameral Legislative Assembly where representatives are directly elected by the people in State elections that are conducted separately.

There was considerable debate before this executive structure was agreed upon. Members of minority communities, fearing an overweening executive, suggested models like the Swiss executive which diffuses power across the executive instead of concentrating it. Similarly, those who wished to empower the executive to carry out socio-economic reform, wanted a powerful, US-type Presidential executive. Neither of these positions was ultimately adopted. There was also a suggestion to have an elected President, but this was rejected by Nehru who insisted that power remain in the Ministries rather than in the office of the President. Nevertheless, the President's office is an important constitutional authority, and is not the ceremonial office of the British monarch. It is the character of this authority that gives the Republic its force.

ii. Federalism

India is both a republic and a federal state, albeit with a stronger central authority than in most federations. In the early stages, it was proposed that India would be a classical federal state, along the lines of the US and Australia, with enumerated powers for Parliament and residuary powers vested in the State legislatures. Once again, minority representatives wanted the States to have residuary powers as a strategy to prevent concentration of power in an all-powerful Union government. Here again, the advocates of having a strong Union government to harness power to effectuate much needed reforms won the argument. India's States thus have much less power than their counterparts in other federal nations. This extends to the lists which enumerate the subjects on which the Parliament or State legislatures can enact laws. The list of Union subjects of the Indian Constitution gives a predominant role to the federal government in relations between the Union and the States. Specific provisions mandate that the executive power of every State be exercised in compliance with the laws made by Parliament and in accordance with the exercise of executive power of the Union. The Union is vested with the power to issue directions to a State to comply with these provisions. The working of the Constitution, however, resulted in India becoming a more federal state in practice, though this change is attributable more to the playing out of practical politics.

As we saw earlier, the colonial government experimented with forms of representation for native Indians in various colonial laws and constitution-like documents from the 1860s till the dawn of independence. Some scholars have argued, based on following this chronology, that India's democracy can be viewed as an inheritance of the British Raj.[37] However, other scholars have noted that the institutions introduced by the colonial regime across the entire period were 'largely a means of co-opting ruling elites and strengthening the colonial state'.[38] While the Constitution of India did persist with aspects of the colonial legal order and in particular the provisions of the Government of India Act 1935, it contained many innovations and novel features which altered its character quite fundamentally. Important changes to the colonial order include a constitutionally-entrenched bill of rights, an independent judiciary and a range of constitutionally empowered technocratic institutions (including the Election Commission, and the Comptroller and Auditor General) which would serve as guardians of the constitutional order.

iii. Fundamental Rights

The 'Fundamental Rights' guaranteed to Indians are outlined in Part III of the Constitution of India which consists of 23 provisions (Articles 12–35). The rights guaranteed by this Part are classified under eight sub-headings. Six of these sub-headings guarantee the following categories of rights: the right to equality (Articles 14–18); the right to freedom (Articles 19–23); the right against exploitation (Articles 23–24); the right to freedom of religion (Articles 25–28); cultural and educational rights (Articles 29–30); and the right to constitutional remedies (Article 32). The remaining two categories include a 'General' section and another that seeks to save certain laws. The General section includes a definitions clause (Article 12) and a significant provision (Article 13) which declares that any laws made in contravention of the rights provisions will be void. This provision, by implication, vests in the Judiciary the power to strike down parliamentary laws. This, then, is the source of the important power of judicial review over legislative and administrative action that is vested in the Indian judiciary. India's judiciary is regarded as one of the most powerful in the world today, but it is generally assumed – wrongly – that the Constitution of India expressly vests the power of judicial review over legislation in the courts. While the Constitution, does vest important powers in the courts, these have been significantly expanded by the courts through judicial interpretation.

[37] See, eg, R Dahl, *Democracy and its Critics* (New Haven, Yale University Press, 1989); and M Weiner, *The Indian Paradox: Essays in Indian Politics* (New Delhi, Sage, 1989).

[38] O Shani, *How India became Democratic* (New Delhi, Penguin, 2018) 14.

A textual analysis indicates that these provisions, where they were not created to respond to indigenous concerns, were inspired in part by the bills of rights in the US and French Constitutions, and by the Universal Declaration of Human Rights. In their terms, however, many of the Indian rights provisions tend to be more elaborate than those that inspired them. In this, they anticipated the later trend of providing elaborate descriptions of rights provisions and the conditions under which restrictions can be legitimately imposed upon them by constitutional authorities.

It is not possible to provide a comprehensive summary of the evolution of each of these provisions here. However, to illustrate how both internal and external forces affected the decision to incorporate specific rights, I focus here on the inclusion of group rights within the fundamental rights chapter. These provisions were seen as necessary to tackle India's heterogeneity in respect of religion, caste and class. Another reason for focusing on this issue is its salience in the contemporary context, which has a direct bearing on current events that are the subject of intense debate.

As we saw earlier, the colonial authorities began taking hesitant steps to involve Indians in their own governance in the aftermath of the revolt of 1857, and especially after the formal transfer of power from the East India Company to the British Government in 1858. The 1872 census was an attempt by the colonial government to better understand the native population, and since they viewed Indians primarily through the lens of religion at the time, the census classified Indians by religion. Religion remained an important marker of the Indian colonial subject's identity throughout the period of colonial rule. Later, the categories of caste, race, and language were added to the potent mix of colonial identity. The overriding tendency of the colonial authorities was to view Indians primarily in terms of group affiliation rather than as individuals. What the colonial authorities learned in India – one of the earliest British colonies in Asia and Africa – about group identities marked by religion and race was repeated across the British Commonwealth with respect to other native populations, and these understandings were reflected in the legal categories that were created as a result and persist in many postcolonial orders across Asia and Africa.

The concessions to self-governance by the native populations took the form of group representation in the colonial legislatures. Attributable both to the colonial imperative of maintaining peace between different sections of the native population, and to the general British tendency to view natives through compartmental units, early British attempts at providing representation was in the form of groups that prioritised minority interests. An early form of this was in the nature of 'separate electorates' which were instituted at the national level by the Government of India Act 1909. These devices had been in place at the local government level in provinces such as the Punjab since the 1880s. Moving beyond the markers of religion and race, the colonial authorities gradually began to provide for legislative representation for groups along social and economic criteria. Through this process, landholders, universities and trade associations came to have representation in legislative bodies over time.

As this process evolved across the early twentieth century, colonial authorities bestowed group representational rights upon a greater variety of groups, along a broader range of institutional options. Beyond separate electorates, these included reserved seats in legislatures, weightage (guaranteed representatives for minorities that was greater than their enumerated share in the population) nomination and combinations of these mechanisms. So, the Government of India Act 1919 catered not only for separate electorates for Muslims but other measures for Sikhs, Indian Christians, Anglo-Indians and Europeans. The colonial government also recognised groups within the Hindu population, granting 'non-Brahmins' reserved seats in legislatures, and enabled members of the 'Depressed Classes' to become nominated members. This was reflected in the scheme of the Government of India Act 1935 which provided reserved seats in provincial legislatures for as many as 13 communal and socio-economic categories.[39] This trend of having reserved seats for religious and caste minorities was already in place in some of the Princely States such as Mysore.

A second measure to improve the representation and involvement of members of minority groups was effected at the executive level. A convention was developed by which minority representation at the cabinet level was secured across the provinces, especially by the time the Government of India Act 1935 was in force. A third strategy towards this overall objective of inclusivity was through group quotas in government employment. It was the Princely States who originated such policies. In 1874, Mysore instituted reservations for backward classes, to counter Brahmin dominance in the public services. Other Princely States such as Kolhapur, Travancore and Cochin, followed suit, and were later emulated by Madras and Kerala. In British India, the government of Punjab introduced a policy of balancing Hindu and Muslim members in government administration as early as in the 1880s. Over the next seven decades and by 1947, various policies were instituted, the consequence of which was that religious minorities (including in some cases caste and linguistic minorities) were 'proportionately represented, often over-represented, in national and provincial government employment'.[40]

Rochana Bajpai identifies three different phases of the evolution of group rights and privileges across the colonial period.[41] In the first stage, lasting until the 1920s, the colonial government's effort was to grant recognition of an entitlement to representation to communities such as Muslims who were seen as an important and distinct element of Indian society. Initially, Congress was not the mass party it became later, and was not unduly concerned about the recognition

[39] G Austin, *The Indian Constitution: Cornerstone of a Nation* (Oxford, Oxford University Press, 1966) 144.

[40] S Wilkinson, *Votes and Violence: Electoral Competition and Ethnic Riots in India* (Cambridge, Cambridge University Press, 2004) 106.

[41] R Bajpai, *Debating Difference: Group Rights and Liberal Democracy in India* (New Delhi, Oxford University Press, 2011) 37–43.

extended to Muslims and the Depressed Classes. By the 1920s, things had changed. The Congress-led national movement, under the charismatic leadership of Gandhi, had expanded greatly in scope and its self-understanding. The colonial government now began to dispense group representation and recognition as a way to 'safeguard' minorities against Congress and Hindu numerical dominance. By doing so, the colonial authorities also sought to legitimise colonial rule by offering protection to various minority groups. The Congress in turn became wary of minority safeguards, viewing them as a colonial device to perpetuate British rule by dividing the Indians. The groups which benefited the most from group rights and understandably championed them were the Muslims and the Depressed Classes/Scheduled Castes. In the months preceding independence and the negotiations over a new constitution, Congress was forced to be open to a range of options in relation to minority groups.

As Bajpai explains, there were two broad types of provisions that were to be negotiated. The first consisted of 'political' safeguards which sought to ensure representation for minority groups in legislatures, executives and government employment positions. These were essentially a continuation of the colonial policies which ensured separate electorates, reserved and nominated seats in legislatures, quotas for minorities in cabinets, government posts and services. The second category consisted of 'cultural rights and privileges' that sought to secure religious, cultural and educational rights for minority groups. This second category was an innovation as they had not been introduced by colonial policies given the British antipathy to rights discourse in general. These rights and privileges did have precursors in the draft constitutions prepared by the nationalist movement since 1895.

According to Bajpai, the convening of the Constituent Assembly in December 1946 marked the third and decisive phase. The Congress party was, at least initially, quite open to both categories of minority provisions, eager as it was to ensure that its actions did not give the Muslim League a reason to boycott the Constituent Assembly. However, things changed drastically within a few months. Jinnah's decision to boycott the Assembly and the fast-paced events that led to the violence of Partition completely altered the relative balance of power between the contestants for constitutional power. Following Partition, the main political parties which had advocated strong group rights for religious minorities – the Muslim League and the Sikh Panthic Party – disintegrated. In general, the supporters of political safeguards for religious minorities were considerably weakened overall. This did not apply to the other minority groups such as the backward classes, whose leader, Dr BR Ambedkar, continued to wield power within the Constituent Assembly and was able to secure political safeguards for the Scheduled Castes and Scheduled Tribes. What this meant was that the political safeguards that had applied during the colonial period to both religious minorities and backward classes were scaled back completely for the former. In the final Constitution, political safeguards applied only to Scheduled Castes and Scheduled Tribes. Religious minorities no longer had any political safeguards in the form of separate electorates, reserved or nominated seats in the legislature. Nor were quotas in the executive or in government posts made available to them. Such political safeguards were extended, as we noted in the previous section, only to Scheduled Castes, Scheduled Tribes and to Anglo-Indians. Religious minorities were instead extended the second category of group rights, that were designed to advance general rights to freedom of religion and cultural and educational rights in tandem. Even here, the final provisions were attenuated when compared to what was originally demanded.

The standard explanation for these limitations is the aftermath of Partition, and how conditions became unfavourable for demands such as political safeguards for religious minorities to be pursued. Bajpai's novel insight is that the liberal, nationalist vision of the nationalist movement in general and the Congress party in particular is an independent explanatory factor that accounts for this change. Through a detailed and careful examination of the preparatory documents and the debates in the Assembly, Bajpai argues that nationalist discourse 'comprised a set of inter-related concepts' including 'secularism, democracy, social justice, national unity and development' all of which were invoked by the nationalists within the Assembly to resist special provisions for groups. In this liberal, nationalist vision, group preference was generally deeply problematic to the vision of nationalism being advanced. However, this nationalist vision was more accommodating to the interests of Scheduled Castes and Tribes since they could be justified as rectifying social disadvantage. Congress and the nationalists generally considered group-differentiated rights legitimate as a temporary measure only for lower castes and tribes, but not for religious minorities. This liberal, nationalist vision was more open to broad liberal guarantees of the right to freedom of religion, and to cultural and educational rights that would enable minority religions to flourish. This explains the commitment to the rights to freedom of religion guaranteed under Articles 25–28 and the rights to cultural and educational rights guaranteed under 29–30. This is also why the political safeguards extended in Articles 33–42 apply only to Scheduled Castes, Tribes and Anglo-Indians, and not to Muslims. These foundational choices continue to be relevant in contemporary India, seven decades on, as we shall see.

iv. Directive Principles and their Separation from the Fundamental Rights

Part IV of the Constitution bears the title, 'Directive Principles of State Policy' and consists of 15 provisions (Articles 36–51). Tellingly, these Principles have not been further divided into sub-categories, perhaps because of the difficulty involved as they contain many different types of provisions. While the rights provisions are, in keeping with general trends elsewhere, often abstract, the Principles tend to focus both on general and very particular issues.

To get a sense of the Principles, let us examine the first few among them. The first provision, Article 36, states that the definition of 'state' applicable to fundamental rights will also apply to the Directive Principles which has important implications that the courts later elaborated upon. Article 37 is significant as it first stipulates that the Principles 'shall not be enforceable by any court' before providing that they 'are nevertheless fundamental in the governance of the country'. It also imposes a duty on the state 'to apply these principles in making laws'. Later in this chapter, we shall see how courts have interpreted the seemingly contradictory motivations of this provision. Articles 38 and 39 can be seen as evidence of the claim of the English constitutional jurist, Ivor Jennings, that 'the ghosts of [the British socialists] Sidney and Beatrice Webb stalk through the pages of the [Indian constitutional] text'.[42] Article 38 exhorts the state to create a social order where the welfare of the people is promoted and all institutions of national life are infused with an overarching ideal of justice. Clause 2 of the provision more specifically targets inequality and urges the state to minimise income inequality and eliminate inequalities of status, facilities and opportunities. The six clauses of Article 39 focus on both general goals ('the ownership and control of the material resources of the community are so distributed as to secure the common good') and more specific ones ('the right to livelihood, equal pay for equal work, the health and strength of workers, the basic rights of children to be protected from exploitation').

The Directive Principles were originally inspired by the much smaller catalogue in the 1937 Constitution of the Irish Republic but, as with the rights provisions, became more extensive and reflective of indigenous concerns by the time they were finalised. Although thought to be irrelevant, even by some of the framers, they have acquired a meaningful existence in their own right, especially when they have been interpreted by the courts to expand the ambit of rights and privileges available to Indians.

It is worth noting that the colonial government, in tune with British political thought about rights more generally even within Britain, remained reluctant to bestow rights upon Indians. One scholar has recently characterised the approach of British colonial authorities to demands for rights provisions raised in the various colonies in the following terms:

> … a bill of rights was ineffective at protecting rights, it limited the actions of the colonial administration, it hamstrung Parliament, it invited litigation, it required skilled judges to interpret, it politicized the judiciary, it was almost impossible to draft effectively, and perhaps most importantly, it was not the British way to protect rights.[43]

[42] I Jennings, *Some Characteristics of the Indian Constitution* (Madras, Oxford University Press, 1953) 35.

[43] COH Parkinson, 'British Constitutional Thought and the Emergence of Bills of Rights in Britain's Overseas Territories in Asia at Decolonization' in H Kumarasingham (ed), *Constitution-making in Asia* (London, Routledge, 2016) 36.

This attitude helps explain why the colonial authorities steadfastly rejected appeals by the Indian nationalist movement for a bill of rights from the time they were first made in 1895, all the way until the grant of independence.[44]

Significantly, there was a shift in the thinking of the nationalist movement concerning the nature of rights over time. It is certainly striking that the distinction between fundamental rights and Directive Principles was made, for the first time, in the deliberations within the Constituent Assembly. In the half century long history of the evolution of rights documents crafted by the nationalist movement, there was an equal emphasis on the civil and political rights as well as the socio-economic rights that owed their respective origins to the liberal and socialist wings of the Indian National Congress. During the drafting process in the Assembly, however, the lawyers BN Rau and Alladi Krishnaswami Aiyar argued that many of the social and economic rights or positive rights were not amenable to judicial review in the same way as classic civil and political rights. Since some members had already objected to the presence of mere 'moral precepts' in the text of the Constitution, the suggestion was that making the socio-economic rights non-justiciable would justify their presence in a separate section of the Constitution.[45] Other members in the Assembly, including the Gandhians and the powerful troika of KM Munshi, KT Shah and Ambedkar strongly urged for the inclusion of strong socio-economic rights as fundamental rights, and were opposed to their being housed in a separate section, which they noted would undermine the importance of socio-economic rights. Eventually, however, the view of Rau and Aiyar prevailed, and Ambedkar himself defended the decision to separate the justiciable fundamental rights from the non-justiciable Directive Principles.[46]

Scholars who have examined the evolution of the Directive Principles across the Assembly have speculated about their overall motivation. Hannah Lerner has argued that the Directive Principles reflect the challenges of constitution-making in a deeply-divided society. She describes the decision to make them non-justiciable as befitting a pattern of what she terms 'constitutional incrementalism' that should be viewed as facilitating 'the adoption of democratic constitutions in emerging democracies, where conflicts over national identity or religion-State relations are at the heart of the constitutional debate'.[47] Tarunabh Khaitan has similarly argued that many controversial issues which could not be

[44] Parkinson notes that the Government of India Act 1935, in ss 275, 298(1) and 299, guaranteed some property rights and provided some protections against discrimination based on religion, sex, place of birth or colour for the purposes of public sector employment, property rights and access to a profession. While this is true, the limited and context-specific nature of these 'rights' should be emphasised.

[45] Rao, *The Framing of India's Constitution*, (n 24), vol 5, 319–333, 322.

[46] For a speculative but illuminating discussion of the reasons that may have motivated the change in Ambedkar's thinking – which also reveal other tensions in the constitution-making process – see Niraja Jayal's excellent analysis of this issue: Jayal, *Citizenship and its Discontents*, (n 27) 144–158.

[47] Lerner, 'The Indian Founding' (n 8).

agreed upon in the Assembly were housed in the chapter on Directive Principles as a way of deferring decision-making.[48]

v. The Judiciary

The Constitution of India contains elaborate provisions relating to the unitary Judiciary. These provisions articulate Ambedkar's overall conception to have 'one single integrated Judiciary having jurisdiction and providing remedies in all cases arising under the constitutional law, the civil law or the criminal law'.[49] This, according to Ambedkar, was 'essential to maintain the unity of the country'.[50] Once again, the temporal concerns of the period surrounding the framing of the Constitution vitally affected the way the role and function of crucial institutions of government would be conceived by the makers of the Indian Constitution. Chapter IV of Part V of the Constitution is titled 'the Union Judiciary' and consists of 23 provisions (Articles 124–147). Another 23 provisions relating to the High Courts and the Subordinate Courts are set out in Chapters V (consisting of Articles 214–232) and VI (consisting of Articles 233–237) under Part VI of the Constitution which deals with 'The States.'

As should be clear from a perusal of the length and detail of the bare provisions relating to the Judiciary, the framers of the Constitution spent considerable time and effort in crafting them. However, unlike in the case of the rights provisions, they were not working from a blank canvas in terms of existing arrangements. The period of British presence in India had witnessed the establishment of an elaborate system of courts from the time of the East India Company. So, for instance, the Mayor's Court was established outside Bombay in 1728. While the Company administered India, there were two sets of courts: one administered by the British Crown, and another by the East India Company.[51] In 1861, after the formal end of Company rule in India, the British Parliament enacted the Indian High Courts Act which authorised the Crown to set up High Courts of Judicature in the 'Presidency towns' of Calcutta, Madras and Bombay. By the time independence was achieved, this system of courts had been in place for nearly a century.

This situation presents a paradox which needs some explanation. The nationalist movement often used the oppressive measures brought about by colonial laws to make its case for, initially, the need for reform in the colonial structures of power, and eventually, the need to reject colonial rule altogether. The sedition trials that the British initiated against important nationalist leaders across nearly 30 years (Jogendra Chandra Bose in 1891, Bal Gangadhar Tilak in

[48] T Khaitan, 'Directive Principles and the Expressive Accommodation of Ideological Dissenters' (2018) 16 *International Journal of Constitutional Law* 389–420.

[49] CAD IX, 21, 787.

[50] CAD VII, 1, 37.

[51] A Chandrachud, *An Independent, Colonial Judiciary: A History of the Bombay High Court during the British Raj, 1862–1947* (New Delhi, Oxford University Press, 2015) 22.

1897, Annie Besant in 1917, Maulana Azad in 1922 and Mohandas Gandhi in 1922) helped mould public opinion in favour of the growing nationalist movement by creating a perception that colonial rule, law and courts were deeply unfair in their application to Indians. However, this impression did not extend to all legal and judicial institutions uniformly. As scholars have argued, while some of the lower courts did become instruments of colonial policy in very clear ways, this tendency did not extend to superior courts in general. Further, the High Courts in particular had begun a process of indigenisation well before independence, so that by the time of independence, the prominent High Courts in particular were considered more Indian than British.[52]

All this goes to explain why the framers of the Indian Constitution did not seem eager to completely supplant the colonial structure of courts and decided instead to continue many parts of that legal order, albeit with important adaptations and modifications, which is the focus here. By the 1920s, the High Courts had become established in several parts of India. Appeals from the High Courts lay to the Judicial Committee of the Privy Council in London, which was an avenue open to very few Indians due to the high expense of such appeals. By the 1930s, the colonial government also established the Federal Court of India under the Government of India Act 1935. This became necessary because that law also introduced a federal element into the colonial Indian legal order for the first time, and the Federal Court was thought to be necessary to resolve disputes between the federal units. Notably, however, the Federal Court had a limited original jurisdiction and its decisions were still subject to appeal before the Privy Council, factors that inhibited its evolution into a robust judicial forum.

Within the Constituent Assembly, deliberations on the judiciary began with some common agreement. The colonial system of courts would be retained, but important changes would be made. Appeals to the Privy Council would be abolished – a decision that was unusual as many other former colonies retained such appeals for long after formal independence – and a new Supreme Court would be established. Although this new institution would retain the role of the Federal Court in being an arbiter of federal disputes, its main purpose would be to safeguard the new bill of rights that would be introduced in Part III of the Constitution. The new Supreme Court was also to have a much wider jurisdiction than the Federal Court in other matters, including in the range of appeals and original cases it would take on. The framers gave this new institution a wider range of powers because of their belief that the unity that the country needed in perilous times could not be achieved exclusively by the strong Union government that they would establish. That process would need additional resources, including, in the words of KM Munshi, 'the unconscious process of

[52] ibid, 299–307. Note that Chandrachud's work focuses on the Bombay High Court but his analysis is plausibly extendable to the other High Courts in Calcutta, Madras, Allahabad, Patna and Lahore.

consolidation which a uniformity of laws and interpretation involves makes the unifying unconscious and more stable'.[53]

As noted earlier, the framers invoked multiple strategies to ensure that the judges of the superior courts would be independent. However, in light of the expansive role undertaken by the judiciary in later years, to which we will turn in the succeeding section of this chapter, it is important to emphasise what kind of role the framers had in mind for the judiciary. One of the great champions of judicial autonomy and independence in the Assembly was Alladi Krishnaswamy Aiyar. On this question, he had a precise explanation:

> While there can be no two opinions on the need for the maintenance of judicial independence, both for the safeguarding of individual liberty and the proper working of the Constitution, it is also necessary to keep in view one important principle. The doctrine of independence is not to be raised to the level of a dogma so as to enable the judiciary to function as a kind of super-Legislature or super-Executive. The Judiciary is there to interpret the Constitution or adjudicate upon the rights between the parties concerned. … the Judiciary as much as the [Legislature] and the Executive, is depending for its proper functioning upon the cooperation of the other two.[54]

It is important to place this statement in context. While the framers of the Constitution were keen to have an independent judicial institution that would safeguard rights and be an important check on the abuse of power, they were equally clear that the main engine of activity in the constitutional scheme was the executive government acting with the support of an active and vigilant Parliament. It appears that their vision sought to combine in hybrid form the parliamentary sovereignty of the British type with judicial review of the US type. In such a vision, the judiciary was to have strong powers and a defined role, but was nevertheless still to play a subordinate role to Parliament and the government of the day which enjoyed a majority in Parliament. This is certainly how the role of the judiciary was envisaged by Prime Minister Nehru who was an ardent champion of judicial review and independence, but also believed that it was Parliament and the government of the day which would have the final say on policy decisions. Interestingly enough, this was also the position of the early judges of the Supreme Court, all of whom had been members of its predecessor, the Federal Court, and had been steeped in the values of the British judiciary which did not have any powers to strike down parliamentary law and viewed the law in 'technocratic' rather than 'political' terms.[55] In later years, as is well known, the Judiciary in India, and the Supreme Court in particular, became a

[53] Munshi, 'Note to the Ad Hoc Committee on the Union Judiciary', cited in Austin, *The Indian Constitution*, (n 7) 184.

[54] CAD XI, 9, 837.

[55] The phrase, technocratic, is used by Professor Sathe to describe the worldview and self-perception of the early Supreme Court. See, SP Sathe, *Judicial Activism in India: Transgressing Borders and Enforcing Limits* (Oxford University Press, New Delhi, 2003) 40.

far more pivotal and central institution in Indian governance and politics, to which brief reference will be made in a subsequent section.

vi. Universal Adult Franchise and Citizenship Rights

One of the most consequential decisions adopted by the framers of the Constitution was to grant universal adult suffrage to all Indian citizens. During the colonial period, the British were very reluctant to grant the right to vote to all Indians. Representation was granted on 'weightage' and separate electorates, which conceived of seats being allocated along religious, community and professional lines, and on a very limited franchise.[56] The small and divided electorate was based principally on qualifications relating to property, gender and education. As a result, under the last colonial statute to govern India, the Government of India Act 1935, only 30 million people, just a fifth of the adult population was eligible to vote.

The nationalist movement headed by Congress demanded universal adult suffrage from at least since the Nehru Report of 1928. Once the Constituent Assembly started functioning, its Secretariat spearheaded the making of the first electoral roll on the basis of universal adult franchise in September 1947, which led to the first General Elections between October 1951 to February 1952. The creation of the electoral roll expanded the electorate more than five-fold, to cover 173 million people, which was about 49 per cent of the country's population.[57] A large proportion of this population exercised its right to vote between 1951 and 1952, while women in parts of Europe still did not have the right to vote. This decision did much to alter the nature and shape of the democracy that was sought to be entrenched within India by the framers.

Interestingly, however, the right to vote is not a fundamental right, and is secured through Article 326 which is housed in Part XV of the Constitution. Originally, it was to be a part of the Rights chapter, but was moved to the section which also housed the Election Commission. There is a similar pragmatic reason for the inclusion of citizenship rights in a separate section of the Constitution, namely, that Partition and other related disturbances required the deferral of final decisions on the question of citizenship by Parliament rather than being embedded in the constitutional text. The consequence of the rights to vote and citizenship not being fundamental rights has been that it has been easier to mould the content and nature of these rights by Parliament. The dilution of the right to vote by the Judiciary, and the subsequent amendments to citizenship laws to change the character of citizenship from *jus soli* to *jus sanguines*,[58] would have been more difficult to achieve if they had been retained as fundamental rights.

[56] Shani, *How India Became Democratic*, (n 38) 2–3.
[57] The details of this 'staggering bureaucratic undertaking' are set out in Shani, ibid.
[58] Jayal, *Citizenship and its Discontents*, (n 27).

vii. Emergency Powers and Preventive Detention

As noted earlier, the framers also felt compelled to include non-liberal and illiberal elements within the constitutional text, because of the surrounding dire political and economic circumstances relating to security and national unity. The irony of course is that this led to the continuation and emulation of those same repressive and draconian emergency powers laws that the colonial government used against the nationalist movement, and which was one of the main rallying points of the nationalist movement against the excesses of colonial rule.

India's emergency laws can be grouped under three broad categories: (i) constitutional provisions and statutes authorising the declaration of formal states of emergency and the use of special powers during those declared powers; (ii) constitutional provisions and statutes authorising preventive detention during non-emergency periods; and (iii) substantive criminal laws which define terrorism and other security related offences and establish special rules to adjudicate those offences during non-emergency periods.[59] This amounts to an extensive array of tools that can enable both central and state governments to suppress civil liberties and thwart transparency in governance. One of most glaring is the presence, within the fundamental rights chapter, of a provision that authorises and legitimates preventive detention, while ostensibly seeking to provide protections against the right of arrest. The provision in question, Article 22, was the subject of sharp criticism from a small minority of members in the Assembly. One of these, Mahavir Tyagi, noted both the problem of continuing colonial era laws that the members of the Assembly had earlier expressed revulsion towards, and the very real possibility that they would be misused by a ruling government in free India against political opponents. The provision was defended by several important individuals within the Assembly including Ambedkar and Aiyar. The latter argued that these provisions were a 'necessary evil' and recalled the principle that liberties can be secured only in a climate where basic security is guaranteed, and emphasised the importance of emergency powers in enabling such a conducive environment.[60] As subsequent events have shown, these provisions have been invoked on numerous occasions, very often on dubious legal premises, and have undeniably dented the efforts at creating a wider culture of free exercise of individual freedoms and a state which governs by respecting principles of transparency and accountability.

[59] A Kalhan et al, 'Colonial Continuities, Human Rights, Terrorism, and Security Laws in India' (2006) 20 *Columbia Journal of Asian Law* 93.

[60] For further details of this exchange and about Emergency Powers laws in postcolonial India, see generally, AK Thiruvengadam, 'Asian Judiciaries and Emergency Powers: Reason for optimism?' in VV Ramraj and AK Thiruvengadam (eds), *Emergency Powers in Asia* (Cambridge, Cambridge University Press, 2010) 466–494.

viii. Broad Goals and Incidental Features

On the substantive content and themes of the Constitution, Upendra Baxi has argued that the Indian Constitution can be viewed as oriented towards four goals: 'rights, justice, development and governance'. Baxi argues that each of these goals is 'intertwined and interconnected with the rest and in contradictory combination … with both the constitutional and social pasts and their images of the future'.[61] Similarly, Uday Mehta has argued that the framers were guided by three broad objectives: (i) an overriding concern with national unity; (ii) a deep and anxious preoccupation with social issues such as poverty, illiteracy, and economic development; and (iii) an intense concern with India's standing in the world.[62] Mehta, like Baxi, suggests that the first two goals identified by him in particular have the potential of moving towards ends which are quite different from those of the anti-colonial struggle which emphasised ideas of freedom. Benjamin's Zachariah's tracing of the intellectual history of ideas of 'development' amongst the nationalist elites between 1930–1950 indicates that the term had an ambiguous quality and could encompass goals that were seemingly common amongst imperialists, capitalists and socialists.[63] These multiple understandings of 'development' had a role to play in the constitutional entrenchment of the goal of 'development' in the text and institutional structures of the Constitution of India.

The length of the Indian Constitution has been the subject of much commentary and speculation. It must be noted that unlike in the case of many federal states, where state Constitutions are housed separately, the Constitution of India sets out the provisions in relation to both the federal and state units. Its length has also been attributed to the anxiety of its framers to set out even minute details in black letter law for fear that failing to do so would lead to the constitutional order being dismantled quite early on. This is a reference to the many unconducive factors for constitutionalism in India: its long history of communal violence, the rampant illiteracy and underdevelopment that characterises its populace, the inequality in Hindu caste society which was exacerbated under the exploitative practices of colonialism, and the persistence of feudal mindsets in large parts of the country. That length has also enabled, as noted earlier, the co-existence of many contradictory features within the overall model of Indian constitutionalism.

[61] U Baxi, '"A Known but Indifferent Judge": Situating Ronald Dworkin in Contemporary Indian Jurisprudence' (2003) 1(4) *International Journal of Constitutional Law* 557–589, 562.

[62] U Mehta, 'Constitutionalism' in N Jayal and PB Mehta (eds), *The Oxford Companion to Politics in India* (New Delhi, Oxford University Press, 2011) 16.

[63] B Zachariah, *Developing India: An Intellectual and Social History* (New Delhi, Oxford University Press, 2005) xv–xvii.

III. BRIEF ANALYSIS OF EVOLUTION OF THE POST-INDEPENDENCE CONSTITUTIONAL ORDER (1947–2019)

This section provides a brief overview of the post-colonial journey of India as a nation that was set on a path ordained by its framers' choices as exemplified in its independence Constitution. It is necessarily truncated and selective, but seeks to aid assessments of the Indian Constitution's achievements and failures.[64]

The historian, Ramachandra Guha, has persuasively argued that India is in danger of becoming an 'elections only democracy'. By this, Guha means that while elections are conducted in a manner that is reasonably free and fair, other aspects of India's democracy are deeply troubling. He points to weak democratic institutions (and deep problems in Parliament, the courts and the police), pervasive corruption and nepotism in political parties, and fundamental weaknesses in the state's capacity to address welfare policies especially for the poor and weak in Indian society.[65]

India's democratic model has been profoundly affected by the decision of the framers of its Constitution to grant universal adult franchise to its vast population, much of which was mired in illiteracy and deep poverty. This unprecedented decision has continued to have a deeply democratising effect on the Indian polity given the importance of elections to its democratic order. Indians have always voted in elections to the state assemblies and Parliament in large numbers. The mobilisation of people through political parties and policies for the purpose of securing electoral victories has had a dramatic effect on the power relations between different sections of India's deeply segregated society. The original text of the Constitution did not mention political parties. This, in retrospect, seems a mistake because there were existing examples such as the Basic Law of Germany (adopted in 1949) which regulated political parties. Political parties have come to play a disproportionately important role in moulding the constitutional order and there is now a clear understanding within Indian constitutional scholars of the need to regulate them by acknowledging the important role they play in the everyday functioning of governing institutions.

Each election in independent India's history – from the first General Elections in 1951–1952 to the 17th held in 2019 – has been the largest electoral exercise in human history. These elections have thrown up different victors from different parties across seven decades, which in turn reflect the rise and fall of different social groupings. The nationalist Congress party – which was the most significant political party seeking independence from colonial rule – dominated

[64] This section draws on a forthcoming co-authored work: P Dann and AK Thiruvengadam, 'Introduction' in P Dann and AK Thiruvengadam (eds), *Democratic Constitutionalism in Continental Polities: Comparing the European Union and India* (London, Edward Elgar, forthcoming 2021).

[65] R Guha, *India After Gandhi: The History of the World's Largest Democracy* (London, MacMillan, 2017) 782–83.

India's political landscape from 1950–1989. Although it was dominant for a long time, in its initial years, it was itself dominated by upper class and upper caste males, which was also reflected in some of the social policies of Congress in the early decades. Over time, the hegemony of the Congress party waned, also as a result of social and economic programmes that enabled members of the most marginalised sections of Indian society – the Dalits – to assert themselves politically.[66] There has unquestionably been a deepening of Indian democracy as members of lower caste groups mobilised themselves into regional parties which were able to gain power in state assemblies, and were also part of national coalitions where they secured significant representation in the Union Cabinet. Most recently, however, India has witnessed the rise of Hindu Right nationalism with the growing electoral power and numbers of the Bharatiya Janata Party (BJP).

From 1989 to 2014, India had either coalition governments or governments with one party being dominant with supporting parties sharing power at the Union level. This included a five-year stint between 1999 to 2004 when the BJP gained power at the Centre at the head of a coalition government. Since 2014, with the rise of Narendra Modi and the resurgence of the BJP, India has experienced a trend in right wing populism, which is increasingly recognised as not just a hegemonic force, but also one that is challenging and seems set to revise the original compact agreed to under the terms of the Constitution of India of 1950. The re-election of Prime Minister Modi's Government in 2019 by a massive majority (the BJP, together with its allies, controls nearly two-thirds of the Lower House of Parliament) presents a watershed moment for India's model of constitutional democracy. The second successive electoral victory by the BJP is viewed as heralding a fundamental rupture with the last seven decades, including a move away from commitments made in the 1950 Constitution which may now be open to question, revision and perhaps wholescale rewriting.[67]

One area where the Constitution and its institutions have come under sharp attack is for the failure of the constitutionally ordained goals of social justice and economic development. Seven decades on, welfarism in India is still at a very primitive level, with vast sections of its populace not having access to even basic social goods such as education, water, health and social security. During the 'socialist' era from 1947 to 1990, the Indian state paid lip service to welfarism, but did not succeed in delivering much. Since 1991, under the thrall of forces of neoliberalism, progress on these welfare goals has been slow despite

[66] J Harriss, 'Political Change, Political Structure and the Indian State since Independence' in P Brass (ed), *The Routledge Handbook of Politics in South Asia* (New Delhi, Routledge, 2013) 55–66; and Y Yadav, 'Reconfiguration of Indian Politics: State Assembly elections 1993–1995' (1996) 31(2–3) *Economic and Political Weekly* 95–104.

[67] S Ruparelia, 'Modi's Saffron Democracy' *Dissent Magazine* (April 2019); AP Chatterji, TB Hansen and C Jaffrelot (eds), *Majoritarian State: How Hindu Nationalism is Changing India* (New Delhi, Harper Collins, 2019); N Jayal, *Re-forming India* (New Delhi, Penguin, 2019); and KS Komireddy, *Malevolent Republic: A Short History of the New India* (Chennai, Context, 2019).

the enactment of specific welfare laws from the mid-2000s onwards.[68] Critics argue that the logic of the market dominates these welfare policies, limiting their application and efficacy. India's continuing abysmally low HDI rates are thus a genuine source of concern.[69]

Other worrying trends also need to be mentioned in brief. As was anticipated by some of the framers, the extensive regime of emergency powers authorised by the Constitution did lead to a situation where they have been frequently deployed and with great frequency across the entire length of the 70 years of the Constitution. Very often, they have been used against the political opponents of the governments in power, and against dissidents and people on the margins of society. Reports from human rights groups and civil society organisations have documented how the Indian state has invoked these emergency powers laws to trample civil liberties of several hundred thousand people over time, especially in troubled areas such as Kashmir, the isolated and politically weak and marginal States in the Indian North East, and the central Indian States where Maoist rebels have taken to armed violence against the consistent failure of the Indian state to deliver on its development goals.

In recent years, and especially since 2014, it is also becoming clear that the Indian state is becoming increasingly majoritarian. This is evident most clearly by the adoption of policies that favour its Hindu population which enjoys an 80 per cent majority. There is equally a discernible hostility in the policies of the Indian state against minorities of all stripes, but especially so against its Muslim population, numbering almost 200 million.[70] In 2006, during the tenure of Prime Minister Manmohan Singh of the Congress Party, a high level committee delivered a report on the socio-economic and educational condition of Muslims in India. Known as the Sachar Committee Report after its Chairperson, the report documented how the Muslim community has been doing worse than many other marginalised sections of Indian society, and backed up its analysis by providing a range of worrying statistics across numerous indices. The Muslim community in India was doing poorly on a range of factors including employment in the better paying formal sector, overall education and literacy rates, and the rates of representation in forms of public employment. Overall, this presented a picture of dramatic and systematic underdevelopment of the Muslim community across the various phases in post-independence India. Although the government of Prime Minister Manmohan Singh took on board the recommendations, and promised action, for a variety of reasons, the Committee's recommendations did not result in policy changes.[71]

[68] Jayal, *Citizenship and its Discontents*, (n 27).

[69] J Dreze and A Sen, *India: An Uncertain Glory and Its Contradictions* (London, Penguin, 2014); Jayal, *Citizenship and its Discontents*, (n 27).

[70] For empirical details and other forms of analysis to back this claim, see generally, Chatterji et al, *Majoritarian State*, (n 67).

[71] For a sobering analysis, see generally, H Kim, *The Struggle for Equality: India's Muslims and Rethinking the UPA experience* (New Delhi, Cambridge University Press, 2019).

The current state of Muslims – who constitute the largest religious minority in contemporary India – raises questions about the health of India's constitutional democracy as a whole. Christophe Jaffrelot has recently drawn attention to the worsening situation.[72] While Muslims have traditionally been under-represented within the institutions of the Indian Republic (the police, the army and public administration), Jaffrelot notes that this phenomenon now extends to elected assemblies owing to the rise of the BJP. Muslims were historically well represented in legislative assemblies and the Parliament, but their numbers have dipped alarmingly. More worryingly, Jaffrelot provides empirical evidence of the targeting of Muslims by Hindu nationalist militias. Very often these militias work in tandem with the police forces and other formal institutional mechanisms.

This is a deeply troubling issue in itself, but also points to the view adopted by Thomas Blom Hansen, an anthropologist who has studied the problem of violence in different regions and parts of Indian society since the early 1990s. He argues that the liberal norms that pervade India's remarkable Constitution 'have neither penetrated everyday political life, nor substantively changed the social and cultural norms among the vast majority of Indians'.[73] Thomas Hansen argues persuasively, and in company with a growing number of other commentators,[74] that the fault for this cannot be laid only at the door of the BJP governments that have governed India during 1999–2004 and since 2014. Blom Hansem notes that almost all of India's postcolonial governments have facilitated a situation where the gap between the ideals expressed in the Constitution and those that exist in the practice of everyday governance is only getting wider across time. Hansen contends – and this takes us back to the first hypothesis of the editors – that this was essentially because of the continuities between the colonial administrative and legal apparatus which, when tasked with implementing the constitutional vision in daily governance, continued with its old ways of thinking and working from the colonial period. This meant, in practice, that

> … the Indian State continued to work through several parallel regulatory regimes, calibrated according to class, caste and region. It also retained and expanded a very extensive regime of secrecy and classification of files and archives. By the 1970s, the Congress had all but abandoned its commitment to liberal principles in favour of a populist reform agenda that reconfigured the political landscape in India. Its main elements were rhetorical embrace of vague socialist Third World-ism, a deep commitment to state sovereignty coupled with several redistributive pro-poor policies, but also harassment of opponents, violent suppression of insurgencies and the systematic build up of a large security state, with more than a dozen different paramilitary services and many armed police forces in each state in India.[75]

[72] C Jaffrelot, 'A De Facto Ethnic Democracy? in Chatterji et al, *Majoritarian State*, (n 67) 41–68.

[73] TB Hansen, 'Democracy Against the Law: Reflections on India's Illiberal Democracy' in Chatterji et al, *Majoritarian State*, (n 67) 19–39.

[74] See, eg, Komireddy, *Malevolent Republic*, (n 67).

[75] Hansen, 'Democracy Against the Law', (n 73) 23.

Blom Hansen contends that the truly worrying feature is that every political party, including the mainstream left, has tacitly supported this policy of large-scale human rights violation in the name of national sovereignty. He notes that there has been no new political formulation for a very long time that has challenged this apparent consensus among all the political groupings, which dampens any prospect that fundamental change is imminent.

Blom Hansen shows that this has happened despite the deepening of democracy in India since the 1990s, when lower caste communities used key elements of liberal democracy – individual and equal rights to vote, to access public goods, to claim affirmative action, the rule of law, etc – to mobilise and gain political and social empowerment. Hansen notes that this did not, however, lead to a questioning of ideas of caste; paradoxically, it led to a sharpening of caste and other forms of identity. He concludes that 'the deepening of democracy in India has produced ever-stronger assertion of majorities, popular power and popular sovereignty, but without any concomitant percolation of liberal-democratic values, and without any stronger assertion of the rule of law as a value in and itself'.[76] Consequently, he emphasises, there seems no contradiction between a strong support for democracy as a form of government, and support for authoritarian styles of governance ruling in the name of the people.

This is a sobering analysis which those concerned about the constitutional order's endurance must ponder over carefully. What provides hope even against this depressing diagnosis is that given that this is India, the numbers involved, even of groups which would be considered small in other places, is huge. In December 2019, in the aftermath of the ruling government's successful enactment of a change to India's citizenship laws that expressly injected an element of anti-Muslim prejudice, protests broke out across the nation. Initially propelled by student groups, they spread to other groups of society, including the influential middle classes, Bollywood celebrities, lawyers associations and corporate leaders. These protests were marked by the reading aloud of the Preamble to the Constitution and the chanting of values enshrined in the text, including that of secularism. Coming as they did a month before the significant 70th anniversary of the Constitution, they provided hope that the battle to maintain and entrench constitutional values, seven decades after a commitment was made in respect of them, continues.

This chapter has focused on the remarkable journey of constitution-making in India, which is characterised by many unique elements, both procedural and substantive. As Madhav Khosla argues in the epigram that appears at the beginning of this chapter, India's constitution-making exercise occurred at a pivotal moment in global history and its experiences captured – and become emblematic of – the reality of a number of nations that faced similar challenges. As the previous section reveals, 70 years on, it is by no means clear that the experiment

[76] Hansen, 'Democracy Against the Law', (n 73) 39.

has been either a clear success or failure. To return to the two hypotheses articulated by the editors, there remain substantial continuities between the colonial legal order and the post-independence legal system developed by the framers. We are living through a period when those continuities seem particularly evident, with the use of coercion, emergency powers and repressive laws across India. This also brings into play the second hypothesis and raises the question whether the attempt by the framers of India's Constitution to entrench a liberal constitution has been successful. While many strands of that founding vision have taken root in the Indian constitutional system, some others are being resisted both by governments and ordinary citizens, leading to a situation where many founding goals remain unfulfilled. Still, there is no question that the Constitution has become the framing device and vehicle for many contestations in the legal and political life of the nation. Its endurance and the fact that it clearly remains relevant for a considerable section of Indians provide hope that it will guide the needs and aspirations of 1.3 billion Indians as they make their way across the difficult times that await us all in the future.

3

From Nation to State: Constitutional Founding in Pakistan

SADAF AZIZ AND MOEEN CHEEMA

INTRODUCTION

THERE IS GROWING appreciation that the processes of constitutional formation in post-colonial states are complicated by the inheritances of colonial governance. Whether that be a haphazard political sphere, hamstrung by colonial powers anxious to retain collaboration or a heavily centralised administrative apparatus, the idea that transitions can be enacted by the law is increasingly called into question. This chapter argues, through a case study of Pakistan's earliest constitutional founding, that the consolidation of sovereignty in moments of transition can act to constrain and bracket the transformative potentiality of a constituent power. Thus, the period in which the first constitution for an independent Pakistan was being formed provides an indicative sense of where and through which mechanisms the transition from an ideational Muslim nationalism was recreated as authorisation for centralised and somewhat immovable executive rule.

This is to acknowledge that there is a considerable degree of uncertainty about the possibilities of constitutionalism in general. The points of variance can be mapped onto competing views that present it as either a set of values or as an institutional formula. For instance, as JE Murkens noted some years ago, constitutionalism is either 'a struggle against the positivist conception of sovereignty and the allied conception of the omnipotent state' or 'the history of the constant pressure to maintain the ultimate authority of the legislature'.[1] For the study of Pakistan's early constitution-making exercises, we tread the ground of ascertaining how these indeterminate views that converge on the necessity

[1] See JEK Murkens, 'The Quest for Constitutionalism in UK Public Law Discourse' (2009) 29(3) *Oxford Journal of Legal Studies* 427, 429 (highlighting two opposing views based on analyses of Friedrich Hayek and Maurice Vile, respectively).

of constitutional primacy were conditioned in their delivery by alternate values and systems.

It is the specific history of how the state, omnipotent and mediated, bizarrely strung together, emerges through the early years of Pakistan that this chapter seeks to investigate. We proceed to unpack the pre-history of the 1956 Constitution, Pakistan's founding constitution, that was enacted after a lapse of nearly eight years following the Partition of British India. While the provisions of the first constitution calling for the establishment of a Westminster-style democracy – replete with guarantees of fundamental rights as well as provisions to enable judicial review – had a very short life in the nation, it served in many ways as a template for the 1973 Constitution that still governs Pakistan. There was an intervening constitution in 1962, functional until 1969, which created an all-powerful president and established a system of indirect elections for a central legislature. However, as opposed to views that tend to see this as an aberrant interlude, there is much evidence to suggest that the events that led to the articulation of the 1956 Constitution equally invigorated the need for a law that would provide cover to executive dominance.

I. CONSTITUENT ASSEMBLIES AS THE SITE OF CONSTITUTIONAL DRAFTING

To read the acts and enactments of a Constituent Assembly alongside the acts of executive actors in a founding moment necessarily entails interrogating where we situate these assemblies on a continuum of whether they possess strong or weak autonomy. The idea of strong autonomy is often a by-product of the idea of capital-C Constitutions, shrouded in an aura of glorious legal and political compacts that enshrine lasting governance arrangements. Such views continue to animate the work of comparative constitutionalists. Relying on the archetype of American, German and a handful of other constitutions in the global North, constitutional lawyers often conceptualise constitution-making as the founding of clean breaks from the past during 'constitutional moments'[2] when the framers representing 'We the people' encode fundamental legal principles and the spirit of 'higher law'.[3] Such a higher law is, thereafter, accorded primacy in the messy business of regulating ordinary politics.

A weaker variant of the story is typified by the work of Jon Elster and others who have paid greater attention to such moments and schematised the constraints and interests which act upon those defining such compacts. Relying to varying

[2] See B Ackerman, *We The People: Foundations* (Cambridge, MA, Harvard University Press, 1991) 6–7, 40–57. For a critique of the concept of constitutional moments in the American context, see MJ Klarman, 'Constitutional Fact/Constitutional Fiction: A Critique of Bruce Ackerman's Theory of Constitutional Moments' (1992) 44 *Stanford Law Review* 759.

[3] V Hart, 'Constitution-making and the Transformation of Conflict' (2001) 26(2) *Peace & Change* 153, 155.

degrees upon insights from behavioural sciences and historical studies, Elster identifies the extent to which the processes of constitutional formation impact the articulation of a constitutional document.[4] This includes the mechanics for the authorisation of constituent assemblies and the processes for ratification of a proposed constitution that have been described as 'upstream' and 'downstream' constraints. Further, Elster has argued that a plethora of contingent features determine the play between private and public interests as they come together to define constitutional design. Although cognizant that the notion of a glorious compact signed by selfless individuals stands to be pierced from all angles, Elster nonetheless seeks to elevate this process through secrecy and by insulating it against the tugs of patrimonial or other loyalties. In his earlier work on the topic, Elster articulates a preference for constitutional founding to be severed in all ways from the ordinary politics of a state.[5]

Other work that firmly avows the thesis of weak autonomy of constituent assemblies investigates both the presumed divide between a higher and lower law and constitutional and ordinary politics. For Hannah Lerner, the depth of conflict in 'divided societies', where schisms can be marked in ideological, religious or ethnic lines, lessens the likelihood that a lasting constitutional compromise can be founded within the institutional structure of an assembly. Even forging an overlapping consensus on a thin, procedural conception of constitutionalism is apt to prove unlikely. Tellingly, then, Lerner provides the specific directive that those 'studying the work of constituent assemblies in divided societies should pay close attention to the politics that preceded the formal stage of drafting'.[6] Her contention is that 'controversial issues that are dividing the society in the pre-drafting stage continue to divide the society during the drafting process as well as in the post-drafting stage of constitutional implementation and interpretation.'[7] This reflects the weak autonomy of constituent assemblies as Lerner is able to show that initial 'procedural disagreements' about the design or composition of the assembly itself could provide the opening for more intractable ideological differences or political conflict to make their way into the forum.

In what might be a companion piece, Mara Malagodi affirms Lerner's views that a more 'open-ended incrementalist method of constitution-making'[8] could have provided a more durable solution to India's problem when she looks closely at the fates of the two successive constituent assemblies of Pakistan that produced the country's first constitution. Malagodi's is one of the few scholarly works

[4] J Elster, 'Forces and Mechanisms in the Constitution-Making Process', (1995) 45(2) *Duke Law Journal* 364.
[5] ibid.
[6] H Lerner, 'Constituent Assemblies and Political Continuity in Divided Societies' in J Elster, R Gargarella, V Naresh and BE Rasch (eds) *Constituent Assemblies* (Cambridge, Cambridge University Press, 2018) 57–78, 60 [hereinafter 'Lerner, '*Constituent Assemblies*'].
[7] ibid.
[8] M Malagodi, 'Constituent Assembly Failure in Pakistan and Nepal' in Elster et al (eds) *Constituent Assemblies*, (n 6) 83.

that looks at the specific processes of constitutional formation in Pakistan. In it, she starts from the premise that 'the process of constitution-making has an intimate relationship with its outcome' so that 'a specific historical and social context bears long-term consequences for constitutional democracy and political stability in any given country'.[9] In this vein, Malagodi indicates the several contextual features that impinged upon the search for a more durable democracy and constitutionally guided state in Pakistan. The features that Malagodi cites are readily familiar to those who have watched constitutions crumble repeatedly in Pakistan: growing militarisation, hostile neighbouring states, and a politically dominant ethnic group in a multi-ethnic state. There is, in fact, little that we can disagree with in Malagodi's account of what led to the purported failure of the first Constituent Assembly of Pakistan to deliver a constitution as well as its subsequent dismissal. We will offer a similar account of the suspension of that Assembly and the constitution of a second one. Where this chapter differs is in elaborating this context.

We are concerned with the pre-history of the first Constituent Assembly in a way that invites a more scrutinising gaze at the formation of Muslim nationalism that was carried through in the party programme of the All India Muslim League (AIML). The AIML, with Mohammad Ali Jinnah at its helm, was the party which from approximately 1940 onwards was most closely associated with the demand for Pakistan. However, prior to that, the AIML had been committed to finding an agreeable formula for Muslim representation within a united India. Amongst the factors that Malagodi and other political historians of Pakistan cite as leading to the enervation of early attempts at constitutional drafting were the relatively ineffectual attempts of the Muslim League to work towards national consolidation while abiding by democratic norms. We certainly also argue that it is from within the gaps and fissures of that project that heavy executive dominance was enabled. This was importantly amongst the features that led the executive to claim legitimacy to guide the state, but which in turn refused to be constrained or constitutionalised by the outcome of Constituent Assembly deliberations. We work through these tensions by reference to the functioning of executive government through cabinet and an assertive bureaucracy. We cite this factor in reference to the Constituent Assembly's operations in its constitutional domain until its suspension, which evidences the tensions between the executive and itself. We also look more closely at the operations of the Assembly in its capacity as an ordinary legislative body. In many ways, all these sites provide some indication of the manifold ways in which the colonial inheritance of over-heavy executive powers and a weak political sphere recreated itself in the period leading to the articulation of the first Constitution in 1956.

A closer and more contextual study of Pakistan's earliest constitution-making exercise reveals a fundamental tension between being the higher law

[9] ibid.

and the equally-pressing objective of encoding sectional and competing interests. Aspirations for a higher law were themselves somewhat denatured as the history of the independence movement provided insufficient grounds for developing a clear, coherent and shared vision (perhaps understandably) of what a territorial nation-state founded on the basis of Muslim nationalism would look like. While acknowledging an array of practical, political and material difficulties that thwarted constitution-making in the first decade of independence, this chapter seeks to highlight an overarching conceptual challenge, which further bedevilled the task of laying down Pakistan's constitutional founding. Part II of this chapter will investigate the constitutional politics of the Muslim League in the late colonial period to show that the idea of Pakistan remained inchoate both in its *temporality* and *territoriality* until the very moment of Partition and beyond. Part III will catalogue the key political challenges that emerged as stumbling blocks in the constitution-making process from 1947–1954 through an appreciation of the Constituent Assembly's legislative and constitutional role. Notably, the disagreement over the incorporation of Islam as the state religion and the representation of the constituent units in legislature were both part of those challenges. Part IV will look at the belated framing of the 1956 Constitution and its brief existence not merely as a failure but also as a founding of three key dimensions which have since remained the core regulatory principles of constitutionalism in Pakistan: parliamentary democracy, federalism, and judicial review.

II. INCHOATE VISIONS OF NATIONHOOD

While they may vary amongst themselves in how far they attribute the growth of a Muslim nationalist consciousness to elite groups or masses, most conventional historians of Pakistan take the 'fact' of a widely held nationalist sentiment as the explanatory basis for the realisation of the idea of Pakistan. For many, this sentiment was born at the point of an initial encounter between Muslims and Hindus in the subcontinent and grew more marked under colonial rule. While exonerating the British from pernicious designs, historians such as Khalid Bin Sayeed acknowledge that systems of divide and rule marked colonial policy but were the consequential effects of the failure to bring about any level of conciliation between the Muslims and the Hindus.[10] Sayeed cites the easier assimilation of Hindus to British rule and, following the 1857 uprising,[11]

[10] KB Sayeed, *Pakistan: The Formative Phase 1857–1948* (Oxford, Oxford University Press, 1968 & 1969).

[11] The 1857 uprising, the so-called Great Indian Mutiny, refers to the revolt by the native troops of the Bengal Army against imperialism, which ultimately led to the end of rule by the British India Company through an enactment – the Government of India Act 1858. See, among others, S David, *The Indian Mutiny 1857* (London, Penguin Books, 2003).

the further marginalisation of Muslims from official offices and employment. For others, the formation of communal nationalism and particularly Muslim nationalism was simply one of the 'internal contradictions of an imperialism which also sought to subscribe to liberal doctrine'.[12] It reflected the incompletion of liberal potentialities presumed to be latent in the making of a national space.

There is of course something to be gained by recognising that Muslim nationalism, which configured the programme of the Muslim League, was influenced by the broader project of rationalisation through the Government of India Act 1858. The Act extended the relations of subjecthood to all Indians and was coupled with administrative reform for creating a fairly uniform apparatus of control.[13] For some, the transformations wrought thereafter were all-encompassing, and some analyses would suggest that these transformations heralded a specific modernity, one that 'came to India by the political route, indeed through the introduction of a new activity called "politics"'.[14] However, understanding this movement in a more detailed fashion requires us to pay attention to the mechanisms that facilitated unities implied in the conception of people's relations with these new governmental 'technologies'. Importantly, for people to conceive of themselves in an evolving national terrain, local identities had to be reconfigured.

Careful historians like Gyanadra Panday show that these were transformations wrought at sites of contest between local groupings. He demonstrates that in the late nineteenth century, inter-community conflict was on the rise at the ritual sites as circulation of 'news' through newly-accessible print technologies as well as the innovation and publicisation of 'hard statistical indices' aided the solidification of such identities. However, people in all cases had to overcome identification with caste, sect and locality for these identities to become salient. It was thus no accident that the earliest precipitative event leading to the formation of the AIML was the colonial government's division of Bengal in 1905. Given that elected Councils[15] (but without meeting the demand for Indian representations in the Councils) had been set up more than a decade earlier and claims of representation could be made at the provincial governmental level, the colonial decision to make the eastern, Muslim majority parts a separate province catered to a Muslim constituency even as it served as a mechanism for fissuring the growing anti-colonial sentiments then gaining expression

[12] S Kaviraj 'The Post-Colonial State in India' in Q Skinner and B Stråth (eds), *States and citizens: History, Theory, Prospects* (Cambridge, Cambridge University Press, 2003) 153.

[13] BM Gandhi and VD Kulshreshtha, *Landmarks in Indian Legal and Constitutional History* (Lucknow, Eastern Book Company, 2005) 346.

[14] Through the Indian Councils Act of 1861, the office of Governor-General came to be associated with a Council which would include at the minimum a number of members with extended service in India and also allow for its discretionary enlargement to include Indians.

[15] See the Indian Councils Act 1861. See further ch 1 on India.

in the Bengal Assembly. The elite signatories of the early Muslim League not only gained access to greater employment in the civil services but affirmed the broader socio-economic issues underlying the Muslim sentiment.[16]

Granted certain concessions to speak for a national Muslim community thereafter, the Muslim League's attention turned to a broader concern with the representation of Muslims in an emergent political scheme with national dimensions. The 'most momentous feature' of the Morley-Minto reforms, which took constitutional shape in the Indian Councils Act 1908, was the acceptance of one of the key demands of the Muslim League by instituting religion-based separate electorates for both the central legislative council and the provincial assemblies on the basis of a very restricted franchise.[17] The Montagu-Chelmsford reform proposals and the resulting Government of India Act 1919 significantly expanded both the franchise and separate electorates.[18] It also devolved power to the provincial tier with Indian ministers responsible for education, agriculture, health and finance in the eight provinces of British India. Thus, from the outset, the politics of the Muslim League was framed around carving a separate and weighted political space within the evolving constitutional structures under the British.

For some, the early concessions of having separate Muslim seats and electors in the Assemblies of the time reflected a form of politics that grew out of the move to disperse rising anti-colonial sentiment by relying on groups the British could easily mark and control. However, it is important to realise that other changes led to the reconfiguration of the bargaining terrain between the colonial government and a plethora of groups emerging within India. Importantly, the Great War precipitated other far-reaching changes in Indian society. By 1918 the Indian army had expanded to half a million men and Indian Muslims – who formed a third of Indian soldiers – became much more important in the Raj's priorities, especially as decommissioned soldiers returned from various campaigns.[19] Jinnah, who joined the Indian Congress in 1906 and the AIML in 1913, was instrumental in the formation of the Lucknow Pact – calling for a joint front against the Raj – between Congress and the Muslim League in 1916. The Congress conceded certain vital constitutional protections to minority Muslims in India including separate electorates, one-third representation in the central legislature and greater weight in government (ie, greater representation than would be secured on the basis of population alone).

[16] JR McLane, 'The Decision to Partition Bengal in 1905' (1965) 2(3) *The Indian Economic & Social History Review* 221, 229–30.

[17] J Chiriyankandath, 'Democracy under the Raj: Elections and separate representation in British India', (1992) 30(1) *Journal of Commonwealth & Comparative Politics* 39, 42.

[18] ibid, 43–44. Five million Indian property owners plus the non-commissioned officers (NCOs) of the army formed the all-male electorate. L James, *Raj: The Making and Unmaking of British India* (London, Little, Brown & Co, 1997) 459.

[19] S Bose and A Jalal, *Modern South Asia*, 3rd edn (London, Routledge, 2011) 104–105.

In 1920, alienated by Gandhi's use of Hindu idiom during the Non-Cooperation Movement and taking exception to the Congress support for the 'particularist' objectives of the Khilafat movement, Jinnah left the Congress. More generally, Jinnah felt alienated by the emergence and tenor of majoritarian politics in the Congress under Gandhi's combined political and spiritual leadership.[20] The Lucknow Pact collapsed soon afterwards. As the protracted negotiations over Dominion status stalled, the Congress expressed its unequivocal rejection of the terms of the Lucknow Pact in the Nehru Report of 1928 and launched another non-cooperation movement in 1930. The constitutional negotiations progressed through a series of Roundtable Conferences in London initially joined by the Muslim League, the representatives of other religious communities, and nearly all the 560 Princely States. As the non-cooperation movement began to falter under a spate of detentions, Congress joined the second session in 1931.[21]

While the Muslim League and the Congress were strenuously engaged in negotiations over the shape of constitutional reforms to pave the way for transition to Dominion status, Choudhry Rahmat Ali, a relatively unknown student at the University of Cambridge, authored a pamphlet in 1933 directed at the delegates of the Third Roundtable Conference.[22] The pamphlet contains the first recorded reference to *Pakistan*, and demanded 'the recognition of their national status, as distinct from the other inhabitants of India, by the grant … of *a separate Federal Constitution* on religious, social and historical grounds' to 'the thirty million Muslims … who live in the five Northern Units of India-Punjab, North-West Frontier (Afghan) Province, Kashmir, Sind, and Baluchistan'.[23] Rahmat Ali's proposal was dismissed out of hand by the Muslim League leadership,[24] even though the poet Muhammad Iqbal had also called for the amalgamation of the four existing Muslim-majority provinces on the western wing of British India (not including the Princely State of Kashmir) in his 1930 presidential address to the AIML at Allahabad. In fairness, Iqbal's proposal appeared to be a call for the constitution of a State within the Federation of India,[25] similar to the size and population of Bengal, which may command greater political weight in the future constitutional structure of India.

[20] A Jalal, *The Sole Spokesman: Jinnah, the Muslim League and the Demand for Pakistan* (Lahore, Sang-e-Meel, 2010) 8 [hereinafter 'Jalal, *Sole Spokesman*']; S Bose and A Jalal, ibid, 114–6, 119.

[21] The second non-cooperation movement was reduced to a battle of attrition between the Congress and the Raj: at its peak 29,000 Congress workers were put behind bars. Of them, only 1,152 were Muslims, revealing the extent to which Congress had alienated Indian Muslims. See Chiriyankandath, Democracy under the Raj, (n 17) 529.

[22] T Kamran, 'Choudhary Rahmat Ali and his Political Imagination: Pak Plan and the Continent of Dinia' in AU Qasmi and ME Robb (eds), *Muslims against the Muslim League: Critiques of the Idea of Pakistan* (Cambridge, Cambridge University Press, 2017) 95 [hereinafter 'Qasmi & Robb'].

[23] ibid.

[24] A Jalal, 'Conjuring Pakistan: History as Official Imagining' (1995) 27 *International Journal of Middle East Studies* 73, 75 [hereinafter 'Jalal, 'Conjuring Pakistan'"].

[25] Kamran, 'Choudhary Rahmat Ali and his Political Imagination' (n 22) 100.

Thus, even as the scope of the Government of India Act 1935 was being negotiated, it is important to consider how the Muslim case for nationhood was tied more to the realisation of the contours of an imagined community than to the control of a demarcated territory. In subsequent decades, the search for a constitutional formula to realise this vision transfigured the terrain such that its geographic form contravened 'the creative expansiveness of its ideological frontiers' and thus hampered this quest from the start.[26]

While some theorists see this as a result of the Muslim League's ahistorical and anti-social constitutional positioning devoid of engagement with broader social forces, others see it more as a consequence of the idea of Pakistan coming to fruition even though it was in fact a mere bargaining chip in Jinnah's arsenal. What is important, however, is that in the years leading to the last constitutional framework proposed for British India, the breach between Indian politicians had widened and both the Muslim League and Congress were forced to reckon with a newly-established platform for national politics as well as with a colonial power that was digging in its heels. From that point on, Jinnah became the voice of a Muslim minority seeking 'sufficient' representation at the centre in a federal structure, but now as a member of the Muslim League. Congress differed radically insofar as it now affirmed an absolutist preference for a unified electorate but shared with the League demands for the abolition of diarchy and a strong federal government. It was also looking for guarantees for self-government or at least formal dominion status for India. The British at this time were playing upon the disaffection between Congress and a Jinnah-led Muslim League, and, as many have noted, it was their interests that were ultimately reflected in the form and content of the Government of India Act 1935.

The new constitutional scheme under the 1935 Act envisioned a weak federation and only if a certain number of the Princely States joined it. The federation did not materialise but the Act nonetheless granted considerably greater powers to the provinces. The 1935 Act reflected the view held by the British elite about the structure of Indian society and the 'ways in which these understandings shaped, and were shaped by, methods and institutions for acquiring information in the colonial state'.[27] Citing the mixture of 'colonial cultural assumptions, a sclerotic intelligence apparatus, and a dynamic Indian political environment', Muldoon suggests that the 1935 Act was engineered to 'seriously hamper any further nationalist unity by attracting Indians worn out by Gandhian-style protests and eager for political office and patronage'.[28] Such hopes were dashed by the 1937 elections in which Congress was voted in by an electorate that had expanded to 35 million, attaining ministerial powers in most provinces.[29]

[26] Jalal, 'Conjuring Pakistan', (n 24) 75.

[27] A Muldoon, 'Politics, Intelligence and Elections in Late Colonial India: Congress and the Raj in 1937' (2009) 20(2) *Journal of the Canadian Historical Association/Revue de la Société historique du Canada* 160.

[28] ibid.

[29] See Jalal, *Sole Spokesman*, (n 20) 15.

The Muslim League fared terribly in the Muslim-majority provinces across India and was exposed as still being largely an elitist party engaging in high politics that was detached from the various Muslim movements, not all of which were nationalist. Separate electorates had not in fact established a ready-made constituency for the Muslim League. Rather, as Faisal Devji notes, the existential burden of having identified separate communities allowed the Muslim Leaguers to work through the notion of this separation without an actual role in governing.[30] This entailed a heightened level of abstraction and a continued focus on achieving a constitutional equipoise.

In March 1940 at its annual session in Lahore, the Muslim League adopted what came to be known as the Lahore Resolution, calling for the establishment of independent 'States' for the Muslims of India. It was not immediately clear, however, what form the independent Muslim-majority States would take. Even in his presidential address Jinnah committed categorically only to the position that 'the whole problem of India's future constitution must be examined *de novo* and the Act of 1935 must go once for all'.[31] He also dismissed the Congress demand seeking an immediate transfer of power by the British simultaneously with the framing of a constitution through an elected Constituent Assembly. He further demanded a say for Muslims in the constitution-making process as a co-equal player, and not as a minority within the Constituent Assembly. This was the essence of the 'two nation theory'. The Muslim League's positioning in constitutional negotiations after World War II lends credence to the claim that Pakistan remained a constitutional imaginary and a bargaining stratagem rather than a poignant demand for a separate territorial nation-state.[32] The biggest challenge was how 'to square the circle of the contradictory interests of Muslims in the Indian subcontinent':[33] that is, to achieve the greatest possible autonomy within a future federation for the Muslim-majority provinces while simultaneously achieving adequate constitutional guarantees for Muslim minorities in the other regions. In dealing with the 1942 Cripps Mission Jinnah appeared willing to accept Dominion status for a united India so long as it accorded the provinces the right to subsequently secede as separate dominions, but the Congress rejected such a proposal.[34]

[30] F Devji, *Muslim Zion: Pakistan as a Political Idea* (Cambridge, MA, Harvard University Press, 2013).

[31] 'Address by Quaid-i-Azam Mohammad Ali Jinnah at Lahore Session of Muslim League, March, 1940' (Directorate of Films and Publishing, Ministry of Information and Broadcasting, Government of Pakistan, Islamabad, 1983) 5–23, available at www.columbia.edu/itc/mealac/pritchett/00islamlinks/txt_jinnah_lahore_1940.html.

[32] For instance, in February 1941, Jinnah conceded that 'the British and Indian newspapers generally have adopted the word 'Pakistan' to describe the Moslem demand as embodied in the Lahore resolution. I really see no objection to it.' RJ Moore, 'Jinnah and the Pakistan Demand' (1983) 17(4) *Modern Asian Studies* 529, 550.

[33] Jalal, 'Conjuring Pakistan', (n 24) 75.

[34] Moore, 'Jinnah and the Pakistan Demand', (n 32) 553.

It was only after this failure that some move was made towards defining a political programme that the League might in fact carry into independence. A broader Muslim dissatisfaction had arisen due to the culturally exclusionary and chauvinistic policies in the Congress-dominated provinces. This included the banning of cow slaughter and the assumption of *bande mataram* as the official anthem of these provinces.[35] These events persuaded many middle-class Muslims to fear simple majoritarianism unbridled by constitutional safeguards.[36] In this context, the young communist worker, Irfan Latifi, was tasked by the AIML with writing the party's manifesto in 1944. The manifesto argued that a separate Muslim state 'would eventually transcend and resolve religious differences in the region, because a Muslim-majority state (or a state constructed by a minority community in India) was inherently more equipped to appreciate religious plurality, harmony and diversity than a state dominated by a large Hindu majority'.[37] The manifesto was intended to counteract the entrenched interests of a 'loyalist' constituency in the Punjab and the efforts of the Congress in Bengal to institute a mass contact campaign to enlist largely poor rural voters as supporters there – also interestingly spearheaded at times by communists belonging to the fold of Congress.[38] While the manifesto named an array of rights that would be available to members of a new state, there was evidence also of grandiose abstraction at play. As Markus Daeschel notes:

> Latifi promised that under Muslim League rule things would change for the better: the enterprising middle classes would find an environment of fairness and meritocracy; the oppressed an end to oppression; the disadvantaged would receive government interference in their favour; there were to be employment programmes, there was to be an end to patronage politics.[39]

In the 1945–1946 elections, which were again held on the basis of a limited franchise, the Muslim League won all of the Muslim seats in the central legislature. The League, however, barely edged out the Congress in the provincial legislatures even in the Muslim-majority western provinces. In accordance with the Cabinet Mission Plan, members of the Constituent Assembly for united India were elected by the provincial legislative assemblies. The Congress had an overwhelming majority (208 out of the total 296 members, excluding 93 seats for Princely States) in the Constituent Assembly, and the Muslim League had 73 seats. The Cabinet Mission laid out two possible bases for proceeding with negotiations for a constitutional compromise: a relatively weak federation in a

[35] James, *Raj*, (n 18) 537.

[36] D Pandey, 'Congress-Muslim League Relations 1937–39: 'The Parting of the Ways'' (1978) 12(4) *Modern Asian Studies* 629, 638–42.

[37] NF Paracha, 'The Idea that Created Pakistan', *DAWN*, 25 Dec 2014, available at: www.dawn.com/news/1153105.

[38] See JP Haithcox, *Communism and Nationalism in India: MN Roy and Comintern Policy, 1920–1939* (New Jersey, Princeton University Press, 2015).

[39] M Daeschel, *The Politics of Self-Expression* (London, Routledge, 2002) 80.

united India or the creation of a territorial Pakistan which would entail the division of the Punjab and Bengal as well. The Muslim League resisted the division of Punjab and Bengal, and Jinnah even supported a subsequent proposal by the Cabinet Mission to group the Muslim provinces into subnational units within the Indian union without parity in constitution-making or a right to secede,[40] but an equal executive position in the interim government. Once again, the Congress rejected this compromise.

III. COMPETING VISIONS OF STATEHOOD

The Indian Independence Act 1947 granted Dominion status to both India and Pakistan. The ambiguities inherent in Muslim nationalism that Jinnah embodied in the lead up to Partition as well as the contradictions it unleashed once the nation had been realised were somewhat displayed in Jinnah's inaugural speech to the Constituent Assembly of Pakistan which will be discussed later. It is important first to be attentive to the mechanisms that gave rise to the first Constituent Assembly of Pakistan.

As noted earlier, late 1946 (July to December) saw the establishment of a Constituent Assembly for the soon-to-be independent India when Partition was not yet a certainty.[41] The provincial assembly members had themselves been elected on the basis of franchise that was limited to a mere 15 per cent of the total population,[42] and thus possessed weak democratic credentials. As seats were also divided on the basis of proportional representation for different communities, 73 Muslim League representatives were also elected.[43] The first session of the Constituent Assembly, tasked with drafting the Constitution of the Union of India, was held on 9 December 1946, which the Muslim League attended but which Jinnah ultimately boycotted, with a clear abstention being announced in July 1947. When the Independence Act 1947 came into force on 15 August, the Constituent Assembly of Pakistan came into being out of the Constituent Assembly of India. However, a little reflected upon fact is that the combined Constituent Assembly for India had passed a forward-looking Objectives Resolution to settle the contours of India's Constitution, thereby adding to Congress members' credentials as experienced legislators hitherto untroubled by the everyday politics in a sovereign state. In Pakistan, the

[40] On the very eve of Partition Jinnah was willing to entertain a proposal for a separate and united state of Bengal and a Pakistan comprising only the western Muslim-majority provinces. See Jalal, *Sole Spokesman* (n 20) 265; and S Wolpert, *Shameful Flight: the Last Years of the British Empire in India* (Oxford, Oxford University Press, 2006) 142.

[41] Lerner, *Constituent Assemblies*, (n 6) 63.

[42] H Alavi, 'State and Class in Pakistan' in H Gardezi and J Rashid (eds), *Pakistan: The Roots of Dictatorship, The Political Economy of a Praetorian State* (London, Zed Press, 1983) 65.

[43] H Lerner, *Making Constitutions in Deeply Divided Societies* (Cambridge, Cambridge University Press, 2011) 125.

Constituent Assembly which first met on 11 August 1947 had no such experience to guide it.

In addition to the 69 members from the provinces of a unified Pakistan on the eve of Partition, there were another 11 members, including representatives of the Princely States and other territories incorporated with varying degrees of sovereignty within the new country. Importantly however, the incorporation of additional seats followed no formula of election or representation. In most cases, office bearers of the Muslim League finalised the selection.[44] The Constituent Assembly of Pakistan was to be the forum for deciding the features and form of the new Constitution to govern these amalgamated territories. In addition, it was to function as a legislative assembly till such a point that a legislature was constituted according to the new Constitution. The Assembly convened as a legislature for the first time in February 1948 after a short session as the Constituent Assembly, a session that declared Jinnah as the Governor-General and sought to settle the shape of an interim constitution.

In his presidential address, Jinnah told the Assembly: 'You are now a Sovereign Legislative body and you have got all the powers.'[45] This statement belies the fact that deep personalisations of power were, in reality, the preferred mode of dealing with a fractious political field: 'It does not require political wisdom to realize that all safeguards and settlements would be a scrap of paper, unless they are backed up by power.'[46] As the preceding section demonstrated, the establishment of Pakistan was not a fully-anticipated outcome of constitutional negotiations. However, the fact that it became a certainty heightened the need to retain power to deal with the multi-valent threats the new nation faced. In this speech as President of the Constituent Assembly, there is considerable insight into what these perceived threats might have been. Jinnah cited the rampant practice of 'bribery and corruption', 'black marketeering', and 'nepotism and jobbery' as urgent problems to be resolved. These were described as 'poison', the 'most grievous of crimes', and Jinnah displayed the gravity of such offences by suggesting that he himself would act 'with an iron hand' to eradicate these crimes.[47]

Jinnah also acknowledged at this moment that the problem of minorities would persist in the new nation. He considered the problem to have been so severe within India as to account for the whole period of colonial rule as the consequence:

> No power can hold another nation, and specially a nation of 400 million souls, in subjection; nobody could have conquered you, and even if it had happened, nobody could have continued its hold on you for any length of time, but for this.[48]

[44] K Callard, *Pakistan: A Political Study* (London, George Allen and Unwin Ltd, 1957) 82.
[45] ibid.
[46] Qasmi & Robb, (n 20) 232.
[47] *Parliamentary Debates*, Constituent Assembly, 11 Aug 1947, (Quaid-e-Azam Muhammad Ali Jinnah, President). Available online: www.na.gov.pk/en/content.php?id=74.
[48] ibid.

By accounting for India's subjugation in these terms, Jinnah declared that from now on the citizens of Pakistan will 'be free' to go to their temples, their mosques 'or to any other place or worship in this State of Pakistan'.[49] Notably, even in this short speech, he read together ethnic, sectarian and broader religious affiliation as capable of dividing the population into minority units. Amongst Muslims, he saw the further divisions of 'Pathans, Punjabis, Shias, Sunnis and so on', and among the Hindus 'Brahmins, Vashnavas, Khatris, also Bengalees, Madrasis and so on'.[50] At this point, rather than suggesting any mechanism to address minority demands in the new entity, or even an apparatus capable of generating agreement amongst these groups, Jinnah's recourse is to affirm the relationship of citizenship within a temporal horizon in which discriminations based on such grounds should somehow cease to exist:

> Thank God, we are not starting in those days. We are starting in the days where there is no discrimination, no distinction between one community and another, no discrimination between one caste or creed and another. We are starting with this fundamental principle: that we are all citizens, and equal citizens, of one State.[51]

In his inaugural speech Jinnah promised freedom for those who would constitute separate nations but did so under the rubric of statehood. He thereby introduced a state that was already constituted and capable of delivering freedoms even before a constitution guaranteeing such freedoms was framed.[52] The origins of the demand for a separate Pakistan were glossed over to the extent that the plight of all nationalities was attributed to colonial governance. Hereafter, the trading of freedom for rights was a subject that would continue to bedevil both the executive and Constituent Assembly. Jinnah himself, in the year that he survived past Partition, continued to cite the 'scourge of provincialism' in several fora and labelled those who sought to bring forth claims for representation on the basis of group allegiances as 'fifth columnists'.

Shortly after assuming the post of Governor-General, a transfer of additional powers to the office was engineered, even though the Crown remained nominally the source of prerogatives.[53] Jinnah relied on the 'extremely wide' power under section 9 of the Indian Independence Act 1947 to bring the Interim Constitution into operation.[54] It was initially granted for a term of seven-and-a-half months but was extended by a year until March 1949.[55] Using this provision, Jinnah removed the power to impose a state of emergency in the provinces from the

[49] ibid.
[50] ibid.
[51] ibid.
[52] See especially, S Aziz, *The State of Knowledge and Knowledges of the State in Pakistan* (PhD Thesis, University of Melbourne, 2020).
[53] ibid.
[54] KB Sayeed, 'The Governor-General of Pakistan' (1955) 8(2) *Pakistan Horizon* 330, 333.
[55] Alavi, 'State and Class in Pakistan', (n 42).

Governors and vested it in the office of the Governor-General.[56] Jinnah himself used this power twice, in Sindh and Punjab, to rein in the provincial leaders of the Muslim League.[57] While there were undoubtedly pragmatic reasons underlying his decision – including the need to supervise the British officials who occupied most of the senior bureaucratic positions and maintain control of the transitional state under the Government of India Act 1935, which served as the Interim Constitution – the demotion of the dignity and position of the Constituent Assembly was surely one of the effects.[58]

The disruptions that Partition caused to the state structure have been understated. One influential view is that 'Pakistan's radical beginning … had nothing to do with the juridical and administrative machinery of the new state, all of which had been inherited from British India.'[59] In actuality, Pakistan faced seemingly insurmountable challenges as a new, post-colonial state with millions of refugees pouring across the as yet un-demarcated border needing rehabilitation and resettlement. Compounding these problems was the fact that Pakistan's share of finances under the Partition Plan was withheld by the Congress government of India until Gandhi forced their transfer to Pakistan under the threat of a fast until death. The administrative structure was effectively non-existent. The socio-economic backwardness of Muslims in colonial India was reflected in the small number of Muslims at the higher echelons of bureaucracy.[57]

This initial administrative reconstruction, which was accompanied by a centralisation of power and policymaking in the federal bureaucracy,[60] was facilitated by a lack of clarity in the juridical framework of the 'new Dominions'. The new Dominions of South Asia were radically different from the old settler Dominions such as Australia and Canada which had experienced a systematic and prolonged transfer of administrative technology and legislative powers. Most of the relatively small numbers of Muslim civil service officers opted to move to Pakistan. Most of them had only attained relatively junior positions within the colonial administration and thus lacked experience in higher policymaking.[61] To reconstitute its administrative services, the new state retained 355 British officers already in Pakistan and acquired the services of 129 officers

[56] The power to impose emergency in the provinces was granted to Governors by s 93 of the Government of India Act 1935. Under s 92A, this power was taken from the Governors and granted to the Governor-General. See Sayeed, 'The Governor-General of Pakistan' (n 54).

[57] L Ziring, *Pakistan in the Twentieth Century* (Oxford, Oxford University Press, 1997) 82–84.

[58] A Jalal, 'Inheriting the Raj: Jinnah and the Governor-Generalship Issue' (1985) 19(1) *Modern Asian Studies* 29.

[59] Devji, *Muslim Zion*, (n 31) 90.

[60] A prime example of this was the creation of the post of the Secretary-General of the Government of Pakistan, an apex bureaucratic office whose holder could co-ordinate the actions of all the departments of the bureaucracy cutting across lines of responsibility and accountability to individual ministers. Alavi, 'State and Class in Pakistan', (n 42) 75.

[61] See RJD Braibanti, *Evolution of Pakistan's Administrative System: The Collected Papers of Ralph Braibanti* (Pakistan Public Administration, Research Centre, 1987) 97 [hereinafter 'Braibanti'].

from England to meet a critical shortfall in administrative human resources. Notably, 'three of the four governors were British and former Indian Civil Service officers and two of these Governors presided over Cabinet meetings'.[62] To add to the administrative difficulties, the 'records and office equipment may have been sent from Delhi were lost in the burning and destruction of trains which accompanied independence'.[63]

With Jinnah's death in September 1948, power shifted to the office of the Prime Minister Liaquat Ali Khan and the prospects of a transition to democratic constitutionalism seemed briefly to have been enlivened. However, as a Muslim League stalwart and one of Jinnah's lieutenants, Liaquat was more comfortable working through the party than through an assembly structure. What we see in the period when Liaquat presided over the Constituent Assembly is a deepening of the protocols of cabinet government and a drawing together of the high bureaucracy. The shift of the centre of power away from the office of Governor-General was largely due to Jinnah's successor, Khawaja Nazimuddin, who occupied the office with considerable rectitude.

However, when Liaquat stepped into the vacuum of power in the Muslim League, he found the eastern branch of the party rebellious and that other fissures in the political landscape had widened. The new Prime Minister was also forced to rely heavily on a bureaucracy and a central party cadre that was slowly being nationalised but was now composed largely of migrants from north-central India. This led to further centralisation of politics and cleavages between the central and the provincial leadership of the Muslim League, especially in East Bengal (later East Pakistan). The Constituent Assembly, comprising mostly those members of the Muslim League who had been elected indirectly by the provincial assemblies, was an insufficient bulwark against the centralisation of power. Keith Callard notably cites high levels of absenteeism along with high levels of cross-appointment of members of the Assembly as diplomats, governors of provinces or even provincial minsters. It was very rare for anyone to give up their seat in the central assembly. Importantly, a venerated leader from the North West Frontier Province, Adbul Ghaffar Khan, was arrested for 'subversion' in 1948 and his seat was left vacant while he remained confined for the term of the first Constituent Assembly.

In fact, central executive dominance became so pronounced that in seeking to arrogate powers from provincial assemblies, as conferred by the terms of the Government of India Act 1935, members of the high executive would confer with, but overrode the concerns of provincial chief ministers. One particularly emblematic case occurred in discussions leading to the promulgation of the Public Safety Ordinance in 1949. Cabinet documents reveal that the Central Government determined firstly that it wished to pass a law to detain persons

[62] KB Sayeed, 'The Political Role of Pakistani's Civil Service' (1985) 31(2) *Pacific Affairs* 131–146, 131.
[63] Braibanti, (n 62) 97.

whenever 'satisfied' that such persons were acting in a manner prejudicial to public safety and public order. Over the objections of three provincial governments, a recommendation was made to the Governor-General to make an order under the India Independence Act 1947 to amend and transfer the executive preventive detention powers from the provincial to the concurrent legislative list. Thereafter, the Ordinance was passed. The manner in which the response in the Constituent Assembly was managed demonstrates the total control the executive was already exercising. In the same file, there is a draft Bill calling for the repeal of the Public Safety Ordinance authored by a Muslim League representative from Sindh, MH Gazdar. Its preambular statement is particularly poignant:

> People of Pakistan have loyally co-operated with the Government since its formation. They have not so far formed even an opposition party which is so essential for a successful working of any democratic institution. They have behaved as most peaceful citizens in present world when there are in other countries all sorts of movements, disturbances and upheavals.[64]

Importantly, the absence of an effective or organised opposition was a direct consequence of both the elections of 1946 as well as the fact that the only bloc of non-Muslim League members comprised largely minority members of the Pakistan Congress Party. The Congress in Pakistan did not have confidence in challenging governmental policy. It, thus, 'had to concern itself with the defense of interests that it might yet lose'.[65] Thus, opposition voices combined for constitutional debates even as the executive remained un-assailed by ordinary legislation and policy. As for MH Gazdar, otherwise a loyal Muslim League member, the Interior Ministry opened a file to ascertain the '[a]ttitude to be adopted towards the non-official Bill by Mr MH Gazdar'[66] and noted that he had eventually withdrawn the Bill and no further action needed to be taken. In this same period, other anti-democratic legislative initiatives were tabled and passed, such as the Public and Representative Officers Disqualification Act, introduced by Liaquat and passed by the Assembly in January 1949. Hereafter, persons could be disqualified from holding public office if they were subject to allegations of corruption or misuse of office.

In such straightened circumstances, the Constituent Assembly took to identifying the basic structure for the upcoming constitution.[67] Ideologically, the main challenge was to ascribe positive meaning to 'Muslim' nationhood beyond an essentially negative assertion of difference from, and parity with, the Hindu majority in the late colonial constitutional tussles. The first significant document to suggest an incorporation of Islam within the constitutional structure was the

[64] Government of Pakistan, Ministry of Interior, Home Division, 'Pakistan Public Safety Ordinance, File No 124/CF/48', National Documentation Centre.

[65] Callard, *Pakistan: A Political Study*, (n 44) 85.

[66] See an 'Office Memorandum' dated 24 January 1950, included in the File No 124/CF/48 (n 64).

[67] GW Choudhury, 'Constitution-Making Dilemmas in Pakistan' (1955) 8(4) *Western Political Quarterly* 589.

Objectives Resolution of 1949. The Resolution was moved by Prime Minister Liaquat and passed after considerable debate and disagreement. It began with a preambular recognition of the sovereignty of Allah over the entire universe and then identified a range of principles on which the future Constitution would be based: 'democracy, freedom, equality, tolerance and social justice, as enunciated by Islam'; 'a Federation wherein the units will be autonomous'; 'guaranteed fundamental rights'; provisions to 'safeguard the legitimate interests of minorities and backward and depressed classes'; and 'the independence of the judiciary'.

The Objectives Resolution raised considerable controversy in the Constituent Assembly, and firm opposition from members from East Pakistan, many of whom were Hindus. They vociferously denounced the references to Islam as undermining the realisation of Pakistan as a multi-faith and secular state, a promise that they recalled Jinnah as having made for a future state during the independence movement. Some of the members felt that the incorporation of religion would curb the possibilities of dissent and lead the country down the path of authoritarianism.[68] Jinnah's inaugural speech to the Assembly was recalled, even as the promises of equal citizenship – minus a mechanism for ensuring this – was now revealed as having been essentially illusory.

The second major challenge for a coming constitution was rather more pragmatic: the nature, form and balance of representation between the more populous eastern wing (today's Bangladesh) and the Western provinces where the Central Government, bureaucracy and military were based. A Basic Principles Committee, set up in 1949, made its first Interim Report in 1950.[69] The Committee proposed a bicameral legislature with both houses having equal power. While there was no mention of a formula for the distribution of membership in the lower house of the people, it proposed an equal division between the constitutive units in the upper house. This would give the four Western provinces overwhelming control in the upper house at the expense of East Bengal, which, in the absence of a land-link, was cut off from the West.[70] With very limited representation in the bureaucracy and with a sizeable non-Muslim minority, the population of East Bengal was rightly anxious about issues of representation. In addition, the report was controversial for its proposal to make Urdu the national language, in line with what Jinnah propounded in his one visit to East Bengal after Partition.[71]

[68] GW Choudhury, *Documents and Speeches on the Constitution of Pakistan* (Dacca, Green Book House, 1967). For objections of East Pakistan members to the Objectives Resolution see ch 4 on Bangladesh in this volume.

[69] ibid, 593.

[70] H Khan, *Constitutional and Political History of Pakistan*, 2nd edn (Oxford, Oxford University Press, 2009) 64–66.

[71] Ziring, *Pakistan in the Twentieth Century*, (n 57) 109. See also ch 4 on Bangladesh in this volume.

At that time, there had also been widespread protests and this in turn engendered an attitude of distrust amongst executive office-bearers and intensified surveillance of universities and other potential sites of protest. Within official communication, proposals were tabled to change the Bangla language script to purge the majority population of Bengal of their Brahmanic legacy. Redeploying a classic colonial device to contain subversion and secure compliance, communists, labour activists and increasing numbers of the Bengali Hindu community were detained under the Public Safety Ordinance. What was clearly working in tandem with the greater insulation of decision-making within the executive branch was the organisation of dissent within the social sphere. The crisis between these two opposing tendencies would play out in the Constituent Assembly, which at first shelved the proposals of the first basic structure committee and invited public proposals instead.

With Prime Minister Liaquat's assassination in 1951, bureaucratic ascendancy became even more entrenched as Ghulam Mohammad, consummate bureaucrat-turned-politician, assumed the office of Governor-General. In its second report the Basic Principles Committee revised the composition and division of powers in the legislature, so that the eastern and western wings would have 'parity' or equal representation in the 120-member upper house and the 400-member lower house.[72] Real legislative power would be vested in the lower house and in a true Westminster fashion the government would be responsible to the lower house.[73] While the proposals did not fully satisfy the demands from East Pakistan, the real resistance came from provinces within the west, especially Punjab. Parity in the upper house was seen as weakening the core principle of federalism in terms of equal representation of the constitutive units.[74] The Constituent Assembly indefinitely postponed its deliberations once again.

Between 1952 and 1953, the accelerated pace of social organisation took on a sectarian-religious character and a local martial law was declared around Lahore to contain a violent anti-Ahmaddiya movement. Soon thereafter the Prime Minister was dismissed from his office. The Governor-General cited the Prime Minister's failure to deal proactively with the disturbances as justification to dismiss him and his Cabinet. This was the first dismissal of a Prime Minister – holder of the most powerful political office – in the country's history. The Constituent Assembly nevertheless accepted the decision and selected Mohammad Ali Bogra as Pakistan's third Prime Minister.

In the provincial elections held in East Bengal in 1954 – the first since Independence – the Muslim League was routed, further delegitimising its status as the founding party and its continuing control over the Constituent Assembly.[75] The progressive coalition that briefly formed a government in East

[72] H Khan (n 70) 64–66.
[73] Choudhury, *Documents and Speeches*, (n 68) 68, 593.
[74] Ziring, *Pakistan in the Twentieth Century*. (n 57) 55, 133.
[75] Alavi, 'State and Class in Pakistan', (n 42) 81.

Bengal – before the hasty imposition of Governor's rule by Iskander Mirza – had campaigned on the demand for complete autonomy for the province in a confederate system and the recognition of Bengali as a national language alongside Urdu.

During this period, the despondency of political actors in the Provinces and in the Constituent Assembly began to lift.[76] Several years had passed and while the disorders of Partition were still acutely felt, issues such as Pakistan's future alignment in a bipolar world as well as the balance of regional interests within Pakistan were widely debated. In this context Prime Minister Bogra managed to develop a creative formula for achieving meaningful parity between the two wings of the country in a future legislature which received extensive support.[77] It was finally agreed that the lower house of the people should be elected on the basis of population, with East Bengal having a clear majority of 165 out of the 300 seats. The 50 seats in the upper house would be divided equally between the federating units, as recommended by the Basic Principles Committee in its first report. Likewise, both houses would have equal legislative powers and any disagreement would be resolved in a joint sitting, with each Wing represented in effect by 175 members.

The Constituent Assembly approved the Basic Principles Committee Report with appropriate amendments in September 1954 and appointed draftsmen to prepare the Constitution Bill. In a proactive move, it made several changes in the Government of India Act 1935 to whittle down the Governor-General's powers by including most notably the grant of writ jurisdiction to the superior courts of Pakistan.[78] A day earlier, the Constituent Assembly repealed the notorious Public Representative Office Disqualification Act 1949 (PRODA), a so-called accountability law first introduced under Prime Minister Liaquat to keep pressure on, and/or disqualify, politicians. This time MH Gazder was unhindered in leading the battle for its repeal. On 21 September, the last day before adjourning its session, the Assembly amended sections 9 and 10 of the 1935 Act to remove the Governor-General's power to dismiss ministers and bind him to act only on the Cabinet's advice. It also granted provincial status to the Princely States of Bahawalpur and Khairpur, thereby increasing the number of the West Pakistan provinces to six.[79] This flurry of legislative activity was done while the Governor-General was on tour and just before the Prime Minister was about to embark on a visit to the US. The Constituent Assembly set 27 October as the date to reconvene in order to take up the Constitution Bill. While it appeared that the Constituent Assembly had finally resolved the longstanding

[76] RS Wheeler, 'Governor General's Rule in Pakistan' (1955) 24(1) *Far Eastern Survey* 1, 1–2 [hereinafter 'Wheeler'].

[77] Choudhury, *Documents and Speeches*, (n 68) 68, 594.

[78] See AS Pasha, *Pakistan: A Political Study Political Study* (Lahore, Sang-e-Meel Publications, 1995) 99 [hereinafter 'Pasha'].

[79] Wheeler (n 76) 2.

issues that plagued its efforts to draft a new constitution, and would finally, even if belatedly, justify its raison d'etre, there was considerable opposition to the draft Constitution especially in Punjab. Likewise, the progressive parties of East Pakistan, in the environment of post-1954 elections there, considered the Constituent Assembly unrepresentative and the draft Constitution an unhappy compromise.[80] Capitalising on this opposition, the Governor-General on 24 October 1954 imposed a state of emergency, dissolved the Constituent Assembly and consequently dismissed the government in a proclaimed exercise of inherent prerogative powers.

The Governor-General's acts relied upon a claim of inherent and meta-constitutional prerogative. This in turn brought the faulty juridical grounds of the new Dominion into relief when Maulvi Tamizuddin Khan, President of the Constituent Assembly, challenged the proclamation of emergency and the dissolution of the Constituent Assembly before the courts.[81] The *Tamizuddin Khan* cases have largely been seen through a political lens and the courts' decisions as mere exercises in strategic and partisan judicial action that ultimately accorded with the essentially administrative executive character of the state, with the Federal Court controversially upholding the Governor-General's decision.[82] The Independence Act had first provided for a transition by making the Government of India Act 1935 the Interim Constitution. However, as noted earlier, it also gave Jinnah wide-ranging powers, including the power to personally amend the interim framework. This was all part of the suite of transitional powers even while he was nominally responsible to the Crown. In hindsight, the most significant ambiguity in the Indian Independence Act 1947 pertained to whether the governors-general after Jinnah would inherit those broad powers to bring the Interim Constitution into operation or would enjoy any other inherent prerogative powers above and beyond what were granted to them.

During its existence, the first Constituent Assembly appeared to have developed a convention whereby any law resulting in a change in the interim constitutional framework was deemed to have been passed by it in exercise of its constituent power, and was therefore not subject to the Governor-General's assent. The passage of ordinary legislation would, of course, still require the Governor-General's assent. Giving credence to that convention, the Sindh High Court rejected the assertion of Governor-General's prerogative in assenting to Bills and unanimously held that the Constituent Assembly was not subject to any limits in the exercise of its constituent powers. The Governor-General appealed the decision to the Federal Court which by a majority decision by Chief Justice Munir compared the role of the Governor-General with those in other Dominion constitutions and held that all acts of the Constituent Assembly, whether in passing ordinary legislation or a constituent law, required his assent.[83]

[80] ibid, 3–4.
[81] *Maulvi Tamizuddin Khan v The Federation of Pakistan*, PLD 1955 Sind 96.
[82] *The Federation of Pakistan v Maulvi Tamizuddin Khan*, PLD 1955 FC 240.
[83] ibid.

The *Maulvi Tamizuddin Khan* case and subsequent decisions of the Federal Court have often been criticised for laying the jurisprudential basis for validating extra-constitutional usurpations of power and embedding the notorious 'doctrine of state necessity' within Pakistan's legal culture. However, such simplistic assertions fail to capture the more nuanced and mediatory role that the courts began to fashion for themselves in the relatively ill-defined legal framework of the new Dominion, with the aim of steering them towards more solid constitutional foundations. While the Federal Court's decision in *Maulvi Tamizuddin Khan* effectively validated the dissolution of the Constituent Assembly, the Court quickly proceeded to correct the misapprehension that the verdict was in any way a licence for the Governor-General to exercise unfettered legislative and prerogative powers.[84] In the further *Governor General's Reference* case,[85] a majority in the Federal Court allowed the Governor-General to temporarily extend the life of the laws that had not received assent on the basis of a doctrine of 'civil and state necessity' until such time and on the condition that a new Constituent Assembly is created as soon as possible. The Governor-General was declared to have no power to amend the constitutional framework in the interim nor any power to nominate any members. The *Reference* case thus compelled the Governor-General to reconstitute a second Constituent Assembly in May 1955 and proceed with the process of constitution-making. However, this was not a significant democratic advance as the new Constituent Assembly was again indirectly elected from provincial assemblies that were themselves a product of rigged and managed elections. The 1954 elections to the East Pakistan Assembly were, however, largely free of complaints of rigging.

IV. COMPROMISE(D) CONSTITUTIONALISM

The contradictions of Muslim nationalism during the late colonial period and the ambiguities about nation and state in Pakistan paralysed early efforts at laying down a constitutional founding. Nonetheless, after the second Constituent Assembly was formed in 1955, it faced less friction in proceeding with its work than its predecessor. Importantly, some of the basic issues, such as the federal structure, had been undertaken by executive acts prior to the establishment of this second assembly, as we shall see. Other contentious issues, such as whether Muslims and minorities would constitute joint or separate electorates, was deferred. Nonetheless, the Constitution framed by the second Constituent Assembly in February 1956 was an exercise in wresting power back to the political sphere from claims of discretionary and arbitrary executive authority.

It adopted a system of parliamentary government but jettisoned the earlier formulas and created a unicameral legislature of 300 members, with both East

[84] *Usif Patel v Crown*, PLD 1955 FC 387.
[85] *Governor-General's Reference*, PLD 1955 FC 435 (advisory jurisdiction).

and West Pakistan having equal representation. It also provided for the addition of 10 women members elected solely by women in their exercise of a dual franchise.[86] This was to accommodate demands from women's organisations that had been mobilised after the dissolution of the first Constituent Assembly, which had two outstanding female representatives; the second assembly had none. The Constitution established an Election Commission, which upon its formation, decided upon separate electorates for religious minorities in East Pakistan and a unified electorate for West Pakistan. However, this proved to be greatly unpopular and went against the expressed desire of minority groups. The office of the President was made largely ceremonial and he was bound to act on the advice of the cabinet. However, the President appeared to have some discretion in appointing from amongst its members a Prime Minster who was 'most likely to command the confidence of the majority of the members of the National Assembly'. In a stable two-party system, such a provision would be merely ceremonial. However, in a divided multiparty political landscape, as Pakistan had become within a few years, this gave the President considerable leeway in dictating the formation of government.

With the representation of new political parties from East Pakistan in the Constituent Assembly, the 1956 Constitution adopted a federal framework. The amalgamation of the West Pakistan provinces into one unit was initially proposed in a session of the first Constituent Assembly where it was vociferously debated.[87] As Saadia Toor noted, the idea of forging a singular identity amongst the West Pakistani population borrowed heavily from the ideas that had earlier been used to unify Muslims across the sub-continent.[88] The irony in arguing that geographical contiguity bred cultural similarities was that it contradicted the characterisation of Muslims – who shared a moral order deriving from common faith – as a distinct nation. Politicians from East Pakistan were quick to point this out and a similar resistance was voiced by political spokespersons of all dominant groups other than Punjabis. It had been enacted by an executive act by Governor-General Ghulam Muhammad and then entrenched in the 1956 Constitution. Legislative powers were divided, again adopting the Interim Constitution's design, between the federation and the provinces such that an extensive list of provincial subjects and residuary powers were vested in the provinces. However, there was also a concurrent list of subjects on which both the federal and the provincial legislatures could legislate. Furthermore, contrary to the demands of the East Pakistan members, no guarantees concerning the equal transfer of fiscal resources between the two provinces were included. A longstanding controversy was, however, resolved when both Urdu and Bengali were constitutionally recognised as national languages.

[86] M Huq, 'Electorates and Elections in Pakistan' (1966) 16(1) *Civilisations* 45–56.

[87] See the Establishment of West Pakistan Act 1955 (3 October 1955).

[88] See S Toor, 'Bengal(is) in the House: The Politics of National Culture in Pakistan, 1947–1971' in MN Chakraborty, *Being Bengali: At Home and in the World* (London, Routledge, 2014) ch 11; and S Toor, *The State of Islam: Culture and Cold War Politics in Pakistan* (London, Pluto Press, 2011).

The Constitution also incorporated detailed Islamic provisions under which all laws repugnant to the injunctions of Islam would be void. In addition, all existing laws would be brought into conformity with Islam within six years. It also provided for the creation of an advisory commission to recommend the Islamisation of laws. However, the power to determine if laws conformed to the injunctions of Islam was vested in the National Assembly and not in the courts or any other independent body. The 1956 Constitution adopted an extensive Bill of Rights and granted judicial review powers to the courts, including a new apex Supreme Court and provincial High Courts. Following the model of the Government of India Act 1935 it dealt with a range of matters not necessarily of a key constitutional import, such as provisions governing the bureaucracy's terms of service and tenure. The 1956 Constitution drew a line between lawful and unlawful detention but made review of detention decisions the purview of executive authorities. It also incorporated explicit provisions for the imposition of an emergency. Thus, while the 1956 Constitution carried over some of the authoritarian legacies of the 1935 Act, it did create the possibility for the transition to more democratic forms of politics. However, for that to materialise, relatively free nationwide elections needed to be held on the basis of universal suffrage to inaugurate a legislature that would adequately represent the interests of East Pakistan and the marginal regions in the west.

General elections were to be held soon after the framing of the Constitution but were delayed.[89] Meanwhile, the Constituent Assembly continued to serve as the interim legislature and the seat of government. With the emergence of new factions and parties within the Constituent Assembly, political turmoil emerged as four different Prime Ministers found it difficult to manage stable coalitions and rotated through that office.[90] As a result, Iskander Mirza, the new President, gained much greater influence over the government in the way previous Governors-Generals did, even though the role of the President had been formally constrained. As such, the only sphere of constitutionalism that was operational during the brief existence of Pakistan's first Constitution was that of judicial review. Pakistan's courts, especially the West Pakistan High Court, took on the task of laying down the foundations of judicial review with a relish. It was during this period that the courts also began questioning legislation and administrative action on the basis of fundamental rights.

Elections were finally scheduled for February 1959 and preparations had been well underway when on 7 October 1958 President Iskander Mirza, citing the political instability brought on by the new Constitution, imposed martial law and abrogated the Constitution. When the Khan of Kalat declared independence for Kalat from Pakistan, President Mirza proclaimed martial law and

[89] H Khan (n 70) 115.

[90] See Pasha (n 78) 121. The provincial governments also suffered from instability. Violent clashes in the East Pakistan assembly contributed to the death of the speaker, while the situation in West Pakistan was not much better either.

named General Ayub Khan the Chief Martial Law Administrator. By a decree on 8 October 1958, Ayub Khan abrogated the 1956 Constitution, assemblies and provincial governments were dissolved, political parties were abolished, group meetings were banned, politicians were arrested, and martial law regulations replaced the Constitution.[91] Previous allies Ayub and Iskander differed on key matters and finally, convinced that the army was unified behind him, Ayub took direct power by displacing Iskander. That this takeover of power did not face widespread or popular opposition was a factor that was cited in the famous *Dosso* case,[92] which effectively legitimised this coup and articulated the now famous revolutionary legality doctrine. Having no precedent in common law, it was a doctrine fashioned from the theoretical postulations of the Austrian jurist Hans Kelsen, who reportedly later decried the *Dosso* judgment for misappropriating his theory.[93] In *Dosso* the court accepted that an effective transfer of power had shifted the highest norm or *grundnorm* – in this case the Constitution – such that a wholly new legal order was now set in place as a consequence of a revolutionary change.

Ayub would institute wide-ranging changes to the structure of government, doing away with the democratic pretensions of early years. In retrospect Ayub characterised defenders of democracy who suggested that his assumption of power retarded its realisation as arguing that 'we did not have a long enough rope to hang ourselves with'.[94] He located the impossibility of realising democracy in the Pakistani terrain as flowing from the fractious nature of the Pakistani political sphere, which spawned endless parties which made the formation of stable coalitions highly problematic. Both this and the somewhat messianic zeal of imparting a programme of multifaceted 'reform' were factors that allowed him to proclaim his economic and political policies as a 'revolution'. The Constitution that Ayub fashioned in 1962 differed in substantial ways from even the conservative recommendations offered by a Constitutional Commission that he himself appointed in 1960.[95] Whereas the Commission members had suggested that parliamentary government was now innately a part of the South Asian genius, given its incremental introduction through the colonial experience, Ayub differed on this matter. As President and Chief Martial Law Administrator, he had by 1960 instituted a system of 'basic democracy' whereby an electoral college could be formed through local elections throughout Pakistan and which in turn gave him an overwhelming mandate to promulgate his constitution from the office of President.[96]

[91] H Khan (n 70) 118.
[92] *State v Dosso*, PLD 1958 SC 533.
[93] See H Kelsen 'Professor Stone and the Pure Theory of Law' (1965) 17 *Stanford Law Review* 1128.
[94] See MA Khan, *Field Marshal Mohammad Ayub Khan: A Selection of Talks and Interviews, 1964–1967*, (Lahore, Oxford University Press, 2010) 133.
[95] See KB Sayeed, 'Pakistan's Constitutional Autocracy' (1963–4) 36(4) *Pacific Affairs* 365–377.
[96] Basic Democracies Order, 1959.

In the early years of the 1962 Constitution's functioning, the passage of the First Amendment Act indicated two areas where Ayub's secular management would not be given primacy. The first was that the name of the state was changed from the original formulation of the Republic of Pakistan to the 'Islamic Republic of Pakistan.'[97] The second was that rights enumerated as principles of law to guide legislators were deemed fundamental rights and held to be justiciable and the power to review laws against their derogation was invested in the superior courts. Whereas a study of how the executive tried to hold back popular political forces in the years leading to the first Constitution evinces their reorganisation in protest and resistance in a regional and patchy fashion, there was a definite expansion and combination of forces demanding a greater dispersal of power across all regions in the Pakistani federation after the enactment of the 1962 Constitution. This led to the establishment of another interim constitutional order in 1969, through the Legal Framework Order, which authorised a general election based on universal suffrage and laid down basic principles for the next constitution of Pakistan to be framed by the returning representatives. The results were such as to indicate that the people of East Pakistan sought a renewal of the national compact, threatening thereby all the power centres that had been built over the preceding two decades. The denial was violent and led to the dismemberment of Pakistan and the establishment of an independent Bangladesh.

V. CONCLUSION

The story of Pakistan's first Constitution is always narrated as one of utter failure. The inability of the first Constituent Assembly to deliver a constitution for more than seven years is seen as emblematic of the entrenchment of authoritarianism – first civil, then military – as well as the beginning of the divide between the east and west wings which ultimately led to a civil war and the secession of the more populous wing, resulting in the creation of the independent nation-state of Bangladesh in 1971. However, a closer inspection of the wrangling over constitution-making in the first decade of Pakistan reveals a more nuanced picture. The first Constituent Assembly did succeed, even if belatedly, in providing a workable solution to the key political challenges that faced the new nation at the moment of its inchoate inception. While these constitutional design principles were only adopted in an insufficient form in the 1956 Constitution, and were never really put into practice, those principles had formed the bedrock of every successive democratic constitutional instrument

[97] See *Report of the Constitution Commission* ('the legal system should only be subject to any Islamisation if the different schools of Islamic law "could evolve unanimity with regards to the fundamentals of Islam as far as traditions are concerned"'). See also, S Mahmood, *The Constitutional Foundations of Pakistan* (Lahore, Publishers United, 1975) 517.

in Pakistan, including the 1973 Constitution.[98] Although they have been deeply contested in form and in practice, and every military dictator has subsequently attempted to jettison them when wielding complete power during periods of martial law, parliamentary democracy, federalism and constitutional judicial review have succeeded in remaining core principles of constitutionalism in Pakistan.

[98] For an analysis of 1973 as a founding moment, see MS Khan, 'What's in a Founding? Founding Moments and Pakistan's "Permanent Constitution" of 1973', in R Albert, M Guruswamy, and N Basnyat (eds), *Founding Moments in Constitutionalism* (Oxford, Hart Publishing, 2019) 201–222.

4

The Founding and Making of Bangladesh's Constitution

RIDWANUL HOQUE*

INTRODUCTION

THE CONSTITUTION OF Bangladesh, adopted by the Constituent Assembly on 4 November 1972, was a revolutionary, autochthonous[1] document established by those who liberated the country from Pakistan in a war of independence. It is a revolutionary document, but its democratic foundation is indeed rooted in the local specificities and moored in the people's lived experiences in the pre-1971 period that raised aspirations for liberal democracy. The framing of Bangladesh's Constitution was quite unlike that of either India or Pakistan,[2] in that no law provided for the state's independence nor for its constitution-making process. It was triggered by the revolutionary act of declaration of independence on 26 March 1971.[3] Although the debates in the Constituent Assembly are documented, there nevertheless is a paucity of literature on the intellectual history of Bangladesh's constitution-making.[4] This chapter seeks to fill this gap to the extent it is possible within the framework of a book-chapter. In particular, I address four questions in this chapter: (a) how was Bangladesh's founding Constitution (1972) made; (b) what were the internal and external factors that influenced the constitution-making; (c) how or to what

*I wish to thank Md. Azhar Uddin Bhuiyan and Raihan Rahman Rafid for their excellent research help.

[1] On this concept, see PC Oliver, 'Autochthonous Constitutions', in R Grote, F Lachenmann and R Wolfrum (eds), *Max Planck Encyclopedia of Comparative Constitutional Law* (New York, Oxford University Press, 2017).

[2] The Indian Independence Act 1947, s 8. See also s 19(3)(a) (modifying the Constituent Assembly of India of 1946 'by the exclusion of the members representing Bengal') and s 19(3)(b) (on Constituent Assembly for Pakistan).

[3] This can somewhat be compared to the Israeli case, where an elected Constituent Assembly to draft a constitution was marred in the 1948 Declaration of Independence itself.

[4] But see AF Huq, 'Constitution-making in Bangladesh' (1973) 46(1) *Pacific Affairs* 59–76; and K Hossain, *Bangladesh: Quest for Freedom and Justice* (Dhaka, University Press Limited, 2013) ch 9 ('The Making of the Constitution').

extent did that Constitution provide a founding for the newly emerged nation-state; and (d) how did it impact subsequent constitutional developments?

I begin by charting a brief history of the emergence of Bangladesh and its constitutional development through the Pakistani period right through to its independence. I then explain the making of the founding Constitution before discussing its impact on the contemporary developments. I conclude with thoughts on the differences between Bangladesh's founding values and the current 'development' agenda of present-day constitutionalism.

I. THE EMERGENCE OF BANGLADESH

Bangladesh – which existed as East Pakistan between August 1947 and March 1971 – emerged as an independent sovereign nation on 26 March 1971,[5] when its independence was declared by its founding leader Sheikh Mujibur Rahman, known as 'Bangabandhu'.[6] His Declaration of Independence – made in the early hours of 26 March after the Army's crackdown the night before – was in these terms:

> This may be my last message, from today Bangladesh is independent. I call upon the people of Bangladesh wherever you might be and with whatever you have, to resist the army of occupation to the last. Your fight must go on until the last soldier of the Pakistan occupation army is expelled from the soil of Bangladesh and final victory is achieved.[7]

Following this Declaration of Independence, Bangladesh endured a brutal nine-month war that saw one of the worst genocides in global history.[8] The country

[5] On Bangladesh's emergence, see, among others, SR Chowdhury, *The Genesis of Bangladesh* (New Delhi, Asia Publishing House, 1972); K Ahmad, *A Socio-Political History of Bengal and the Birth of Bangladesh,* 4th edn (Dacca, Zahiruddin Mahmud Inside Library, 1975); C Baxter, *Bangladesh: A New Nation in an Old Setting* (Boulder, CO, Westview Press, 1984); R Sisson and LE Rose, *War and Secession: Pakistan, India, and the Creation of Bangladesh* (Berkeley, CA, University of California Press, 1990); AMA Muhith, *Bangladesh: Emergence of a Nation* (Dhaka, University Press Limited, 1992); M Anisuzzaman, *Creativity, Reality and Identity* (Dhaka, International Centre for Bengal Studies, 1993); S Raghavan, *1971: A Global History of the Creation of Bangladesh* (Cambridge, MA, Harvard University Press, 2013); and R Sobhan, *From Two Economies to Two Nations: My Journey to Bangladesh* (Dhaka, The Daily Star Books, 2015). See also D Ludden, 'The Politics of Independence in Bangladesh' (2011) 46(35) *Economic & Political Weekly* 79, 81–85.

[6] Sheikh Mujibur Rahman was also known as 'Bangabandhu', meaning 'Friend of Bengal'. It was an affectionate nickname given to him by the students on 23 Feb 1969 in the aftermath of a mass upsurge in demands for self-autonomy in East Pakistan. He is also popularly known as 'Sheikh Mujib', which is used in this chapter to refer to him in the pre-1969 period. The term 'Bangabandhu' is used for the post-1969 period.

[7] The Declaration of Independence, originally made in Bangla, has recently been recognised as a constituent instrument. See the 6th Schedule to the Constitution, inserted via the 15th Amendment of 2015.

[8] On the 1971 genocide, see generally GJ Bass, *The Blood Telegram: Nixon, Kissinger, and a Forgotten Genocide* (New York, Knopf Doubleday, 2013). See also AK Blood, *The Cruel Birth of Bangladesh: The Memoirs of an American Diplomat* (Dhaka, University Press Limited, 2002).

attained its physical liberation on 16 December 1971 – Victory Day – when the occupying Pakistani forces surrendered in Dhaka. The war was fought by the (Bangladesh) Awami League[9] under Bangabandhu's leadership.[10] It was the first opposition party in Pakistan, and it won a landslide victory in the 1970 general elections that were held for the purposes of framing a constitution for undivided Pakistan.

A. Bangladesh and the 1947 Partition of British India

Bangladesh's constitution-making history does not begin in 1971 but dates to its days during the British Raj.[11] Before the partition of British India in August 1947, Bangladesh was part of the province of Bengal.[12] The Indian Independence Act 1947 granted India and Pakistan independence from the colonial rule in the form of two nations, India and Pakistan.[13] The 1947 Act also created a new province of 'East Bengal'[14] with territory comprising present-day Bangladesh. This province was to become the eastern wing of Pakistan – known since 14 October 1955 as East Pakistan[15] – albeit separated from its western wing by over 1,200 miles of Indian territory. Following the 1947 partition, East Bengal legislators joined

[9] The Awami League was founded on 23 June 1949 with the name of the East Pakistan Awami Muslim League by some progressive and secular-minded Bengali leaders of the Pakistan Muslim League. In October 1955, the party's name was changed to the East Pakistan Awami League, arguably to reflect its stance for secular politics.

[10] Sheikh Mujibur Rahman was a Joint Secretary of the Awami League in 1949 and was its President in 1971.

[11] This phase of colonial and pre-colonial history of Bangladesh's constitutional past is not covered in this chapter, for which see chs 2 and 3 on India and Pakistan in this volume. For a brief colonial politico-constitutional history in the context of Bangladesh's founding, see Chowdhury, *The Genesis of Bangladesh*, (n 5) ch 1.

[12] See The Government of India Act 1935, s 46(1). Along with Bengal there were ten other provinces.

[13] Along with other similar pre-1947 instruments, the two colonial statutes of 1935 and 1947 had notable influences, at least with respect to certain aspects, on the founding constitutions of Bangladesh, India, and Pakistan. The 1935 Act was Pakistan's interim Constitution until 1956. See MA Matin, *Unwritten Constitution of Bangladesh* (Dhaka, Mullick Brothers, 2019) (noting that the 1935 Act and Pakistan's 1956 and 1962 Constitutions are parts of Bangladesh's unwritten constitution).

[14] See the Indian Independence Act 1947, s 3 (creating two provinces out of Bengal – East Bengal and West Bengal). According to the First Schedule to the 1947 Act, 'East Bengal' 'provisionally' included the following districts: Chittagong, Noakhali, Tippera, Bakarganj, Dacca, Faridpur, Mymensingh, Jessore, Murshidabad, Nadia, Bogra, Dinajpur, Malda, Pabna, Rajshahi and Rangpur. Of these districts, the Bengal Boundary Commission (led by Sir Cyril Radcliffe; award published on 17 August 1947) assigned Murshidabad to West Bengal, while Nadia and Malda were divided in a way to assign some areas of them to East Bengal. Following the result of 7 July 1947 referendum, Sylhet (of Assam Province) joined East Bengal and hence went to Pakistan's jurisdiction. Moreover, the Chittagong Hill Tracts were allocated to Pakistan by the Boundary Commission.

[15] The provinces that were in the western wing were all merged as the Province of West Pakistan by the Establishment of West Pakistan Act 1955 (3 October 1955). As for East Pakistan, there was no such law, but article 1 of the 1956 Constitution defined 'East Pakistan' as 'the Province known immediately before the Constitution Day as the Province of East Bengal'.

Pakistan's Constituent Assembly.[16] East Bengal joined Pakistan with the legitimate expectation that its autonomy would be respected but the constitutional terms governing its relationship with the western wing were not categorically spelled out.[17] Soon after independence from the British, West Pakistani leaders adopted a policy of discrimination and de-recognition vis-à-vis East Bengal and thus sowed the seeds of its eventual secession.[18]

Immediately after independence, Pakistan was overcome by one constitutional crisis after another, and the process of framing a democratic constitution fell into disarray.[19] In view of the emerging autocracy and rapid 'erosion of parliamentary democracy',[20] pro-democratic Bengali leaders left the Muslim League, which spearheaded Pakistan's independence, and established the Awami League in 1949.[21]

Since its inception, the Awami League demanded provincial autonomy of East Bengal (later East Pakistan).[22] It 'adopted a 42-point-programme' that emphasised the recognition of Bangla as the state language,[23] universal franchise, and a democratic constitution for Pakistan based on economic and political equality between its two parts. Three democratic movements were particularly catalytic to the emergence of Bangladesh as a sovereign state and thus provided the bedrock of its constitutional foundings: (a) the language movement of 1948–1952; (b) the 1954 provincial elections based on the 21-point-programme; and (c) the mass upsurge in 1965–1969 against autocracy based on Sheikh Mujibur Rahman's six-point demand. The impact of these movements can be

[16] On 20 June 1947, 107 out of 141 East Bengali legislators from the Bengal Legislative Assembly supported East Bengal's joining Pakistan.

[17] Although 'provincial autonomy' was not detailed in the Government of India Act 1935, which was a constituent instrument, the principle was in the Simon Commission that outlined the post-partition governance system. See Chowdhury, *The Genesis of Bangladesh*, (n 5).

[18] On this see A Jalal, *Democracy and Authoritarianism in South Asia: A Comparative and Historical Perspective* (Cambridge, Cambridge University Press, 1995) ch 1 ('The Colonial Legacy in India and Pakistan').

[19] The crises had indeed lingered at least until the dismemberment of Bangladesh in 1971. Writing as early as 1972 on Bangladesh's independence, Chowdhury saw constitutional crises in Pakistan in four phases – erosion of parliamentary democracy (14 Aug 1947 to 24 Oct 1954), advent of military oligarchy (25 Oct 1954 to 27 Oct 1958), political experiments of a military dictator (27 Oct 1958 to 25 Mar 1969), and the strategy of deception (25 Mar 1969 to 25 Mar 1971). See Chowdhury, *The Genesis of Bangladesh*, (n 5) 22–75. Since 1947, Pakistan has experienced four extra-constitutional military regimes, eleven constitutional arrangements, and three formal Constitutions of 1956, 1962 and 1973. On the impact of Pakistan's constitutional crises on Bangladesh, see GW Choudhury, *Constitutional Development in Pakistan* (Lahore, Longman, 1969).

[20] Chowdhury, *The Genesis of Bangladesh*, (n 5) 22.

[21] See above note 9.

[22] The first manifesto of the party stated that its motto was to secure 'the right of self-determination of the regional units'. See M Rashiduzzaman, 'The Awami League in the Political Development of Pakistan' (1970) 10(7) *Asian Survey* 574–587, 585 (citing S Huq, *East Pakistan Awami Muslim League Draft Manifesto* 13 & 17).

[23] Harun-or-Rashid, 'Bangladesh Awami League', in *Banglapedia:* http://en.banglapedia.org/index.php?title=Bangladesh_Awami_League.

seen in the speeches of Bengali leaders in the Constituent Assemblies and parliaments of Pakistan.

B. Bangladesh as Part of Pakistan (1947 to 1971): The Pre-independence Years of Constitution-making

i. 'Bangla' and the Language Movement of 1948–52

The first impetus for Bangladesh's constitutional founding came from the resistance of Bangalee (Bengali) leaders to the western wing's attempt in 1948 to impose Urdu as the national language of Pakistan. Several East Bengali members of the Pakistani Constituent Assembly urged inclusiveness and demanded that Bangla be one of the languages of the Assembly. Veteran legislator Dhirendranath Datta (1886–1971)[24] argued that '[t]he State language ... should be the language which is used by the majority of the people of the State'.[25] However, Mohamed Ali Jinnah – Pakistan's founding father – declared Urdu to be Pakistan's national language at a meeting in Dacca (Dhaka) on 21 March 1948.[26] East Bengal's representatives in the Constituent Assembly were initially denied a right to speak in Bangla. When Prime Minister Nazimuddin declared that Urdu was to be Pakistan's sole state language on 28 January 1952, an all-party movement advocating Bangla as a state language took off. Protests culminated in bloodshed during a procession on 21 February 1952[27] when several protesting students were killed by police. The Language Movement (1947–1952) in which nationalist party leaders including Maulana Bhasani and Sheikh Mujibur Rahman[28] played key roles not only heightened the identity of the Bengali nation but also signalled the start of the nation's struggle for liberation.[29] The movement continued until 1956 when Pakistan's first Constitution acknowledged Bangla as one of the state languages. Thereafter the erstwhile nationalists created an even stronger movement for East Bengal's provincial autonomy.[30]

[24] Mr Datta, a member of the then Bengal Legislative Council in 1937 and 1946 as well as of the Pakistan Constituent Assembly, was tortured to death by the Pakistani Army on 29 March 1971. See MA Salam, 'Datta, Dhirendranath', in Banglapedia: http://en.banglapedia.org/index.php?title=Datta,_Dhirendranath.

[25] Speech at the Second Session of the Assembly, 25 Feb 1948.

[26] He declared: 'Urdu is going to be the lingua franca of this country. Anyone who says anything else is an enemy of Pakistan', cited in SC Sen, 'The Constitution of Bangladesh and a Short Constitutional History' (1974) 7(3) *Law and Politics in Africa, Asia and Latin America* 257–273, 257.

[27] Following a UNESCO announcement on 17 November 1999, 21 February is observed globally as the International Mother Language Day.

[28] In 1952, Sheikh Mujibur Rahman along with other leaders was arrested and sent to jail from where he was elected Joint Secretary of Awami League.

[29] On the history and the impact of the language movement, see A Anwary, *National Language and the Dynamics of a Social Movement of East Bengal: Framing, Opportunities and Outcomes* (PhD Thesis, University of Minnesota, 1987); SA Akanda, *Language Movement and the Making of Bangladesh* (Dhaka, University Press Limited, 2013); and A Dil and A Dil, *Bengali Language Movement and Creation of Bangladesh* (Dhaka, Adorn, 2011).

[30] Anwary, ibid, iv.

ii. The 1954 Provincial Elections, the Twenty-One-point Programme, and Pakistan's First (Islamic) Constitution of 1956

The second building block for the founding Constitution was lent by the 1954 elections for the 309-seat East Bengal Legislative Assembly,[31] the very first elections in East Pakistan.[32] The ruling Pakistan Muslim League faced several opposition parties with manifestos for democratic and secular politics.[33] The Awami League along with Krishak Sramik Party (peasants and workers' party) formed the famous 'Jukta Front' (United Front) and laid down a 21-point electoral programme[34] demanding a federal system of parliamentary government with full autonomy for East Pakistan. Point 19 is worth noting:

> In accordance with the historic Lahore Resolution,[35] to secure full and complete autonomy and bring all subjects under the jurisdiction of East Pakistan, leaving only defence, foreign affairs, and currency under the jurisdiction of the center.[36]

Other notable demands were the recognition of Bangla as a state language, independence of the judiciary, and free and fair elections. The main objective was to attain economic, linguistic, educational, and military parity between the eastern and western wings of Pakistan. Unsurprisingly, the United Front's electoral programme was welcomed by the public as a 'Charter of Freedom' for East Pakistan,[37] while the West Pakistani leaders saw it as a blueprint for incipient secession. The programme has since become the basis of all subsequent political and constitutional movements in East Pakistan.

The United Front won a landslide victory, capturing 223 of the 309 seats, and formed the provincial government with Abdul Kashem Fazlul Huq as Chief Minister of East Bengal. Top leaders, including Sheikh Mujibur Rahman – General Secretary of the Awami League – were elected and co-opted as members of the second Constituent Assembly which had the responsibility of making Pakistan's first Constitution. Unfortunately, Huq's government was dismissed

[31] The East Bengal Legislative Assembly (EBLA) (1947–1955) and the East Pakistan Provincial Assembly (1955–1971) were Bangladesh's pre-independence legislatures. The EBLA was created with 141 East Bengali members of the Bengal Legislative Assembly and legislators elected for Sylhet to the Assam Legislative Assembly before 1947. The predecessor of the EBLA was the Bengal Legislative Council (1861–1935) (with a few nominated Indian members) and the Legislative Assembly for Bengal (1935–1947), with the Legislative Council as a permanent upper chamber).

[32] Absent a Constitution at the time, these elections were held in accordance with the Government of India Act 1935. See 'East Bengal Goes to the Poll', *The Economic Weekly* (Delhi, 13 March 1954) 303.

[33] Also formed was a right-wing party, the Nizami-i-Islam, 'with the objective of establishing an administration based on the principles of Islam'. See Rashiduzzaman, 'The Awami League', (n 22) 576.

[34] For this, see AKM Shamsul Huda, *The Constitution of Bangladesh* (Chittagong, Rita Court, 1997) 169–171.

[35] Lahore Resolution is the resolution of the All India Muslim League passed in 1940, rejecting the federal constitutional plan in the Act of 1935 and proposing instead the division of India into two nations based on two major religions, Islam and Hindu. See, among others, Chowdhury, *The Genesis of Bangladesh*, (n 5) 5–6.

[36] The 21-point Programme, as in note 34 above.

[37] Rashiduzzaman, 'The Awami League', (n 22) 577.

by the Central Government only after two months in office, and Huq was placed under house arrest. In its place was imposed a coalition government.

In the meantime, Pakistan's first Constitution was adopted by the 2nd Constituent Assembly on 23 March 1956[38] which did not provide for East Pakistan's long-standing demand for autonomy. Sheikh Mujibur Rahman rejected it as a 'halfway provincial autonomy'.[39] In the 1st Constituent Assembly, the East Bengal members[40] vehemently opposed the transforming of Pakistan into a theocratic state on the ground that it breached Jinnah's clear promise of a secular constitution.[41] At the 2nd Constituent Assembly, Sheikh Mujib continued to protest vociferously. He also expressed his dismay in continuing to have separate electorates on the basis of religion, and argued for a secular, plural constitution. He also sought a place for the Bengali language as a state language, thus drawing the framers' attention to the consequences of excluding the nationalist demands for linguistic recognition. Most importantly, Sheikh Mujib warned the Assembly that the East Bengalis would reject the Constitution if it ignored their desire for full autonomy.[42] But his words went unheeded and Pakistan's 1956 Constitution was an Islamic constitution that denied East Pakistan full autonomy.

It has been argued that had this inaugural Constitution been secular and accommodated Bengali demands for autonomy, Bangladesh might probably not have come into being.[43] As a result, the struggle for self-rule continued in East Pakistan. In 1957, the East Pakistan Provincial Assembly passed a unanimous resolution demanding full autonomy for the province. However, on 8 October 1958, the Army Chief (General Ayub Khan) took over the state as President, imposed 'martial law', abrogated the 1956 Constitution, and banned all political parties.

[38] See ch 3 on Pakistan in this volume.

[39] Sen, 'the Constitution of Bangladesh', (n 26) 258.

[40] On 11 August, KS Roy, for example, hoped that the new state would be 'a secular democratic State'.

[41] It is beyond the scope of this chapter to enter a detailed discussion on this, but a reference can be made to the oft-quoted 11 August 1947 speech of Mr Jinnah, the founding leader of Pakistan, in which he had this to say: 'You are free; you are free to go to your temples, you are free to go to your mosques or to any other place or worship in […] Pakistan. You may belong to any religion or caste or creed – that has nothing to do with the business of the State. […] [I]n course of time Hindus would cease to be Hindus and Muslims would cease to be Muslims, not in the religious sense, […], but in the political sense as citizens of the State.' See G Allana, *Pakistan Movement: Historical Documents* (Karachi, Department of International Relations, University of Karachi, 1967) 407–411.

[42] Dubbing the Constitution as dictatorial, he concluded with these words: 'If you frame the Constitution on the basis of 21-point programme, we will cooperate with you, we will join you, but if you go against the wishes of the people we will mobilize opinion not only in East Pakistan but also in West Pakistan against this dictatorial and undemocratic Constitution.' See S Iqbal, *Sheikh Mujib in Parliament: 1955–58* (Dhaka, Agami Prakashani, 1997).

[43] See M Guruswamy, 'Constitution Crafting in South Asia: Lessons on Accommodation and Alienation' in D Landau and H Lerner (eds), *Comparative Constitution Making* (Cheltenham, Edward Elgar, 2019) 464–487; and R Jahan, *Pakistan: A Failure in National Integration* (New York, Columbia University Press, 1972).

iii. Bangladesh's Post-1956 Struggle for Self-rule, Public Upsurge of the 1960s and the Six-point Demand

The third impetus for a democratic constitution came from the anti-Ayub and autonomy movements of the 1960s. After assuming power, President Ayub Khan continued and strengthened the policy of discrimination against East Pakistan. In 1962, he imposed a new constitution for Pakistan.[44] Sheikh Mujib took a definitive stance against that 'imposed' Constitution and initiated an agitation, for which he was arrested and detained without trial for some time. When the military government withdrew restrictions on political parties in 1966, Sheikh Mujib launched the Six-point Programme/Movement on 7 June 1966 for East Pakistan's full autonomy through a federal democratic constitution.[45] Point 1 of the programme, relevant for the present purposes, reads as follows:

> The Constitution should provide for a Federation of Pakistan in its true sense based on the Lahore Resolution, and the *parliamentary form of government* with *supremacy of a Legislature directly elected* on the basis of *universal adult franchise* (emphasis added).

Point 2 restricts the federal government to dealing 'with only two subjects' – defence and foreign affairs. All other residual subjects would be reserved for the 'federating' states.

The central government viewed the six-point programme as a demand for the separation of the eastern wing from Pakistan and threated stern actions 'with the language of weapons'[46] against any attempt for dismemberment. At the same time, Awami League leaders began mobilising the public in support of the six-point demand. Sheikh Mujib was arrested along with 54 other people and implicated in the infamous 'Agartala Conspiracy Case'[47] for treason by conspiring with foreign enemies to break down Pakistan. The trial took place inside the Dhaka Cantonment, and this added fuel to the fire of the province-wide movement against Ayub Khan. In 1967, the opposition leaders formed 'the Democratic Action Committee' demanding the restoration of parliamentary democracy and direct franchise, while student parties formed the 'Students' Action Committee' based on a 11-point demand for autonomy of East Pakistan.[48]

[44] See generally Y Roznai, 'Internally Imposed Constitutions' in R Albert, X Contiades, and A Fotiadou (eds), *The Law and Legitimacy of Imposed Constitutions* (London, Routledge, 2019) 58–81.

[45] See Rashiduzzaman, 'The Awami League', (n 22) 583; Hossain, *Bangladesh: Quest for Freedom and Justice*, (n 4) 136.

[46] S Bhuiyan, P Sands, and NJ Schrijver, 'An Interview with Kamal Hossain' in *International Law and Developing Countries* (Dhaka, University Press Limited, 2014) 17.

[47] The case was titled as *State v Sheikh Mujibur Rahman and others*, bringing a charge against 35 individuals under the Defence of Pakistan Rules 1965. See S Begum, 'Agartala Conspiracy Case', in *Banglapedia:* http://en.banglapedia.org/index.php?title=Agartala_Conspiracy_Case. There was an unsuccessful writ petition in the Dacca High Court for the release of Sheikh Mujib, which challenged the legality of the formation of a special tribunal for the trial.

[48] Rashiduzzaman, 'The Awami League', (n 22) 585.

The central government gave in to what came to be popularly known as the 'mass movement' of 1966–69 for regional autonomy and released Sheikh Mujib who was vaunted to the stature of a national figure able to dominate public opinion. Unfortunately, even he was unable to persuade Ayub Khan to change his mind.[49] Ultimately, the 'mass movement' led to the fall of Ayub Khan who handed over power to General Yahya Khan on 25 March 1969, another military dictator.[50]

General Yahya Khan imposed martial law the same day he assumed power, but immediately declared that he would transfer power to elected representatives. He promised a general election on 5 October 1970[51] and a new constitution after the formation of a National Assembly. On 30 March 1970, Khan promulgated the Legal Framework Order (LFO) laying down the rules for the conduct of elections 'as well as the role of the future National Assembly' that was to consist of 313 members, 169 of whom would be from East Pakistan. The LFO also lay down five key principles that would be adhered to, including Islam as the state religion, and empowered the President to reject the constitution and dissolve the National Assembly. The Awami League protested these undemocratic conditions. Fearing that the President might scrap the constitution-making process,[52] the party began a massive preparation based on its six-point-programme for the second-ever direct general elections in Pakistan.[53]

iv. The 1970 General Elections: The Way to Independence

The keenly-awaited general elections were held in December 1970, and the Awami League won all but two seats in East Pakistan.[54] Instead of transferring power to the elected representatives of the winning party, President Yahya Khan postponed calling the National Assembly time and again. At some point, the postponed meeting of the National Assembly was scheduled for 25 March 1971, but on 7 March Bangabandhu demanded that the transfer of power to the elected representatives took place before the Assembly met. The concluding part of his 7 March Speech called for independence:

> But if moves are made to exterminate the people of this country, Bengalis must act with caution. In every village, every neighbourhood, set up Sangram Parishad under the leadership of the Awami League. And be prepared with whatever you have.

[49] Bhuiyan et al, 'An Interview with Kamal Hossain', (n 46) 18.

[50] Ayub Khan, while handing over power, alleged that Sheikh Mujib's proposal for constitutional amendment 'would liquidate the Central Government and Army'. See Rashiduzzaman, 'The Awami League', (n 22) 585.

[51] On 28 November 1969, Yahya Khan announced that elections would be held in October 1970.

[52] Interestingly, after independence, Bangladesh repealed the LFO via The Representation of the People Order 1972 (PO No 155 of 1972), art 95.

[53] First general elections were held in 1962 under the military ruler Ayub Khan.

[54] The number of seats for National Assembly was 313 (300 general seats and 13 reserved seats for women), of which 169 seats (162 general seats and 7 reserved women seats) were for East Pakistan. See the Legal Framework Order 1970 (Pakistan), sch 1.

> Remember: Having mastered the lesson of sacrifice, we shall give more blood. God willing, we shall free the people of this land. The struggle this time is a struggle for emancipation. The struggle this time is a struggle for independence.[55]

Dhaka became increasingly tense and protests turned more violent. On the night of 25 March 1971, the Pakistani Army commenced an all-out crackdown on the Awami League and its supporters, and arrested Bangabandhu. However, he managed to transmit Bangladesh's Declaration of Independence in the early hours of 26 March. Then followed a bloody and brutal war for Bangladesh independence that ended on 16 December 1971 with the surrender of Pakistani forces in Dhaka. After 26 March 1971 senior Awami League leaders crossed the border and formed a provisional presidential-style government on 10 April 1971[56] with Bangabandhu Sheikh Mujibur Rahman as the President (then in a Pakistani prison); Syed Nazrul Islam as the Vice-President (who was Acting President); and Tajuddin Ahmed as the Prime Minister. The war-time government was sworn in on 17 April 1971 at Meherpur in Kushtia – a district bordering India. Meherpur was later renamed Mujibnagar ('City of Mujib'), and the provisional government (26 March 1971 to 12 January 1972) has since been known as the Mujibnagar Government.

II. THE PROCLAMATION OF INDEPENDENCE AND THE PROVISIONAL CONSTITUTION: THE FIRST FOUNDINGS

A. The Proclamation of Independence: The First Interim Constitution

When the elected leaders gathered to form the provisional government, they formed themselves into a Constituent Assembly and promulgated the Proclamation of Independence on 10 April 1971 (made retrospective to 26 March 1971).[57] The Proclamation was drafted by a leading lawyer and 'the elected whip', M Amir-Ul Islam,[58] with guidance from Prime Minister Tajuddin Ahmed and assistance from economist Rehman Sobhan.[59] It was signed by Professor Yousuf

[55] See the Constitution of Bangladesh, 6th Schedule, inserted in 2015.

[56] On 10 April 1972, all available Awami League leaders who were elected met in a parliamentary session in a place within the Indian territory to discuss and approve the formation of a provisional government, in which the draft Proclamation (drafted on 8 April) was also adopted, although it was made public on 17 April 1971.

[57] See below, especially at section III.

[58] For an interview of Mr Islam on this, see the *Daily Star*, 'The Proclamation of Independence: Context and Multiple Purposes', *The Daily Star*, Dhaka, 17 April 2010 www.thedailystar.net/law/2010/04/03/index.htm. See also MH Khan, 'Genesis of Bangladesh's Constitution', *The Daily Star*, Dhaka, 17 April 2016 www.thedailystar.net/op-ed/genesis-bangladeshs-constitution-1209718.

[59] R Sobhan, *Untranquil Recollections: The Years of Fulfillment* (New Delhi, Sage, 2016) ('Along with Amirul Islam, I was entrusted by Tajuddin Ahmed with the task of drafting the independence proclamation. Amirul, by virtue of his qualifications as a barrister, took on the substantive responsibility for preparing the [proclamation] and with subsequent inputs from some senior lawyers in Kolkata, such as Barrister Subroto Roy Chowdhury, completed this historic task.')

Ali in his capacity as the Constituent Assembly's 'duly constituted' plenipotentiary. The proclamation was effectively the first and interim Constitution of Bangladesh,[60] making 'provisional arrangements' for the country's governance.[61] It formally proclaimed Bangladesh a 'sovereign people's Republic' and established the nation's constitutional foundation on the basis of 'equality, human dignity and social justice' as well as 'democracy'.[62] It also accorded constitutional legitimacy to the founding leader's informal declaration of independence of 26 March 1971 and to the 'provisional' government. Accordingly, it outlined the powers and functions of the state organs, although it left a gap regarding the judicial function that was later plugged by the Provisional Constitution.[63] A relevant part of the preamble of the Proclamation of Independence is worth quoting here:

> We the elected representatives of the people of Bangladesh, as honour-bound by the mandate given to us by the people of Bangladesh whose will is supreme[,] duly constituted ourselves into a Constituent Assembly, and having held mutual consultations, and in order to ensure for the people of Bangladesh equality, human dignity and social justice, declare and constitute Bangladesh to be sovereign Peoples' Republic ....[64]

It is important to note how the Proclamation of Independence drew its legitimacy from the 'constituent people' and the deliberative process through which their remit was determined. The Proclamation declared Bangabandhu to be the President of the newly-independent nation and empowered him to 'exercise all the Executive and Legislative powers of the Republic' until 'a Constitution is framed' and to appoint a Prime Minister and other ministers. The President was also empowered 'to summon and adjourn the Constituent Assembly' and 'do all other things that may be necessary to give to the people of Bangladesh *an orderly and just Government*' (emphasis added).[65]

[60] The Proclamation of Independence is widely regarded as the first Constitution of Bangladesh. See Islam's interview, 'The Proclamation of Independence', (n 58); E Azad, 'The Proclamation of Independence: The First Constitution of Bangladesh', *The Daily Star*, 10 April 2018, www.thedailystar.net/law-our-rights/bangladeshs-first-constitution-1560727; and ME Haque, 'Formation of the Constitution and the Legal System in Bangladesh: From 1971 to 1972: A Critical Legal Analysis' (2016) 27(1) *Dhaka University Law Journal* 41–56.

[61] Provisional Constitution of Bangladesh Order 1972, preamble, first paragraph.

[62] Tajuddin Ahmed's radio speech on 10 April 1972. See Khan, 'Genesis of Bangladesh's Constitution', (n 58).

[63] On the same day the Proclamation was issued, the then Acting President Syed Nazrul Islam promulgated the Laws Continuance Enforcement Order 1971 (with effect from 26 March 1971), which was the first law made under the legislative authority of the new state. This Acting President's Order is arguably a constituent document as it adopted all 'existing laws' that were in force before 26 March 1971 as laws of Bangladesh subject to their compatibility with the Proclamation, on which see *Mullick Brothers v Income Tax Officer* (1979) 31 DLR (AD) 165.

[64] See the Constitution of Bangladesh, 7th Schedule, inserted in 2015 via the 15th Amendment.

[65] As Mr Islam, the drafter of the Proclamation, reminisced, there was a resolution in the parliamentary meeting of the Awami League on 1 March 1971, authorising Bangabandhu to lead the nation and its government with necessary constitutional powers. It is also known that the mention of

The proclamation legitimised Bangladesh's independence on the basis of 'the legitimate right of self-determination of the people of Bangladesh' and declared that it would accept all legal obligations arising from its statehood and comply with the United Nations Charter. This appeal to international law was necessary to solicit international support.[66] By invoking the principle of self-determination under international law and the constituent people as the source of plenary powers, the proclamation laid down a solid basis of legitimacy both for Bangladesh's unilateral declaration of independence and the founding constituent instrument.[67]

B. The Provisional Constitution Order: The Second Interim Constitution

The next constituent instrument was the Provisional Constitution of Bangladesh Order (PCO). It was promulgated by Bangabandhu in his capacity as the President on 11 January 1972, the day after his return following his release from Pakistan. It was an instrument put together in a hurry because of the impending meeting of the first Cabinet following Bangabandhu's return. Drafted in about an hour or so,[68] the PCO supplemented and extended the scope of the Proclamation of Independence. It changed the form of the provisional government to a parliamentary one[69] and constituted the judiciary.[70] Notably, it used, for the first time, 'People's Republic of Bangladesh' as the official name of the new country.

Under the PCO, the Prime Minister would be appointed by the President.[71] In appointing other ministers and discharging all other functions, the President would act on the Prime Minister's advice. After this new arrangement, Tajuddin Ahmed resigned as head of the provisional government and Bangabandhu became the Prime Minister. However, the legislative power of the state

the 'armed forces' in the Proclamation was inserted on 14 April. See his interview, 'The Proclamation of Independence', (n 58).

[66] See Islam's interview, ibid.

[67] It should be noted that the International Court of Justice in an advisory opinion (10 to 4) of 22 July 2010 observed that Kosovo's unilateral declaration of independence of 17 February 2008 'did not violate international law'. See the summary of the ICJ's advisory opinion on the question of accordance with international law of the unilateral declaration of independence in respect of Kosovo www.icj-cij.org/files/case-related/141/16010.pdf.

[68] Hossain, *Bangladesh: Quest for Freedom and Justice*, (n 4) 136.

[69] In an interesting case, the change of form of government by the Provisional Constitution Order (PCO) (arts V to VIII) was unsuccessfully challenged as incompatible with the Proclamation of Independence. See *AKM Fazlul Hoque v State* (1974) 26 DLR (SC) 11. The Appellate Division overruled the challenge, holding that the Proclamation empowered the President to make any law including a constituent law like the PCO.

[70] By default, the then Dacca High Court continued as the country's Supreme Court from 26 March 1971.

[71] It was also provided that the member of the Constituent Assembly commanding the confidence of the House would be appointed Prime Minister by the President.

continued to be vested in the President. The PCO provided for a 'High Court of Bangladesh' but did not elaborate on its powers and functions as a constitutional court, a gap that was later filled by the High Court of Bangladesh Order 1972 of 17 January 1972.[72] The Chief Justice and other judges were to be appointed by the President.[73]

III. THE MAKING OF BANGLADESH'S FOUNDING CONSTITUTION: THE DRAFTING PROCESS

A. The Constituent Assembly and the Wider Political Policy for Foundings

Bangladesh's founding Constitution was enacted by the 'Constituent Assembly of Bangladesh' (CAB),[74] the legal formation of which was of *sui generis*. It derived its existence from the Proclamation of Independence of 10 April 1971 which in turn drew its legitimacy from those 'elected representatives of the people of Bangladesh' who were victorious in 1970–1971 elections[75] and who constituted themselves into the Constituent Assembly. Importantly, the Proclamation of Independence established CAB retrospectively, dating it from the day of independence. Later, the Provisional Constitution of Bangladesh Order (12 January 1972) formally defined CAB to be composed of elected representatives 'not disqualified by or under any law'.[76] On 23 March 1972, the Bangladesh Constituent Assembly Order 1972 was enacted to provide for structure, powers and functions of CAB.[77]

There were 469 elected representatives, 169 of whom were from the National Assembly and 300 from the Provincial Assembly. Among them, 12 members had died, 2 accepted Pakistani citizenship, 46 were declared disqualified by law, five were arrested and disqualified under the Collaborators Order,[78] and one member resigned to accept a position in the Foreign Service. The remaining 403 members initiated the process of constitution-making.[79] Of these,

[72] High Court of Bangladesh (Second Amendment) Order 1972 (PO No 5 of 1972), art 2 (effective 11 Jan 1972).

[73] Article 9. Justice Abu Sadat Mohammad Sayem of the then Dacca High Court was sworn in as the country's first Chief Justice on 12 January 1972. Mr Kamruddin Ahmad, a senior advocate, was first asked to be the Chief Justice, an offer he politely declined for personal reasons. See Hossain, *Bangladesh: Quest for Freedom and Justice*, (n 4) 137.

[74] This official title of the Assembly was first given by the Bangladesh Constituent Assembly Order 1972, art 2(a).

[75] These elections were scheduled to be held from 7 December 1970 to 1 March 1971 but were actually held on 7 & 17 December 1970 and 17 January 1971.

[76] The Provisional Constitution of Bangladesh Order 1972, art 4.

[77] PO No 22 of 1972. Articles 4 & 7 provided for the formation of the Constituent Assembly.

[78] The Bangladesh Collaborators (Special Tribunals) Order 1972 (PO No 8 of 1972) (repealed on 31 December 1975 by the first military government).

[79] According to another account, of the elected members, 10 died, 5 were killed by Pakistani forces, 23 were expelled from the party and thus lost their seats, 2 were disqualified for their

400 members belonged to the Awami League, one to the opposition National Awami Party (NAP) and two were independents.

Within weeks of the victory day, 16 December 1971, Bangabandhu as the newly installed Prime Minister made the following policy statement on constitution-making on 14 January 1972:[80]

> While we set about to tackle the urgent task of relief and rehabilitation and economic reconstruction, we shall not delay a single moment more than is absolutely necessary in *convening the Constituent Assembly* in order to place before it the draft constitution of *the People's Republic of Bangladesh. The preparation of the draft constitution is already under way.*
>
> ...
>
> The people of Bangladesh had always aspired to establish on their soil a *just society, free of exploitation.* The Bengali people have had to pay very dearly in order to attain this aim. Having regard to our population, our resources and the basic economic realities with which we are confronted, it will be possible to fulfil the aspirations of the people by establishing *a socialist economy.*
>
> ...
>
> I would like to assure our people that those who are responsible for committing atrocities and for collaboration will not go unpunished. At the same time, it should not be forgotten that *one of the fundamental aims of our national liberation struggle* was to establish *the rule of law and respect for fundamental human rights.* The culprits will be duly punished in accordance with the due process of law. I would, therefore, appeal to all concerned to remain patient while *the due process of law* takes its course.

Bangabandhu's statement made it clear that the aspirations for a socialist-democratic society based on the rule of law, and a guarantee of fundamental human rights for the citizenry, would be the foundations of the imminent constitution.

B. The Constitution Drafting Committee

On 10 April 1972, the CAB commenced a two-day first session at a house that is now within the Office of the Prime Minister in Tejgaon, Dhaka.[81] At its first meeting, the Assembly elected Shah Abdul Hamid – its eldest member – as Speaker and Mohammed Ullah as the Deputy Speaker and adopted its rules

allegiance to Pakistan, and 4 were in prison on charge of collaborating with Pakistani forces. See Huq, 'Constitution-making in Bangladesh', (n 4) 60.

[80] See *the Bangladesh Observer*, Dacca, 15 January 1972, p 5 (italic added). See also Sen, 'The Constitution of Bangladesh', (n 26) 264–265.

[81] With a current signpost of 'Old Parliament House', that building was indeed a torture-house maintained by the Pakistani Forces during the war of liberation. A separate room within the House was provided for the translators and others.

of procedure. The next day, the CAB established a 34-member Constitution Drafting Committee (CDC) chaired by Dr Kamal Hossain – Bangabandhu's trusted aide and then Law Minister.[82] Hossain oversaw the drafting process intensely and drafted some initial provisions himself. Among the leading drafters were the finest jurists of the country,[83] of whom only two members were members of the Hindu community – Dr Kshitish Chandra Mandal and Suranjit Sen Gupta (the only opposition member).[84] There was no opposition party in the Assembly.[85] Ms Begum Razia Bano, who had been elected to one of the women's seats in the National Assembly, was the only female member. Interestingly, the only indigenous community member of the CAB, Manabendra Narayan Larma (1939–1983), representing the Chittagong Hill Tracts (CHT), was not co-opted onto the Drafting Committee. Whilst the Constituent Assembly was a revolutionary body, its composition was criticised for the 'non-participation of the various [social] groups'.[86]

The CDC was required to submit the draft Constitution to the Awami League Working Committee for consideration before being placed before the Constituent Assembly by 10 June 1972.[87] The draft was to take the form of a Bill.[88] It appears that the CDC completed most of its work by the designated time, although there is evidence of its work extending till September.[89] The drafters took their lead from Bangabandhu's 10 April speech in the Constituent Assembly, which provided guidance on 'nationalism, socialism, democracy and secularism' as fundamental 'ideals' of the nation and the Constitution.[90]

[82] Dr Hossain was Sheikh Mujibur Rahman's legal adviser especially during the political and constitutional negotiations with the Pakistani Government in January to March 1969 and January to March 1971. He was also a defence counsel in the historic Agartala conspiracy case against Sheikh Mujib in 1969. See Dr Hossain's interview entitled 'I Believe in the Power of Human Beings to be Agents of Change' in Bhuiyan et al, 'An interview with Kamal Hossain', (n 46) 18.

[83] There were nine lawyers on the Committee. Other eight lawyers were Asaduzzaman Khan, Badal Rashid, Faqueer Shahabuddin Ahmed (First Attorney-General), M Amir-Ul Islam, Serajul Haq, Suranjit Sen Gupta, Shaukat Ali Khan, and Tajuddin Ahmed.

[84] Mr Gupta, elected to the then National Assembly from the National Awami Party (Pro-Moscow), was also the only opposition member in the Constituent Assembly in which there was no formal opposition party.

[85] The Leader of the House and the Prime Minister hoped that there would be an opposition party emerging from the first general elections scheduled to be held in March 1973.

[86] MA Hakim and AS Huque, 'Governmental Change and Constitutional Amendment in Bangladesh' (1995) 2 *South Asian Survey* 255–270, 257.

[87] Sen, 'The Constitution of Bangladesh', (n 26) 266.

[88] A resolution proposed by Mr Mansur Ali and passed in the Assembly on 11 April 1971.

[89] For example, Mr Rahman, a member of the CDC, sent his note of dissent on certain provisions on 11 Sep 1972.

[90] Hossain, *Bangladesh: Quest for Freedom and Justice*, (n 4) 140 notes that there was a resolution asking the CDC to make these four principles as constitutional cores, but no record of such a resolution is found in the Constituent Assembly proceedings. As he recalls (at 144), 'Our efforts, in the Constitution Drafting Committee, had been directed towards, as faithfully as possible, preparing a draft … by working out specific provisions on the basis of four principles.' The meaning of the principles of nationalism, socialism, democracy and secularism were described in, respectively, arts 9, 10, 11 and 12.

The Drafting Committee held 74 meetings and several public consultations.[91] By a resolution adopted on the first day they met on 17 April 1972, the CDC asked for public proposals and suggestions to be submitted by 18 May 1972 and received a total of 98 memoranda and 2 presentations from the various political parties. One possible reason for the poor public response was that there arguably was already a consensus about the fundamentals of the Constitution.[92] Importantly, the CDC met formally twice with Bangabandhu, the Leader of the House, and consulted other founding leaders, ministers, and local experts.[93] A fuller draft in English was readied by 10 June 1972. The Constitution was translated into Bangla by Professor Anisuzzaman (1937–2020),[94] who besides being an authoritative translator, exerted a great intellectual influence on the drafting of the Constitution, especially on the principles of secularism and Bengali nationalism.

The work of translation was done daily as the CDC prepared the draft. In many instances, the drafters first consulted Anisuzzaman to determine the most meaningful and appropriate terms to be used in English as well as in Bengali before proceeding. He attended all of the CDC meetings, and was assisted by two other noted linguists, one of whom, Neamaal Bashir, had earlier drafting experience. Earlier on, the CDC resolved to form a Committee of Eminent Scholars on Bengali language[95] and to appoint one Robert Guthrie as a technical draftsman. Guthrie was at the time with a London-based organisation involved in drafting private members' Bills in the British Parliament.[96] Following the CDC Chair's trip to London on 13 June 1972, Guthrie was appointed technical drafting adviser and was asked to provide his input on the draft by 7 September.[97] The CDC then finished the draft by early October and had its last meeting on 11 October 1972 when the draft Bill was approved. The draft had been sent to the Awami League Parliamentary Committee for discussion on 9–10 October. The Constitution Bill, along with the CDC's Report, was laid before the Constituent Assembly on 12 October 1972 at its second session.[98] Six members appended their notes of dissent to the report. Most dissents were on articles 42 and 47 that dealt with socialism and the right to property broadly.

[91] According to Anisuzzaman, the CDC had met for 85 days altogether. See Anisuzzaman, *Bipula Prithibi (The Vast World)*, 6th reprint (Dhaka, Prothoma Prokashan, 2015) 56.

[92] Huq, Constitution-making in Bangladesh, (n 4) (critiquing the Committee's general invitation as inadequate to invoke public interest and arguing that it would have done better by issuing a survey-questionnaire on major aspects of the proposed constitutional order).

[93] For example, as regards the structure of the Supreme Court, Chief Justice Sayem was consulted. He opposed the idea of establishing two divisions in the Supreme Court and proposed two separate courts – Supreme Court and the High Court. Moreover, Dr Kamal Hossain consulted his prominent lawyer friends such as Syed Ishtiaq Ahmed. Anisuzzaman, *Bipula Prithibi*, (n 91) 36–37.

[94] See art 153, which accords primacy to the Bengali text in case of any conflict between it and the English text.

[95] Its members were: Prof Syed Ali Ahsan, Dr Mazharul Islam, and Prof Anisuzzaman.

[96] Anisuzzaman, *Bipula Prithibi*, (n 91) 91.

[97] ibid, 56.

[98] See *Report of the Constitution Drafting Committee*, *Bangladesh Gazette*, Extraordinary, Thursday, 12 October 1972, Dhaka, at 2615 ff [hereafter 'Constitution Drafting Committee Report'].

C. Adopting the Founding Constitution

The Constituent Assembly held 17 meetings from 12 October to 4 November 1972. Members debated and deliberated on the nation's founding constitution assiduously.[99] Altogether, 157 members took part in the deliberations. The most debated provisions were those relating to socialism, secularism,[100] and the unenforceability of social rights. The first reading of the Bill spanned from 19 to 30 October while the second lasted from 31 October to 3 November. After the third reading, the Constitution Bill was adopted on 4 November 1972. The Leader of the House proposed that the Constitution come into force on 16 December 1972 on the first anniversary of Victory Day. The Constitution was reduced into a handwritten master copy (in both Bangla and English) and signed by 357 members of CAB. It was authenticated by the Speaker of the Assembly on 14 December.[101] The signing ceremony was held on 14 and 15 December 1972. When the Constitution came into operation on 16 December 1972, the Constituent Assembly became functus officio and dissolved.[102] The Constitution, although blessed with overwhelming popular support and legal-democratic legitimacy, was adopted without a national referendum.[103] The founders, thus, missed an opportunity to add further legitimacy to the Constitution by engaging the people beyond the Constituent Assembly process.[104]

IV. THE CONSTITUTION'S FOUR IDENTITY PRINCIPLES AND THE POLITICAL FOUNDING

At the core of Bangladesh's constitutional order lie certain basic normative principles. These include constitutional supremacy, popular sovereignty, responsible government, periodic elections based on universal adult franchise, judicial

[99] The dates are as follows: 12–14, 19–21, 23–27 & 30–31 October and 1–4 November.

[100] See DM Siddiqi, 'Secular Quests, National Others: Revisiting Bangladesh's Constituent Assembly Debates' (2018) 49(2) *Asian Affairs* 238–258.

[101] On how the Constitution was hand-written, illustrated and bound and printed, see Anisuzzaman, 'On How the Constitution Was Written in Bangla', in Shahiduzzaman et al (eds), *Forty Years of the Constitution and the Judiciary* (Dhaka, Law Reporters' Forum, 2013) 90; and Anisuzzaman (n 91).

[102] The Constitution of Bangladesh, 4th Sch (transitional and temporary provisions), para 1.

[103] There were criticisms that the Constitution of Bangladesh was adopted through an inadequate consultation with the public, which Hossain, *Bangladesh: Quest for Freedom and Justice*, (n 4) 144 claims were not true. For a critique, see F Ahmed, 'Bangladesh Constitution: Colonial Legacy' (in Bangla), in *Rashtrochinta Blog*, 9 June 2020 http://rashtrochinta.net/blog-post/. On public participation in constitutional adoption, see Z Elkins, T Ginsburg, and J Blount, 'The Citizen as Founder: Public Participation in Constitutional Approval' (2008) 81 *Temple Law Review* 101–121.

[104] When the draft Constitution was laid before the CAB, two members (Gupta and Larma) proposed for a referendum, which was refused. The referendum-based wider public participation in constitution-making, however, is largely a post-1972 phenomenon. See, eg, J Blount and T Ginsburg, 'Participation in Constitutional Design: Asian Exceptionalism', in R Dixon and T Ginsburg (eds), *Comparative Constitutional Law* (Cheltenham, Edward Elgar, 2011) 38.

independence, public participation, and social inclusion. The Constitution provided for a parliamentary democracy based on direct elections and 'universal franchise', in which the executive 'would be collectively responsible to Parliament'.[105] Apart from participatory democracy, another aspect that 'engaged the greatest amount of attention' in the formulation of detailed provisions of the Constitution was the attainment of a social and economic system that would end exploitation and inequality in society.[106]

The Constitution had an enforceable Bill of Rights and a group of judicially unenforceable social rights in the form of 'fundamental principles of state policy' that were to be the basis of all state actions. It established a unitary, two-tiered Supreme Court with a strong form of judicial review power to check the legality of government actions and laws as well as to enforce fundamental constitutional rights.[107] All its 'basic features' seem to be based on the overarching principle of democracy. As the CDC Report noted, the commitment to democracy and the rule of law finds expression in provisions protecting fundamental human rights and independence of the judiciary, ensuring accountable government, and establishing 'certain other constitutional offices considered necessary for the proper functioning of a parliamentary democracy, *viz*, the offices of the Attorney-General, the Comptroller and Auditor-General, the Election Commission and the Public Service Commissions'.[108]

As the Constitution was being drafted and debated,[109] the framers were fully conscious and alive to the recent tumult of the war of liberation as well as the causes which the people fought for over the years: democracy, social justice, equality, and the rule of law. The people's aspirations are reflected in the Preamble:

> Pledging that the high ideals of nationalism, socialism, democracy and secularism, which inspired our heroic people to dedicate themselves to, and our brave martyrs to sacrifice their lives in, the national liberation struggle, shall be the fundamental principles of the Constitution.

Arguably, the framers intended these four 'high ideals' to be something of a higher normative value.[110] Indeed, as noted above, constitution-making proceeded taking

[105] Constitution Drafting Committee Report (n 98) 2617.

[106] Hossain, *Bangladesh: Quest for Freedom and Justice*, (n 4) 144.

[107] The Supreme Court comprises two divisions, the High Court Division (HCD) and the Appellate Division (SCAD). The HCD has the original jurisdiction of judicial review, while the SCAD hears appeals from any order or decision of the HCD. See for details R Hoque, 'Constitutional Positioning of the Supreme Court of Bangladesh', in *The Supreme Court Day Book* (Dhaka, Supreme Court of Bangladesh, 2018) 284–304.

[108] Constitution Drafting Committee Report (n 98) 2617, para 11.

[109] For the Constituent Assembly Debates, now see MA Halim, *The Constituent Assembly Debates* (Dhaka, CCB Foundation, 2015).

[110] I had elsewhere argued that these principles were, therefore, unamendable. See R Hoque, 'Eternal Provisions in the Constitution of Bangladesh: A Constitution Once and For All?', in R Albert and BE Oder (eds), *An Unconstitutional Constitution?: Unamendability in Constitutional*

those principles collectively as a pole-star. Article 8 thus provided that these four constitutional fundamentals, together with other state policy principles,[111] shall form the basis of legislation, interpretation of the law and the Constitution, and the actions of the state and its citizens.

A. Nationalism

The first foundational principle was 'nationalism', more specifically Bengali nationalism, which was inseparable from the people's identity and their belief in non-communalism and secularism. As Hossain argues, '[n]ationalism represented an assertion by the people of their identity, which evolved during the course of its historical struggle into the right to their language, culture, traditions and history'.[112] He continues:

> In declaring independence, the people of Bangladesh had emphasised that they were exercising their right to self-determination to create a nation state. [...] Now that Bangladesh had been established as a nation state, and was recognised as such by the world, their national identity could no longer be questioned.[113]

Accordingly, the Constitution adopted an interesting approach to citizenship and nationalism in article 6 by declaring the people of Bangladesh as 'Bengalis' and citizens as 'Bangladeshis' and, 'Bangla' was accorded the status of state language (article 3), thereby diminishing the status of other languages. As Bangladesh is nationalistically and linguistically plural, such an approach was exclusionary. The non-recognition of other nations in the Constitution and politics made a serious dent on notions of inclusivity.

B. Socialism

Another founding principle was 'socialism', which the Constitution sought to achieve through the democratic process. Article 10 heralded as follows: 'A socialist economic system shall be established with a view to ensuring the

Democracies (Cham, Springer, 2018) 195– 229. See also S Alam, 'The State-Religion Amendment to the Constitution of Bangladesh: A Critique' (1991) 24(2) *Verfassung und Recht in Übersee (Law and Politics in Africa, Asia, and Latin America)* 209–225, 224 ('those ideals [...] have taken roots from [...] blood of the people [and hence] cannot be changed').

[111] These principles are set out in Part III, arts 8 to 25, of the Constitution.

[112] Hossain, *Bangladesh: Quest for Freedom and Justice*, (n 4) 141. See further AFS Ahmed, *Bengali Nationalism and the Emergence of Bangladesh: An Introductory Outline* (Dhaka, International Centre for Bengal Studies, 1994). For a general view of Bengali identity, see MN Chakraborty, 'Being Bengali at Home and in the World: Some Speculations', in MN Chakraborty (ed), *Being Bengali: At Home and in the World* (London, Routledge, 2014) ch 1.

[113] Hossain, *Bangladesh: Quest for Freedom and Justice*, (n 4) 141.

attainment of a just and egalitarian society, free from the exploitation of man by man.' Consequently, the Constitution contained several 'principles of state policy' aiming at establishing an exploitation-free society[114] where everyone would have a right to work and be paid according to their work and no one would be allowed to enjoy 'unearned incomes'.[115] While the Constitution guaranteed the right to property, it also allowed for nationalisation or appropriation of private properties against 'compensation'.[116]

In both the CDC and Constituent Assembly meetings, the principle of socialism was intensely debated, but the Committee was confident it would break 'new ground' by making provisions for a 'socialist society, free from exploitation'.[117] To further the goal of socialism and inclusiveness, the Constitution established a substantive concept of legal equality of all citizens (article 27), with provision for affirmative state action in favour of various minority groups including the indigenous people. Article 28 provided that the principles of equality and non-discrimination would not prohibit the making of a special provision 'for the advancement of any backward section of citizens' or 'for the purpose of securing their adequate representation in the service of the Republic'.[118] Unlike the Indian Constitution, Bangladesh's independence Constitution did not specifically mention 'tribal communities' or communities that are known as 'scheduled castes' in India.

The Constitution did not make social and economic rights judicially enforceable. These social rights – including the right to basic necessities or the people's right to equal economic development – were declared to be judicially unenforceable 'fundamental principles of state policy'.[119] It was left to the state to honour these rights through progressive realisation. On the question of property or the socialist goal, the framers seem to have quietly borrowed from India by modelling its social rights provisions along the lines of India's 'directive principles'.

C. Democracy

As a founding feature of the Constitution, democracy would ensure the people's 'effective participation' in governance.[120] Democracy would co-exist with socialism.

[114] Article 14 provided as follows: 'It shall be a fundamental responsibility of the State to emancipate the toiling masses, the peasants and workers, and backward sections of the people from all forms of exploitation.'

[115] Constitution of Bangladesh, art 20.

[116] ibid, art 42.

[117] Constitution Drafting Committee Report (n 98) 2617.

[118] Constitution of Bangladesh, arts 28(4) & 29(3)(a). The Constitution, however, did not define what a 'backward' section is. Nor has Bangladesh yet adopted any systematic affirmative action programme for the disadvantaged and excluded sections of society, although there are certain ameliorative schemes such as free education for schoolgirls and the reserved quotas in government employments.

[119] Constitution of Bangladesh, art 8.

[120] Constitution of Bangladesh, preamble and art 11 ('The Republic shall be a democracy in which fundamental human rights and freedoms and respect for the dignity and worth of the human person

As Bangabandhu remarked: 'We want such a democracy that would promote social welfare and protect the suffering masses of this country and the exploited people from the exploiters.'[121] To entrench democracy, the founding Constitution underscored the need for a system of fair, free, and multi-party elections, by establishing an independent Election Commission.[122] There are no specific provisions for political parties except that the elections were required to be contested on a party line. It did, however, define a 'political party'[123] and prohibited parties organised along religious lines.[124]

D. Secularism

One of the biggest debates in both the CDC and the Constituent Assembly concerned whether it was politically correct to adopt 'secularism' as a founding principle. Given the debate and the context of Islam being the religion of the majority, the framers were cautious in constitutionalising secularism. Bangabandhu was 'aware of the religiosity of the people' and reassured them that secularism did not mean 'the absence of religion'.[125] During the drafting process, he emphatically instructed the CDC to adopt 'secularism' and twice spoke on this issue in the Constituent Assembly. On the first day of the Assembly, he focused on the functionality of secularism in the elimination of communal politics and exploitation of the people in the name of religion.[126] On 4 November 1972 when the Constitution was adopted, he made it clear in his concluding speech that people of all religions would be free to perform their religious rites and that the main purpose of secularism was 'to prevent the use of religion as a political tool'.[127] In the end, articles 12 and 38 banned religion-based politics but guaranteed the right to freedom of religion, respectively.[128]

shall be guaranteed and in which effective participation by the people through their elected representatives in administration at all levels shall be ensured').

[121] My own translation of Bangabandhu's speech of 4 November 1972, as in note 127 below.

[122] See clauses 4 and 5 of art 118 of the original Constitution, which provided that the Election Commission would be independent in the exercise of its functions and that the Commissioners would be subject to removal in accordance with the provisions applicable for judges of the Supreme Court. The only opposition member in the CAB, Mr Gupta, doubted the efficacy of the Election Commission in ensuring free and fair elections and he unsuccessfully proposed that Supreme Court judges be appointed as election commissioners.

[123] Constitution of Bangladesh, art 152.

[124] Ibid, art 12, which made it a state policy that the 'abuse of religion for political purposes' would be eliminated to establish secularism.

[125] T Fazal, 'Religion and Language in the Formation of Nationhood in Pakistan and Bangladesh' (1999) 48 (1&2) *Sociological Bulletin* 175–191, 190–191; and Hossain, *Bangladesh: Quest for Freedom and Justice*, (n 4) 142–143.

[126] For Bangabandhu's speech of 12 October 1972, see *Constituent Assembly Debates* (Dhaka, Parliamentary Secretariat, 1972) 20. See also JT O'Connell, 'Dilemmas of Secularism in Bangladesh' (1976) 11 *Journal of Asian & African Studies* 64–81, 69.

[127] *Constituent Assembly Debates* (n 126), Bangabandhu's speech of 4 November 1972.

[128] Article 12 explained secularism in these words: 'The principle of secularism shall be realised by the elimination of – (a) communalism in all its forms; (b) the granting by the State of political status

On this normative aspect of secularism, the Chairman of the CDC recently wrote that 'secularism' 'was to maintain a separation between the state and religion and to create an environment in which all religious communities could coexist in harmony, free from discrimination and religious intolerance [...]'.[129]

V. THE FOUNDINGS AND THE PROBLEM OF INCLUSIVE CONSTITUTIONALISM

Even though the Constitution embraced rule-of-law ethos, it was nevertheless insufficiently inclusive[130] as several non-Bengali *adivasi* (indigenous/aboriginal) communities were not included. Instead, the framers dismissed their demand for recognition as a distinct constitutional community. In the Constituent Assembly, the only elected representative of CHT, Manobendra Narayan Larma, expressed his dismay at the absence of a minority protection clause in the draft Constitution, stating that it 'did not reflect the hopes and aspirations of the tribal population'.[131] He proposed the incorporation of a clause in the fundamental rights chapter recognising the autonomous status of CHT 'so that the tribal population could establish its political, economic, social and religious rights'.[132] To press their demand, a delegation of the indigenous people led by Larma met Bangabandhu and demanded that their autonomy be protected constitutionally and a legislature for CHT be allowed.[133]

Their demands were summarily rejected on the grounds that they went against national sovereignty and the principle of Bengali nationalism. Unfortunately, Bangabandhu reportedly asked the *adivasis* to assume the Bengali identity by shunning their own. When the Constitution was adopted, all citizens were collectively identified as 'Bangalee' in article 6. Larma objected to this and walked out.[134] This aggressive assimilative Bengali identity may have arisen from the war-time mandate in 1971 that ultimately subsumed and delegitimised all other identity claims.[135] Bangladesh thus began a troublesome constitutional journey

in favour of any religion; (c) the abuse of religion for political purposes; (d) any discrimination against, or persecution of, persons practising a particular religion.'

[129] Hossain, *Bangladesh: Quest for Freedom and Justice*, (n 4) 142.

[130] See for details R Hoque, 'Inclusive Constitutionalism and the Indigenous People of the Chittagong Hill Tracts in Bangladesh', in *Indian Yearbook of Comparative Law 2016* (New Delhi, Oxford University Press, 2017) 217–248.

[131] See Mr Larma's speech in *Constituent Assembly Debates*, (n 126) 536.

[132] ibid.

[133] Other demands were as follows: the constitutional protection of the 1900 Chittagong Hill-Tracts Regulation, continuation of the tribal chiefs' offices, and the restriction of in-migration of 'non-tribal people' to the CHT. See BU Khan and MM Rahman, *Protection of Minorities: Regimes, Norms and Issues in South Asia* (Newcastle upon Tyne, Cambridge Scholars, 2012) 72–83.

[134] Anisuzzaman, *Bipula Prithibi*, (n 91) 59.

[135] See L Yasmin, 'The Tyranny of the Majority in Bangladesh: The Case of the Chittagong Hill Tracts' (2014) 20 *Nationalism and Ethnic Politics* 116–132.

with an assimilative/integrational approach to indigenous autonomy and identity, rather than an accommodative/inclusive one.[136]

The exclusion of indigenous communities was a grave constitutional mistake and failure,[137] as they were deprived of the right to cultural identity and equal citizenship. Indeed, this planted the seeds of conflict in the CHT in later years when Larma established a political entity in 1972 with an armed wing in 1973 to fight for autonomy, if not secession, and commenced a protracted insurgency.[138] A constitution in a diverse society should unify or rally power to strengthen unity amidst diversity.[139] This attribute was missing in the founding Constitution's design.

VI. EXTERNAL INFLUENCES ON THE FOUNDING CONSTITUTION

Like other constitutions that emerged in the 1970s, Bangladesh's founding Constitution was passively influenced by external sources.[140] The Drafting Committee examined 'constitutions of different countries'[141] but there was no direct international involvement in the making of the Bangladeshi Constitution in the way, as for example, Sri Lanka's first Constitution was drafted. Unlike the case of the Indian Constitution, there was no overt attempt to learn from others by, for example, appointing any commission to travel abroad. Kamal Hossain, the Drafting Committee Chair, was, however, cognisant of constitutional

[136] The 'integration' approach to diverse identities seeks to promote one single public national identity and is often considered the key 'to political stability, public unity, and the transcendence of group-based chauvinism', while the 'accommodation' approach seeks to promote dual or multiple public identities based on the principle of equality with institutional respect for a 'deep' diversity. See J McGarry, B O'Leary, and R Simeon, 'Integration or Accommodation? The Enduring Debate in Conflict Regulation' in S Choudhry (ed), *Constitutional Design for Divided Societies: Integration or Accommodation*? (Oxford, Oxford University Press, 2008) 41–88. Bangladesh's abrupt denial of indigenous identity can be called a resistant approach to ethnic diversity.

[137] As the Chairman of the Constitution Drafting Committee has recently acknowledged, the adoption of Bangalee nationalism 'led to smaller ethnic communities, in particular those living in the Chittagong Hill Tracts, feeling excluded'. See Hossain, *Bangladesh: Quest for Freedom and Justice*, (n 4) 141. See also Anisuzzaman, *Bipula Prithibi*, (n 91) 168.

[138] The insurgency grew intense in subsequent years, lingering for over 25 years, arguably as a consequence of the majoritarian imposition of a hegemonic national identity on indigenous peoples. See, among others, L Karim, 'Pushed to the Margins: Adivasi Peoples in Bangladesh and the Case of Kalpana Chakma' (1998) 7 *Contemporary South Asia* 301–316; and A Mohsin, *The Politics of Nationalism: The Case of the Chittagong Hill Tracts, Bangladesh* (Dhaka, University Pres Limited, 2002).

[139] HP Lee, 'A Unifying Constitution for a Diverse Nation' (2001) 24(3) *UNSW Law Journal* 605–610.

[140] On types of external influences see also Z Al-Ali, 'Constitutional Drafting and External Influence' in Tom Ginsburg and Rosalind Dixon (eds), *Comparative Constitutional Law* (Cheltenham, Edward Elgar, 2011) 77–95 (passive external influence occurs 'through the impact of a series of norms or rules').

[141] Constitution Drafting Committee Report (n 98) 2616, para 3.

developments elsewhere and conversant in international law. He travelled personally to India and London while the drafting was in progress. While in Delhi, he was in dialogue with leading constitutional experts and 'benefited' from discussions with Subrata Roy Chowdhury, India's leading international lawyer at the time.[142] In London, he met Robert Guthrie, an Irish-born legal drafting expert, who eventually came to Dhaka and provided technical assistance to the drafting team with reference to the English language.[143]

It was desirable that Bangladesh's founding Constitution reap the benefits of the international human rights regime and global principles of constitutionalism. Sources of inspiration included the constitutions of the UK, US, and India. Ireland was a source of inspiration too, albeit vicariously through the Indian experience. Bangladesh adopted the model of constitutionalism that was a mix of the British and American traditions. As for the goal of a socialist democracy, in addition to a more direct source of inspiration from India, there was some but no significant reliance on Russia, the major superpower that supported Bangladesh's independence.[144] Bangladesh's adoption of the principle of secularism was also arguably influenced by the discourse in the Indian Constituent Assembly over 20 years earlier.[145]

Although Bangladesh became a member of the United Nations in 1974,[146] its founding document endorsed in 1972 the basic principles of the UN Charter and adopted a fundamental state policy to comply with international law obligations (article 25), an approach that began with the Proclamation of Independence. In entrenching fundamental rights in Part II of the Constitution, the drafters closely observed the UN instruments[147] and relied upon the language of the international Bill of Rights, especially the Universal Declaration of Human Rights 1948.[148] The Constitution incorporated some social, economic and cultural rights as non-justiciable state policy principles in Part II.[149] The adoption of this

[142] I learned about the fact that Dr Hossain discussed with his friend Subrata Roy Chowdhury via my communication with Dr Hossain himself. On Roy Chowdhury's influence on the drafting of independence proclamation, see Sobhan, *Untranquil Recollections*, (n 59).

[143] Anisuzzaman, 'On How the Constitution', (n 101); *Bipula Prithibi*, (n 91) 35–36.

[144] In his inaugural speech at the CA, Bangabandhu thanked Russia and India. Earlier (14 January 1972) he made a statement expecting that China 'would now come forward to recognise the reality of' Bangladesh's independence.

[145] On this, see S Jha, 'Secularism in the Constituent Assembly Debates, 1946–1950' (2002) 37(20) *Economic & Political Weekly* 3175–3180.

[146] Bangladesh acquired UN membership on 17 September 1974.

[147] Brandt et al think that apart from offering guidance as to the content of the Bill of Rights, international law has very little to offer in the making of a constitution. See M Brandt, J Cottrell, Y Ghai, and A Regan, *Constitution-making and Reform,* 1st edn (Geneva, Interpeace, 2011) 192.

[148] As the Chairman of CDC, Dr Kamal Hossain, reminisced, the drafters consulted international human rights treaties. See PK Sikder, 'The Role of Comparative Law in the Making of the Constitution of Peoples' Republic of Bangladesh' (2017) 5 *Jahangirnagar University Journal of Law* 85–106, 98.

[149] For an argument that Part II does not contain only social rights, see ME Haque, 'Does Part II of the Constitution of Bangladesh Contain Only Economic and Social Rights?' (2012) 23(1) *Dhaka University Law Journal* 45–50.

division between enforceable and unenforceable rights was notably influenced by the Indian Constitution.

To what extent was the founding Constitution a complete break away from Pakistan's founding Constitution of 1956? Having envisioned an autochthonous constitution, the framers of Bangladesh's Constitution made a conscious effort not to look to the Pakistani constitutions. Moreover, the country's liberation struggle was against undemocratic orders sanctioned by the Pakistani constitutions. However, no founding constitution is an absolute separation from the country's past. Bangladesh's Constitution bears similar democratic norms such as the scheme of reserving seats for women in Parliament entrenched in Pakistan's first Constitution. In complete contrast, article 63(3) of the Constitution empowered Parliament 'to enact any law' for public safety and protection of the state during war, aggression, or 'armed conflict' and nothing in the Constitution would 'in any manner, restrain the Parliament from making such laws'.[150] This provision – now replaced by emergency provisions[151] – was a carryover of the overweening executive power exercised by the colonial regime under the Government of India Act 1935 or under the emergency provisions of Pakistan's first Constitution (articles 191–95).[152] It may nevertheless be argued that Bangladesh's constitution-making adopted the 'national ownership' model congruent with the existing international constitutional standards.[153] This can be seen, for example, in its adoption of 'secularism' and its rejection of the 1956 and 1962 'Islamic' constitutions of Pakistan.

VII. POST-1972 DEVELOPMENTS AND THE IMPACT OF CONSTITUTIONAL FOUNDINGS

This section examines the role of the founding Constitution during Bangladesh's state-formative years and its impact on post-1972 developments. The 1972 Constitution that has endured to present date can be seen through the lens of five periodic phases: the first spans between 1972–1973, the second between 1973–1975, the third runs from 1975–1990, the fourth from 1991–2014, and the fifth and the current phase consists of the years since 2014.

[150] B Umar, 'The Proposed Constitution: A Fundamental Measure Against Socialism, Democracy, Secularism, and Nationalism' in R MacDermott et al (eds), *Sources of Indian Tradition: Modern India, Pakistan and Bangladesh*, 3rd edn (New York, Columbia University Press, 2014) vol 2, 864, 866.

[151] Article 63(3) was repealed, and emergency provisions were replaced, in 1973. See note 154 below.

[152] A set of provisions in the founding Constitution that are similar, in a negative way, to those in the 1956 Pakistani Constitution are those that attach conditions to some fundamental rights.

[153] This is the model which Saunders thinks is more acceptable in terms of international influence in national constitution-making. See C Saunders, 'International Involvement in Constitution Making' (2019) University of Melbourne Legal Studies Research Paper https://ssrn.com/abstract=3414698.

As noted above, the founding Constitution entrenched the 'high ideals' of nationalism, socialism, democracy and secularism, based on the values of popular sovereignty and rule of law. Its overarching principle has been one of a liberal and deliberative democracy. Unfortunately, however, democracy followed a chequered trajectory. The first sign of constitutional decay emerged within a year of the Constitution's commencement when provisions for state of emergency and preventive detention were internalised in 1973.[154] Then followed the most drastic constitutional deformation in 1975 when the parliamentary form of democracy was replaced with a one-party presidential system. The 4th Amendment,[155] the vehicle for this constitutional replacement, was pushed forth by the same party that led the war of independence and constitution-making process. It destroyed many other founding values such as the independence of judiciary, judicial review, and the protection of fundamental rights including the freedom of the press.

After the brutal assassination of Bangabandhu on 15 August 1975, the nation fell prey to unconstitutional forces and remained under the grip of military and civil autocracies until its transition to democracy in 1991. Even after that, Bangladeshi democracy continued to remain unconsolidated, illiberal, and quite exclusionary. During the autocratic regimes, the Constitution's basic foundational core was drastically compromised and defaced. Occasionally there were parliaments, but the general elections were a sham and engineered.

Since independence, Bangladesh's state identity has been continuously contested, especially the concepts of 'Bengali nationalism' and 'secularism'.[156] After independence, 'religion soon became an important component'[157] and the far-right forces and religious groups tried to Islamise the Constitution and the body politic. The Awami League believed in socialism, secularism, and Bengali nationalism but not the Bangladesh Nationalist Party – founded in 1978 – which based its political vision on the Islamic ideal and 'Bangladeshi' nationalism. This conflict over national identity and religion became increasingly tense during and throughout the post-1975 military regimes.

In the post-1975 period, the Constitution was suspended for many years during the two successive military and extra-constitutional governments. When revived, the Constitution had been drastically changed. It constitutionalised 'Bangladeshi

[154] See the Constitution (Second Amendment) Act 1973, inserting arts 141A–141C and amending art 33, respectively. The amended art 33 provided that certain major constitutional protections in criminal matters would not apply to people detained under the preventive detention laws. The 2nd Amendment, thus, had 'a substantial impact' on the democratic system. See Hakim and Huque, 'Governmental Change', (n 86).

[155] The Constitution (Fourth Amendment) Act 1975 (25 January 1975).

[156] SK Bhardwaj, 'Contesting Identities in Bangladesh: A Study of Secular and Religious Frontiers' (Asia Research Centre Working Paper No 36, 2011, LSE, London) www.lse.ac.uk/asiaResearchCentre/_files/ARCWP36-Bhardwaj.pdf.

[157] A Mohsin, 'Religion, Politics and Security: The Case of Bangladesh' in SP Limaye, M Malik, and RG Wirsing (eds), *Religious Radicalism and Security in South Asia* (Honolulu, Asia-Pacific Center for Security Studies, 2004) 467–488.

nationalism', redefined 'socialism', replaced 'secularism' with the principle of belief in Almighty Allah as the source of state power, and adopted Islam as the state religion. At the same time, governance was plagued by increasing corruption and terrorisation in politics, dealing a serious blow to the rule of law.

In the post-1990 period, democracy has been equally non-deliberative and unstable. In 1991, the greatest challenge to democracy was to ensure effective popular participation through fair and competitive elections, but all Bangladesh's post-1990 governments succumbed to democratic decay as they weakened all the democratic institutions such as the judiciary and the electoral commission while also whittling down the founding democratic values of the nation. The constitutional amendment process was used to introduce amendments mostly 'in sectarian or party interest,'[158] giving 'electoral advantage to the ruling party'.[159] There have been seventeen constitutional amendments, most of which are driven by narrow party interests aimed at consolidating and perpetuating power.[160] For example, several constitutional amendments increased the tenure and the size of the foundational scheme of reserved seats for women in Parliament.[161] In 1996, a new system of an apolitical caretaker government was introduced by the consensus-driven 13th Amendment that required the appointment of a neutral caretaker government upon the dissolution of Parliament to conduct general elections.[162] This exceptional system came about after successive incumbent governments failed to hold free and fair elections at the end of their terms. However, this did not stop politicians from trying to manipulate the system. In 2004, the 14th Amendment[163] was passed to raise the retirement age for the Supreme Court judges because the ruling party wanted a particular chief justice to lead the forthcoming caretaker government.

In 2007, a two-year emergency was declared and imposed, but after it was lifted, a general election was held in December 2008. It was won by the Awami League which remains the government in power at the time of writing. A major

[158] *Anawar Hossain Chowdhury v Bangladesh* (1989) BLD (Special) 1, 156 (per Shahabuddin Ahmed, J).

[159] AA Khan, 'The Politics of Constitutional Amendments in Bangladesh: The Case of the Non-political Caretaker Government' (2015) 9 *International Review of Law* 1–16. On politics of constitutional amendments generally, see S Akhter, *Amendments to the Constitution of Bangladesh 1973–2011: Background, Politics and Impacts* (MPhil Thesis, University of Dhaka, Department of Political Science, 2016).

[160] On earlier accounts of the constitutionalism and amendment nexus, see Hakim and Huque, 'Governmental Change', (n 86); MR Islam, 'The Quest for Constitutionalism in Bangladesh: A Reflection on Its First 25 Years', in M Alauddin and S Hasan (eds), *Bangladesh: Economy, People and the Environment* (Queensland, the University of Queensland, 1996) 131–144; and MH Rahman, 'Our Experience with Constitutionalism' (1998) 2 *Bangladesh Journal of Law* 115–132.

[161] These were the 10th, 14th, and 17th Amendments of the Constitution.

[162] See the Constitution (13th Amendment) Act 1996. For a detailed account of the caretaker government system, see SZ Khan, *The Politics and Law of Democratic Transition: Caretaker Government in Bangladesh* (London, Routledge, 2017); and N Ahmed, *Non-Party Caretaker Government in Bangladesh: Experience and Prospect* (Dhaka, University Press Limited, 2004).

[163] See the Constitution (14th Amendment) Act 2004.

attack on the foundational vision of a free and fair election system, however, came in 2011 when the 15th Amendment arbitrarily abolished the caretaker government system.[164] However, it simultaneously restored the founding principles of secularism, socialism, and collective Bengali nationalism, but curiously kept intact 'Islam' as the state religion. In protest against the abolition of the caretaker government system, major opposition parties boycotted the January 2014 general election, effectively turning it into a one-party race. Indeed, 153 out of 300 representative seats were elected unopposed and there was no opposition in the tenth Parliament of 2014.[165] Unsurprisingly, a dangerous pattern of democratic backsliding ensued, replete with increasing breaches of human rights and the constitutional goal of sustainable development. While the major parties contested the December 2018 elections, the fairness of the electoral process remained widely questioned.[166] The ruling Awami League and its allies won 293 out of 300 directly contested seats, and Parliament was once again deprived of any serious opposition.

In the last decade or so, Bangladesh witnessed many democratic deviations. Since the 2014 elections, it has edged towards becoming an illiberal democracy as a result of the massive informal constitutional changes that altered the course of democracy and participatory elections.[167] As we have seen, this back-paddling was engineered by the ruling party to secure its dominance. At the same time, incidents of corruption have risen alarmingly. Today, Bangladesh may well be in a state where there is a constitution without constitutionalism or 'civilian authoritarianism'.[168]

VIII. CONCLUSION

From a comparative point of view, Bangladesh presents a unique case of revolutionary constitution-making. Also notable is the brief span of time, just seven months (10 April–4 November 1972), that the Constituent Assembly took to draft, debate, and adopt the first Constitution. As already noted, the Constituent Assembly derived its legitimacy from the popular mandate of the 1970 general

[164] The Constitution (15th Amendment) Act 2011. Earlier, by a preliminary judgment of 10 May 2011, the Supreme Court's Appellate Division in a 4 to 3 judgment in *Abdul Mannan Khan v Bangladesh* (2012) 64 DLR (AD) 169 held that the caretaker government system was unconstitutional.

[165] See R Hoque, 'Judicialization of Politics in Bangladesh: Pragmatism, Legitimacy and Consequences', in M Tushnet and M Khosla (eds), *Unstable Constitutionalism: Law and Politics in South Asia* (New York, Cambridge University Press, 2015) 261–290.

[166] See, among others, S Ganguly, 'The World Should be Watching Bangladesh's Election Debacle' (*Foreign Policy*, 7 January 2019) https://foreignpolicy.com/2019/01/07/the-world-should-be-watching-bangladeshs-election-debacle-sheikh-hasina/. See further A Riaz, *Election in a Hybrid Regime: Explaining the 2018 Bangladeshi Election* (Singapore & New York, Palgrave McMillan Pivot, 2019).

[167] For a pre-2014 account, see D Lewis, *Bangladesh: Politics, Economy and Civil Society* (Dhaka, Prothoma Prakashan, 2013) 90–108.

[168] See A Riaz, 'The Legislature as a Tool, Executives' Power Grab, and Civilian Authoritarianism: The Bangladesh Case', in I Khmelko, R Stapenhurst, and ML Mezey (eds), *Legislative Decline in the 21st Century: A Comparative Perspective* (New York & London, Routledge, 2020) 105–117.

elections which had been called to draft a constitution for undivided Pakistan. In this context, the making of the founding Constitution was largely participatory and inclusive. There was nevertheless a problem in the exclusion of indigenous communities and other minority groups from the process. Even so, the process and substance of constitution-making might be said to accord with global standards and best practices.[169]

Several internal and external factors influenced the constitution-making process. Internally, these included demands from the indigenous community for constitutional recognition of their cultural autonomy; Bangladesh's past experiences during the Pakistani and colonial regimes; and the post-war urgency of nation-building. Externally, Bangladesh's constitution-making was significantly influenced by international politics, especially from the world's super-powers and India. Its unilateral declaration of independence required international support, and the Constitution made an express commitment to abide by international law. International human rights instruments were another source of influence and inspiration, as seen in the entrenchment of an enforceable Bill of Rights and a set of unenforceable social and economic rights. On the other hand, like any other constitution, Bangladesh's first Constitution was not a complete break from the nation's past experiences but was rather informed and influenced by its societal and political histories.

The founding Constitution provided democratic, social, and political moorings for the nation. Despite the many derelictions in subsequent years, that first Constitution has largely endured. It also had a positive impact on subsequent developments even if its positive influences were not always as durable as hoped. In 1975, the founding Constitution endured a major democratic decline when the multi-party parliamentary democracy was replaced by single-party, authoritarian presidentialism.

With the country's democratic transition in 1991, the damaged foundational values began to be restored, albeit on a piecemeal basis. The most notable impact of this restoration was the return of the country to parliamentary democracy in 1991. Unfortunately, democratic practices and the culture of rule of law have declined noticeably in recent years. The January 2014 general election marked the beginning of a sharp decline in multi-party democracy, while the December 2018 election effectively ushered in a de facto one-party government. Almost 50 years into the Constitution's founding, its transformative aspirations for a democracy based on the higher values of social justice, rule of law, and popular sovereignty have largely remained unfulfilled.

See also WB Milam, 'Bangladesh – On the March to Authoritarianism?', *The Express Tribune*, 13 January 2014 https://tribune.com.pk/story/658535/bangladesh-on-the-march-to-authoritarianism/.

[169] See United Nations, *Guidance Note of the Secretary-General: United Nations Assistance to Constitution-making Processes* (United Nations, 2009) www.un.org/ruleoflaw/blog/document/guidance-note-of-the-secretary-general-united-nations-assistance-to-constitution-making-processes/. See further V Sripati, *Constitution-Making under UN Auspices: Fostering Dependency in Sovereign Lands* (New York, Oxford University Press, 2020).

5

Dominion Status and Compromised Foundations: The Soulbury Constitution and Sinhalese Buddhist Nationalist Responses to the Founding of the Ceylonese State, 1931–1956

ROSHAN DE SILVA-WIJEYERATNE

INTRODUCTION

PARADOXICALLY, IT MAY be possible to trace the origins of Ceylon's descent into communalism some ten years after independence in 1948 to the Donoughmore Commission's recommendation to abolish communal representation in the interests of progressive liberal constitutional development in the colony. Indeed, this was imagined as the continuation of a process that began in the 1830s. It may be argued that the Colebrooke-Cameron Reforms of the 1830s in the areas of judicial, fiscal and administrative organisations set the colony on the path of becoming a territorially bounded nation-state, albeit one that would later fragment as these broadly secular reforms could not withstand the politics of nationalist (both Sinhalese and Tamil) renewal from the second half of the twentieth century. The antecedents of this religious and nationalist renewal may, however, be traced back to the Buddhist cultural and religious reform movement of the late nineteenth century.

Ceylon's independence as a Dominion within the British Commonwealth of Nations under the 1948 Soulbury Constitution marked the evolution of Ceylonese self-government which had been formalised under the terms of the 1931 Donoughmore Constitution. The constitutional settlement of 1931 established the institutional frame for debates for further reform among the Ceylonese elites and the colonial state and the British Government, and between themselves *inter se*. Having achieved internal self-government under the Donoughmore Constitution the view among the Anglophile Ceylonese elites was that Dominion status was the natural next step in the process initiated by the Colebrooke-Cameron Reforms. This was the preferred option among the elites who eschewed the increasingly dominant republican strand of the Indian National Congress.[1] Indeed the latter was a mass movement, whereas the Ceylon National Congress (founded in 1919) was a wholly-elite Anglophile enterprise that actively discouraged mass participation in reform politics. The legal politics surrounding the transition from Dominion to Republic in India thus stand in sharp contrast to that experienced in Ceylon. In Ceylon it was the very elite nature of both internal self-government under the Donoughmore Constitution and the elite process that led to the granting of Dominion status in 1948 which established the canvass for the popular Sinhalese Buddhist and later Tamil revolt against the elite settlement of 1948 that fashioned in political terms the classic *imitation* Dominion.[2]

From the perspective of popular Sinhalese Buddhist sovereignty, a vision that had its origins in the textual (*vamsa*) tradition of the Sinhalese, the 1948 settlement was both liberal and secular and conceded too much (in terms of constitutional guarantees) to the ethno-religious minorities.[3] Sinhalese Buddhist nationalist and more secular Left opposition to the 1948 Soulbury Constitution coalesced around populist readings of the *Mahavamsa* 'regarding Sri Lanka's privileged status as the Buddhist promised land',[4] a land that would fulfil its promise to the Sinhalese majority in the form of a Republican state, free of the residual legal and symbolic ties to the British state.[5] While a civic republican constitution could have eschewed ethno-religious privileging, what emerged in the early 1970s was a majoritarian republican constitution that relegated to the past the relatively strong defence of judicial review enshrined in the 1948

[1] H Kumarasingham, 'Eastminster – Decolonisation and State-building in British Asia' in H Kumarasingha, *Constitution-Making in Asia* (Abingdon, Routledge, 2016) 1–35, 1 [hereinafter 'Kumarasingham 'Eastminster''].

[2] H Kumarasingham, 'The Tropical Dominions: The Appeal of Dominion Status in the Decolonisation of India, Pakistan and Ceylon', *Transactions of the Royal Historical Society* (US, Palala Press, 2013) 242–245. [hereinafter 'Kumarasingham, 'The Tropical Dominions''].

[3] The symbolic order of Buddhist sovereignty, while centralising in intent, lent itself to a *galactic* polity that was in terms of the distribution of power devolved in structure and process. *Vamsa* alludes to 'lineage' or 'descent'. In the Hindu-Buddhist tradition, ideas and knowledge are recited by one generation in order to be learnt by the next, this being the means by which practices and institutions survived in historical consciousness through the Brahman teachers. See S Kemper, *The Presence of the Past: Chronicles, Politics and the Culture in Sinhala Life* (Ithaca, Cornell University Press, 1991) 31–32.

[4] TJ Bartholomeusz, *In Defence of Dharma: Just-War Ideology in Buddhist Sri Lanka* (London, Routledge Curzon, 2002) 34.

[5] The *Mahavamsa* represents the most significant text among the *vamsa* literature in Sri Lanka and constitute the principal source of mytho-history in Sinhalese Buddhism. See Kemper, *The Presence of the Past*, (n 3) 34–41.

Constitution. Judicial review had, at least in a limited sense, constrained the desire of an increasingly Sinhalese dominated state from pursuing policies to undo the secular constitutional settlement that had been jointly constructed by Sir Ivor Jennings and Chief Minister DS Senanayake. I say limited as the domestic courts missed many opportunities to function as a bulwark against the Sinhalese nationalist sentiments of both the executive and legislative branches of government in the period following the demise in 1952 of DS Senanayake, Ceylon's first Prime Minster. However, in a limited sense, the anti-communal sentiments expressed in the 1948 Constitution (section 29) guaranteed minority participation and protection in the public life of the post-colony.[6]

Somewhat paradoxically the foundational text of the post-colony and its performative force in the Ceylonese courts and the Privy Council in London also provided the interpretive horizon for the Sinhalese Buddhist nationalist mobilisation against the Dominion Constitution of 1948 and the campaign for an ethno-religious republican constitution that was eventually promulgated through a Constituent Assembly in 1972. If the secular Indian Republican Constitution of 1950 has (at least until the current phase of Bharatiya Janata Party rule in India) enabled state institutions including the judiciary to counter the Hindutva politics of sections of the Indian political class, the ethno-religious republicanism that dominated Ceylonese politics in the 1970s accelerated the ethno-religious violence and discrimination against the Tamil minority. This then led to a civil war between the state and the extra-constitutional Tamil nationalism of the Liberation Tigers of Tamil Eelam (LTTE) from the 1970s to 2009.[7]

My focus is on the 1948 Constitution as a foundational text that established the post-colonial Ceylonese State. Its significance lies in its fulfilment of the Colebrooke-Cameron Reforms, a participatory democracy that privileged an enumerated logic – of course this logic in the absence of a political culture that rotated on the axiom of ideological differences (Left verses Right verses Liberals)

[6] A Welikala, '"Specialist in Omniscience"? Nationalism, Constitutionalism and Sir Ivor Jennings' Engagement with Ceylon' in H Kumarasingham (ed) *Constitution Making in Asia: Decolonisation and State-Building in the Aftermath of the British Empire* (London, Routledge, 2016) 127–129 [hereinafter 'Welikala, 'Specialist in Omniscience''].

[7] R de Silva-Wijeyeratne, *Nation, Constitutionalism and Buddhism in Sri Lanka* (London, Routledge, 2014) 135–192. If it is possible to point to one moment that precipitated the eclipse of constitutional Tamil nationalism that had since the early 1950s coalesced around the Federal Party and their campaign for a federal/devolved reordering of the *unitary* state that the Soulbury Constitution had bequeath the island – a state which contra the rhetoric of Sinhalese nationalism had only been consolidated since the Colebrooke-Cameron Reforms of the 1830s – it is arguably the promulgation of the 1972 Constitution which marks that moment. Gunathilike provides a detailed account of the extent and nature of political violence in the recent period since 2009 and suggests that the Republican constitutions of 1972 and 1978 have in effect constitutionalised ethno-religious violence directed at non-Buddhists, in effect severing the causal connection with the government of the day, rendering the latter unable to act effectively against such violence. See, G Gunatilleke 'The Constitutional Practice of Ethno-Religious Violence' (2018) 13 *Asian Journal of Comparative Law* 359–387.

gave way to ethno-religious majoritarianism.[8] The argument I develop proceeds by first outlining the expansion of constitutional government in the colony from the 1830s when the Colebrooke-Cameron Reforms were implemented up to the establishment of self-government following the Donoughmore Commission of 1929. The Colebrooke-Cameron Reforms were motivated by a Benthamite zeal directed at the utilitarian transformation of the logic of sovereignty. Its focus was on *governmentalising* the relation between the colonial state and the colonised to arrange things so that people 'following their own self-interest, will do as they ought'.[9] With respect to judicial, administrative, and constitutional matters, it ushered in reforms such as an independent judiciary and a system of political representation based on ethno-communal identity.

Communal representation and what would become communal domination by the Sinhalese majority framed constitutional evolution in Ceylon in its transition from colony to internal self-government to Dominion to Republic. Initially this was by design but later, as independence dawned, it was by default. By the 1920s political elites found themselves compromised and shackled by appeals to ethno-religious populism. Critically what characterises the period of political reform in the nineteenth and early twentieth centuries is the expansion of the public sphere, the medium through which bourgeois civil society expanded, not only to hold the colonial state to account, but also facilitate an indigenous cultural renewal.

In the first part I explore the constitutional significance of the Colebrooke-Cameron Reforms as that moment in Whiggish reform of the state that initiates colonial modernity – but only to the extent that the *modern* can ever have an origin. In the second part I offer a genealogy from the Colebrooke-Cameron Reforms to the Donoughmore Constitution of 1931. In the third part I argue that the *telos* of the Donoughmore Constitution was the Dominion Constitution of 1948. The Dominion Constitution of 1948, after an initial period of commitment to the principles of a Westminster model of government, proved incapable of withstanding the Sinhalese nationalist populist assault on both the constitution and liberal cultural forms that the elites were seeking to popularise. The forces of popular Sinhalese sovereignty proved irresistible and like a Leviathan consumed both institutions and people, especially the ethnic and religious minorities.[10] The secular motives that inspired the Colebrooke-Cameron Reforms underpinned the Donoughmore Reforms (the abolition of communal representation being indicative of this) and reached their fulfilment in the Dominion Constitution of 1948 with its carefully crafted

[8] Such logic is one informed by the simple majoritarian ethos of an ethno-representative democracy, in which the political is reduced to a zero-sum game.

[9] D Scott, 'Colonial Governmentality' (1995) 43 *Social Text* 21–49, (n 2) 103 [hereinafter 'Scott, 'Colonial Governmentality''].

[10] The Commission of Inquiry into constitutional reform that led to the Dominion Constitution confirmed the pre-eminence of the territorial form of representation mandated by the Donoughmore

anti-discrimination clause. Paradoxically, this process of liberal reform allowed for the bottom-up re-sacralisation of the social and cultural horizon of popular Sinhalese forms of representation – particularly Buddhism thus setting in motion a series of events that led to the demise of the 1948 Dominion Constitution.

I. THE COLEBROOKE-CAMERON COMMISSION

Following the eviction of the Dutch in the Maritime Provinces of Ceylon in the late eighteenth century, the Kandyan kingdom – last remaining redoubt of autonomous Sinhalese Buddhist power (even this was circumscribed by the near economic collapse of the kingdom) – remained outside of British jurisdiction until 1815. When the British militarily defeated the last rulers of the Kandyan kingdom (who in fact happened to be of Tamil lineage from South India), the terms of surrender obliged the colonial state to protect the institutional links between Buddhism and what had been the Kandyan kingdom.[11] The colonial Governor morphed into the Buddhist King (or *cakkavatti* monarch) thus maintaining the legitimating nexus between kingship and Buddhism that was an intrinsic feature of Buddhist kingship in South and Southeast Asia.

However, opposition to the state's protection of Buddhism in what was now a *virtual* Kandyan kingdom increased as European Christian missionary activity gathered strength in the colony. Pressure from an increasingly powerful Anglican Church grew, alongside a Westminster-inspired commission of inquiry into the British administration of the Cape Colony, Mauritius and Ceylon. The Commission of Eastern Inquiry was tasked with examining the structures and cost of the civil government, the economy and the administration of justice of each colony.[12]

The logic of the Reforms was Benthamite and the Colebrooke–Cameron Reforms sought to induce 'improving effects on colonial conduct'[13] in three areas: the economy, the government and the judiciary. The reforms were motivated by a Whig concern for the expansion of a colonial public sphere and a concomitant increase in the democratic accountability of the state through, for example, the establishment of Executive and Legislative Councils that would (at least in the case of the latter) admit native members. The public sphere would be guaranteed through the 'great Whig principles of an English education and a free press',[14] as well as a number of institutional changes to hold the state to account in the court of public opinion.[15]

Commission and this served only to further consolidate opposition to the secular liberal constitutional settlement of 1948 given the numerical supremacy that the Sinhalese had.

[11] The terms of surrender became known as the Kandyan Convention.

[12] de Silva-Wijeyaratne, *Nation, Constitutionalism and Buddhism*, (n 7) 85.

[13] Scott, 'Colonial Governmentality', (n 9) 44.

[14] ibid, 45.

[15] ibid, 45–46.

It was in the arrangement of things and the organisation of institutions to this purpose, that the logic of modern (or *governmentalising*) power was to be directed. In Ceylon it revealed itself in the adoption of instrumentalities that supported the emergence of a system of individual property, market-based labour, and an independent judiciary under a Charter of Justice to adjudicate disputes over land and labour. Modernity had entered the life of the colonised – it was both discursive and pragmatic. Through these reforms, the features of a modern civic and commercial society came into being. However, the mode of political engagement made possible by the Reforms was essentially anti-modern in that it elevated ethnos over civil-national modes of identity associated with secular political projects.[16] The Legislative Council was appointed on the basis of ethnic identity and fundamentally ascriptive attributes of the community/nation. The Executive Council, which appointed members of the Legislative Council, placed special emphasis on native membership, and in 1833, three of the 15 members were native Ceylonese. They were nominated by the Governor to represent the low-country Sinhalese, Burghers and Tamils.

At the same time the Reforms implemented the abstract principles of liberal imperialism 'in which imperial domination was argued to be an effective and legitimate tool of moral and material progress'[17] for colonised peoples.[18] Critically the Reforms removed the Governor's near-absolute powers[19] and set up a unified structure for the colony's administration. Sinhalese Buddhist historiography had a conception of 'unity' which did not necessarily relate to territorial 'unity', but a sense of 'unity' based on the principles of righteous Buddhist kingship. But with these reforms, they now had a concrete unity one could almost touch.[20]

The colony was divided into five provinces, with each province divided into four or five districts. A Government Agent (GA) was in charge of each province and an Assistant Government Agent (AGA) in charge of each district, but answerable to the provincial GA. Following the Charter of Justice in 1833, the coastal areas and the interior Kandyan provinces were all brought under the umbrella of an administrative system that organised the island into a unified

[16] Wickramasinghe suggests that they 'brought a change in the life of the people and their perceptions, anchoring them firmly in modernity'. See N Wickramasinghe, *Sri Lanka in the Modern Age – A History of Contested Identities* (London, C Hurst & Co, 2006) 27.

[17] K Mantena, *Alibis of Empire: Henry Maine and the Ends of Liberal Imperialism* (Princeton, Princeton University Press, 2011) 28–29.

[18] US Mehta, *Liberalism and Empire: A Study in Nineteenth-Century British Liberal Thought* (Chicago, Chicago University Press, 1999); J Pitts, *A Turn to Empire: The Rise of Liberal Imperialism in Britain and France* (Princeton, Princeton University Press, 2005); A Sartori, 'The British Empire and its Liberal Mission' (2006) 78(3) *Journal of Modern History* 623–642; Wickramasinghe, *Sri Lanka in the Modern Age*, (n 16) 28–29; and Mantena, *Alibis of Empire*, ibid, 1.

[19] It was in the colonies that the prerogative powers of the Crown appeared most unlimited. A cursory reminder of the causes of the American Revolution confirm this fact.

[20] Kemper, *The Presence of the Past*, (n 3) 196–198.

territory. It was now a nation-state in the making that would in the late nineteenth century and beyond be re-imagined and recast by the Sinhalese Buddhist nationalist movement as a *monist* Sinhalese Buddhist nation-state that existed from time immemorial.

With these Reforms and under pressure from the Anglican establishment, the colonial state gradually began to dissociate itself from Buddhism and its rituals.[21] The apparent breach of the colonial state's undertakings to protect Buddhism underwritten in the Kandyan Convention fomented a Sinhalese cultural revival in the late nineteenth century. This revival would, however, be circumscribed by an increasingly modernist understanding of Buddhism which drew on the dominant strand of Buddhist historiography, Orientalism and Indology.[22] In time, the revival turned into a Sinhalese Buddhist nationalist movement that flourished not just through the print media, but also through the proliferation of lay Buddhist associations such as the Buddhist Theosophical Society (BTS), patronised by the emerging Sinhalese Buddhist bourgeoisie.[23] The Reforms facilitated the emergence of a native multi-ethnic and multi-religious bourgeois elite who were products of a Maucaulayite emphasis on educational policy as a means of creating a political class that fashioned their political objectives through the lens of liberal imperial constitutional reform. Such reforms were informed by the language of tutelage shared by the colonial state and the emerging native Anglicised elites.[24]

As in British India – until Gandhi entered the scene – the bourgeois and multi-ethnic Ceylonese elites supported incremental constitutional change. In 1911, for example, one native member was elected to the Legislative Council: Sir Ponnambalam Ramanathan a prominent member of the Tamil minority. Significant minority representation in the Legislative Council at the time augured well for 'minority relations with the Sinhalese majority, and make a powerful inter-communal vanguard for independence'.[25]

[21] N Casinader, R de Silva-Wijeyeratne and L Godden, 'From Sovereignty to Modernity: Revisiting the Colebrooke-Cameron Reforms: Transforming the Buddhist and Colonial Imaginary in Nineteenth Century Ceylon' (2018) 16(1) *Comparative Legal History* 34–64, 65.

[22] It is worthwhile signposting that a distinctive Orientalist reading of Buddhism, one dominated by the Indologists of Oxford and Heidelberg, would fashion the discursive and disciplinary frame that Sinhalese Buddhist nationalism would occupy. See de Silva-Wijeyeratne, *Nation, Constitutionalism and Buddhism*, (n 7) 88–96.

[23] M Roberts, *Exploring Confrontation: Sri Lanka – Politics, Culture and History* (Geneva, Harwood, 1994) 304–305 [hereinafter 'Roberts, *Exploring Confrontation*'].

[24] Royal College and St Thomas's College were established in 1835 and 1851 respectively as institutions designed to train the children of the local elites and impart to them Anglicised bourgeois sensibilities. Collectively, the purpose of a fledgling press and an education system designed to inculcate a specific corpus of English bourgeois sensibilities was directed at putting in place a 'public sphere in which only certain kinds of knowledge – and not others – could circulate with any efficacy'. See Scott, 'Colonial Governmentality' (n 9) 46.

[25] H Kumarasingham, 'The Jewel of the East Yet Has its Flaws: The Deceptive Tranquillity surrounding Sri Lankan Independence' (Heidelberg Papers in South Asian Comparative Politics, Working Paper No 72, 2013) 1–18, 3.

With the British promising India greater self-rule, the Ceylonese elites established the Ceylon National Congress (CNC) in 1919, initially under the leadership of Sir Ponnambalam Ramanathan (1851–1930) and later Sir Ponnambalam Arunachalam (1853–1924). Both were distinguished but conservative Tamils, who had little desire for the entry of the masses (Sinhalese or Tamil) into participatory politics. In the 1920s, under the governorship of Sir William Manning, there was an expansion of native representation on both the Executive and the Legislative Councils. At the same time, the number of elected representatives in the Legislative Council was further increased. Initially, electoral competition was not so much between Sinhalese and Tamils, but between the various caste communities among the Sinhalese, as the *goyigama* slowly gained numerical superiority over the *karāva*.[26]

The CNC leaders were wealthy men of property who were keen to restrict the electoral roll. As a consequence of the communal constituencies set up under the reforms of the 1920s, ethnic cleavages between the Sinhalese and Tamil elites increased and representation was adjusted to favour the minorities. The CNC's scepticism towards further enlarging the franchise was driven by the fear that ethno-nationalist sentiments would simply increase at the expense of the bourgeois inter-ethnic Ceylonese nationalism the CNC initially espoused. Until now, the elites had eschewed – at least in public – ethno-religious claims to political privilege, but this was soon to change. The gradual disintegration of the CNC into various ethno-communal groups anticipated the ethno-religious disintegration that was to come after independence. By 1925, many Kandyan leaders had left the CNC and formed the Kandyan National Assembly (KNA). In 1927, the KNA became the first organisation to advocate a federal reordering of the colonial unitary state as a mechanism to guarantee autonomy for the Kandyan Provinces – a reflection of its fear of dominance by the Sinhalese and ethnic *others* from the island's Maritime Provinces.[27]

After independence, such fears were echoed by the Tamil political leadership. This was the backdrop against which the Commission of Inquiry – chaired by the Anglo-Irish peer, the Earl of Donoughmore – began proceedings in 1927 to determine what further reforms were needed.[28] The Commission recommended

[26] Caste among the Sinhalese is occupational. The *goyigama* work the land and are historically people from the interior of the island and the *karāva* historically worked the oceans. While there are many caste groups among the Sinhalese these are the two dominant groups and democratic logic also facilitated the growth of caste competition among the Sinhalese in the late colonial period. See M Roberts, *Caste Conflict and Elite Formation: The Rise of a Karava Elite in Sri Lanka, 1500–1931* (Cambridge, Cambridge University Press, 1982).

[27] The ethnic Kandyan Sinhalese and their leadership had ever since the rebellions against British rule in the mid-19th century and their subsequent economic marginalisation developed a sense of consciousness that positioned themselves as preserving a Sinhalese Buddhist culture and heritage that had been denuded and made somewhat impure by Sinhalese and ethnic *others* in the coastal Low Country. The coast and its immediate hinterland were the location for the emergence of decidedly hybrid cultural forms that were informed by European cultural and religious transformation.

[28] Scott, 'Colonial Governmentality', (n 9) 164–165.

a diarchic form of power-sharing between the Ceylonese and the British that led to the unforeseen consolidation of the territorial and administrative unification of the polity fashioned by the Colebrooke-Cameron Reforms through the evolution of ethno-Sinhalese Buddhist political agency.[29] The institutions of the Donoughmore Constitution – especially the executive committee system – were integral to this process as pure numerical superiority enabled the Sinhalese Buddhists to dominate the Executive. The expansion of native participation in colonial state institutions became a vehicle that enabled the consolidation of Sinhalese hegemony in the post-colonial period. This was clearly not what the Whiggish architects of the Colebrooke-Cameron Reforms had anticipated as the natural *telos* of their reforms.

II. THE DONOUGHMORE REFORMS

The Donoughmore Commission's report was published in 1928.[30] Its most controversial recommendation was the introduction of universal suffrage for the colony, and the abolition of communal representation.[31] The Ceylon Tamil leadership feared losing its advantage under the system of communal representation, and the Kandyans feared that universal suffrage would render them a minority vis-à-vis the Indian Tamils who worked on the tea plantations in the Kandyan highlands.[32] This lay at the core of their petition to the Donoughmore Commission to consider the merits of a *federal union* in Ceylon.[33] To placate the fears of the Ceylon Tamils, key Sinhalese politicians such as SWRD Bandaranaike and George E de Silva pleaded with the Delimitation Commission in 1930 to allocate extra seats to the Tamil majority Northern Province, but other Sinhalese leaders of the CNC – who envisaged a Sinhalese Buddhist nationalist future – spoke against such concessions to the Tamils.[34] In the end, the Delimitation

[29] Welikala, 'Specialist in Omniscience', (n 6) 335.

[30] Donoughmore Report: *Ceylon: Report of the Special Commission on the Government of Ceylon*, Cmd. 3131, London: HMSO, 1928. The Commission was established by Lord Passfield (Sidney Webb), the Secretary of State for the Colonies in Ramsay MacDonald's Labour Government.

[31] The Donoughmore Report described communalism in Ceylon a 'canker on the body politic … poisoning the new growth of political consciousness and effectively preventing the development of a national or corporate spirit' (cited in Kumarasingham, 'The Tropical Dominions', (n 2) 3).

[32] O Hollup, *Bonded Labour, Caste & Cultural Identity Among Tamil Plantation Workers in Sri Lanka* (New Delhi, Sterling, 1994). The Report hypothesises that there could be 'no hope of binding together the diverse elements of the population in a realisation of their common kinship and an acknowledgment of common obligations to the country of which they are all citizens so long … communal representation, with all its disintegrating influences, remains a feature of the constitution' (Donoughmore Report: 18–39).

[33] R Edrisinha, 'Federalism: Myths and Realities' in R Edrisinha and A Welikala (eds), *Essays on Federalism in Sri Lanka* (Colombo, Centre for Policy Alternatives, 2008) 86–87. While federal constitutional arrangements became a key demand of the political platform of Tamil nationalists after 1948, its earliest advocates were representatives of the Kandyan Sinhalese, and they would reiterate these arguments in the 1940s in petitions to the Soulbury Commission.

[34] J Russell, *Communal Politics under the Donoughmore Constitution, 1931–1947* (Colombo, Tisara Praksakay, 1982) 32.

Commission rejected what it saw as a proposal that went against utilitarian values and which favoured communal representation.[35]

The Donoughmore Commission established a constitutional system based, not on a cabinet-government model, but on a system of executive committees – it was a model informed by the executive structure of the London County Council. As a harbinger of the Sinhalese Buddhist disenfranchising strategy after 1948, the *Kandyan National Association* successfully lobbied against granting the franchise to the Indian Tamil tea estate workers in the Kandyan Highlands of the interior. The colonial government modified their proposals for a universal franchise and Governor Stanley in 1931 by an Order-in-Council disenfranchised the majority of the Indian Tamils.[36] For non-British subjects resident on the island, eligibility to vote required 'either a literacy or property and income qualification, or a Certificate of Permanent Settlement which could be granted on proof of five years residence'.[37] While few Indian Tamils actually met these requirements, the Kandyans agitated for even further restrictions. These were operationalised in 1948 when new citizenship legislation further denuded the ability of the Indian Tamils to participate in the post-colonial polity.

The Donoughmore Constitution established a unicameral legislature of 61 members. In the first election in 1931, 28 of the 38 Sinhalese members returned were Buddhists. The State Council had both legislative and executive power over specified areas such as agriculture, industry, health and education. While the system of seven executive committees allowed all legislators to participate in executive decision-making, this period saw the growing fissure between Sinhalese and Tamils. This fissure intensified when the Board of Ministers acquired a Sinhalese majority after the 1936 elections.[38] The executive committee model of government was thus compromised once a pan-Sinhalese majority was established across all the departmental committees. This negated the need to seek compromise with the representatives of the ethno-religious minorities. The struggle between the Sinhalese and Tamil leaderships for both symbolic and real capital ensured that 'centripetal social forces within each community were not powerful enough to counteract … fissiparative tendencies'.[39] Democratic reason simply encouraged Sinhalese politicians – particularly in the south – to appeal to loyalties of caste and religion. The ethno-religious cleavages that would intensify in the later post-colonial future were thus established at this key juncture.

The institutional forms of a secular rational order actually intensified Sinhalese Buddhist ethno-religious sensibilities. Self-government under the

[35] ibid, 33–34.

[36] The key provisions were incorporated into ss 7 and 9 of the Ceylon State Council (Elections) Order-in-Council, 1931.

[37] KM de Silva, *Managing Ethnic Tensions in Multi-Ethnic Societies: Sri Lanka 1880–1985* (Lanham, MD, University Press of America 1986) 54).

[38] Russell, *Communal Politics*, (n 34) 243–288; and A Jeyaratnam-Wilson, *The Break-Up of Sri Lanka* (London, C Hurst & Co, 1988) 16.

[39] Russell, ibid, 334.

Donoughmore Constitution centralised power in the hands of the CNC's Sinhalese elites and generated the fateful consequences of pure majoritarian rule and the electoral subordination of Tamil and other minorities. The Donoughmore Constitution thus offered the increasingly-racialised Sinhalese Buddhist nationalist narrative a political platform through the State Council. For example, SWRD Bandaranaike's policy positions of the 1950s with respect to the legal privileging of the Sinhala language may be traced back to the path he trod in the 1930s. By the early 1930s, Bandaranaike had appropriated the cultural narrative of the Buddhist revival and started to echo Anagarika Dharmapala, leader of the revival, by seeking to give the revival political purchase.[40] In 1939, as Minister for Local Government, he echoed Dharmapala's own sentiments about majority rule when he stated that he did not know of 'any country which had progressed to the goal of freedom by embracing all communities and all cultures',[41] a view that caused increasing anxiety among the Tamil leadership. By this time, the latter was dominated by the Tamil Congress led by GG Ponnambalam an urbane and brilliant Kings Counsel.

Bandaranaike also used the *Sinhala Maha Sabha* (Chief Sinhala Council) – a loose Sinhalese Buddhist nationalist alliance he founded in 1935 – as a vehicle for his explicit aligning of Buddhism and political activism.[42] In 1936, addressing the *Sinhala Maha Sabha*, he gave voice to the trope that became integral to the Sinhalese nationalist narrative: 'Sinhalese history was a record of constant wars. They either killed each other or killed the Tamil invader … Dutugemunu … did not practice ahimsa when it came to getting rid of King Elara.'[43] From the late 1930s, Sinhalese Buddhist leaders began to adopt an increasingly trenchant ethno-chauvinist tone and Bandaranaike and others after him would reap the rewards of this populist appeal from the 1950s.

Rare attempts at reaching a common position between the Sinhalese and Tamil political leadership were often undone by pressure from Sinhalese Buddhist opinion that was simpatico with the markers of the Buddhist cultural revival. For example, in May 1944, when JR Jayewardene (a future president) initiated a debate in the State Council requesting that Sinhala and Tamil be made official languages, he was supported somewhat ambiguously by Bandaranaike.[44] However, activist Buddhist monks and organisations such as the *Sinhala Maha*

[40] de Silva-Wijeyeratne, *Nation, Constitutionalism and Buddhism*, (n 7) 92–96).

[41] Russell, *Communal Politics*, (n 34) 146, 147–150.

[42] Roberts, *Exploring Confrontation*, (n 23) 258–259.

[43] Roberts, ibid 151–152. Russel notes that the Dutthagamani/Elara story refracted 'the whole tenor of Sinhalese–Tamil relations in Ceylon in the Donoughmore period. It was the fulcrum on which both the past and present rested' (p 153) and would form the foundation upon which competing claims for power and resources between the two communities would manifest themselves after independence. Dutthagamani, a 2nd century BCE Sinhalese ruler vanquished the ruler of Anuradhapura, King Elara, who was from the Tamil South Indian Chola dynasty. Anuradhapura was the site of one of the earliest Sinhalese Hindu-Buddhist polities that dominated the island before Portuguese colonisation in the 16th century.

[44] de Silva, *Managing Ethnic Tensions*, (n 37) 77–80.

Sabha vociferously opposed any such concessions, which in turn provoked what would become the increasingly familiar response of Tamil foreboding. That said, the Sinhalese leadership remained committed up to this point to a policy of parity of status for both the Sinhala and Tamil languages, an approach that lasted till 1956.

This begs a question: How could the Donoughmore Commission have not recognised the tentative capture of the Sinhalese Buddhist political imaginary by the Buddhist nationalist movement? The Commissioners had envisaged that government by executive committee would be a natural progression of the Benthamite reforms of 1832, in a direction now motivated by a democratic logic. They did not envisage that democratic politics would give rise to a form of political agency motivated by Sinhalese populism. In spite of all the evidence to the contrary (and here I have in mind the cultural transformation of the *political* that the Buddhist revival had engendered by the 1920s), the Commissioners seemed to believe that religion could be contained within the private realm. Given that religion was profoundly public in South Asia, this was a rather naïve expectation on the part of the Commission. Such an expectation depended on the systematic embedding of both colonial civil society as well as a muscular 'secular rationality',[45] which the colonial state had tried to effect since the Benthamite reforms of the 1830s. Thus universal suffrage was to have 'an educative, or rather, a *governing*, effect on the conduct of the political elites'.[46] It was envisioned that by making the Sinhalese Buddhist political elites dependent on the Sinhalese Buddhist masses, the former would refashion the political inclinations of the latter 'in the direction of acquiring a more democratic egalitarian ethos'.[47] It had exactly the opposite effect. Instead, it enabled the racialised narrative of Sinhalese Buddhist nationalism and that engendered Sinhalese Buddhist political dominance by the late 1930s.[48]

Democratic structures and institutions – such as those created by the Colebrooke-Cameron Commission – were no guarantee against the forces of popular sovereignty which in the case of Ceylon increasingly took on a distinctly Buddhist nationalist persona. By the late 1930s, the radical wing of the CNC began to demand full independence from Britain. Chief Minister, DS Senanayake, had to contend with Bandaranaike and the *Sinhala Maha Sabha*'s demand that the Ceylonese state cease being religiously neutral, and that the policies of the putative independent state be framed within a Sinhalese Buddhist cultural milieu. Senanayake was, however, conscious that the CNC had by this stage lost the support of the minorities, and that the Colonial Office was not sympathetic to such demands. In December 1941, Whitehall announced,

[45] Scott, 'Colonial Governmentality', (n 9) 169.

[46] ibid, 168.

[47] ibid.

[48] Russell, *Communal Politics*, (n 34) 195–226; and Roberts, *Exploring Confrontation*, (n 23) 213–248.

through Governor Caldecott, that further constitutional reform would only be considered after the end of the War. The Board of Ministers, led by Senanayake, often reminded both the colonial government and London of Ceylon's valuable role in the defeat of Japanese fascism in Southeast Asia.[49]

The uncritical support that the Board of Ministers (comprised of the chairs of the executive committees) provided to the Allied war effort against Japanese expansionism persuaded the Governor and the Commander-in-Chief of the island, Sir Geoffrey Layton, to petition the Colonial Office for further reform of internal self-government. In addition, Senanayake had the active support of Lord Mountbatten who as Supreme Head of Allied South-East Asian Command was headquartered in Kandy for the duration of the Pacific war.[50]

London's declaration of intent in December 1942 failed to satisfy either Caldecott or Layton. In turn they responded with their own policy document on constitutional reform, which they sent to London for approval. The principles enunciated in this document were approved by the Colonial Office and published in Colombo in May 1943. The Colonial Office was committed to offering Ceylon's political leadership 'full responsibility for government under the Crown in all matters of Civil administration',[51] with London retaining responsibility for external affairs and defence. From the perspective of the British wartime coalition, Ceylon was still undergoing tutelage, and fully responsible self-government was still some time away. Events would, however, dictate that independence be granted at a time the Colonial Office did not necessarily envisage. In the final section I situate the debates that led to the Dominion Constitution of 1948 against the background of the proposals for constitutional change proposed by the State Council in the early 1940s, as well as the consolidation of Sinhalese Buddhist nationalist arguments in favour of Sinhalese privilege in any new post-British dispensation.

III. THE SOULBURY COMMISSION AND THE DOMINION CONSTITUTION

The Colonial Office hoped its 1942 declaration of intent would force the Sinhalese leadership to accommodate the Indian Tamil minority, a majority of whom had been disenfranchised at the behest of the Sinhalese leadership. However, the reality of the democratic logic of numbers (consolidated by the Donoughmore Constitution) was not lost on Oliver Stanley, the Secretary of State for the Colonies, who also feared that further conversations about constitutional reform would intensify tensions between the respective political leadership of the Sinhalese and Tamils.

[49] Kumarasingham, 'The Tropical Dominions' (n 2) and *Constitution Making in Asia* (n 6) 3–4.
[50] ibid.
[51] de Silva, *Managing Ethnic Tensions*, (n 37) 127.

In 1944 the Colonial Office sent the Soulbury Commission to Colombo to devise further constitutional reforms. The Board of Ministers was 'adamant that full independence was their objective, but they were equally resolute that Sri Lankan independence meant the status akin to the white Dominions – a cabinet based parliamentary system within the Commonwealth'.[52] The onus was now on the Board of Ministers to respond to London's initiative. Any draft constitution would need the support of three-quarters of the State Council, and with this in mind Joseph AL Cooray set about drafting a constitution that contained a justiciable Bill of Rights. This was a radical departure for someone like Cooray, a lawyer steeped in the Diceyan (unitary) traditions of British public law.[53] Of course, Cooray (who was associated with the more radical wing of the CNC) was not immune from constitutional debates in the Indian National Congress which showed greater sympathy to American constitutional traditions as a counter to the *monistic* outlook of the British Constitution. Senanayake, however, was not sympathetic to the inclusion of a Bill of Rights as a means of reassuring the minorities of their status and in this he found a sympathetic ear in Sir Ivor Jennings.

It is at this stage that Sir Ivor Jennings enters the constitutional scene – indeed his work in Ceylon sets the ground for his wider legacy as the doyen of British Commonwealth constitutional law.[54] Jennings arrived in Ceylon in 1941 as the new principal of the University College of Ceylon – he was mandated by the Colonial Office to create a university which he duly did, becoming the first Vice-Chancellor of the University of Ceylon. At the London School of Economics, he had a reputation as an exponent of the functionalist school of public law as a response to Diceyan orthodoxy which neutralised the question of political value. The new functionalists led by Jennings, Harold Laski and William Robson sought to restore the status of political value as integral to the question of sovereignty.[55]

The colonies were an apt place for the new functionalism in public law to be tested and a model Benthamite colony like Ceylon was the ideal test bed for Jennings' vision of the *telos* of public law as a modernist project intimately tied to the task of progressive nation-state building.[56] Jennings' functionalist

[52] Kumarasingham, 'The Jewel of the East', (n 25) 4.

[53] Cooray, a Sinhalese *karava* Catholic was the young JR Jeyewardene's loyal lieutenant and a member of the State Council. In the State Council JR Jayewardane voiced reservations about the proposals for Dominion status and instead put forward a resolution in the State Council that Ceylon should demand total independence.

[54] Kumarasingham, 'The Jewel of the East', (n 25) 9.

[55] M Loughlin, *Public Law and Political Theory* (Oxford, Oxford University Press, 1992) 175–176. Whereas Laski was committed to a humanist Marxism, Jennings was committed to Fabian socialism, which courtesy of Sydney and Beatrice Webb had become the dominant intellectual tradition at the LSE in the inter-war years (Kumarasingham, 'Eastminster', (n 1) 8).

[56] M Loughlin, 'Modernism in British Public Law, 1919-1979' (2014) *Public Law* 56–67, 59. Jennings like the Donoughmore Commissioners deplored the propensity of the Ceylonese political class to gravitate towards the populism associated with appeals to cultural communalism.

approach made him hostile to an entrenched Bill of Rights because such a liberal normative device would give the courts a paramount role in mandating and limiting the agency of the state.[57] The functionalists saw in the common law method the propensity of judges to defend the interests of private property over the 'common good' and an approach that smacked too much of American rights jurisprudence.

Yet, Jennings – who became Senanayake's principal if unofficial adviser on constitutional affairs – accepted the inclusion of judicial review in the Soulbury Constitution and a mechanism for the enforcement thereof against legislation that was inconsistent with the Constitution, in particular section 29 (anti-discrimination clause). Welikala speculates that Jennings opted for the narrow focus of section 29 as an alternative to a 'fully formed bill of rights'[58] to pre-empt the emergence of a litigious culture. Section 29 was a variation on section 5 of the Government of Ireland Act 1920, which prohibited 'legislation infringing on religious freedom or discriminating against persons of any community or religion'.[59] Similarly section 29(2)(b) of the Soulbury Constitution barred Parliament from passing laws that 'make persons of any community or religion liable to disabilities or restrictions to which persons of other communities or religions are not made liable'.[60] Later I will return to the significance of section 29 both as a protective mechanism designed to offer non-Sinhalese citizens of Ceylon a sense of confidence in the independence settlement, and as the constitutional tool that facilitated Sinhalese Buddhist nationalist opposition to the liberal promise of independence.

Communal tensions were on the ascent and the pan-Sinhalese Board of Ministers comprised figures in the majority community with varying perspectives. Some, like Bandaranaike, proved adept at exploiting Sinhalese populism. The question of the nature of the unit of political representation was ripe for such exploitation. The Donoughmore Commission had consigned communal representation to the past. In response the draft constitution incorporated a principle of weightage in favour of the minorities as well as the Sinhalese Buddhist rural heartland. Jennings himself met 'Tamil demands for communal representation as an institutional protection against Sinhalese dominance with the argument that they would obtain sufficient representation under territorial democracy because of their preponderance in the north and east'.[61] The Board of Ministers also included a provision for the head of state to appoint

[57] Welikala, 'Specialist in Omniscience', (n 6) 117.

[58] Kumarasingham, 'Eastminster', (n 1) 118.

[59] de Silva, *Managing Ethnic Tensions*, (n 37) 130.

[60] Furthermore, under s 29(2)(c), Parliament was barred from passing laws that 'confer on persons of any community or religion any privilege or advantage which is not conferred on persons of other communities or religions'.

[61] I Jennings, *The Constitution of Ceylon* 3rd edn (Bombay, Oxford University Press, 1953) 6–8; Welikala, 'Specialist in Omniscience' (n 6) 112–136.

up to six members to represent the even smaller Burgher, Malay and European communities.[62] Jennings' rather bland dismissal of Tamil political representatives' concerns proved ill-judged in light of the communal turn under the Donoughmore Constitution.

In a gesture that anticipated the future, the Tamil Congress was not consulted on the formulation of the draft constitution. Indeed, it would become a common and important refrain of the Tamil leadership that their consent to constitutional evolution was not sought. A draft constitution was submitted to Whitehall in February 1944. In response, in July 1944 Whitehall announced the establishment of the Soulbury Commission (chaired by Lord Soulbury, a former Conservative minister) to look into further constitutional reform. The Commission's remit to consult with 'various interests, including the minority communities'[63] alienated Senanayake and the Board of Ministers who argued that the remit breached London's May 1943 declaration. However, Senanayake's argument was difficult to sustain, given that London had never excluded the possibility that it would consult the minority communities about any constitutional settlement.[64]

When the Commission arrived in Colombo, Senanayake and the Board of Ministers boycotted its public sessions, although Senanayake corresponded with it in private. The CNC, however, boycotted the Commission in its entirety and Bandaranaike (ever the cynical operator) took up a position at odds with Senanayake's. Bandaranaike sought to counter the Commission's inquiry by drafting the 'Free Lanka Bill', which placed both external relations and defence in the purview of the Cabinet and not the Governor-General as envisaged by the Whitehall draft. The Colonial Office did not respond to Bandaranaike's manoeuvring, but neither did the Soulbury Commission take on board the petitions of the Tamil leadership with respect to their possible marginalisation under an inevitable Sinhalese dominated polity.[65] Consistent with the majoritarian logic of the universal franchise ushered in by the Donoughmore Constitution, Lord Soulbury, like Jennings, believed that the fears of Ponnambalam's Tamil Congress were grossly exaggerated.[66]

[62] The Burgher community were descendants of European (Portuguese, Dutch, French, and German primarily) settlers and the European community was primarily made up of British planters and service personnel (Kumarasingham, 'The Jewel of the East', (n 25) 5).

[63] de Silva, *Managing Ethnic Tensions*, (n 37) 132.

[64] ibid, 132–133.

[65] Jeyaratnam-Wilson, *The Break-Up of Sri Lanka*, (n 38) 1–22. Ponnambalam's advocacy of special weightage for the Tamil minority that he made both in the State Council and to the Colonial Secretary drew on other British Commonwealth historical precedents from asymmetric compromises for French Canadians in 1867, the Maori Representation Act of the same year in New Zealand or the position of Muslims from Cyprus to Mauritius as reasons for such protection. Such potential concessions were regarded by the Commission as running counter to British constitutional history. See H Kumarasingham, 'Written Differently: A Survey of Commonwealth Constitutional History in the Age of Decolonisation, (2018) 46(5) *Journal of Imperial and Commonwealth History* 874–908.

[66] The Soulbury Commission, in addition to rejecting the Tamil Congress's proposal for guaranteed representation for the Ceylon Tamils, also received 'proposals from minority groups as diverse

Lord Soulbury wrote to the Colonial Secretary Oliver Stanley supporting Senanayake's position. He warned the British war-time coalition government that there were

> ... younger, more radical and socialist Ceylonese nationalists that not only thought Dominion status was a 'sham independence', but also would align their republican agenda with the expulsion of British personnel from the island's [military] bases.[67]

As the Cold War gathered pace and the Left movement in Ceylon gathered popular support, Senanayake stressed the extent to which he was a safe pair of hands with respect to guaranteeing British economic interests on the island. Writing to Soulbury:

> ... Senanayake complained that if power was not transferred soon he would lose his majority to the Communists who had already 'published a complete rejection of Dominion status' and who believed in withdrawal from the Commonwealth and expulsion of the British from the bases'.[68]

Consistent with the telos of the secular-liberal project initiated with the Colebrooke-Cameron Reforms, the Soulbury Commission saw Ponnambalam's request for specific constitutional protection as running counter to the democratic (anti-communal) ethos of the unit of representation mandated by the Donoughmore Constitution. The irony that universal suffrage created the preconditions for ethno-religious political mobilisation was lost on the Soulbury Commission. The Commissioners simply chose to shield itself from the rising tide of Sinhalese Buddhist nationalist sentiment that the mechanics of the Donoughmore Constitution had facilitated and, in a sense, helped consolidate.[69]

Similarly, the Commission brushed aside the petitions of the Ceylon Indian Congress (later the Ceylon Workers' Congress) about the disenfranchisement of the Indian Tamils and their fears regarding continued disenfranchisement

as the Ceylon Moors' Association, the All-Ceylon Scheduled Castes' Federation, the Catholic Union of Ceylon, the Ceylon Malayali Mahajana Sabha, the Ceylon Muslim League, the Dutch Burgher Union, the Malay Political Association and even the Central Fisheries Union of Ceylon, who, using different methods argued for separate and legally stipulated representation in parliament'. See Kumarasingham, 'The Tropical Dominions', (n 2) 13.

[67] Lord Soulbury was at pains to stress that British interests aligned well with DS Senanayake's interests in ensuring an orderly transfer of power that in the short term at least limited the capacity of the well organised Left movement to appeal to popular rural and working class sentiments against what would prove to be in the tumult of the mid to late 1950s an unpopular Anglicised elite. The Left itself was led by an urbane and intellectually gifted group of Ceylonese men and European women (NM Perera, Colvin R de Silva, Pieter Keuneman, SA Wickremasinghe, Hedi Keuneman and Doreen Young Wickremasinghe) who had all studied at either Cambridge or the London School of Economics (both centres of anti-imperial and anti-fascist activism). At the LSE these Ceylonese Marxists fell under the intellectual tutelage of Harold Laski who had been Jennings' nemesis – Jennings while a member of the Labour Party was a classic modernist of Fabian lineage while Laski's intellectual inheritance was more radical finding a path to RH Tawney's ethical and Christian socialism. See, Kumarasingham, 'The Tropical Dominions', (n 2) 244.

[68] Kumarasingham, ibid, 8.

[69] Such was Jennings' hold over Senanayake and Ceylonese elites that he successfully shielded them from constitutional debates in British India where through the LSE and Columbia trained

under majority Sinhalese rule.[70] The Indian Tamil leadership argued that in view of the discriminatory impact of the 1931 legislation, both the franchise and immigration (principally from South India) should be reserved for the British Government under any new constitutional settlement. The Commission rejected their argument and the failure of Ceylonese and Indian delegations to resolve the residency period under which all Indian Tamils would acquire citizenship resulted in Senanayake's government imposing its own settlement. This settlement took form in grossly discriminatory citizenship legislation which targeted the Indian Tamils by disenfranchising a significant proportion of this community. It was a moment when judicial review failed to strike down such legislation.[71] It was the Left – in the form of the recently established Communist Party of Ceylon (CPC) – and the representatives of the Kandyan Sinhalese that resurrected the federal model of government first articulated by the KNA in the late 1920s in their dealings with the Donoughmore Commission.[72]

Senanayake arrived in London in July 1945 only to find that Clement Attlee's Labour Party had replaced Churchill's wartime coalition, with George Hall the new Secretary of State for the Colonies. Senanayake received the findings of the Soulbury Commission in London in August 1945. Satisfied that the concerns of the minorities had not been addressed in a manner detrimental to the position of the Sinhalese leadership, he now sought to persuade Whitehall that Ceylon was ready for full Dominion status.[73] This would place both defence and external affairs in the hands of the Cabinet rather than retaining them within the jurisdiction of the Governor-General. In September 1945, Hall conveyed to Senanayake that the British Government would approve the Commission's findings but remained opposed to the grant of Dominion status. However, while in London, Whitehall conceded to Senanayake that the issue of the citizenship status of the Indian Tamils would be a matter for the State Council and its successor body. It was with respect to citizenship that the newly independent polity would most disappoint the Soulbury Commissioners as the task of post-colonial nation-building would be undermined by legislation that disenfranchised a

BR Ambedkar, a civil rights based constitutional law would combine with the Westminster system of government as part of India's post-Dominion Republican Constitution.

[70] de Silva, *Managing Ethnic Tensions*, (n 37) 143–148); SJ Tambiah, *Sri Lanka: Ethnic Fratricide and the Dismantling of Democracy* (London, IB Tauris, 1986) 109. In somewhat of a contradictory gesture the Commission was a roving enterprise. It was an exercise in deliberative democratic practice in that the Commissioners took evidence from rural communities and from those well outside elite circles. I would argue that they did not take the concerns of those on the political margin seriously.

[71] de Silva-Wijeyeratne, *Nation, Constitutionalism and Buddhism*, (n 7) 112–116.

[72] As in the late 1920s the representatives of the Kandyan Sinhalese also took advantage of the presence of the Commission and once again proposed a federal scheme where the Up-country region, the Low-country, and the Tamil dominated north would comprise the three federal administrative units of Ceylon. The Soulbury Commission found no merit in these proposals for a constitution that validated a federal state in which sovereignty was shared.

[73] de Silva, *Managing Ethnic Tensions*, (n 37) 141–142.

large proportion of the Indian Tamil community – ethno-centric post-colonial nation-building was not the kind that Jennings envisaged the new constitutional order would be tasked with.[74]

Senanayake returned to Colombo in triumph, and the Soulbury Report was passed by the State Council by 51 votes to 3 in November 1945 – with two of the three negative votes coming from the Ceylon Indian Congress. As a sign of the kind of *modernist* Buddhist politics that would envelop the island in the 1950s, monks of the *Vidyalankara pirivena* (founded in 1875)[75] staged a protest outside the State Council, targeting the conservative nature of Senanayake's settlement with Whitehall.[76] Once it became clear that India was going to be offered Dominion status (and here was a rare occurrence when British Indian policy developments influenced affairs in Ceylon), Senanayake sent Sir Oliver Goonetilike to Whitehall to negotiate the transfer to full Dominion status. Arthur Creech Jones, Hall's successor as Secretary of State for the Colonies, was also sympathetic to the immediate grant of Dominion status. In June 1947, London announced that Ceylon was to receive 'fully responsible status within the British Commonwealth of Nations' under a unitary or monist state model that centralised power and administrative decision-making in Colombo at the expense of the Provinces and the smaller regions of the island.[77]

[74] Later in the 1960s once legislated discrimination was entrenched by the Ceylonese State, Lord Soulbury would publicly regret the failure of the Commission to take into account the concerns of the Tamil leadership with respect to the constitutional protection of the minorities.

[75] The *Vidyalankara* monks gave expression to the Sinhalese Buddhist nationalist sentiments that Dharmapala had evoked as the core of his project of cultural renewal.

[76] HL Seneviratne, *The Work of Kings: The New Buddhism in Sri Lanka* (Chicago, University of Chicago Press, 1999) 131–188. An intrinsic feature of *modernism* is that premodern categories were subject to a revaluation that generated interesting consequences for state–society relations and the wider constitutional imaginary in the decades after independence. As a consequence of the Orientalist encounter with Buddhism, Buddhism is first denuded of its cosmological and ritual base, and reimagined as rational, logical and scientific within an Orientalist/*modernist* frame that privileged religious, racial and linguistic markers of identity. R Gombrich and G Obeyesekere, *Buddhism Transformed: Religious Change in Sri Lanka* (Princeton, Princeton University Press, 1990). This new hybrid phenomenon of *modernist* Buddhism was appropriated by the Sinhalese Buddhist middle class in the revivalist and nationalist movement and gave it political purchase. *Modernist* Buddhism was pivotal to the secularisation of the ethical framework of Buddhism, and through it the Buddhist revivalist movement was able to look 'to the past for evidence that their faith provided an effective base for action in the modern world' (Rogers 1990: 94). Myths, customs and rites – which all had localised origins – were thus transformed into the emblem of a *unified* ethnic cum racial identity. See de Silva-Wijeyeratne, *Nation, Constitutionalism and Buddhism*, (n 7) 3–10, 91–92. This would have devastating and violent consequences in the years after independence.

[77] Such was the popular force of the *modernist* Buddhist narrative that while for Jennings and local constitutional lawyers the *monistic* state that the Soulbury Constitution bequeathed was the teleological consequence of the secular administrative reforms initiated by the Colebrooke–Cameron Commission, in the evolving rhetoric of Sinhalese Buddhist nationalism the *monistic* state was imagined as giving contemporary institutional validation to the forms of state and government that had prevailed under the Buddhist kings of pre-colonial Ceylon. As outlandish as such claims were, they developed significant purchase on the evolving Sinhalese Buddhist imaginary and underpin much of the Sinhalese opposition to re-designing the *unitary* state in the contemporary moment.

IV. WITHER ELITISM

Under the Soulbury Constitution the Dominion of Ceylon would have a bi-cameral legislature.[78] Uniquely Ceylon became a Dominion without the British Parliament passing an enabling Act. Instead, Ceylon's new Constitution was delivered by an Order-in-Council from Buckingham Palace and it 'even explicitly mentioned the need "as far as may be" to follow the constitutional conventions of another country – the United Kingdom'.[79] Even more interesting and constitutionally odd, Dominion status was formally granted in February 1948, some three months after Senananyake's United National Party (successor to the conservative wing of the CNC) won the general election of 1947. The LSE-educated Dr NM Perera, a former student of Harold Laski and leader of the Troksyite Lanka Sama Samaj Party, became Leader of His Majesty's Loyal Opposition.[80]

By the late 1940s and just before Dominion status was granted, radical monks began advocating the 'birth of a new order envisaged in Dharmapala's work'.[81] At the core of this new order was the outline of social practice for monks and a call for full independence from the British Crown and the Privy Council as Ceylon's final court of appeal.[82] As Seneviratne notes, this was a 'declaration of war'[83] on the CNC's Christianised Sinhalese Buddhist leadership who were about to inherit the state.[84] While the first Cabinet that governed until DS Senanayake's death was multi-ethnic and multi-religious and there were no communal riots, there were signs that even before Senanayake's death in March 1952, that all was not as it seemed.[85] As Kumarasingham notes, 'beneath

[78] The House of Representatives would have 101 members 'of which 95 were elected by a majoritarian voting system and the remaining six nominated by the Governor-General. The Senate would have typical checking powers, but lacked a veto, and would have 15 members selected by the Governor-General and 15 elected by the lower house.' See Kumarasingham, 'The Tropical Dominions', (n 2) 4.

[79] A Westminster Act of Parliament as had been passed with respect to Indian independence would have required more time and debate, and Senanayake and the CNC were too impatient for that – this all added to the sense of the elite nature of the enterprise that was Ceylon's progress to Dominion status. Kumarasingham, 'Eastminster', (n 1) 7.

[80] The leader of the Communist Party of Ceylon, Pieter Keuneman declared that Dominion status was nothing other than a 'sham independence', but in a fateful move that would compromise the Left's ability to counter the tide of Sinhalese Buddhist nationalism after independence, during the course of the 1947 general election the Left and Buddhist monk activists formed an alliance of mutual benefit which in the long term would precipitate the demise of the old Left as it succumbed to the tide of Sinhalese Buddhist populism.

[81] Seneviratne, *The Work of Kings*, (n 76) 136.

[82] ibid, 136–143.

[83] ibid, 141.

[84] A Abeysekara, *Colours of the Robe: Religion, Identity, and Difference* (Columbia, University of South Carolina Press, 2002) 81–85.

[85] Ponnambalam, the leader of the Tamil Congress was bought off by the promise of a seat in the Cabinet, but his prescient observations in favour of substantial protection for the minorities (in a manner that would have been a substantive variation on the British Constitution) proved accurate as the new Dominion set about in its first act of legislation, to further place citizenship and voting

the veneer of continuity and tranquillity lay very deep problems. The Ceylon National Congress was undoubtedly an elite organisation and never succeeded (if it even really attempted) in becoming a mass movement that excited and mobilised the masses in the fashion of Gandhi's revitalised INC in the 1930s.'[86] The cause of the Soulbury settlement's demise lay in its lack of a normative anchoring – after all, it was an elite compromise between the colonial state and the Anglicised Ceylonese elites who all too often imagined themselves as mere reflections of bourgeois Englishness.[87] The foundational text of the nation-state lacked credibility vis-à-vis the masses. Constitutions as foundational documents must, in a classically contradictory gesture, be both 'descriptive of the polity that it seeks to govern and at the same time as it is constitutive of the polity'.[88] It is imperative that a constitution in a democratic polity reflects the social conditions of the territory it seeks to institutionally organise. In a democratic polity citizens

> … enjoy affinity with and ownership of the constitution, and it is especially important in a communally plural polity that minority communities feel secure and represented in the constitutional order.[89]

Fundamental to the decolonising moment is the constitutive role of constitutions; that foundational document through which the 'nascent and contested national identity of the new state is symbolically constituted'.[90] But Jennings ensured that the Soulbury Constitution remained silent in describing the Ceylonese nation-state, its religio-cultural forms and pre-European history – the normative foundations that would have given the nascent post-colony a shared identity (however illusory it might prove to be). Liberal legalism, much like political liberalism, seeks to etiolate the political forms of the post-colonial state (insofar as this was a project about social or legal representation of cultural and religious identity).

Independence was based on pure faith; British faith in 'one individual to keep the peace and maintain the constitutional settlement. Senanayake and his reassuring creed were seen as 'the best bet'.[91] Patrick Gordon Walker, reporting from the Independence Day celebrations, told the Attlee Cabinet that Ceylon's first Prime Minister 'is in the genuine tradition of Dominion Prime Ministers:

disabilities on the Indian Tamil estate workers who also it should be noted had voted overwhelming for the Left in the 1947 general election. See Kumarasingham, 'The Tropical Dominions', (n 2) 13–14.

[86] Kumarasingham, ibid, 7.

[87] Sir Oliver Goonetilleke, a leading member of the local elite, and a future Governor General pronounced publicly that the world should 'think of Ceylon as a little bit of England'. Cited in J Manor, *The Expedient Utopian: Bandaranaike and Ceylon* (Cambridge, Cambridge University Press, 1989) 199.

[88] Welikala, 'Specialist in Omniscience', (n 6) 120.

[89] ibid.

[90] ibid, 121.

[91] Kumarasingham, 'The Tropical Dominions', (n 2) 8.

deeply committed to the British connexion'.[92] British interests in the island were, for the time being, secure.[93]

The general election campaign of 1947 saw the contours of future conflict manifest itself. The influential monk, Walpola Rahula, was to be at the centre of this response for the next 40 years as he tried to frame Buddhist activism by harking back to the role played by monks throughout South and Southeast Asia prior to European colonisation. The ambiguity of the Buddhist *modernist* response is acknowledged in Rahula's observation (in a rejoinder to Senanayake and other conservative Buddhist politicians who felt that monks should desist from political activity) that 'it was nothing but fitting for *bhikkhus* to identify themselves with activities conducive to the welfare of the people – whether these activities be labelled as politics or not – as long as the activity did not impede the religious life of a *bhikkhu*'.[94] Democratic participation gave the monks political agency as well and this would foment an overtly political form of Buddhism in the decades after independence that would unravel the elite settlement of the Soulbury Constitution.

The liberal veneer that Senanayake and Jennings had established as intrinsic to the rationale of independence quickly evaporated during the debates about the citizenship status of the Indian Tamil estate workers. This key moment saw the mobilisation of section 29 of the Constitution in defence of the citizenship rights of the Indian Tamils. Bandaranaike argued in 1954 that Senanayake had committed himself to disenfranchising a significant number of the Indian Tamils as early as 1940.[95] Motivated by Kandyan hostility to the presence of the Indian Tamils in the highland tea growing districts, the new government introduced the Ceylon Citizenship Bill to further disenfranchise the large body of Indian Tamil labourers, a significant vote bloc for the Left.[96] In its foundational moment, the Ceylonese (Sinhalese) state revealed its profound anxiety about the presence of Indian Tamils in its midst, and excluded them through the use of citizenship law. In the post-colonial period, this anxiety would be extended to Ceylon Tamils, Burghers and Muslims. Kandyans and their parliamentary representatives drew on Kandy's legacy as the last seat of autonomous Buddhist kingship as rhetoric

[92] ibid.

[93] While the Dominion of India established a Constituent Assembly in order to fashion in a more deliberative process an autochthonous Constitution that went well beyond the Government of India Act 1935, Ceylon's independence Constitution lasted until 1972. By the time a deliberative process was established in Ceylon to draft a Republican Constitution that in the event was deeply hostile to judicial review (perversely taking Jennings' scepticism towards judicial review to its logical functional conclusion) the state had been captured by a singular commitment to a document whose normative gesture was Sinhalese Buddhist. This singular gesture was saturated in epistemological violence and one which the contemporary Sri Lankan state perpetuates.

[94] Cited in SJ Tambiah, *Sri Lanka: Ethnic Fratricide and the Dismantling of Democracy* (London, IB Tauris, 1986) 26.

[95] Jeyaratnam-Wilson, *The Break-Up of Sri Lanka*, (n 38) 49.

[96] A Shastri, 'Estate Tamils, the Ceylon Citizenship Act of 1948 and Sri Lankan Politics' (1999) 8(1) *Contemporary South Asia* 65–86.

against the Indian Tamils, blaming them for the loss of 'Kandyan Buddhist dignity' and the 'theft of material success'. These were powerful metaphors and the parliamentary debates on Ceylonese citizenship became a narrative about ethnic roots. For the Kandyan, the nation-state could be made whole once again after expunging the Europeans and the Indian Tamils whom they held responsible for their imagined disfigurement of the Kandyan landscape.

The Ceylon Citizenship Act of 1948 and other voting rights legislation effectively denied this group the ability to organise their political representation. The majority of a population that numbered 780,000 in 1946 lost their ability to choose their representatives, and the courts – both domestic and the Privy Council – were unable to protect the Indian Tamils. Section 29(2) of the Constitution – which Jennings had such faith in – failed to guarantee non-discrimination on the grounds of race or religion.[97]

By legally disenfranchising the Indian Tamils, Senanayake unwittingly opened a rich vein that would be exploited by Sinhalese Buddhist nationalist opposition against the Ceylon Tamils and Burghers. They also successfully challenged the dominance of English as a language of advancement and later on, the place of Christianity within Ceylon's social fabric. The citizenship legislation represented a breach in the avowedly liberal promise of section 29 of the Soulbury Constitution to outlaw indirect discrimination.

The passage of the Citizenship legislation split the Tamil Congress, and SJV Chlevanayakam led a dominant group of MPs out of the Congress. Ponnambalam could not effectively defend 'the Indian Tamils from the other groups including the Sri Lankan Tamil parties.[98] The lessons of how easily rights could be taken away were not learnt in this case. However, it would not be long before the communal corollary was evident' – it became self-evident that the political task of advancing Sinhalese interests would take place at the

[97] The constitutionality of ss 4 and 5 of the Ceylon Citizenship Act and s 4 of the Ceylon (Parliamentary Elections) Act 1949, which excluded those who were non-citizens from the electoral register, were challenged in the courts in *GSN Kodakan Pillai v Mudanayake* [1952] NLR 433. The argument was that they were ultra vires of Art 29(2)(b) of the Constitution. Under Art 29(2)(b), Parliament was barred from passing laws that 'make persons of any community or religion liable to disabilities or restrictions to which persons of other communities or religions are not made liable'. In the Privy Council, the Crown conceded that a large number of Indian Tamils could not become citizens because neither their fathers nor grandfathers were born in Ceylon. The appellant contended that these provisions were indirectly discriminatory, their effect being to make members of the Indian Tamil community subject to a disability to which those of other communities were not subject. The Privy Council held that, '[i]t must be shown affirmatively by the party challenging a statute which is upon its face intra vires that it was enacted as part of a plan to effect indirectly something which the legislature had no power to achieve directly' (p 438). The Privy Council went on to hold that 'the legislature did not intend to prevent Indian Tamils from attaining citizenship provided that they were sufficiently connected with the island' (p 439).

[98] Under Chelvanayakam's leadership, the Federal Party which he established in 1949 came to embody the claims of constitutional Tamil nationalism, with its central aim being a 'federal (Dominion) union of Ceylon' through a redrafting of the Soulbury Constitution (A Jeyaratnam-Wilson, *SJV Chelvanayakam and the Crisis of Sri Lankan Tamil Nationalism* (London, C Hurst & Co, 1994) 30, 50–51).

expense of gradually denuding the Tamil people of their sense of place in the post-colony. It would be unsustainable and eventually lead to civil war.[99] It was a moment rich in irony. Having sought to quell the communal tide through a series of constitutional reforms in the 1930s and the 1940s, Sinhalese political dominance was such that it ripped a hole in the edifice of a constitution designed to strengthen nation-building and resist ethno-religious factionalism.[100] Jennings hoped that section 29(2) would privatise religion and race but it had the opposite effect. The silence about Buddhism in the Soulbury Constitution merely mobilised Buddhist activists to create a form of Buddhist Republicanism that would wreck the 'mistake' of constitutional neutrality concerning religion.

Post-colonial nation-building would restore the Sinhalese Buddhist majority to their rightful place at the apex of the state's structures. The policy on official languages would be the next test for the Soulbury Constitution's secular rationale. In May 1951, the UNP established the Official Language Commission under the chairmanship of Sir Arthur Wijewardene. The Commission was to implement the 1944 policy on official languages that called both Sinhala and Tamil to be established as official languages (*swabasha*). Within a month, Bandaranaike and his supporters had left the UNP and formed the Sri Lanka Freedom Party (SLFP). Initially, Bandaranaike maintained a commitment to the 1944 policy, but during the 1952 election campaign, he argued for a speedy implementation of *swabasha*. Dudley Senanayake, on the other hand, advocated a gradualist approach.[101] However, Buddhist organisations such as the Buddhist Theosophical Society and the Young Men's Buddhist Association wanted English to be replaced by 'Sinhala only'. Their demands received support from an unlikely quarter when Sir Arthur Wijewardene succumbed to the rising tide of Buddhist activism and in 1953 advocated *swabasha* for Sinhala only.

Sinhalese linguistic nationalism found an even more unlikely advocate in SWRD Bandaranaike, who hailed from one of the most prominent and wealthy Sinhalese families in Ceylon.[102] In the 1930s he had advocated a federal

[99] Kumarasingham, 'The Tropical Dominions', (n 2) 12.

[100] Senanayake was hostile to political Buddhism, but on this issue he succumbed to Kandyan Sinhalese whims.

[101] DS Senanayake's son Dudley succeeded his father as leader of the UNP and as Prime Minister following the former's death in March 1952. The manner of the succession raised questions about the nature of political interference regarding the way in which the Westminster convention on the appointment of a Prime Minister was applied by Lord Soulbury on DS Senanayake's death. Kumarasingham notes that rather 'than follow the practices and conventions of the Westminster system Sri Lanka had very proudly adopted and admired, DS Senanayake's son Dudley became prime minister without passing the all-important Westminster litmus test of demonstrating he had the confidence of the popularly-elected House'. See Kumarasingham, 'The Tropical Dominions', (n 2) 11. If a Tory grandee could breach a constitutional convention it would not be long before the local elites took notice of the said example.

[102] Bandaranaike was Christened an Anglican 'with the Governor, Sir Joseph West Ridgeway as his godparent (and from whom two of his middle names come from)[,] and his knighted father was famously the highest ranked "native" with a highly pro-English sensibility, which manifested itself in sending his son Solomon to Christ Church, Oxford where he studied Classics and ended as Secretary of the Union'. See Kumarasingham, 'The Tropical Dominions', (n 2) 15.

decentralised constitution for Ceylon as a means of giving voice to ethno-religious pluralism. By the 1950s his strategy changed – 'there was more political capital to be made from appealing to the Sinhalese only – just as the Tamil politicians were departing the main parties to form their own ethnic based ones and appeal directly to their own constituency'.[103] In the 1956 election the SLFP-led coalition campaigned for 'Sinhala only' and won an overwhelming victory, reducing the UNP (now led by Sir John Kotelawala) to 8 seats. While Bandaranaike found appeals to communalism antithetical to his core liberal instincts he allowed his vanity to delude him into 'thinking that the chauvinists he was manipulating could be tamed after obtaining power'.[104]

Bandaranaike made good his promise to Buddhist activists on the status of the Sinhala language. In 1956 the Official Language Act was passed. Regulations passed under the Act required entry into the Ceylon Civil Service and public service, as well as promotion within the Service, to be determined by an examinable knowledge of Sinhala. While these new regulations clearly placed non-Sinhala-speaking minorities in the public service at a disadvantage, the only legal challenge to the legislation was by Kodeswaran, a Tamil clerical officer, who commenced his legal challenge in 1962.[105] Kodeswaran had been refused promotion, and the salary increment that went with it, after he failed to appear for a Sinhala language test that was mandated under the terms of a Treasury Circular introduced under the Act in 1961. He claimed that this was a breach of the contract he had entered into with the Crown prior to the Act coming into force. In the Colombo District Court, Justice OL de Kretser rejected the Crown's argument that under the common law a civil servant did not have an enforceable contract with the Crown and held the Official Language Act to be *ultra vires* Article 29(2)(b) of the Soulbury Constitution. Accordingly, the 1961 Treasury Circular was invalided. The Crown appealed successfully, but Kodeswaran made a further appeal to the Privy Council. By the time the Privy Council gave judgment in 1970, the denial of a salary-increment to civil servants who failed the Sinhala language test had been resolved by a UNP-led government.

In the first ten years after the Soulbury Constitution gave post-colonial Ceylon its legal foundation, Buddhist activists and Sinhalese politicians began chipping away at the Constitution's liberal core. While Bandaranaike was an insincere Sinhalese nationalist, his decisions heralded the demise of the Soulbury Constitution, all within 15 years of the passage of the Official Language Act. When Bandaranaike tried to compromise and mitigate the worst effects of the legislation by reaching an accommodation with the Tamil leadership, riots ensued

[103] Kumarasingham, ibid.

[104] As a sign of how cynical Bandaranaike was, he said in 1956 'You know, my dear fellow [smiling broadly], I have never found anything to excite the people in quite the way this language issue does' (cited in Manor, (n 87) vi). See also N DeVotta, *Blowback – Linguistic Nationalism, Institutional Decay, and Ethnic Conflict in Sri Lanka* (Stanford, CA, Stanford University Press, 2004) 55.

[105] *Attorney-General v Kodeswaran* [1967] NLR 121.

against the Tamils in Colombo and beyond.[106] The ensuing riots and disorder compelled the government to enact a State of Emergency, the first of many that would become a common feature of Ceylon's political life and Bandaranaike was assassinated by a Buddhist monk. If murder by a saffron-clad monk should have jolted the Sinhalese Buddhist political class out of the religious nationalism that they were embracing, it did not. Kumarasingham identifies three key points flowing from the Official Language Act and the ensuing riots that created the conditions for an even more flawed Republican constitutional settlement:

> Firstly despite giving one language a privileged status above others, including as the language of government and administration – even in Tamil areas, the constitution was judged not to have been breached. Minority rights were therefore unprotected. Secondly, with the exception of the Communists no party targeted support from all communities. As a recent theoretical framework of multinational democracies concluded, Sri Lanka 'ceased to have any major polity-wide parties after the aggressive nation-state-building policies were initiated in 1956' as the 'temptation increased for winner-take-all outbidding among Sinhalese parties for the votes of Sinhalese for the control of their nation-state'.[107] Thirdly, and related to the preceding point, Sri Lankan nationalism meant Sinhalese nationalism. The UNP and SLFP would begin from this point the dangerous ethnic outbidding of the Sinhalese masses where there was little political or institutional incentive to make concessions to the Tamils – and if the concessions were made they were robustly protested against by their rival parties.[108]

I have outlined a series of communal events that led to the gradual erosion of commitment to the Soulbury Constitution. The Constitution failed to 'anticipate the rise of Sinhala-Buddhist nationalism laying claims to the ownership of the entire nation-state.'[109] Jennings' approach to constitution-making was consistent with the LSE functional school of public law. He brooked no compromise with petitions (from the Tamil leadership in particular) for embedding communal representation into the Constitution. For Jennings, section 29 was a concession to the 'context, in the nature of an exception, to the heuristic model of modern, civic nationhood that decolonising constitution-making must not only reflect but also actively promote'.[110] In the end the failure of the Soulbury Constitution to withstand the Sinhalese Buddhist communal turn signalled the limits of adapting the Westminster system to its South Asian context.

[106] Nira Wickramasinghe notes that 'the 1958 riots were the first major outbreak against the Tamils and in many ways a point of no return'. See Wickramasinghe, *Sri Lanka in the Modern Age*, (n 16) 273.

[107] A Stephan, JL Linz and Y Yadav (eds), *Crafting State-Nations – India and Other Multinational Democracies* (Baltimore, Johns Hopkins Press, 2011) 150–152.

[108] Kumarasingham, 'The Tropical Dominions', (n 2) 15–16.

[109] Welikala, 'Specialist in Omniscience', (n 6) 121.

[110] ibid.

V. CONCLUSION

Ceylon's brush with self-government dates back to the introduction of the Donoughmore Constitution in 1931. That experiment was motivated by the increase in nationalist sentiments among various ethno-religious communities on the island which were exacerbated by the establishment of communal constituencies under the reforms of the 1920s. The period of government under the Donoughmore Constitution provided a canvass for ethnic tensions to emerge and find parliamentary voice. By the time Lord Soulbury arrived in the island in 1944 as chair of the Soulbury Commission, Sinhalese nationalist sentiments had found a political platform through the reforms that the Donoughmore Commission had bequeath.

The resultant Dominion Constitution that the Soulbury Commission helped shape was the first migration of the British Westminster model to a non-settler colony in the British Empire. It was presented as the natural evolution of state reform going back to the 1830s. In the 1830s the cold and calculating hand of Benthamite utilitarianism shaped the foundations of the modern Ceylonese state. At the time, the one concession to an Actonian concept of nationality was the establishment of communal representation. By the 1920s such notions were out of favour with the Millian view of nationality that favoured the unitary whole at the expense of the constituent parts of the nation-state.[111] Such a view found expression in the scheme of the Soulbury Constitution. It was envisaged that the extensive judicial review the Constitution allowed (which went against the grain of Jennings' statist lineage) would enable the Ceylonese elites to manage the propensity of sectarian ethno-religious nationalism to undo what had been put in place. Instead the Dominion Constitution provided a platform for both Sinhalese nationalists and the secular Left to mobilise opposition to the residual symbolic, and real links to the British Crown, Parliament and superior courts that Dominion status left in place. Given the nature of the transactional relationship between DS Senanayake and the colonial state and the British Government, the success of the Constitution rested very much on Senanayake's statecraft. Following his early death in 1952, his successors 'possessed neither his reputation nor his political skill to contain the explosive forces of ethno-religious nationalism that would overwhelm the modernist project in Ceylon'.[112] The Soulbury Constitution and the residual links to the British Crown therein established a canvass on which Sinhalese Buddhist nationalism would articulate a project for wholesale evisceration of the post-colonial state.

[111] ibid, 122–123.
[112] ibid, 124.

6

Constitutional Foundings in Nepal: Experience with Changing Parameters

BIPIN ADHIKARI

INTRODUCTION

NEPAL IS THE only one of the eight South Asian countries never to have been colonised.[1] A mountainous, landlocked state with a population of over 28 million people, Nepal is predominantly a Hindu country; over 80 per cent of its population are Hindu and about 9 per cent Buddhist. Historians typically date its modern history to 1769, when the territory was conquered and unified by the Kingdom of Gorkha led by Prithivi Narayan Shah.[2] Shah instituted a hereditary kingship over the whole territory and ruled with absolute power. For the next 80 years or so, politics was the exclusive province of a few high-caste Hindu families, and until the emergence of the Rana family in 1846, the elite factions involved four prominent Kshatriya noble families – the Shahs (the ruling royal family), the Pandes, the Thapas and the Basnyats.[3]

However, succession problems, post-unification instabilities and court intrigues led to the rise of Jang Bahadur Rana (1817–1877) as Prime Minister in 1846.[4] Jang Bahadur's primary concern after becoming Prime Minister 'was to consolidate his new position and make it secure as much against any danger

[1] On South Asia, see generally SS Wadley, *South Asia in the World: An Introduction* (London, Taylor & Francis, 2015); see also MJ Gilbert, *South Asia in World History* (Oxford, Oxford University Press, 2017).

[2] J Whelpton, *A History of Nepal* (Cambridge, Cambridge University Press, 2005) 34–39 [hereinafter 'Whelpton, *A History of Nepal*'].

[3] See BL Joshi and LE Rose, *Democratic Innovations in Nepal: A Case Study of Political Acculturation* (Berkeley, University of California Press, 1966) 23 [hereinafter, 'Joshi & Rose, *Democratic Innovations in Nepal*'].

[4] Whelpton, *A History of Nepal*' (n 2) 39–46; and S Kumar, 'The Nepalese Monarch From 1769 to 1951' (1962) 4(1) *International Studies* 46–73, 48–58.

from other chieftains as against any possible encroachment' by the royal family.[5] To consolidate his own power and that of his family, Jang Bahadur reduced the King to a political non-entity and succeeded in forcing the King to share power with him. This 'divided kingship' between the King and the Prime Minister 'became institutionalized during the rule of Jang Bahadur himself and it continued as such up to 1951'.[6] Henceforth, the office of Prime Minister would be occupied by members of the Rana family on a hereditary basis. Rana also ingratiated himself with the British who, though initially suspicious, later supported him and even conferred a knighthood on him after 1858.[7] Although the British never colonised Nepal, it nonetheless exerted some influence over the kingdom through the Treaty of Sugauli of 1815.

Nepal's political awakening began with the anti-British movements before, after and during World War II and especially after Mahatma Gandhi called for 'an orderly British withdrawal' from the Indian sub-continent.[8] The feudal and oppressive Rana regime (1846–1951) was a major stumbling block to Nepal's progressive political development. For more than a century, the Rana regime had rendered the King of Nepal titular and symbolic but wielded real power, exercising executive powers autocratically. This political awakening resulted from the work and agitations of groups like the Gorkha League (1921), Prachanda Gorkha (1930), Nepal Praja Parishad (1936), Civic Rights Committee (1937), Nepali National Congress (1947) and Nepal Democratic Congress (1948).[9] Nepal's educated elites were involved in these organisations, and Gurkha soldiers, returning from serving the British in World War II, created a positive wave with their message about democratisation. The major concern for all parties was the establishment of a constitutional democracy in Nepal in place of the preceding Rana regime.[10]

This chapter discusses Nepal's constitutional foundings,[11] starting with the Nepal Interim Government Act 1951 or the 1951 Interim Constitution. I will also consider various political efforts in the subsequent 70 years or so to build new 'foundings'. These efforts include changing the parameters established by each of the seven constitutions enacted up until 2015, when a republican Constitution was adopted through the Constituent Assembly II. I argue that the inability to seriously implement the Nepal Interim Government Act, which embodied the spirit of the 1950–1951 revolution, led to prolonged, nation-wide

[5] Kumar, ibid, 59.

[6] ibid.

[7] Whelpton, *A History of Nepal*, (n 2) 46–47.

[8] M Gandhi, *Quit India*, RK Prabhu and UR Rao (eds) (Bombay, Padma Publications, 1942).

[9] P Basnet, *Nepali Congress ko Itihansko Prarup* [*An Outline History of Nepali Congress*] (Kathmandu, Purushottam Basnet, 2009) 8–145 [(hereinafter, 'Basnet, *Nepali Congress*').

[10] See A Sever, *Nepal under the Ranas* (New Delhi, Oxford & IBH Publishing Co., 1993).

[11] For a summary of the early history of Nepal's constitutional development, see M Malagodi, *Constitutional Nationalism and Legal Exclusion: Equality, Identity, Politics, and Democracy in Nepal (1990–2007)* (Oxford, Oxford University Press, 2013) 54–93 [hereinafter 'Malagodi, *Constitutional Nationalism*'].

instability. And, although Nepal now has a new Constitution[12] that reflects the foundational constitutional aspirations of the political parties of 1951, the lack of serious and effective implementation may again lead to another constitutional misfortune and cast the constitutional foundings further adrift.

I. THE 1950–1951 REVOLUTION AND THE FOUNDING CONSTITUTION OF 1951

The anti-British sentiments brewing in India were to have a significant impact on Nepal and on the Ranas. In 1945, Padma Shamsher Rana (1882–1961) became the 8th hereditary Prime Minister of Nepal. In 1947, opposition to Rana rule came in the form of the Nepali National Congress (Nepali Rashtriya Congress) founded by Bishweshwar Prasad (BP) Koirala (1914–1982),[13] whose key objective was 'the overthrow of the Rana regime by nonviolent *satyagraha* tactics and its replacement by a democratic government under the constitutional leadership of the King'.[14] The Rana regime was further jeopardised in February 1947 when the British publicly declared their intention to withdraw from India by June 1948. The withdrawal of the Rana's allies deprived them of a vital external source of support, and they were compelled to respond to the call for constitutional democracy.[15] In 1947, the Prime Minister constituted a Constitution Reform Committee[16] to draft a constitution, which was eventually enacted as the Government of Nepal Act. To assist in the drafting, two experts from India – Sri Prakash Gupta and Ram Udgar Singh – were brought in by the government.[17] The result was a hybrid document that drew heavily on the British institutional framework that was adapted to the immediate requirements of the Ranas. The Act was promulgated on 26 January 1948 in the name of the Prime Minister Padma Shamsher Rana as Nepal's first written constitution (and is often referred to as the Rana Constitution).[18]

[12] The Constitution of Nepal 2015 was promulgated on 20 September 2015.

[13] BP Koirala was the second of Krishna Prasad Koirala's (d 1945) three sons who were to become Prime Ministers of Nepal. The others were Matrika Prasad (MP) Koirala (1912–1997) who served as Prime Minister twice (1951–1952; and 1953–1955) and Girja Prasad (GP) Koirala (1924–2010) who was Prime Minister four times (1991–1994; 1998–1999; 2000–2001; and 2006–2008). BP Koirala was Prime Minister from 1959 to 1960.

[14] Joshi & Rose, *Democratic Innovations in Nepal*, (n 3) 61.

[15] Available at www.lawcommission.gov.np/en/wp-content/uploads/2018/09/government-of-nepal-act-2004-1948.pdf.

[16] Members of the Committee were: Bahadar Shamsher; Singh Shamsher; Krishna Shamsher; Mrigendra Shamsher; Brahma Shamsher; Sharada Shamsher; Vijaya Shamsher; Nayab Bada Guruju Shree Heramtha Raj Pandey; Badakaji Ramaman Singh; Sardar Shree Gunjaman Singh; Sardar Narendra Mani Acharya Dixit; Subarna Shamsher; and Kul Nath Lohani. See S Bhandari, *Self-Determination & Constitution Making in Nepal* (London, Springer, 2014) 213 [hereinafter 'Bhandari, *Self-Determination*'].

[17] See *Nepal Parichaya (An Introduction to Nepal)*, 3rd edn (Kathmandu, Department of Information and Broadcasting, 2020) 110.

[18] See, TB Singh, Nepalko Samvidhan ra Samvaidhanik Kanoon [The Constitution of Nepal and Constitutional Law] (1970) at 504.

The Government of Nepal Act gave continuity to the Rana system of hereditary prime ministership and retained the titular monarch, while providing for some fundamental rights to the people.[19] The Act laid out the framework of a parliamentary system with a bicameral legislature as the form of government and established a Supreme Court and a Judicial Committee comprising of members of the legislative body and legal experts. The entire membership of the upper house and a majority of the lower house were to be selected by the Prime Minister who was vested with the power to reject or/and veto any legislative measure.[20] This move was welcomed by the Nepali National Congress as a healthy start, but hardliners within the Rana clan were not prepared to accept even this mild 'constitutional' document. In April 1948, fearing for his life and pleading 'health concerns', Padma Shamsher crossed into India and submitted his resignation as Prime Minister. On 30 April 1948, he was succeeded by his hard-line Commander-in-Chief and son of Chandra Shamsher, Mohan Shamsher (1884–1967), who did not support these reforms and did what he could to delay their implementation.[21] Indeed, as Joshi and Rose have noted, the 1948 Constitution (the Act) 'was eventually nullified, not by opposition from the Nepali people but by the insincerity and duplicity of the dominant wing of the Rana family – the sons of Chandra Shamsher – who refused to allow its implementation in form or spirit'.[22] The new Indian Government in Delhi, which had pushed the Ranas towards reform, was disappointed.

Mohan Shamsher ruled with an iron fist and succeeded not only in alienating the Nepali National Congress members but also some members of his own clan, and this set Nepal on the road to revolution.[23] Early in 1950, two nephews of former Prime Minister Padma Shamsher funded the establishment of the Nepali Democratic Congress in Calcutta, India with the aim of overthrowing the Rana regime by way of an armed struggle.[24] And in March 1950, this organisation merged with the Nepali National Congress to form the Nepali Congress.

The revolution started in November 1950, when King Tribhuvan (1906–1955), who sided with the revolutionaries, left the palace and took refuge in the Indian embassy in Kathmandu with most of his family members. They were then taken to Delhi. The Nepali Congress Liberation Army, the militant wing of the Nepali Congress Party, then commenced an armed revolution throughout the country, with the people supporting the uprising.[25] Unable to contain the insurrection, the Ranas agreed to negotiate. The revolution ended with a

[19] Part II, Government of Nepal Act 1948.

[20] See Joshi & Rose, *Democratic Innovations in Nepal*, (n 3) 66–68.

[21] ibid, 66.

[22] ibid.

[23] Whelpton, *A History of Nepal*, (n 2) 69–70.

[24] ibid, 70; see also SPS Dhungel, B Adhikari, BP Bhandari and C Murgatroyd et al, *Commentary on the Nepalese Constitution*, (Kathmandu, Nepal Consulting Lawyers Inc, 1998) 14–47 (dealing with the constitutional history of Nepal until 1997) [hereinafter 'Dhungel, *Commentary*'].

[25] ibid, 389–90 (dealing with the establishment of the Nepali Congress and its political, economic and social justice-oriented platform and announcement of revolution).

compromise between the Ranas and King Tribhuvan, which was brokered by the Indian Prime Minister Jawaharlal Nehru during the time the King took refuge in Delhi.[26] Nehru dealt with the revolutionary Nepali Congress separately, which, by this time, had lost its independent clout as the King was under India's influence.[27] The compromise, often hailed as the Delhi Compromise, was reached between the Ranas, the Nepali Congress and the King, although there is no document showing that it was consensual.[28] Nevertheless, King Tribhuvan returned to Nepal as a dignified head of state, the Ranas agreed to surrender hereditary powers, and the Nepali Congress declared the end of the armed rebellion at the King's call. A space was, thus, created for these three centres of power to collaborate for a democratic change.[29]

The compromise ushered in the following solutions: (a) an elected constituent assembly to frame a democratic constitution within two years; (b) an interim cabinet of ten ministers, five of whom would be drawn from the Nepali Congress, under the prime-ministership of Mohan Shamsher, thereby creating the Rana Congress Coalition Government; (c) no restriction on the establishment of political parties; (d) release of all political prisoners and the agreement by agitators to surrender arms; and (e) the retention of King Tribhuvan as monarch but with real executive power.[30]

Very soon after his return to Kathmandu on 15 February 1951, King Tribhuvan endorsed the aforementioned commitments by way of a Proclamation. The King formally declared an end to the Rana family rule and established a democratic governance system. In the transition and in the spirit of national reconciliation, the Nepali Congress accepted the last Rana Prime Minister Mohan Shamsher as the leader of the new Council of Ministers. The Cabinet would work as a team to continue the democratisation process aiming a new political order 'based on a democratic constitution framed by a constituent assembly elected by the people'.[31] The King further stipulated that the Prime Minister and other ministers 'would hold office as his pleasure and be collectively responsible to him for their actions'.[32] This Proclamation – bereft of any constitutional

[26] King Tribhuvan was in Delhi from 10 Nov 1950 to 8 Feb 1951.

[27] See B Adhikari, 'Successive Constitutions and Geopolitical Pinches' in DN Dhungel and MK Dahal (eds), *Nepal: A Country in Transition* (New Delhi, Rupa Publications, 2018) 63–105 [hereinafter, 'Adhikari, 'Successive Constitutions''].

[28] Since then, geopolitical issues have pervasively influenced national politics and the politics of constitution-making in Nepal. This includes the making of the 2015 Constitution by the Constituent Assemblies I and II. This issue has not been further explored in this chapter.

[29] Joshi and Rose remarked that 'it was on this mixed note of hope, disappointment, and uncertainty that the first experience under the new "democratic order" was launched in February 1951'. See Joshi & Rose, *Democratic Innovations in Nepal*, (n 3) 80.

[30] GB Devkota, *Nepalko Rajnitik Darpan* [Political Mirror of Nepal] (Kathmandu, KC Gautam, 1959) 39.

[31] Quoted in CP Singh, 'Rise and Growth of Anti-Rana Movement in Nepal' (2004) 65 *Proceedings of the Indian History Congress* 992–1002, 1000–1001.

[32] Joshi & Rose, *Democratic Innovations in Nepal*, (n 3) 84.

principle or political convention – thus provided the 'sole legal basis for the new government'.[33]

This compromise did not go far enough for the revolutionary Nepali Congress, who wanted a parliamentary form of government with a constitutional monarchy, in which the King would reign but not rule, as well as a government answerable to a legislature elected by the people. Above all, the manifesto of the Nepali Congress called for an accountable government and a society that would be free of exploitation and based on equality, political freedoms, and justice.[34] Going beyond democracy, however, it pledged to restructure Nepal on the basis of social justice, which included land reforms and the empowerment of peasants. It was these ideological platforms that endeared the Congress to the masses who supported the revolution.[35] BP Koirala, the erstwhile leader of the Nepali Congress and Prime Minister from 1959 to 1960, recalled the spirit of the revolution in the following words:

> The revolution of 1950–51 and the subsequent historical royal proclamation of February 18, 1951 established the consensual principle that the country is not any single person's private property, but a commonwealth of all, including of the King and all people. It was something akin to the induction of a god into a stone statute via the process of *pran pratistha* [in Hindu traditions] in a temple. In this case, one considers the country as a temple and the stone statute thereby spiritualised, as the theory of a commonwealth. A *yagyna*, or a sacred establishment ... should not be allowed to be contaminated. I joined the revolution of 1950–51 because of this overwhelming sacred feeling of the greatness of nationalism and democracy, and I committed myself to that *yajnya* because of my love for the country .... This is the central inspiration of my political life. All my activities, successful or unsuccessful, intelligent or unintelligent, have been bound together by strong threads of this feeling and have been taken in clear conscience.[36]

II. THE 1951 INTERIM CONSTITUTION AND CONSTITUTIONAL FOUNDINGS: THE POINT OF DEPARTURE

On 30 March 1951, King Tribhuvan, acting on the advice of his Council of Ministers, promulgated the Interim Government of Nepal Act, which had been drafted by its members.[37] The Preamble of this Act made clear its temporary

[33] ibid.

[34] Basnet, *Nepali Congress*, (n 9) 139.

[35] See R Gautam, *Nepalko Prajatantrik Andolan ra Nepali Congress* [Democratic Movements of Nepal and Nepali Congress], (Kathmandu, Bhairab Apset Press, 1998) 281–344.

[36] PR Pokharel, *BP Koiralako Adalatko Bayan* [Court Statements of BP Koirala] (Kathmandu, BP Sangrahalaya Samiti, 2012) 3–4 [author's translation].

[37] Dhungel, *Commentary*, (n 24) 22–24. Members of the 1951 Drafting Committee were: Mohan Shamsher (Prime Minister); Babar Shamsher; Bisheshwar Prasad Koirala; Subarna Shamsher; Chandra Raj Shamsher; Ganesh Man Singh, Nirpanjung Rana; Bhandra Kali Mishra; Yagya Bahadur Basnet; and Bharat Mani Sharma. See Bhandari, *Self-Determination* (n 16) 214.

nature by stipulating that it was meant to operate until a new constitution was 'framed and promulgated'. Under this Act, the King was given tremendous power, with the executive power being exercisable by him 'either directly or through ministers or other officers subordinate' to the King.[38] And the legislative too vested in the King who would 'continue[] to have sovereign and plenary powers to make laws for the peace, order, and good government of Nepal'.[39] Under Article 22 (2), the King was also proclaimed the Supreme Commander of the Defences Forces of Nepal. The Cabinet and the Prime Minister would all be nominated by him, and their sole role would be 'to aid and advise the King in the exercise in his function'.[40] In the interim period, the King would appoint an Advisory Assembly, a body comparable to a Parliament, with a Speaker, internal structures, powers and privileges, and legislative and financial procedures. However, the Advisory Assembly was only allowed to discuss legislative matters and make recommendations to the King.[41] In principle,[42] therefore, the sovereign legislative powers rested with the King.[43] The Act also provided for a Supreme Court.[44]

To further the people's 'welfare', the Act enjoined the government to 'promote the welfare of the people by securing and protecting effectively as it may, social order in which justice, social, economic and political, shall inform all the institutions of the National life'.[45] The interim Constitution also contained various provisions guaranteeing fundamental rights, including equality before law, political freedoms such as freedom of assembly and the right to form unions, freedom of speech and expression, guarantees in criminal justice, and the right to personal liberty. The Act also contained some provisions on directive principles. The government was obliged to direct its policy toward securing social conditions for citizens, including the right to adequate means of livelihood and distribution of the ownership and control of material resources, as best to serve the common good.[46] These directive principles were not to be enforceable by any court, and no law was deemed to be invalid only for being inconsistent with them.[47] However, they were considered as being fundamental in the governance of the country, and the government was to adapt the existing laws based on these principles as early as possible as well as in framing new laws.[48]

[38] Article 22(1), the Government of Nepal Act 1951.
[39] Article 30, ibid.
[40] Article 24, ibid.
[41] Arts 33–59, ibid.
[42] Article 31, ibid.
[43] Article 22(2), ibid.
[44] Article 32, ibid.
[45] Article 4, ibid.
[46] Article 5, ibid.
[47] Article 3(1), ibid.
[48] Article 3(2), ibid.

The aim of the Interim Government was to 'create conditions, as early as possible, for holding elections for the Parliament'[49] on the basis of adult suffrage.[50] The Act created an Election Commission and provided for a Comptroller and Auditor General of Nepal to audit the government accounts.[51] It also provided for a Public Service Commission to conduct examinations for appointment to all civil services of the government. All of these commissions were supposed to be independent constitutional functionaries. However, hopes for an early general election and the appointment of a constituent assembly to draft a new constitution were dashed by the fluid and volatile political situation in the immediate post-Rana period.

One of the biggest challenges came from the attempt to reconcile the feudal and modern political leadership through the coalition government. The Rana-Congress coalition simply could not embark on the process of implementing the constitutional ideals of the Revolution. There were frequent clashes between BP Koirala, the popular Nepali Congress leader, and Prime Minister Mohan Shamsher. At one stage, the King was forced to accept the demand of the Nepali Congress for a government under its leadership. On 16 November 1951, the government of Mohan Shamsher was replaced by the Nepali Congress Government led by BP Koirala's elder brother, Matrika Prasad Koirala. King Tribhuvan's choice of MP Koirala as Prime Minister instead of BP Koirala created trouble in the Nepali Congress. The King's choice may well have been the result of pressure from the Indian Government that did not trust BP Koirala.[52] In any case, MP Koirala's government lasted only till 14 August 1952 when it, too, collapsed after internecine fighting within the Nepali Congress that led to the expulsion of MP Koirala and his supporters.[53]

From 14 August 1952, following the dissolution of the MP Koirala government, King Tribhuvan ruled the country for ten months with an advisory committee of five royal advisors belonging to the army and civil service. General Kesar Shamsher was the chief advisor of the committee. On 15 June 1953, in response to pressure from the political parties, the King announced the formation of a five-member party government headed again by MP Koirala, who had established his own Rastriya Praja Party (RPP). Meanwhile, in 1954, King Tribhuvan amended the Government of Nepal Act 1951 and arrogated to himself even greater royal powers. The entire chapter dealing with the judiciary, save for the continuance of a Supreme Court, was repealed. The RPP government was replaced by a seven-member National Coalition Cabinet (NCC) on 17 February 1954 under the prime-ministership of MP Koirala. In the meantime, King Tribhuvan was ailing. He had suffered a heart attack in 1953, and another in 1954. On 13 March 1955, while on a convalescence trip

[49] Article 66, ibid.
[50] Article 71, ibid.
[51] Articles 60–63, ibid.
[52] Whelpton, *A History of Nepal*, (n 2) 89.
[53] ibid.

to Zurich, King Tribhuvan died and thus ended the first four years of the post-revolutionary period of political instability in Nepal.[54]

The late King Tribhuvan's son, Mahendra (1920–1979), succeeded his father as King and carried out several political experiments and governmental changes. Politically, he was very ambitious and wanted to wield power personally. After accepting the resignation of MP Koirala on 2 March 1955, he announced on 14 April 1955 the establishment of a five-man Council of Royal Advisors, with Sardar Gunjman Singh as the Principal Royal Advisor. Less than a year later, on 26 January 1956, King Mahendra dissolved the advisory council and announced the formation of a new government consisting of four ministers from the Nepal Praja Parishad (NPP) party and three royalists and independents. The government was led by NPP leader Tanka Prasad Acharya as the Prime Minister. Archarya undermined the holding of elections for the Constituent Assembly that had been promised by King Tribhuvan[55] and even declared that such a body would divide royal authority by having 'two sovereigns in the country'. The forthcoming elections would thus only be for electing members of Parliament.

BP Koirala, President of the Nepali Congress, had initially expressed doubts about the legitimacy of a constitution that was not drafted by a constituent assembly, having the 'firm conviction' that 'people should have the choice to decide a political system, which they like to adopt'.[56] However, the growing political rivalry between political parties and increasing Indian interference in public issues compelled Koirala to compromise with the King.[57] Soon he drastically changed his position and claimed that a Constituent Assembly would be 'highly unnecessary'.[58] On 16 March 1958, the King appointed a five-member Constitution Drafting Commission, with Bhagwati Prasad Singh – who later became Chief Justice of Nepal – as chairman; the long-promised election for a constituent assembly evaporated. On 15 May 1958, King Mahendra formed a six-member cabinet without a Prime Minister and gave it the task of holding general elections and helping the framing of a new constitution.[59]

The Revolution of 1950–1951 had been a major step in setting Nepal on the road towards constitutional democracy, if not liberalism. However, the nascent ideals of democracy and of a plebiscitarian-style constituent assembly were thwarted by incessant bickering between the main political parties that did little to stabilise the political situation in the country in the post-Rana era. This led first to a reform-minded King Tribhuvan taking the reins of power and mediating between the key political leaders. Upon Tribhuvan's death, Mahendra, his politically-ambitious son, abandoned Tribhuvan's democratising vision and

[54] RK Dahal, *Constitutional and Political Developments in Nepal* (Kathmandu, Ratna Pustak Bhandar, 2001) 26–28 [hereinafter, 'Dahal, *Constitutional and Political Developments*'].

[55] Whelpton, *A History of Nepal*, (n 2) 91.

[56] Quoted in Bhandari, *Self-Determination*, (n 16) 39.

[57] Adhikari, 'Successive Constitutions' (n 27).

[58] ibid, 40.

[59] Dahal, *Constitutional and Political Developments*, (n 54) 29–32.

moved swiftly to centralise power, marginalise the political parties and establish the monarchy as the centre of power.

III. PROMULGATION OF THE FOUNDATIONAL 1959 CONSTITUTION

Just as the Interim Constitution of 1951 had been promulgated by the King in the exercise of his inherent plenary powers, so too was the 1959 Constitution.[60] The Constitution Drafting Committee was comprised of Bhagwati Prasad Singh (Chairman), Ramraj Pant, Surya Prasad Upadhyaya, Ranadhir Subba and Hora Prasad Joshi. The government sought the expertise of the renowned British constitutional expert Sir Ivor Jennings (1903–1965) to help draft the constitution.[61] Jennings had in fact been approached by the British Foreign Office as early as May 1956 'with a proposal from the Nepali prime minister and minister for education to set up a new residential university in Nepal and assist in the drafting of a new constitution'.[62] Jennings responded to the Foreign Office with two option on constitution-making: 'settling a constitutional draft with the Government', which would take only a few months, or 'getting a draft through a Constituent Assembly', which would 'take much longer'.[63] In any case, Jennings informed the Foreign Office that he would not be available until mid-1958 for the job and instead recommended Sir Robert Drayton QC.[64] However, in December 1957, the Foreign Office contacted Jennings again, urging him to accept King Mahendra's invitation to visit Nepal. On 19 January 1958, Jennings accepted the instructions from the Foreign Office. King Mahendra was thus able to issue a Royal Proclamation on 1 February 1958 outlining the road-map for Nepal's constitution-making process and naming the five-member drafting committee.[65]

Jennings worked with the members of the Constitution Drafting Commission and the King to evolve a draft during his short stay in Kathmandu, which lasted from 28 March to 24 April 1958.[66] From Jennings' accounts of his work in Nepal, he was the principal draftsman, although he received a 'parallel draft' from the Commission's secretary, Hora Prasa Joshi. Jennings was unimpressed

[60] Dhungel, *Commentary* (n 24) 22–29.

[61] R Dhungel *Pandhra salko sambidhan masyaudaka gopya patraharuko khulasa* [*Exposure of Confidential Letters Regarding the 1959 Constitution*] (Kathmandu, Human Rights Organization of Nepal, 2011). See also, M Malagodi, 'Constitution Drafting as Cold War Realpolitik: Sir Ivor Jennings and Nepal's 1959 Constitution' in H Kumarasingham (ed), *Constitution-making in Asia: Decolonisation and State-Building in the Aftermath of the British Empire* (London, Routledge, 2016) 154–172 [hereinafter 'Malagodi, 'Constitution Drafting'].

[62] Malagodi, 'Constitution Drafting', (n 61) 158.

[63] ibid.

[64] ibid.

[65] ibid, 159–160.

[66] Malagodi has detailed the work of Jennings in Kathmandu, ibid, 160–165.

by Joshi's draft, which he called a 'pathetic document' that was 'a collection of bits from other constitutions strung together amateurishly'.[67] Jennings met six times with members of the Drafting Commission to discuss his various drafts. He also met the Chairman of the Election Commission and the King himself. In all, Jennings produced three drafts, which he completed on 7 April, 15 April and 20 April, respectively.[68] Jennings submitted an 81-article draft for the Commission's consideration. Inputs were received from 15 political parties as well. The final draft was submitted again after discussions with these stakeholders. Jennings preferred a short and simple constitution and thought that 'the reality of life in Nepal should make it possible for a modified "Westminster model" easily to be transplanted'.[69] He noted that most provisions in the draft 'contained the more or less standard formula necessary to bring the Cabinet government into operation'.[70] The draft Constitution was first approved by the coalition cabinet of BP Koirala before being submitted to the King for promulgation. Jennings had left Kathmandu in late April 1958, but it was not until 12 February 1959, just a week before the scheduled inaugural general election, that the Constitution was finally brought into law by a royal promulgation.[71] Some substantive additions were made to Jennings' final draft, 'most likely by the king and his entourage, especially with regard to the ethnocultural elements of the document', since none of these elements were present in Jennings'.[72]

The 1959 Constitution entrenched and augmented features of the monarchical system that was first institutionalised in the interim Constitution by the Government of Nepal Act 1951. The lengthy preamble of the 1959 Constitution incorporated the 'historical nationalist narratives legitimising the wide powers of the king: the historical dynastic continuity of the Shah monarchy as the symbol of the unity of the nation, Hinduism, and the Nepali language'.[73] Article 1, the constitutional supremacy clause, declared the Constitution to be 'the fundamental law for Nepal' and that 'all laws inconsistent with it, shall, to the extent of the inconsistency … be void'. However, it further stipulated that nothing in the Constitution 'shall affect the law, customs and usage relating to the succession to the throne'. The Constitution could be amended by Parliament by a Bill passed by each house by not less than two-thirds of all of its members and assented to by the King, who had absolute discretion on whether or not to sign the Bill.[74]

Legislative power was vested in a bicameral legislature comprising of a Senate and a House of Representatives, but the King, as stated above, had the

[67] ICS/125/B/xiii/5/ii, cited in Malagodi, ibid, 162.
[68] Malagodi, ibid, 161–165.
[69] Dhungel, *Commentary* (n 24) 27.
[70] ibid.
[71] Malagodi, 'Constitution Drafting', (n 61) 164.
[72] ibid, 165.
[73] ibid.
[74] Constitution of the Kingdom of Nepal 1959, Art 53.

ultimate authority to withhold his assent to any Bill.[75] He could return the Bill to the House in which it originated for further consideration.[76] The King also had the discretion to exercise emergency powers if he was 'satisfied that a grave emergency exists whereby the security or economic life of Nepal, or any part thereof, is threatened by war or external aggression, or by internal disturbance'.[77] This allowed him, among other things, to assume all or any of the powers vested in or exercisable by Parliament or any other governmental body or authority.

Under the 1959 Constitution, executive power was vested in the King and could have been exercised by him personally or through ministers or officers subordinate to him.[78] The Cabinet was led by the Prime Minister and comprised ministers appointed by the King upon the recommendation of the Prime Minister. The Cabinet was charged with 'the general direction and control of the Government ... and shall be collectively responsible to the House of Representatives' – the lower House of Parliament.[79] In addition to the Cabinet, the Constitution provided for a Council of State comprising of the King, the President and Deputy President of the Senate, the Speaker and Deputy Speaker of the House of Representatives, Ministers of the Crown, persons who have previously held office as ministers and such other persons as the King may appoint.[80] The Council of State acted as an advisory body to the King and had no independent powers of its own. The King, however, was obliged to 'consult' the Council when exercising his discretion in the following matters: (a) declaring that the Prime Minister had ceased to hold office;[81] (b) exercising the functions of the Cabinet after suspending it;[82] (c) determining whether or not to withhold his assent to any Bill;[83] and (d) proclaiming a state of emergency.[84] Jennings explained that the Council of State – which he based on the old British Privy Council – was intended to serve as a buffer for the King against popular discontent. In relation to the Royal Assent, he stated:

> On the question of the King's discretionary power to refuse Royal Assent, I carried the draft by pointing out that it would be difficult [for the King] to refuse unless he had the Council of State with him. Kings, like politicians, have to keep their popularity.[85]

The Constitution guaranteed the rights to life and personal liberty, equality, religion, property and political freedoms.[86] The right to file a petition in the

[75] Article 42, ibid.
[76] ibid.
[77] Constitution of the Kingdom of Nepal 1959, Art 55.
[78] Article 10(1), ibid.
[79] Article 10(2), ibid.
[80] Article 11(1), ibid.
[81] Article 13(5(d), ibid.
[82] Article 17(1)(a), ibid.
[83] Article 42(2), ibid.
[84] Article 55(5), ibid.
[85] ICS 125/B/xiii/5/I, quoted in Malagodi, 'Constitution Drafting', (n 61) 163.
[86] Articles 3–9, Constitution of the Kingdom of Nepal 1959.

Supreme Court for appropriate proceedings for the enforcement of constitutional fundamental rights was also guaranteed. The Supreme Court enjoyed the power to issue directions, orders or writs, including writs in the nature of habeas corpus, *mandamus*, prohibition, *quo warranto* and *certiorari* for the enforcement of fundamental rights.[87] However, the laws made for the public good were to be protected from judicial review.[88] In other cases, without prejudice to any other remedy, a person who alleges that any law is void because of inconsistency with the Constitution may also move the Supreme Court, which may declare the law invalid and grant incidental remedies.[89]

The 1959 Constitution is a key foundational document for two main reasons. First, it institutionalised Nepal's post-Rana constitutional ethos that returned power to the monarch, who remained essentially unaccountable to the masses. Second, the people were provided with a nominally democratic Westminster-style parliamentary system with a bicameral legislature, which received legislative power for the first time.[90] Unfortunately, however, the transfer of power moved from one autocrat to another, rather than to the people. And, as we shall see below, this pattern of governance was to secure the primacy of the monarchy's role in national and constitutional politics for the next half century.

A week after the Constitution was promulgated, Nepal had its first-ever general election on 18 February 1959, when voters cast their ballots for representatives for the 109 seats in Parliament under a single-plurality system of voting. Of the approximately 4.47 million eligible voters, only about 1.8 million voters (44 per cent) cast their votes. The Nepali Congress, with 37.2 per cent of the votes, won 74 seats, while the Nepal Rashtrabadi Gorkha Parishad, with 17.1 per cent, won 19 seats. The fourth most popular party was the Nepal Communist Party, with 7.2 per cent of the votes and four seats.[91] BP Koirala, the leader of the Nepali Congress, was sworn in as Prime Minister on 27 May 1959.

IV. THE PANCHAYAT CONSTITUTION OF 1962: UNDOING THE FOUNDING?

Despite the fact that the Nepali Congress won an overwhelming majority of seats, the political situation in Nepal remained volatile both because of party

[87] Article 9, ibid.

[88] Article 8(2) provides: 'A law shall be deemed to be made for the public good within the meaning of sub-clause (b) of clause (1) if it is expressed in the preamble thereto to be made for the maintenance of law and order within Nepal, maintenance of security of Nepal, good relations between Nepal and other countries, good relations among different classes or sections of the people, or between the people, or between the people of different areas, or generally good manners, health, comfort or convenience or decency or morality and economic welfare or the citizens of Nepal, or to prevent internal disturbance or any attempt to subvert this Constitution or any law in force for the time being or any other like attempt or for the prevention of contempt of court or House of Parliament.'

[89] Article 54, Constitution of the Kingdom of Nepal 1959.

[90] This point was also made by Malagodi, 'Constitution Drafting', (n 61) 165.

[91] Whelpton, *A History of Nepal*, (n 2) 96.

infighting and opposition from the communists and other political parties. Things came to a head in October 1960 after King Mahendra returned to Kathmandu after a world tour. The King was greeted by open clashes between members of Congress and the Gorkhar Parisad and disgruntled refugees from the Nuwakot region. Citing the fall of the law and order, corruption, and 'encouragement of anti-national elements', King Mahendra removed the Koirala Government on 15 December 1960, suspended the 1959 Constitution, and declared a state of emergency. Whelpton has suggested that the political instability was more of an occasion rather than the cause for the King's action:

> Concern over public order was in fact probably a pretext rather than a principal motivation for Mahendra … [who] had really hoped to retain effective control of the government all along and had probably agreed to the 1959 elections only because he believed that they would lead to a hung parliament which he could easily manipulate. Faced with Congress majority in parliament and a strong-willed prime minister, he hoped initially to use the Grokha Parisahd and party dissidents to unseat the government and, when it was clear this would not happen, he finally used his emergency powers and control of the army to arrest BP Koirala and his colleagues at a public meeting on 15 December.[92]

The dissolution of the elected government was, for all intents and purposes, a royal coup. King Mahendra could not legally become active in politics once more and wield the reins of power. Following the repeal of the 1959 Constitution, the King promulgated a new constitution, called the Panchayat Constitution, on 16 December 1962, and this Constitution consolidated power in the King's hand instead of opening the space for democracy and accountability.[93] This Constitution was drafted by a six-member Committee chaired by Finance Minister Rishikesh Shah. The drafting committee included Attorney-General Shambhu Prasad Gyanwali, Chief Judge of the Tax Court Prakash Bahadur Khatri, Principal of Padma Kanya Campus Angur Baba Joshi, Danbar Narayan Yadav and Kul Shekhar Sharma.[94]

Ditching the parliamentary democracy adopted by the 1959 Constitution, this 'partyless' Royal Constitution built on the so-called traditional panchayat system (grassroots self-government institutions),[95] banned all political parties and reduced the fundamental rights and political freedoms to a bare minimum. Interestingly, the country was declared a monarchical Hindu kingdom.[96] There was an illusory separation, if at all, of the powers of the three state organs. The legislature was without organised political opposition. The power was basically concentrated in the hands of the King.[97] A new system of indirect

[92] ibid, 98.

[93] Constitution of Nepal 1962.

[94] Bhandari, *Self-Determination*, (n 16) 215.

[95] See UN Sinha, *Developments of Panchayats in Nepal* (Aligarh, PC Dwadash Shreni & Co, 1972).

[96] Article 3(1), Constitution of Nepal 1962.

[97] Dhungel, *Commentary*, (n 24) 30–35.

election was ordained to sustain 'guided democracy', which seemingly borrowed from Pakistan's 'controlled' or 'basic democracy' in the 1960s or Indonesia's 'guided democracy'. The King clarified his intentions even further by stating at the time of the first amendment to the Panchayat Constitution that democracy was 'possible only through the "partyless" democratic panchayat system rooted in the life of the people in general, and in keeping with the national genius and tradition, as originating from the very base with the active cooperation of the whole people, and embodying the principles of decentralization'.[98]

The King's involvement in each branch of government meant, therefore, that there was no system of checks and balances of any kind between the three branches of government, and the concept of a separation of power was in effect meaningless.[99] Some constitutional functionaries were also created like the Auditor General,[100] a Public Service Commission,[101] an Election Commission[102] and an Attorney-General.[103] Later, the Second Amendment to the Constitution introduced a Commission for the Prevention of Abuse of Authority, an anti-graft body.[104] Again, an enabling environment for them to perform as independent institutions was lacking.

The 1962 Constitution provided for some 'guaranteed' fundamental rights,[105] but it maintained that laws could be made for the sake of the public good to regulate or control the exercise of these fundamental rights. Additionally, it was provided that if the preamble of any Act stated that it had 'been made for [the public good], such Act, as well as any rule, order or by-laws made under such Act and having the force of law, shall be deemed to be a law made for the public good'.[106] The third amendment to this Constitution in particular internalised the single plurality electoral system and partially recognised the ministerial responsibility to the unicameral legislature. The 1962 Constitution nevertheless remained an authoritarian and royal Constitution with the King as the sole source of authority and power to amend or even suspend the Constitution invoking an emergency situation. Although extremely unpopular, the 1962 Constitution, with its three amendments, was enforced for 28 long years.

[98] ibid, 30.

[99] Article 20(2) of the Panchayat Constitution states: 'The sovereignty of Nepal is vested in His Majesty and all powers – executive, legislative and judicial emanate from him. These powers are exercised by His Majesty through the organs established by or under this Constitution and other laws for the time being in force keeping in view the interest and wishes of His Majesty's subjects according to the highest traditions of the Shah dynasty.'

[100] Articles 75–76, Constitution of Nepal 1962.

[101] Article 77–78, ibid.

[102] Articles 78A–78B, ibid.

[103] Articles 79–80, ibid.

[104] Articles 67C, 67D, and 67E, ibid.

[105] Constitution of Nepal 1962, Part III.

[106] Article 17, ibid.

Unrest and demonstrations erupted sporadically throughout the period of the Panchayat Constitution. In May 1979, as a background to the third amendment to the Constitution, King Birendra (1945–2001), who succeeded King Mahendra on his death in January 1972, announced a nationwide referendum that would determine the future form of government.[107] The question of the referendum was whether to continue with the panchayat system (with certain prospective reforms) or to install a multi-party system. The majority voted to retain the panchayat system. Following this, the King formed a Constitution Reforms Commission, chaired by the Acting Chief Justice of the Supreme Court and comprising eleven members. Subsequently, the King decreed three constitutional amendments to provide for the following: (a) direct elections for the national legislature to be held every five years (with 112 elected seats and 28 seats to be filled through the King's personal nomination); (b) election of the Prime Minister by the National Panchayat; and (c) the appointment of a Cabinet accountable to the national legislature by the King on the Prime Minister's recommendation.[108] The pro-royal outcome of this referendum did little to quell opposition to the Panchayat system, and ultimately, inevitably, it failed. The Panchayat Constitution would be enforced only up to early 1990, when the pro-democracy movement called for the restoration of democracy, political freedoms and a multiparty system.[109]

V. THE 1990 CONSTITUTION: RESTORING THE 1959 FOUNDINGS?[110]

King Birendra withdrew the Panchayat Constitution following what is described as the Mass Movement I,[111] which was launched on 8 February 1990 and called off on 9 April 1990. The Movement was initiated by the Nepali Congress and the United Left Front and was supported by many others. Besides political grounds, 'local discontent caused by the Indian trade embargo [against Nepal] coincided

[107] The King said that for the purpose '[of] clearly ascertaining what type of changes our countrymen desire in the context of the situation prevailing in the country today, and taking appropriate steps thereafter we hereby proclaim that arrangements will be made to hold a referendum by secret ballot of the entire Nepali people throughout the Kingdom of Nepal on the basis of adult franchise. Such a national referendum will be held on two basic questions: should the existing Panchayat system be retained and gradually reformed; or should it be replaced by a multiparty system of government.' See the 24 May 1979 issue of *The Rising Nepal*. Quoted in Dhungel, *Commentary*, (n 24) 33–34.

[108] See DP Kumar, *Nepal: Year of Decision* (New Delhi, Vikas Publishing House, 1980), dealing with the referendum and its aftermath.

[109] W Raeper and M Hoftun, *Spring Awakening: An Account of the 1990 Revolution in Nepal* (New Delhi, Penguin Books, 1994).

[110] See generally, M Hutt, 'Drafting the Nepal Constitution, 1990' (1991) 31(11) *Asian Survey* 1020–1039; M Malagodi, 'Constitutional Developments in a Himalayan Kingdom: The Experience of Nepal' in S Khilnani, V Raghavan and A Thiruvengadam (eds), *Comparative Constitutionalism in South Asia* (Oxford, Oxford University Press, 2012) 86–115, especially 98–110; and M Malagodi, *Constitutional Nationalism and Legal Exclusion: Equality, Identity Politics and Democracy in Nepal (1990–2007)* (New Delhi, Oxford University Press, 2013) ch 4.

[111] The Mass Movement II has been discussed later in the chapter.

with the international wind of democracy caused by the East European revolutions only a few months earlier'.[112] At the height of the Movement I, security forces shot dead several dozen unarmed demonstrators in the streets outside the Royal Palace on 6 April. Thereafter, the law and order situation deteriorated rapidly. Two days later, the embattled monarch lifted the 30-year-old ban on political parties and removed the term 'partyless' from the 1962 Constitution. Several provisions of the 1962 Constitution that affected democracy and human rights were suspended. Later, on the advice of Ganesh Man Singh, leader of the mass movement, the King invited KP Bhattarai of the Nepali Congress to become Prime Minister. Bhattarai formed a consensus government giving ministerial portfolios to the United Left Front as well as the King's nominees. The Cabinet was vested with all executive power as well as the power of the dissolved national legislature, thereby creating a very powerful interim government.[113]

This government forced the King to appoint a Constitution Recommendation Commission led by Supreme Court Justice Bishwanath Upadhyay. It comprised of experts and political representatives who were respected by the Mass Movement. The Commission was to rationalise constitutional monarchy with parliamentary democracy in Nepal, which required it to agree on the nature of the polity to be established and to constitutionalise that consensus as precisely as possible.[114] In drafting the 1990 Constitution, the Commission tried and built on the basic values established by the 1950–1951 revolution and the Government of Nepal Act 1951. They also counted on features of the 1959 Constitution.

Adopted on 9 November 1990 as an Act promulgated by the King 'with the consent of the Council of Ministers' that represented the first Mass Movement, this Constitution reduced the kingship to a constitutional monarchy,[115] declared the people as the sovereign source of authority and re-introduced the parliamentary system of government, adult franchise, multi-party politics, periodic elections and the independence of judiciary. It also established an elaborate scheme of entrenched fundamental rights and political freedoms, such as freedom of speech and the right to associate and form political parties, and announced the commitment to the rule of law.

The preamble of the 1990 Constitution was very different from that of its predecessors.[116] For the first time in Nepal's history, it explicitly stated that 'the source of sovereign authority of the independent and sovereign Nepal is inherent in the people', and 'in keeping with the desire of the Nepalese people expressed through the recent people's movement to bring about constitutional changes, we are further inspired by the objective of securing to the Nepalese

[112] M Hofton, 'The Dynamics and Chronology of the 1990 Revolution' in M Hutt (ed), *Nepal in the Nineties: Versions of the Past, Visions of the Future* (New Delhi, Oxford University Press, 1994) 14–27, 20.

[113] Dhungel, *Commentary*, (n 24) 35–37.

[114] ibid.

[115] The term 'constitutional monarchy' was included in the preamble.

[116] Dhungel, *Commentary*, (n 24) 35–36.

people social, political and economic justice long into the future'. In promulgating the Constitution, the King hoped that, 'keeping in view the desire of the people', 'the State authority and sovereign powers shall, after the commencement of this Constitution, be exercised in accordance with the provisions of this Constitution'. The core paragraph of the Preamble states:

> Whereas, it is expedient to promulgate and enforce this Constitution, made with the widest possible participation of the Nepalese people, to guarantee basic human rights to every citizen of Nepal; and also to consolidate Adult Franchise, the Parliamentary System of Government, Constitutional Monarchy and the System of Multi-Party Democracy by promoting amongst the people of Nepal the spirit of fraternity and the bond of unity on the basis of liberty and equality; and also to establish an independent and competent system of justice with a view to transforming the concept of the Rule of Law into a living reality.[117]

The 1990 Constitution encouragingly declared Nepal to be a multi-ethnic, multilingual, democratic, independent, and indivisible sovereign entity that would be a Hindu and constitutional monarchical kingdom.[118] Recognition of such an ethnic diversity was demanded by many indigenous and minority communities during the constitution-making process. While all mother tongue languages were recognised as languages of the nation, Nepali became the national and official language.[119] This has been a unique case of constitutional accommodation of linguistic pluralism. While announcing Nepal to be a Hindu state, the Constitution at the same time guaranteed religious and cultural freedoms to other religious groups.[120] It guaranteed the right to promote and preserve one's language, script and culture as well as the rights to education in the mother tongue and manage and protect religious places.[121]

The 1990 Constitution entrenched certain basic human rights,[122] and innovatively guaranteed the right of access to information of public importance[123] and the right to privacy regarding one's personal affairs.[124] Additionally, forced labour, child labour, human trafficking for slavery, and serfdom were all prohibited.[125] The 1990 Constitution also promised to transform the concept of the rule of law through the establishment of an independent and competent justice system.[126]

[117] Constitution of the Kingdom of Nepal 1990, Preamble (para 3).
[118] Article 3, ibid.
[119] Article 6, ibid.
[120] Article 19, ibid.
[121] Article 18, ibid.
[122] See Part 3, ibid (dealing with fundamental rights).
[123] Article 16, ibid (dealing with the right to information).
[124] Article 22, ibid (dealing with the right to privacy).
[125] Article 20, ibid (dealing with the right against exploitation).
[126] See Pt 11, dealing with the judiciary. Article 84 clearly stated that '[p]owers relating to Justice in the Kingdom of Nepal shall be exercised by courts and other judicial institutions in accordance with the provisions of this Constitution, the laws and the recognized principles of justice'.

The 1990 Constitution recognised the people's aspirations for social, political and economic justice.[127] It sought to promote the principles of an open society and to transform Nepal's economy into an independent and self-reliant one through the equal distribution of economic gains. To further this objective of social justice, several directive principles in reference to matters of political, economic and social development and foreign policy (such as the policy of international relations that enhances the nation's dignity and independence) were included.

Importantly, the 1990 Constitution emphasised the provision of favourable conditions for the enjoyment of the principles of democracy by maximising the people's participation in governance.[128] It legalised and legitimised all registered political organisations or parties.[129] At the same time, it was provided that parties that are established 'on the basis of religion, community, caste, tribe or region' would not be registered.[130] Promoting the notion of inclusive governance, the Constitution provided that at least five per cent of the candidates of any party contesting elections in the House of Representatives must be women.[131] Additionally, political parties could be de-registered if they failed to secure at least three per cent of the total votes cast in the previous general election.[132]

The Constitution could be amended or repealed by a two-thirds majority in both Houses of Parliament,[133] provided the proposed amendment did not contradict the spirit of the Constitution's preamble.[134] This is a plausible but ambiguous amendment rule, since it was unclear what the 'spirit' of the preamble was. This Constitution, however, is critiqued for not meeting the demands for secularism, the rights of indigenous people and minorities and other social, economic, and cultural rights. On this, Dennis writes:

> While proclaiming a return to democracy and asserting as a first principle that all Nepali citizens are equal, the 1990 constitution retained many features of earlier Nepali constitutions that validated a system of social and legal exclusions on the basis of gender, ethnicity, caste, and language. The tension between these constitutional principles, combined with a rising tide of ethnic identity politics throughout the 1990s, contributed to the following two decades of political instability, Maoist insurgency, and royal autocratic takeovers that finally culminated, in 2008, with the expulsion of the last king of Nepal.[135]

[127] Preamble (para 2), ibid.

[128] See Pt IV, ibid (dealing with Directive Principles and Policies of the State).

[129] See Pt 17, dealing with political organisations. Additionally, the establishment of a one-party system was deemed unconstitutional.

[130] Article 112(3).

[131] Article 114.

[132] Article 113(1)(d).

[133] Article 116.

[134] Article 116(1) states: 'A Bill to amend or repeal any Article of this Constitution, without prejudicing the spirit of the Preamble of this Constitution, may be introduced in either House of Parliament: Provided that this Article shall not be subject to amendment.'

[135] DK Dennis, 'Review of Constitutional Nationalism and Legal Exclusion: Equality, Identity Politics, and Democracy in Nepal' by M Malagodi (2014) 34(1) *Himalaya* 34.

Certain articles in the 1990 Constitution can also be said to be discriminatory against women. Those provisions pertained to the areas of citizenship, inheritance, penal laws, marriage and divorce and rape, among other issues.[136] Previous laws that discriminated against marginalised groups remained in force even after the 1990 Constitution. On the other hand, politics seemed to disregard the constitutional directive to adopt policies for the social and economic benefit of marginalised communities[137] or to enact new laws in view of the constitutional deletion of 'untouchability', or racial discrimination or race-based social exclusion.[138] Informal institutions like patronage and nepotism were also argued to have contributed to the exclusion of minorities in governance, in addition to the dominance of certain castes and gender.[139]

The 1990 Constitution provided a free political environment to the critics of the system to expose the fallacies of Nepal's nation-building process and its weaknesses in addressing them. Though not popularly made, this Constitution nevertheless incorporated some democratic principles and built on the positive values of the two founding constitutions of 1951 and 1959.

VI. THE MAOIST ARMED REBELLION

On the sixth year of the restoration of democracy, a Maoist armed insurrection broke out.[140] The Maoists, organised as the Communist Party of Nepal (CPN-Maoist), challenged the 1990 Constitution and its democratic system, stating that the parliamentary system of government could not fulfil the expectation of the people and that a 'people's democracy' of the Maoist model was the only solution.[141] A civil war broke out on 13 February 1996, with the CPN vowing to overthrow the monarchy and establish a people's republic. On 13 February 1996, the Maoists carried out seven attacks in six districts, marking the beginning of the armed conflict. Throughout what they named the 'people's war', teachings of the Maoist brand of communism was spread throughout the countryside. While the Maoists were prevalent in rural Nepal, the government more or less maintained control of urban areas. Hopes for an end to conflict came with a

[136] M Lawoti, 'Exclusionary Democratization in Nepal, 1990–2002' (2008) 15(2) *Democratisation* 363–385, 377.

[137] ibid, 371.

[138] ibid.

[139] ibid, 377.

[140] See D Thapa and B Sijapati, *A Kingdom under Siege: Nepal's Maoist Insurgency, 1996 to 2004* (London, Zed Books, 2005).

[141] RS Mahat, *Trials, Tremors and Hope: The Political Economy of Contemporary Nepal* (New Delhi, Adroit Publishers, 2020) 50–52 (dealing with enabling conditions and Maoist tactics). Ideals such as these socio-political issues and the overall developmental scenario have generally remained bleak in Nepal. See R Bajracharya, P Najracharya and MD Manadhar, *Nepal's Economy in Disarray: The Policies and Politics of Development* (New Delhi, Adroit Publishers, 2019).

declaration of a ceasefire on 25 July 2001, but the talks broke down and fighting resumed.

As the Maoist rebels refused to recognise the constitutional monarchy, the government began banning anti-monarchy statements. Journalists were jailed and publications were shut down. During subsequent rounds of peace talks, ceasefires and the resumed conflict, the government constantly rejected the insurgents' call for an election to establish a constituent assembly. In November 2004, the government rejected the Maoist call for a direct negotiation with King Gyanendra (instead of the Prime Minister) and a third party (eg the United Nations) facilitation of the peace talks.

On 1 February 2005, seeing how the semi-democratic government failed to restore order, King Gyanendra (b 1947) – who succeeded his brother King Birendra and his nephew King Dipendra after they died during the royal massacre of 1 June 2001 – assumed full control of Nepal. The new King proclaimed that democracy and progress were in conflict with each other. Following his declaration, the UK and India suspended their economic support to Nepal. On 5 May 2005, seven political parties formed the Seven Party Alliance (SPA). On 22 November 2005, with the support of the Indian Government, the SPA and the Maoists issued a joint 12-point resolution.[142] Among other things, they blamed the autocratic monarchy as the biggest stumbling block to Nepal's path to democracy, peace and prosperity. The SPA committed to hold elections for a constituent assembly and for Maoists to renounce violence altogether. The issue of restoring democracy was once again on the forefront.

By 2006, violence had subsided considerably, and pro-democracy demonstrations dominated the public space. On 21 April, King Gyanendra proposed the return of a Prime Minister-led system, but this was rejected by both the SPA and Maoist rebels. Then on 24 April, the King proposed reinstating the House of Representatives. This was accepted by the SPA but rejected by the Maoists. Then, on 2 June in Kathmandu, the largest pro-democracy demonstration was organised by the Maoists and was attended by about 200,000 people. Finally, on 9 August, both the government and the Maoists agreed that the United Nations would monitor the peace process and manage arms of both sides. This led to the signing of the Comprehensive Peace Accord that ended the Civil War and provided for an Interim Constitution as well as a promise of an elected Constituent Assembly to draft a new Constitution for Nepal.[143]

[142] See PP Khatiwada, *The Nepalese Peace Process: Faster Changes, Slower Progress* (Berlin, Berghof Foundation, 2014) 7.

[143] Interim Constitution of Nepal 2063 (2007) (English version), available at http://constitutionnet.org/sites/default/files/interim_constitution_of_nepal_2007_as_amended_by_first_second_and_third_amendments.pdf.

VII. CONSTITUTION-MAKING BY THE PEOPLE AT LAST?

A. The Interim Constitution 2007

Mass Movement II, which was launched in 2006 in the wake of King Gyanendra's exercise of authoritarian power in the name of combating the Maoist rebels, proved catalytic in bringing the decade-long Maoist insurgency to an end. This Movement not only brought the Maoists into the peace process, but it also ended Nepal's monarchy and helped the government organise the election for a constituent assembly in April 2008. The 2007 Interim Constitution was drafted by a team led by Supreme Court Judge Laxman Aryal[144] in the most unpropitious circumstances amidst heightened identity consciousness and politics based on caste, creed and ethnicity.[145] It was discussed in and adopted by the House of Representatives. Its preamble expressed a determination towards 'progressive restructuring of the state in order to resolve the existing problems of the country relating to class, caste, region and gender'. It also expressed 'full commitment to democratic norms and values including a system of competitive multiparty democratic rule, civil liberties, fundamental rights, human rights, adult franchise, periodic elections, full freedom of the press, independence of the judiciary and concepts of the rule of law'.[146] Its purpose was to guarantee the basic rights of the Nepali people to frame a constitution for themselves and to participate in the free and impartial election of the Constituent Assembly in a fear-free environment. The Preamble was later amended to declare Nepal a federal democratic Republic and to abolish the ruling/absolute monarchy. The Interim Constitution, although not adopted by the Constituent Assembly, was important from the viewpoint of democratic constitution-making, because all other previous constitutions were promulgated by the King acting on his own or, at best, on the recommendation of the Council of Ministers.[147]

B. Constituent Assembly I

The 2007 Interim Constitution created the basis for the election to the first Constituent Assembly of Nepal, a unicameral body of 601 members that served from 28 May 2008 to 28 May 2012. Of the Assembly, 240 members were elected in single seat constituencies, 335 through proportional representation, and the

[144] The Interim Constitution Drafting Committee comprised Justice Laxman Prasad Aryal (Coordinator) and Harihar Dhal, Sindhunath Pyakural, Sambhu Thapa, Mahadev Yadav, and Khimlal Devkota, all lawyers.

[145] Bhandari, *Self-Determination*, (n 16) 53–73.

[146] Preamble, para 4.

[147] Bhandari, *Self-Determination*, (n 16) 12–15.

remaining 26 were from reserved nominated seats. It was the most inclusive house, in terms of language, religion, culture, ethnicity, caste and region, to ever be elected in Nepal's history. In the election, the CPN won half the constituency seats and about 30 per cent of the proportional representation seats and emerged as the largest party in the Assembly. The rest of the seats were split between the traditional parliamentary parties. At the first meeting of the Constituent Assembly in 2008, the Assembly decided to dismantle the monarchy and adopt republicanism for Nepal. The Assembly also worked as the interim legislature, exercising control on the parliamentary government and public purse. The constitution-making process that began was not only comprehensive, but also participatory, at least in principle.

Efforts were made to involve the common people in the constitution-drafting process, with Assembly members conducting field visits and reaching out to the people through the use of media, public debates and consultation, questionnaires, written submissions, and electronic communication. International experts and civil society groups were also involved in discussions with the Assembly members. However, the Assembly failed to deliver a constitution despite multiple extensions to its initial two-year term, largely due to political differences on ideological, socio-political, ethnic and geo-political issues.[148] The political parties' views differed vastly on a multitude of issues, including the form of government, federalisation of the state and ethnic empowerment.[149] There were contradictory positions, dissenting opinions and gaps and overlaps in the preliminary drafts.[150] The environment was unbearably ethnicised.[151] Despite efforts to resolve these problems, the political leaders failed to reach a compromise on all contentious issues. As Malagodi observed, the life of the Constituent Assembly 'was marred by political instability from its inception' largely because of major disagreements between the majority CPN leaders and the leaders of the other political parties, especially the Nepali Congress that was 'mostly concentrated on political power play for government posts and on the arm integration process' and 'did not give the constitution-making process [its] personal time or priority'.[152]

[148] See B Adhikari, *Nepal Constituent Assembly Impasse: Comments on a Failed Process* (Kathmandu, Nepal Consulting Lawyers Inc, 2012) 33–98 [hereinafter 'Adhikari *Nepal Constituent Assembly*'].

[149] See, eg, M Bishwakarma, 'Federalism in Nepal: Identity Politics and Pragmatic with Dalit Community' (2012) 14(13) *Participation: A Nepalese Journal of Participatory Development* 1–124, 80–86 (for a discussion about the importance of unification among the Nepali Dalit community during the process of federalisation and constitution-building).

[150] See B Adhikari, *Constitutional Crisis in Nepal: Ensuring Democratic Governance During the Transition to a New Constituent Assembly* (Kathmandu, Nepal Consulting Lawyers Inc, 2013) (suggesting a framework for transition to resolve the constitutional crisis).

[151] See, eg, J Strasheim and S Bogati, *Nepal's Quest for Federalism: A Driver of New Violence* (Hamburg, GIGA Focus, 2016) 3.

[152] M Malagodi, 'Constituent Assembly Failure in Pakistan and Nepal' in J Elster et al (eds), *Constituent Assemblies* (Cambridge, Cambridge University Press, 2018) 79–108, 101–102.

C. Constituent Assembly II

In November 2011, the Constituent Assembly extended its term a third time, but this was greeted with a legal challenge by two lawyers. On 26 November 2011, the full bench of the Supreme Court ruled that it was a violation of Article 64 of the 2007 Interim Constitution and instructed the government to complete the drafting of the new constitution before the expiry of the six-month extension.[153] This could not be accomplished, and the Constituent Assembly was dissolved on 28 May 2012, leaving Nepal not only without a constitution-drafting body but also without a legislature. Elections for a new constituent assembly and legislature were scheduled for 22 November 2012 but postponed until the following year. On 24 March 2013, a new 'consensus government', comprising of ministers appointed by the political parties and headed by the Chief Justice Khil Raj Regmi, was established. Calling itself the Nepal Interim Election Council, this body – which violated all the rules of constitutional separation of powers – nonetheless governed Nepal until 19 November 2013, when the postponed elections were held.

The Nepali Congress emerged as the largest party, winning 196 of the 575 elected seats. The CPN established itself as the second largest party. The Maoists, charged for being uncompromising as far as ethnicity-based federalism was concerned, came third in the re-elected house. In the second Constituent Assembly, efforts were made to build on the foundations of the work of the Constituent Assembly I. This time, the political parties were more accommodating, and some compromises were made by the Maoists with the Congress and CPN. On 23 August 2015, a draft Constitution with a seven-province model was tabled in the Assembly for approval, but members representing the marginalised groups stormed out in protest. Street protests and communal violence broke out across the Terai lowland region in the south.[154] Eventually, however, the final version of the Constitution was adopted by the Constituent Assembly II on 16 September 2015 and promulgated by the President on 20 September 2015.

VIII. THE 2015 CONSTITUTION

The Constitution of Nepal 2015, which established a secular, democratic, and federal republican state, is a document of compromise between the Nepali Congress, the CPN, the UCPN (Maoist) and some fringe parties.[155] Being a document of compromise, it could not accommodate many of the more radical and

[153] *Adv Bhara Mani Jamgam & Adv Bal Krishna Neupane v Prime Minister and Cabinet Office et al*, Writ No 068-WS-0014, cited in Malagodi, ibid, 104.

[154] Malagodi, 'Constituent Assembly Failure' (n 152) 106.

[155] When put to split voting after the endorsement of individual articles and schedules, the Constitution Bill garnered support from 507 out of 598 members of the Constituent Assembly. As many as 25 Assembly members, however, cast their vote against the Bill. Altogether, 532 members cast their votes, while 65 others did not take part in the voting process. While the Rastriya Prajatantra

extreme views. The new Constitution had an improved form of parliamentary government,[156] a system of proportional inclusion of all indigenous and marginalised communities in the state governance[157] and a mixed single-plurality and proportional electoral system,[158] with proportional voting for 40 per cent of the members of the House of Representatives in the federal Parliament[159] and provincial assemblies.[160] Parties contesting the House of Representative elections must field a closed list of candidates that included women, *dalits*, indigenous peoples, Khas Arya, Madhesi, Tharu, Muslims and those from backward regions, all on the basis of population.[161] More specifically, 33 per cent of parliamentary and provincial assembly seats were reserved for women.[162]

The 2015 Constitution is liberal in its incorporation of socio-economic and cultural rights and the principle of secularism. The system of a unitary state has been abandoned in favour of a cooperative model of federalism. A novel three-tier system of federalism – a federation, seven provinces and 753 local governments – has been instituted, together with an articulated division of the state power and concurrent powers. The third tier comprises of local villages, municipalities and districts and is entitled to its own separate list of constitutional powers.[163]

The judiciary remains unchanged with a clear provision for the creation of a constitutional bench[164] and the pre-existing power of judicial review.[165] Progressive state policies are internalised in the Constitution through its directive principles,[166] which include policies relating to social and cultural

Party-Nepal, which is known for its advocacy of the restoration of the monarchy, voted against it, most of the Madhes-based parties boycotted the voting process. The CA Chairman Subas Chandra Nembang did not have to take part in the voting because there was no tie to break. See, *The Himalayan Times* (2015), 'Constituent Assembly endorses Nepal's Constitution 2072 with two-thirds majority, to promulgate on Sunday,' available at https://thehimalayantimes.com/kathmandu/constituent-assembly-endorses-constitution-bill/.

[156] Two important improvements over the Nepali traditions, and aimed at stability, are: (1) a motion of no confidence cannot be tabled until the first two years after the appointment of the Prime Minister and until another one year after the date of failure of the motion of no confidence once tabled; and (2) a motion of no confidence to be tabled under shall also indicate the name of a member proposed for the Prime Minister. See Art 100.

[157] Article 42(1) guarantees that the 'economically, socially, or educationally backward women, Dalit, indigenous nationalities, Madhesi, Tharu, Muslims, backward classes, minorities, marginalized communities, persons with disabilities, gender and sexual minorities, farmers, labourers, oppressed or citizens of backward regions and indigent Khas Arya shall have the right to participate in the State bodies on the basis of the principle of proportional inclusion'.

[158] Article 84 (federal Parliament) and Art 176 (provincial assembly).

[159] Article 84(1)(b).

[160] Article 176(1)(b).

[161] ibid (see the proviso).

[162] Articles 176(9) and 176(9).

[163] See D Adhikari, *Nepal's Road to Federalism: From the Perspective of Grassroots Democracy* (Kathmandu, RTI International, 2020).

[164] Article 137.

[165] Article 133.

[166] Articles 49–55, dealing with 'Directive Principles, Policies and Obligations of the State.'

transformation,[167] social justice and inclusion[168] and the basic needs of citizens.[169] This Constitution is the first in South Asia to make socio-economic and cultural rights enforceable, subject of course to the condition of resource-availability and through statutes to be enacted under the Constitution. These changes are very important for the stability of politics in Nepal, as they address the issues of identity, diversity and inclusion.

During the making, and following the promulgation, of the Constitution, many critical issues were raised by various groups.[170] For example, some ethnic communities criticised the smaller percentage of parliamentary members to be elected by proportional representation compared to what was provided under the Interim Constitution (45 per cent versus 58 per cent, respectively).[171] Proportional representation allowed more members of marginalised communities to be elected into the Parliament. Similarly, members of the Tharu and Madhesi communities disputed the provincial boundaries established under the Constitution, arguing that it limited their political representation, since various Terai districts were merged with the Brahmin-Chettri-dominant hill districts.[172] Some groups, including the Rastriya Pranjatantra Party-Nepal, opposed the adoption of secular constitutional identity and wanted the restoration of constitutional monarchy. Some were fiercely against the federalisation of the country. Women rights activists also pointed out the added difficulty for single Nepali mothers to pass citizenship to their children, and for Nepali women who are married to foreign men to gain Nepali citizenship (a restriction that does not apply to their male counterparts).[173] In terms of public participation, research has shown that many Nepalis from marginalised groups, including indigenous and deprived populations in Nepal's far-western region, felt socially excluded from the process and were not even aware of the Constituent Assembly elections that promised representation of diverse sects of the country.[174]

IX. CONCLUSION

Nepal is experimenting with its seventh Constitution in just over 70 years. Unlike neighbouring India, where its 1950 Constitution remains the first and

[167] Article 51(c).

[168] Article 51(j).

[169] Article 51(h).

[170] See Adhikari, *Nepal Constituent Assembly* (n 148), shedding light on the creation and demise of the Constituent Assembly I due to irreconcilable positions and demands.

[171] Available at www.bbc.com/news/world-asia-34280015.

[172] Available at https://ijrcenter.org/2015/09/30/nepal-adopts-secular-constitution-amid-violence-and-deadly-protests/.

[173] Available at www.bbc.com/news/world-asia-34280015. See also, S Tamang, 'Exclusionary Process and Constitution Building in Nepal' (2011) 18 *International Journal on Minority and Group Rights* 293–308.

[174] D Khadka et al, 'Knowledge and Perception among Indigenous, Marginalized and Deprived People of Far Western Region about the Constitution of Nepal' (2018) 6(3) *Asian Research Journal of Arts & Social Sciences* 1–5.

the only constitution to have governed the country, Nepal's constitutional journey has been a long and arduous one. Thus, one would be hard put to pinpoint a founding moment or a foundational constitution in Nepal. Based on the discussion above, the development of Nepali constitutionalism may be divided into three broad periods or movements, starting with the Revolution 1950–1951.

The first period dates from 1950 to 1961 when the revolt against the Ranas signalled a shift away from traditional absolute autocratic rule. It is always tempting to ask the counter-factual 'what if' question. In this case: 'What if the reform-minded King Tribhuvan had not died prematurely in 1955? Would Nepal have progressed more quickly towards instituting a democratic constitutional order?' The ideals and aspirations of the 1950–1951 Revolution had certainly laid the first foundations for such an order, except that when King Mahendra took the throne, he did what he could to push back on reforms and arrogate powers to himself. The drafting of the 1959 Constitution, which as I argue had the second line of foundings, was the high-water mark of this period, but even this document, which conceded so much residual executive power to the monarch proved insufficient for the King, who suspended it in 1961. The struggle between the people and the aristocrats was over, and the locus of power shifted both in fact and in law to the King, and this was to establish Nepal's constitutional ethos and trajectory for the next 70 years.[175]

The second period runs from 1962, when the Panchayat Constitution came into force, up until 1990 when a new constitution was promulgated. During this period, the royal family consolidated its hold on power and ruled autocratically, just as the Ranas had done before. It was only with Mass Movement I that King Birendra relented and agreed to cut back on most of his powers through the 1990 Constitution. The compromises attained through the 1990 document allowed the democratic system to continue dominating the Nepalese state and society for another 25 years, until the Maoist rebellion broke out.

And this takes us to the third period, which begins broadly with the eclipse of royal power following Mass Movement II and the promulgation of the Interim Constitution of 2007 – laying the foundation for relinquishing monarchy – and leading right up to the promulgation of the 2015 Constitution. This period signals a clear revolutionary break from the past, with the abolition of the monarchy and two genuine attempts at forging a national consensus between the country's disparate groups and regions. From the viewpoint of constitutional theory and history, this must be considered the most important of the three epochs we have been discussing.

As we have seen, the Interim Constitution of 2007 added new dimensions to the smouldering embers of 1959 – secularism, political inclusion and

[175] See M Malagodi, 'The Locus of Sovereign Authority in Nepal' in M Tushnet and M Khosla (eds), *Unstable Constitutionalism: Law and Politics is South Asia* (Cambridge, Cambridge University Press, 2015) 45–85.

non-discrimination and emphasising the need for 'the progressive restructuring of the state in order to resolve the existing problems of the country relating to class, caste, region and gender'.[176] It also declared Nepal to be a secular state, while also guaranteeing economic, social, and cultural rights as conditionally enforceable rights. The 2015 Constitution builds on these values[177] and offers the Nepali people the promise of a constitutional system that might actually work. In this sense, the 2015 Constitution is both revolutionary and foundational.[178]

[176] Interim Constitution of Nepal 2007, Preamble.

[177] For the analysis of the 2015 Constitution, see SK Bhattarai, *Samvaidhanik tatha Prashashanik Kanoon: Samvaidhanik siddhanta, Nyayik Dristikon ra Samvaidhanik Abhilekhharu* [Constitutional and Administrative Law: Constitutional Theory, Judicial point of View and Constitutional Records] (Kathmandu, Sopan Masik, 2019).

[178] This can be compared to the characterisation of Pakistan's 1973 Constitution as a foundational document. See S Khan, 'What's in a Founding? Founding Moments and Pakistan's "Permanent Constitution" of 1973' in R Albert, M Guruswamy and N Basnyat (eds), *Founding Moments in Constitutionalism* (Oxford, Hart Publishing, 2019).

7

Making Bhutan's Constitution: Institutionalising a 'Traditional' Monarchy

WINNIE BOTHE

INTRODUCTION

THE DRAFTING AND enactment of Bhutan's founding Constitution in 2008 is often celebrated as a liberal triumph. It was widely conceived as the foundation of a participatory social order based on the principles of equity, freedom of expression and equal access to participate in the political process. However, a closer look at the process of its creation and of its immediate legacy raises deeper questions as to the nature of this triumph. I argue that although significant changes have taken place, it provides for neither democratic institutions nor respect for those deemed less worthy as citizens in Bhutanese society, especially the farmers and non-Buddhists. A study of the constitutional debates and how they were conducted will demonstrate how, in addition to popularising the Constitution, they serve as a stage to constitutionalise the state in the image of the King. Thus, instead of it being a venue for critical debates, it served as a platform for the praising of the governors. The constitutional process thus represents a missed opportunity to increase local political engagement in deciding important issues for Bhutan's future. Instead, it reproduced and reinforced the position of the locals as supplicants of the state. A study of Bhutan's constitutional founding requires us to understand legal change from the wider perspective of the enduring legacy of Bhutan's monarchy and the cultural basis for this.

This points towards how social change needs to be understood from a larger platform than that which a contractual understanding of sovereignty offers. Rather, of equal, or even greater importance is understanding the events from a cultural perspective of sovereignty. In effect, the Bhutanese case can best be understood by the famous quote by Giuseppe Tomasi di Lampedusa in his novel,

The Leopard, which describes the Italian move to constitutionalism: 'If we want things to stay as they are, things will have to change.'[1]

The following analysis begins by considering the process of state formation as respectively a political process of creating participants and a cultural process of creating nationals, and proceeds to discuss its consequences for how citizenship is perceived and constructed.

I. HISTORICAL TRAJECTORIES OF THE BHUTANESE CONSTITUTION[2]

The Bhutanese state was established by monastic rulers who fled to Bhutan from local conflicts, most famously Ngawang Namgyal (1594–1651), and the Zhabdrung Rinpoche,[3] who was a high prince abbot from the important Ranglung monastery. Parallel with the reunification of Tibet under the fifth Dalai Lama, Ngawang Lobsang Gyatso (1617–1682),[4] the Drukpa Karguypa lineage[5] asserted a dominant position in Bhutan under the Zhabdrung's leadership in the seventeenth century. The Zhabdrung managed to fend off several Tibetan attacks and establish a religious Buddhist state in Bhutan based on feudal principles. Buddhism thus assumed a principal position in Bhutan's political and cultural landscape. The Zhabdrung established a dual system of government which divided administration into civil and religious divisions with the Je Khenpo heading the religious branch, and the Druk Desi heading the civil administrative branch. Drukpa lamas thus functioned as governors of religious, economic and temporal affairs and has done so since.[6] For 256 years, Bhutan was ruled by 57 successive Druk Desis until 1907 when the theocracy went into decline. In 1907, Ugyen Wangchuck (1862–1926) – with British backing – was elected hereditary ruler of Bhutan and installed as the Druk Gyalpo (Dragon King). In 1910, King Ugyen signed the Treaty of Panakha with the British under which the British agreed not to interfere in Bhutan's internal affairs provided it accepted British advice on external relations.

[1] G Di Lampedusa, *The Leopard: A Novel*, Archibald Calhoun (trans) (New York, Pantheon, 2007).

[2] For this section, I have drawn heavily on my 'Gross National Happiness and Inequality' in J Dragsbaek Schmidt (ed), *Development Challenges in Bhutan: Perspectives on Inequality and Gross National Happiness* (New York, Springer, 2017) 49–68, 52–56. See also V Iyer, 'Constitution-Making in Bhutan: A Complex and Sui Generis Experience' (2019) 7(2) *Chinese Journal of Comparative Law* 359–385 [hereinafter, 'Iyer, 'Constitution-Making in Bhutan''].

[3] This title refers to the great lamas of Tibet but in Bhutan, this title invariably refers to Ngawang Ngamgyal, founder of the Bhutanese state. He was also known as 'The Bearded Lama'.

[4] LE Rose, *The Politics of Bhutan* (Ithaca, Cornell University Press, 1977) 26.

[5] The Drukpa refers to the 'Red Hat Sect' and is a branch of the Kagyu School of Tibetan Buddhism that was established in the 13th century.

[6] M Aris, *The Raven Crown: The Origins of Buddhist Monarchy in Bhutan* (London, Serindia, 1994) 18 & 53 [hereinafter 'Aris, *The Raven Crown*'].

As part of subsequent state-building efforts, the ruling Wangchucks invited large numbers of Nepalese immigrants – most of whom were Hindus – to cultivate the southern plains. They provided cheap labour for the development plans of the third Druk Gyalpo, King Jigme Dorji Wangchuk (1929–1972) in the 1960s.[7] Because the Nepalese were more exposed to ideas of modernity, they prioritised education and therefore gained an educational edge over the Buddhist segment. At the same time, they lagged behind the majority Buddhist population of Drukpa origin, in terms of political influence, access to development, exposure and education.[8]

Bhutan's precarious geostrategic position as one of the most sparsely populated regions located between the world's two most populous countries became evident when India annexed Sikkim in 1975 and Nepal became increasingly assertive. When a census in 1988 revealed that the Nepalese population might soon become the majority population in Bhutan, Bhutanese sovereignty and identity, as well as the supremacy of the Drukpa elite came under threat. Thereafter, differences between the Nepalese-origin Bhutanese (known as Lhotshampas) and the Drukpas – including their cultural/religious differences – became the main source of conflict.[9]

To defend Bhutan's sovereignty and maintain the status quo, the Drukpa elite adopted an essentialist strategy and started projecting Bhutan as a culturally unique nation-state even though the state was anything but homogenous. A militant version of this strategy made Buddhism the dominant ideology of the state.[10] As a result, the Nepalese population was 'othered' and increasingly identified as an internal threat. Central to these efforts was the promotion of *driglam namzha*, an official dress code, that served as a tool for educating 'the people' on how to dress and act 'as true Bhutanese'. The Hindu population, to whom this culture was even more alien than to the rural Buddhists, spearheaded a movement for the recognition of cultural rights and democracy and in the process ironically became the force of change that the Drukpa elite feared they would become,[11] with the first overt mass demonstrations for democracy and human rights in Bhutan's history.[12] Political upheavals in Nepal from 1989 onwards led to even greater politicisation amongst Bhutan's ethnic Nepali population, and thousands of people (Lhotshampas) from the southern districts left Bhutan for refugee camps in Eastern Nepal.

[7] AC Sinha, *Himalayan Kingdom Bhutan: Tradition, Transition and Transformation* (New Delhi, Indus Publishing, 2001) [hereinafter 'Sinha, *Himalayan Kingdom Bhutan*'].

[8] ibid.

[9] ibid.

[10] Aris, *The Raven Crown*, (n 6) 17–18.

[11] See Sinha, *Himalayan Kingdom Bhutan*, (n 7); and M Hutt, *Becoming Citizens: Culture, Nationhood and the Flight of Refugees from Bhutan* (Oxford, Oxford University Press, 2003).

[12] D Rizal, *The Semi-Authoritarian Democracy of Bhutan* (London, Lexington, 2015) 109 [hereinafter 'Rizal, *The Semi-Authoritarian Democracy*'].

In 1997, a small 'rebellion' broke out in the East. It was a rather subtle and uncoordinated protest that was met by a relatively harsh reaction by the state, perhaps in order to prevent a similar escalation which had previously taken place in Southern Bhutan. The protest seems to have originated in the Nyingmapa religious establishment, where lay monks and semi-divine figures initiated a protest against what they perceived as 'Drukpa attempts' at streamlining the Nyingmapa lineage to align with the Drukpa's. The Nyingmapa order thus challenged state attempts at influencing, and even coercing the Nyingmapa Buddhists to follow Drukpa Kargyupa practices, and government efforts at controlling the succession and visits of religious leaders. This included attempts to replace paintings of Guru Rinpoche – the founder of Buddhism in the region – with 'The Drukpa guru, the Zhabdrung' (Bhutan's founder). This was tantamount to swapping the worship of Buddhism with that of the state's founder. The conflict escalated with Easterners' demands to reinstate as spiritual leader, Jigme Ngawang Namgyal – they believed to be the reincarnation of the Zhabdrung – who was at the time living in exile in India.[13]

The danger of such demands needs to be understood against the ambivalent relationship between the Zhabdrung and the Wangchuck Monarchy. On the one hand, the monarchy had very efficiently appropriated the Zhabdrung as a symbol to legitimise monarchical power.[14] Further, the Zhabdrung's reincarnations were seen as a latent threat to the monarchy. It appears that the myth of the Zhabdrung is more valuable to the monarchy with him in his grave than when he inconveniently reincarnates from time to time. From its initially religious origins, the protests in the East developed into a more comprehensive movement against the undemocratic and exclusivist approach to governance, and the lack of development in Eastern Bhutan. The leader of this movement was Rongthong Kinley Dorji who later fled to India and established the Drukpa National Congress (DNC) while in exile and spearheaded demands for political reform, religious freedom and the return of the Zhabdrung's latest incarnation.[15]

The rebellion was effectively crushed in its infancy with a number of monks and political leaders exiled or imprisoned and students expelled from schools. Monasteries believed to be at the centre of the protests were closed.[16] Subsequent development activities continued in the East, but in Southern Bhutan, these were discontinued, partly due to the unrest in the region and partly due to animosity towards the Lhotshampas – Bhutanese of Nepalese descent – who came to be seen as disloyal traitors. A large number of well-educated Lhotshampas were also dismissed from public service.[17]

[13] ibid, 46.

[14] Aris, *The Raven Crown*, (n 6) 109.

[15] Rizal, *The Semi-Authoritarian Democracy*, (n 12) 109.

[16] See J Acharya, 'Bhutanese Refugees: The Struggle in Exile' in R Hofmann and U Caruso (eds), *Minority Rights in South Asia* (Frankfurt, Peter Lang, 2011) 23–46, 32.

[17] Sinha, *Himalayan Kingdom Bhutan*, (n 7).

It is tempting to ask what kind of constitution might have been written had the Constitution included the groups who rebelled against the monarchy in the late 1980s. Indeed, had one-sixth of the population not been driven into exile in Nepal, the process might well have been very different. But the prevailing culture was one of silence and fear and the resulting constitutional process would have little room for critical scrutiny and contestation. One might therefore expect to find a constitution devoid of democratic content, but that is not the case as the King genuinely sought to introduce an element of competition and rights into the Constitution. This is most clearly expressed by the fourth Druk, King Jigme Singye Wangchuk (b 1955), who initiated the constitution-making process when he presented the Constitution to the public in 2005:

> Bhutan, through good fortune and fate, could not hope for a better moment than now for this historical development and would never find another opportunity like this to introduce a Constitution that would provide a democratic system of government best suited for the future well-being of the nation. Today, the King, government, clergy and the people of all sections of society, enjoyed unprecedented level of trust and fidelity. The security of the country was ensured[,] and the people enjoyed peace and stability …. In many countries, constitutions were drafted during difficult times, under pressure from political influences and interests, but Bhutan was fortunate that the change came about without any pressure or compulsion.[18]

Even when King Jigme Singye abdicated in 2006, 'the people' were too intimidated to take on the role as critics and the constitutional process instead became a process for praising the monarchy. When the Crown Prince took over, the monarchy was further deified and strengthened, instead of 'the people' assuming greater plebiscitarian power. What emerges from this process is the codification of monarchical power and legitimacy with certain elements of a Schumpetarian elite democracy,[19] strongly enmeshed in Buddhism. Although the Constitution contains some elements of democracy, its drafting and endorsement was characterised by a process of homogenising the population, sacralising the monarchy and Buddhism, and distilling these exclusionary ideals as fundamental pillars of an emerging Bhutanese nation-state. I will subsequently describe how this took place based on my own observation of events in Bhutan during this period.

II. THE CONSTITUTIONAL COMMITTEE

The present Constitution is not Bhutan's first fundamental law regulating the relation between citizens and the state. Such a law had been initiated by the Zhabdrung back in the seventeenth century and inscribed on stone plates, which can still be seen in the Bhutanese National Museum. The decision to initiate a

[18] *Kuensel*, 5 Nov 2005.

[19] J Schumpeter, *Capitalism, Socialism and Democracy* (New York, Harper & Row, 1975) [hereinafter 'Schumpeter, *Capitalism*'].

constitution written in contemporary language must be understood against the backdrop of the conflicts described above. As the monarchy weathered a period of turbulence and threats, it determined that the way to ensure its stability and contemporary power institutions (formal as well as informal): the monarchy, the political leadership of the Drukpa Karguypa elite and the monastic bodies and secure Buddhism's dominant role in society was to institutionalise a constitutional monarchy. The latter could then be formulated in the language of the monarch and the elite rather than in the language of the democratic movement, noted above.

The move to draft a constitution for Bhutan was initiated by King Jigme Singye Wangchuk. He reigned as Druk Gyalpo from 1972 to 2006 when he abdicated in favour of his eldest son, Jigme Khesar Namgyel Wangchuk, the present Druk. On 4 September, just months after the tragic massacre of the Nepali royal family in June, Jigme Singye, who was 'acutely conscious … of the vulnerability of his own family to the kind of stresses and strains that had led to the demise of the Nepali monarchy' issued a Royal Proclamation commanding that a written constitution be promulgated.[20] At the same time, he established a 39-member Constitution Drafting Committee headed by Chief Justice Lyonpo Sonam Tobgye. Other members included the Speaker of the National Assembly; one member from each of the 20 *dzongkags* (districts), seven Royal Advisory Council members including its head, the Zhung Kalyon, two nominees of the clergy and three lawyers of the High Court.[21]

Since members from the government, judiciary and Royal Advisory Council were appointed by the King, its 'popular component' lies in the elected representatives of the 20 districts. However, members who were selected to draft the Constitution were, according to the editor of *Kuensel* (Bhutan's only newspaper at the time) and academics, all loyal supporters of the monarchy. Many of them were in fact appointed rather than elected. It is therefore unsurprising that they saw the constitutional process as one that was steered by the enlightened monarch. The Speaker, for example, epitomised this spirit when he said: 'As we play the humble role in Bhutan's journey through time, His Majesty the Druk Gyalpo's extraordinary vision will be our guiding light.'[22]

The King inaugurated the drafting process with the *Zhugdrel Pheunsum Tsokpai* – a traditional ceremony for the acquisition of 'grace, glory and wealth' during a formal and auspicious occasion – on 30 November 2001.[23] Immediately after the ceremony, the first drafting session was convened at the Royal Banquet Hall in Thimphu (capital of Bhutan). This session lasted until 14 December, and in the interim, members discussed the right to freedom of thought, conscience

[20] See LS Tobgye, *The Constitution of Bhutan: Principles and Philosophies* (Thimphu, N.P., 2008) 14–15 [hereinafter 'Tobgye, *The Constitution of Bhutan*'].

[21] ibid.

[22] 'Bhutan starts drafting a written constitution', *Kuensel*, 30 Nov 2001.

[23] Tobgye, *The Constitution of Bhutan*, (n 20) 15.

and speech as well as provisions highlighted by the King's 4 September speech. In all, the Drafting Committee held nine drafting sessions between November 2001 and 26 May 2003.[24] The Committee also appointed Kottayan Katankok (KK) Venugopal (b 1931), a senior advocate from India 'with long and distinguished experience, and highly respected by the [j]udges and the lawyers in India' as a constitutional expert.[25]

According to Chief Justice Lyonpo Sonam Tobgye, who chaired the Drafting Committee, a copy of the first draft of the Constitution was sent to Venugopal through the Indian Ambassador, who then held eight consultative meetings with the Committee. Thereafter, a corrected draft was submitted to the King who sent it back to the Committee on 15 October 2004. This was analysed and resubmitted to the King on 18 October 2004 and after making extensive revisions the King sent the draft to the Council of Ministers on 1 November 2004. Thereafter began a series of revisions in consultation with the King whereby the Chairman of the Drafting Committee submitted corrections 'in the form of "submissions" with justifications, analysis and background' to the King.[26] The first of 30 submissions was tendered on 4 December 2004.[27] Tobgye recounts the process vividly:

> His Majesty devoted considerable time in improving the document and meticulously studied every word, phrase and sentence. Thereafter, His Majesty sent the revised draft to the Chairperson of the Constitution Drafting Committee on 15th October 2004 to be reviewed by the Legal Committee formed under the Chairperson of the Constitution Drafting Committee. The process of corrections between His Majesty and the Legal Committee was phenomenal. The Chairperson submitted to His Majesty the corrections in the form of 'submissions' with justifications, analysis and background. The first submission was submitted on 4th December 2004. There were more than four hundred submissions in total. Meanwhile, His Majesty sent the draft to the Council of Ministers on 1stNovember 2004. The copy of the corrections of the draft submitted to His Majesty by the Council of Ministers was received by the Committee on 19th January 2005. The Legal Committee incorporated relevant changes based on their recommendations and comments.[28]

After all the changes were made, a special session of the *Lhengye Zhungtshog* (Council of Ministers) was convened on 21 March 2005 where the King shared his views on the draft Constitution – his final formal discussion before the

[24] The sessions were: First Session (Thimpu) 30 November to 14 December 2001; Second Session (Punakha) 4–8 Feb 2002; Third Session (Thimphu) 27 March to 11 April 2002; Fourth Session (Thimpu) 10–19 June 2002; Fifth Session (Bumthang) 9–18 October 2002; Sixth Session (Thimphu) 23–25 November 2002; Seventh Session (Thimphu) 12–14 March 2003; Eighth Session (Thimphu) 7–11 April 2003; and Ninth Session (Thimphu) 14–26 May 2003. See Tobgye, *The Constitution of Bhutan*, (n 20) 15–16.

[25] Tobgye, *The Constitution of Bhutan*, (n 20) 16. Venugopal made headlines when he was appointed Attorney-General of India in 2017 at the age of 86.

[26] ibid, 17.

[27] ibid.

[28] ibid.

second draft was distributed to the people.[29] The King's reasons for this were made clear:

> The Draft Constitution will be distributed to all the twenty Dzongkhags next year so that our people can study it and be fully aware of its contents. Following this, I will be personally visiting every Dzongkhag to meet with our people and hold discussions and consultations on all issues regarding the Constitution. Only after completing the consultations with our people in all the Dzongkhags will the adoption of the Constitution take place.[30]

This mass consultation was clearly intended to transform the Constitution into a popular document, but as Lyonchen Jigme Yoser Thinley (Prime Minister from 2003 to 2004) wondered: 'His Majesty will definitely give us a good constitution but what is worrying is whether the people of Bhutan can take on the task in a responsible manner?'[31]

III. CONSULTING THE PEOPLE

A. Distributing the First Draft: Ceremony and Symbolism

On 26 March 2005, the draft Constitution was distributed to the people. I was on site in Gasa Dzong (about 70 km north of Thimphu) to observe the historic event as the country took its first steps in constitutionalising the state. The Constitution is distributed in the formal venue of the Dzong, situated close to the Tibetan border. It was once a fortress against Tibetan invasions and is today the centre of administrative and religious power. The stage is set in the gigantic Dzong, the players wearing their unique costumes signalling the formality and sanctity of the event. Gathered to observe the happening are the top administrative personnel, the monks and the people's representatives: the Chimis,[32] the Gups[33] and the Mangmis.[34] All present followed strictly the dress code of *driglam namzha*, signifying their respect for the state. The female participants dressed in silk kiras and wore the obligatory rachu (a narrow, embroidered cloth) over their left shoulders while the men dressed in ghos and wore the formal kabney (scarf) around their necks. The colours of the men's kabneys denote their rank: the Chimis (state representatives) wear a blue scarf and the Gups (local elected officials) a red one, symbolising their position as interlocutors between the state and the 'people'. State officials wear tshoglhams (traditional boots) with a coloured band around the top, indicating their rank in the civil service. The only exception to the dress code was a few foreigners in western clothes,

[29] ibid.
[30] *Kuensel*, 20 Dec 2004.
[31] *Kuensel*, 17 Dec 2004.
[32] Elected members of the National Assembly.
[33] Elected leader of the Geog (group of villages).
[34] Elected members of the Geog (group of villages).

and the representatives from the remote areas, who are excused due to the five-day-long journey and difficult terrain they needed to traverse to attend the event.

The participants gathered in a row as Dasho Dzongdag, the Governor, approached. He had the privilege of wearing a patang (symbolic sword) as well as a full red scarf. The participants lined up in a row running towards the ceremonial room. As the Dasho proceeded past the line of attendants, they respectfully stepped backwards in prostration, whilst stretching their kabneys and rachus forward and displaying their palms, all as a mark of respect. The procession proceeded into the main temple, where the monks performed a series of prayers and religious rituals. The highest-ranking monk, Lem Neten, initiated the prayers in a profoundly deep voice. The walls were covered by depictions of the Buddha. Holy water, tea, delicacies and a coin were distributed, whilst the prayers continued. In the background, the national television video camera beeped. Dasho Dzongdag stood on a podium flanked by the elected chair of the district on his left and by the monks of high rank on his right. The local representatives were seated in a central position in the middle of the room.

The Chairman of the *dzongkhag yargye tshogchung* (district development committee) or DYT opened the proceedings by stating:

> Today is a historic occasion to take the constitution due to the King's kindness. Therefore we have to be grateful for the King for his visionary leadership. Normally you get power through fighting and pressure groups, but here you get power from the throne. People feel this constitution is too early. But on the other hand, if the constitution is delayed people will start thinking it will not change and this will hamper development. However, we cannot say the constitution is early or late, but we must support the King's initiative. It is the responsibility of the DYT members to read the constitution and give feedback. It is also the responsibility of DYT members to give feedback on the constitution to the ministers. It is important for us to provide feedback to the King with all our commitment and dedication.[35]

Dasho Dzongdag, the Governor then explained the reason for distributing the Constitution and the review process:

> The King has made a royal command to read out the constitution. In 2002 the people's representative was called into the Assembly. It was decided in the National Assembly. The people's representatives took responsibility to write a constitution. The members of the Royal Advisory Council, the representatives of the Districts, the Chief Justice was the Chair. The constitution was written and took a long time and convenience. Many changes were made[,] and the ministers checked the document based on the people's feedback. Today we present the well-made document to the DYT members. This is the noble thought of the Royal Government. We are going to distribute the copies of the Constitution to the people through the Gups. The Gups and Chimis will read out and explain the Constitution to the people. The people will have to

[35] W Bothe, 'The Monarch's Gift: Critical Notes on the Constitutional Process in Bhutan' (2012) 40 *European Bulletin of Himalayan Research* 27–58.

> understand clearly and provide feedback to the Government. This is a very important responsibility. After this is done the DYT will commence to decide on the feedback. It is not for the people to doubt the negative impact of the constitution. The King will visit all the 20 Dzongkhags to speak about the constitution to the people. The people will have to provide feedback to the King during his visits. We hope to fulfil the vision of gross national happiness![36]

The Dasho finally holds the Constitution high above his head, before distributing it to the elected representatives, who ritually receive it with their heads bowed and palms turned upwards. After a group photograph is taken outside, a meal is served.

B. The Construction of Citizens as 'Participants'[37]

A few days later a local Geog meeting is held, in which the Constitution is given to the people's representatives, the *tshogpas*. The discourse that follows casts the citizen in the role of responsible participants whose responsibility is to understand the Constitution and provide feedback to the King or government with commitment and dedication. Notably the Dzongdag does not characterise 'responsibility' as influencing, discussing and criticising the Constitution.

This notion of citizen responsibility is repeated when the Chimis present the Constitution to the villagers: 'When you get a copy, instead of keeping it in the safe you should read it thoroughly and explain it to the people.' However, this idea takes on a slightly different tone in his next sentence: 'Then the King will come to all the Geogs [lowest unit of local government] and discuss. He will visit all the Geogs including ours. He will hear if the people have understood the constitution.' Responsibility has now been turned into a duty. He proceeds: 'If you feel there are certain doubts to clarify in the constitution, you will have to clarify to the King. You will have to raise the question to the King.' The word 'clarify' indicates the possibility of posing questions to the King insofar as this does not imply critical views. The Chimi continues: 'Otherwise it will seem as if I have not explained about it to the people. In that case you and I will have to debate about it.' This carries the subtle expectation that questions are discussed with him prior to the King's arrival.

At the end of the meeting the Tshogpas (local representatives) joke about the gravity of the task before them. Because they are illiterate, or only have a few years of schooling, it would be impossible for them to read, much less explain the Constitution to the 'people'. Their isolated existence offers them barely any exposure to the outside world and, as such, liberal notions such as rights, opposition and political parties are likely to be meaningless to them. In any case, at the end

[36] ibid.

[37] The following account is based on the author's field notes, published as Bothe, 'The Monarch's Gift' (n 35).

of the meeting, the villagers give their thumbprints to document their participation and avoid the fine equivalent to a day's salary.[38]

This thick descriptive account illustrates how the constitutional debate constructs the villagers as citizens with the duty, rather than the right, to understand and participate in the debates. Moreover, they are expected to participate, regardless of their competence to do so. That begs the question: Why engage the locals in an obviously impossible task? The answer may lie in the way in which the Constitution is seen as a 'royal command' that should be followed regardless of its impossibility. Given the inequality in cultural capital, the process is captured and controlled by the local representatives. Thus, the people have the duty to participate but are expected to do so under the control of the local authorities. Through this process, the relationship between the King and the 'people' is articulated as a bond between the benevolent King, 'committed … to the service of the people' and his loyal subjects who invest their 'complete trust and faith' in the constitutional project of the King. In such a relationship, there is little room for influence or discussions, let alone criticism. The event also serves one further purpose – to heap praise on the benevolence and wisdom of the King and the government. In all, the scene for the constitutional debates serves purposes other than that of popularising the people's constitution; it equally serves as a stage for nationalising Bhutan in the image of the Monarch. As a consequence, instead of it being a venue for critical debates, it tends to become a stage for praising the King and, in his image, the state officials. The constitutional process thus misses the opportunity for increasing local political engagement in deciding important issues for the future of the country. It reproduces and even reinforces the position of the locals as supplicants of the state. This points towards how the change needs to be understood from a larger platform than that which is a contractual understanding of sovereignty offers. Rather, of equal, or even greater importance, is understanding the events from a cultural perspective of sovereignty. As a consequence, the theory adopts a dual perspective in the analysis of how citizens are constructed respectively as 'political beings' and as 'national beings'.

Below I analyse the events of the distribution of the Constitution and the first election that followed.[39]

IV. THE CONSTITUTIONAL DEBATES

During 2005 and 2006 the process of discussing the Constitution carried on in all Dzongkhags. What is interesting in the whole exercise is the absence of opposition or rejection, especially from the intelligentsia. I met a number

[38] ibid, 45.

[39] Participant observation of the nationwide distribution of the Constitution, 26 Mar 2005, Gasa Dzong, on file with the author.

of intellectuals during my fieldwork[40] – mostly academics and public officials, and most of them were sceptical about the democratic impact of the Constitution. The absence of critical remarks is particularly noticeable in Thimphu, the capital and base of the educated and middle classes. This paradox is explained by Kinley Dorji in these words:

> Some of the comments were predictable, meaning that speakers focused on broad compliments and on His Majesty's own phenomenal achievements more than the issues in the draft Constitution itself. Some of the speakers were far off the mark. And the general public seemed a little oblivious to the core issues. It would have been unfair to expect serious academic or political vision from the general public. But many of the people who attended the Thimphu meeting were not simple farmers by any means. Some of them are already effective players in both rural and national politics. Rural elections have shown us that local leadership is not new to politics. We had expected at least some practical concerns and views on important issues like the electoral process, political parties, even corruption in politics …
>
> There is, of course, the dilemma that we all face. We all know that the draft Constitution of the kingdom of Bhutan is a special document. Not only has it been initially drafted by a committee of selected representatives of Bhutanese society, it has been done so under the close guidance of His Majesty the King himself. The contents had been strengthened through the study of numerous other Constitutions … Many of the citizens attending the Thimphu meeting did say that, given this formidable background to the Constitution and their complete trust in it as an initiative of His Majesty the King, they did not even see the need to question any aspect of it. Many people were, understandably, overwhelmed by the magnitude of the issue.[41]

Therefore, proposals for minor changes can be raised but criticism that goes against the image of the benevolent and enlightened King is normatively unacceptable. In this way the discourse on democracy is revisited but under the control of the power holders unlike in the previous popular movement that claimed democracy from below.

These meetings come across as a site for disciplining the locals into the role of nationalised subjects of a state that is personified by the King. But, where there is power, there is also resistance, as Foucault insists. The intellectual's absenteeism from the meeting in Thimphu is a subtle exercise of resistance against being drawn in as participants in a process over which they hold little influence. Equally importantly, the sarcasm expressed by the Tshogpas at the local meeting in Gasa can be seen as a protest against their involuntary participation in a task beyond their capabilities and comprehension. The most outspoken protest, however, is posed at the meeting in Thimphu when an old man walked up to the King and told him that the Constitution should stipulate how many wives the King should be allowed to marry in future.[42] Not only did the old

[40] Interviews with academics and public officials, 2005 – author's field notes.

[41] 'Editorial', *Kuensel*, 29 Oct 2005.

[42] Recounting the experience of academic and confirmed by a journalist at *the Bhutan Times*. Author's field notes.

man breach the official code of conduct expected, but more seriously broke an official taboo: the question of the King marrying four sisters and thereby positioning this family as the most powerful family in Bhutan. These were issues that were not discussed openly, even though it was a continuous source of internal criticism behind closed doors.[43] The question touches upon the taboos of the King's personalised power circles, something which only 'a commoner' had the temerity to question.

In all, the constitutional process served to thicken the national hegemony rather than to open new spaces for local empowerment. The lack of critique is perhaps unsurprising in a normative context where the King's command was seen to be 'as heavy as the golden Yoke',[44] and where groups expressing such aspirations were historically imprisoned or exiled. However, local political engagement was arguably not the main strategic purpose of the constitutional debates. Instead, the event served the implicit strategy of socialising the locals into their roles as nationals and as loyal and obedient subjects of the state, as supplicants.

V. DISCUSSIONS BETWEEN THE KING AND THE PEOPLE

On 9 December 2006, King Jigme Singye publicly declared that he intended to abdicate the throne in favour of his eldest son, Jigme Khesar. The Crown Prince was given full responsibility of running the country with immediate effect. Jigme Khesar was officially crowned as the new King only on 6 November 2008. This announcement came in the midst of the King's direct constitutional consultation and dialogue with the people. Thus, the initial debates in the nationwide consultations were headed by the fourth King, Jigme Singye but later handed over to Crown Prince, Jigme Khesar. King Jigme Singye personally participated in public consultations in seven *dzongkhags* – Thimphu, Haa, Paro, Panukha, Wangduephodrang, Mongar, and Trashigang – while Prince Jigme Khesar covered the remaining 13 *dzongkhags* between 24 December 2005 and 24 May 2006.[45] The draft Constitution was translated and read in three dialects – Dzongkha, Tshangla and Lhotshamkha.

The scene changed drastically after the King set the Crown Prince in charge of the debate. It meant that the Crown Prince began to lead the debates as future King. My principal argument is that it was more of a performance in praising the monarchy than one of democratising Bhutan or empowering its people. However, there is a significant difference between the debates between the King and the people, and those between the Crown Prince and the people.

[43] Author's interviews, 2005.
[44] Interview with Gup, Punakha, 2005, on file with the author.
[45] Tobgye, *The Constitution of Bhutan*, (n 20) 20–21.

In the discourse between the King and the people he came across as a ruler with the genuine wish to alter the premises of sovereignty. Throughout his meetings he stressed that the Constitution was being established 'for the future well-being of the country and the people' because monarchy was 'not the best form of government for Bhutan as it has many flaws'.[46] There is no reason to doubt that this reflects the King's genuine intention. In support of the idea of the citizenry as holders of sovereign power, he continually encouraged them to speak their views freely. As such, the meetings are often opened in the spirit of the good governance discourse, reflected in the way in which the royals repeatedly stress the importance of electing competent leaders.[47]

Meanwhile, however, the fact that the King decided to give power away places him at a level of a deified character, as if the myth of the divine King had finally come true. From the perspective of local citizens, it is therefore difficult to accept the idea that the Constitution sets a retirement age for the King. In the words of a Gup from Paro: 'The Druk Gyalpo is a precious symbol of the nation. He should remain on the Throne even if he is not active in his old age … we pray that our King will live for at least 100 years.'[48] This question, which was repeated in all the debates, most likely reflected a genuine response to a change that went against the social imaginary of the public representatives and local citizens generally. With an age limit placed on the reign of a monarch, his status is downgraded to that of a mortal, running completely counter to the core narrative of the King as a divine being. Meanwhile, these questions gave the Royal family a welcome opportunity to legitimise the Constitution.

However, the argument changed as the debates shifted from one King to another. In the debates with the incumbent King, his very presence was sufficient to legitimise the Constitution. However, the Crown Prince did not yet have the same degree of legitimacy and needed to draw upon his father's legitimacy in his defence of the retirement age: '… the inclusion of this clause is only one of countless such acts that reflect His Majesty's dedication to the nation and its future'. These views must be understood in light of the fact that the Constitution was not the outcome of a popular process. As such, the debates served the strategic purpose of legitimising the Constitution by the reference to the public narratives of the monarchy.[49]

Even if there is a genuine attempt at introducing an element of popular control in the debates, this stands somewhat at odds with the elected representatives' own interpretation, as they ritually confirm their faith in the monarchy:

> … His Majesty has commanded the drafting of the Constitution and initiated political reform despite repeated pleas of the people who believe that Monarchy is the best form of government for Bhutan. Therefore, today, in the presence of His Majesty

[46] *Kuensel*, 5 Nov 2005.
[47] ibid.
[48] Interview with retired Gup, *Kuensel* Paro, 12 Nov 2005.
[49] Bothe, 'The Monarch's Gift', (n 35) 27–58.

> the King, the representatives of Punakha dzongkhag pledge their full support for the Constitution although it represented a change that they had not even imagined in their dreams.[50]

This quote refers to an understanding of social order as established by a legal contract. However, as the word 'pledge' indicates, the representatives support the contract, not necessarily because they feel ownership over it, but rather because of their loyalty to the King. This is unlikely to be coincidental but reflects the general discourse on the constitutional process as something guided by the King, more than it is wished for by the people.

Therefore, the debates served a higher purpose than that of discussing the Constitution; they served the purpose of establishing the legitimacy of the state without the absolute power of the monarch. This discourse had important repercussions for the way in which citizenship was constructed. In spite of the encouragement to be open and frank in raising questions, the norms *associated with the monarchy* carved out for the locals bear a striking resemblance to one of passive subjects.

VI. ADOPTION AND CONTENT OF THE CONSTITUTION

Even before the Constitution was formally adopted, Bhutan's new bicameral legislature was inaugurated. The year before, the long-standing ban on the formation of political parties was lifted and a mock election was in April 2007 held to prepare the people of Bhutan for democracy. On 24 March 2008, elections were held for the very first time in Bhutan. Two parties – Druk Phuensum Tshogpa (DPT) and the People's Democratic Party – were registered to take part in the elections. The Bhutan National Party was refused registration and could not contest the election which the DPT won overwhelmingly, capturing 45 of the 47 seats and 67 per cent of the popular vote. Parliament convened from 9 to 29 May 2008 in a special joint-session to debate the provisions of the draft Constitution.[51] On 18 July 2008, at a grand ceremony, the Constitution for the Kingdom of Bhutan was officially adopted.

The Bhutanese Constitution is one of the most comprehensive constitutions in the world. This analysis will not give full credit to the many nuances and innovations of the Constitution, which make it a unique document, but rather focus on its effect in constructing the citizen's constitutional role in the Bhutanese context. I argue that the Constitution represents significant continuities in the distribution of power, through the constitutionalisation of the power of the King and of the state to overrule citizens' rights when this is deemed doable in their interest. Moreover, the Constitution falls short of reflecting popular democracy

[50] *Kuensel*, 30 Nov 2005.
[51] Iyer, 'Constitution-Making in Bhutan', (n 2) 376.

but can better be understood as one that was drawn up to serve Schumpeter's ideal of an 'elitist democracy'.[52] Finally, by one interpretation, the Constitution tends to depoliticise politics and this set the stage for a highly depoliticised first election. It is thus surprising when the Bhutanese applied their new voting rights to protest informal power structures which they saw as highly oppressive.

In a style familiar in South Asia, the preamble of the Constitution begins with these words: '*We the people of Bhutan*'. Further, the first Article of the Constitution draws on a liberal understanding of social order: 'Bhutan is a Sovereign Kingdom and the sovereign power belongs to the people of Bhutan.'[53] This idea is linked in Western democratic thought to the normative ideas of 'popular control over collective decisions and political equality in its exercise'.[54] These principles are reflected in a number of articles in the Constitution, and institutionalised in paragraphs on political competition and political and civil rights. Simultaneously, however, this is challenged by articles and electoral regulations and practices that tend to undermine these same principles.[55]

The idea of popular control is inscribed in the division between the executive, the legislative and the judicial powers. At the same time, however, the monarch retains a highly prominent role. He enjoys the power to award titles, grant citizenship and land, as well as to propose Bills and exercise undefined powers 'not provided for in the Constitution'.[56] Furthermore, the monarch holds considerable direct political power such as the agenda-setting power in Parliament, the right to reject a Bill, and power to command a national referendum.[57] Importantly, the monarch is vested with wide-ranging powers to appoint high-ranking judicial officers and, to a lesser degree, central administrative offices like the Election Commission.[58]

These prerogatives are likely to maintain an elevated position for the King as a central political actor. Given that the monarch equally possesses considerable legislative power, the separation between the legislative and the judicial powers thus become blurred. This is compounded by Article 20(7) which states that the government is collectively responsible to the monarch and the Parliament. Moreover, the King is ascribed the role of protector of the Constitution: 'The Druk Gyalpo shall protect and uphold this Constitution in the best interest and welfare of the people of Bhutan.'[59]

Finally, the King may appoint those responsible for the interpretation of the Constitution. This is accentuated by his influence on the second chamber,

[52] See J Medearis, *Joseph Schumpeter's Two Theories of Democracy* (Cambridge, MA, Harvard University Press, 2013).

[53] Constitution of Bhutan 2008, Art 1(1).

[54] D Beetham, *Democracy and Human Rights* (Cambridge, Polity Press, 1999) 5–6.

[55] W Bothe, 'In the Name of King, Country, and People on the Westminster Model and Bhutan's Constitutional Transition' (2015) 22(7) *Democratization* 1338–1361.

[56] Constitution of Bhutan 2008, Art 2(16).

[57] ibid, Art 13(10).

[58] Bothe, 'In the name of King' (n 55).

[59] Constitution of Bhutan 2008, Art 2(18).

the National Council, which consists of 25 members without party affiliation, five of whom are directly selected by the King.[60] Thus, one fifth of the members in this chamber are not elected by the principle of 'popular control'. Indeed, this provides the monarch with even more elaborate constitutional powers than those enjoyed by American presidents. Since the monarchy is hereditary, considerable power thus lies outside of popular control. As such, the extent to which the Constitution is democratic or monarchic is a question of whether the glass is half full or half empty. However, much will depend on constitutional practice in the ensuing years. To give an example, the Danish democratic Constitution states that all laws must have the approval of the King, which is a clause that might have been used to reassert monarchy in the past, but which few Danes today regard as a potential threat to democracy. However, a similar clause, naming the Nepali King as the protector of the Nepalese Constitution, was interpreted by King Gyanendra (who reigned from 2001 to 2008) as a carte blanche to arrogate power in his hands. This presents an even larger risk, given the King's wide-ranging powers to appoint the most important constitutional positions. A lot will, therefore, depend on the succeeding Kings' understanding of their role.[61]

The principle of political competition is codified in the introduction of a party system.[62] This is unique in the sense that Bhutan is the first country in the world to deliberately establish a diarchic party system by law, with a maximum of two parties represented in the National Assembly, ie the governing party and the opposition.[63] This reflects an attempt to avoid ethnic cleavages. It may, however, equally result in the exclusion of significant voices in Parliament, especially in a country with three major ethnic groups.[64] The risk entailed is the production of what Beetham calls a 'permanent minority'; a position most likely to be held by the Lhotshampas minority. However, the clause that all parties must represent an all national composition might have the potential of preventing such a situation from occurring. Nevertheless, the risk is that the diarchic party system might turn out to be an apolitical body[65] much like the earlier 'partyless' Panchyat system of Nepal, due to the King's restriction on the free formation of parties.

This risk is enhanced by an electoral system which prioritises sparsely-populated districts. The National Assembly comprises a maximum of 55 elected members elected from each dzongkhag 'in proportion to its population, provided that there shall be at least two and no more than seven representatives from each district'.[66] Since the sparsely-populated districts are mostly populated

[60] ibid, Art 11(1).
[61] Bothe, 'In the name of King' (n 55).
[62] Constitution of Bhutan 2008, Art 23.
[63] ibid, Art 15(5)–15(8).
[64] ibid, Art 15(1)–15(4).
[65] Bothe, 'In the name of King' (n 55).
[66] Constitution of Bhutan 2008, Art 12(1).

by Ngalongs, and the districts in the South and in the East are the most populous (except for Thimphu), the Ngalongs are likely to be overrepresented, especially in the National Council where each district has one elected representative. Nevertheless, even though the party system appears to discriminate against the Lhotshampas and the Sharchops (Easterners primarily following the Nyingmapa line of Buddhism), it is still likely to provide these groups with substantially more influence than they enjoyed in the past. Further, there is an argument for providing the sparsely-populated districts with larger representation, in order to ensure the rights of minorities.[67]

Whilst Bhutan's first Constitution maintains a strong role for the monarch, it also represents a renewal of the Bhutanese political system. For the first time in history, it codifies the rights of individuals. This promotes the idea of political equality, inscribed as a 'fundamental right' of the citizens. Here the Constitution takes a major leap in constructing the citizens as bearers of political rights such as the (limited) freedom of religion[68] or the freedom of assembly, movement and speech, and the right not to be deprived of property without fair compensation.[69] The latter could have an important impact on farmers who find themselves in a vacuum when it comes to rights over their land. However, Article 20 emphasises the rights of the state at the expense of the individual rights:

> 20. – Notwithstanding the rights conferred by this constitution, nothing in this Article shall prevent the State from subjecting reasonable restriction by law, when it concerns:
>
> 1. The interest of sovereignty, security, unity and integrity of Bhutan;
> 2. The interest of peace, stability and wellbeing of the nation

The section guaranteeing rights to individuals contains a substantial paragraph giving the state the right to overrule these rights if they go against the interest of the state, even in the absence of a national emergency. As a result, the principle of minority protection risks being reversed into the protection of the ones who hold the power over the state. The idea of Bhutan as a culturally united nation is repeated in the paragraphs codifying 'all national orientation' of the political parties, which are obliged to 'promote national interest' and 'national unity' and ensure that the party is 'broad-based with cross-national membership' (Article 15(1–4)). These clauses formed part of the basis for excluding the Bhutan People's Unity Party (BPUP) from participating in the elections, which advocated the rights of the Nyamchung (the downtrodden people).[70]

In sum, citizens with the right to vote can do so for an approved candidate, but not necessarily for their preferred candidate or party if these are deemed

[67] Bothe, 'In the name of King' (n 55).

[68] Constitution of Bhutan 2008, Art 3(1), subject to Art 8(3).

[69] ibid, Art 7.

[70] The applicant 'party had waived off membership fees on the grounds that it was a party for the Nyamchung (downtrodden people) but that went against the Constitution of Bhutan, which was for a united, not divided based on religion, economic or social status'. See *Kuensel*, 28 Nov 2007.

against the unity of the country. Thus, in spite of the new spaces that are opened for local influence, the Constitution opens new opportunities for the control of the local citizens. In combination with the lack of access for NGOs seeking to promote civil and political rights, locals are effectively prevented from becoming politicised to challenge their position at the bottom of society. As such, the Constitution and its practice consolidates the idea of the nation-state as a unified entity where every citizen is a microcosm of the larger national will, as opposed to being individuals separated by differences of interests and views.

Besides these formal changes, Bhutan reasserts its sovereignty with the new bilateral treaty with India that emphasises an equal relation of friendship instead of the previous unequal relation. This is most significantly seen in Article 2. The original 1949 Treaty states:

> The Government of India undertakes to exercise no interference in the internal administration of Bhutan. On its part, the Government of Bhutan agrees to be guided by the advice of the Government of India in regard to its external relations.

In contrast, and referring to the 2007 bilateral treaty, Article 2 of the Constitution emphasises the equality of the relation in these terms:

> In keeping with the abiding ties of close friendship and cooperation between Bhutan and India, the Government of the Kingdom of Bhutan and the Government of the Republic of India shall cooperate closely with each other on issues relating to their national interests. Neither Government shall allow the use of its territory for activities harmful to the national security and interest of the other.

As such, India gave Bhutan a much-desired gift in return for its democratisation process, ie, the full recognition of its independence, something that was probably the strategic purpose of the Constitution.

It could therefore be expected that the Constitution carried little change. Most significant of these changes was the silent rebellion against the structure of a dual monarchy, where the elite forged an alliance with the rural inhabitants in putting a halt to the future domination of the dual monarchy under the new system. Although this was presumably an elite driven rebellion, the courage it must have taken for the local citizens to vote against the candidates from the members of the Queen's family, experienced as an oppressive power structure, should not be underestimated.

VII. THE TRADITIONALISATION OF THE CONSTITUTION

At first sight the constitutional process seemed to serve more national purposes of celebrating the monarchy, and, through this process, to establish a national bond between the monarch and local citizens. As such the reform of the state is legitimised through the image of the benevolent and divine Kings, with the attributes of bodhisattvas. The introduction of elements of popular control, however, opened a window of opportunity for change. The democratisation of the system introduced new processes of accountability, which provided the locals with the tools to contest the highly overt power structures associated with the King's family, ones they had come to view as extremely oppressive. This, in combination with the constitutional definition of who is royal and who is not, may indeed provide for more accountable governance practices, not least at the local level.[71]

Thus, although the Constitution deviates in a number of ways from the standard Western liberal democratic model, in terms of Dahl's polyarchy,[72] it nevertheless effectively provides the citizens with a choice in deciding the leadership of the country, as well as a mechanism for holding it accountable. However, this choice is confined by institutional limitations as to who can stand for elections and who cannot, where only people with a bachelor's degree or with five years of government experience can run for office. This limits the voting power of the local citizens to a choice between the incumbent Chimi and an elite candidate. Most retrogressively, this arrangement limits the ordinary citizens' right to participate in state governance.[73]

These practices rank citizenship hierarchically. At the apex are the elite who qualify as citizens with full rights to participate in political competition; in the middle are the less well-educated section of the population, who hold identity cards and qualify as voters. At the bottom are those of primarily Lhotshampa origin, without citizenship, and accordingly no rights to participate. This divides the citizens between what Aristotle refers to as 'bios', ie, human beings with political rights as opposed to 'zoe', ie, humans who are simply 'beings' without rights (distinctions taken from Foucault's reference to Aristotle). Situated in the middle are the vast majority, who only enjoy the passive right to vote. In all, the idea of democracy thus resembles more a Schumpeterian-type elite democracy, unlike the popular form usually associated with the term 'democratic'.[74]

Ultimately, this limits the role of democracy as a means for representing and mediating conflict of interests and turns it into a forum for the building a national consensus by the intellectual avant-garde and straitjacketing the democratic experiment. Therefore, debates in Parliament operate less as a platform for debates but instead serve the same purpose as the constitutional debates, ie, as a venue for consolidating the national character of the state, unified under a King with the attributes of a bodhisattva. This is even more pronounced in the local districts where the King's compassionate image is even more aggressively promoted than in the past.[75] In this manner the potential threat of national disintegration – which the elite believe 'democracy' presents – is countered by elevating the state's only unifying symbol, the King,

[71] Bothe, 'In the name of King' (n 55).
[72] R Dahl, *Polyarchy: Participation and Opposition* (London, Yale University Press, 1971).
[73] Bothe, 'In the name of King' (n 55).
[74] Schumpeter, *Capitalism*, (n 19).
[75] An academic's e-mail correspondence with the author, 2010.

to a divine position. At the same time, this has the side-effect of elevating the state representatives to a position above the mundane citizens. It is therefore uncertain if the new opportunities for accountability can be fully realised, given the prevalence and continuation of traditional practices. Although the option of legal sanctions is abandoned, the disciplinary mechanism continues largely unchanged. Given the fear which the local citizens have of the state, the change is likely to have little bearing on their lives in the short run, especially in cases where they are prevented from knowing what rights they have under the Constitution. Instead, there is continued re-emphasis on the symbolic practices that distinguish the state officials from the rest of the general citizenry. Moreover, tradition continues to be reinvented and new colours to be introduced and scarves redesigned to denote the status of those holding new positions in Parliament. Most notable among these are the scarves of the Chimis (assembly members), which were changed from white with a blue stripe to full blue, signifying their symbolic promotion to a superior position as superiors. Juxtaposed with the limitation on local citizens contesting elections, the Chimis risk becoming more representative of the state than representatives of the people. Drawing an analogy to Hobsbawm and Ranger's example of the reinvention of tradition in Britain, the idea of the superior and inferior was thus smuggled into a context of legal equality, via symbolic practices that elevate the Chimis to a position of superiority.[76] This demonstrates the highly politicised character of tradition, which reconfigured the value of capital attributed to agents on the ground, with the disguised effect of concealing inequalities and hierarchies. More peculiarly, there is an ongoing process of constitutionalising tradition, one that continuously adjusts tradition to practices perceived as historically more authentic. The higher one's position is in the hierarchy, the more traditionalised is his or her code of conduct. As such, tradition continues to be a potent tool of power.

The process of advancing popular control and individual rights (however limited), represents notable progress in providing local citizens with a larger say over their lives. Simultaneously, however, the national processes that are at play, arguably reproduce and possibly even thicken the existing hegemony. However, it is doubtful in the longer run whether the locals can continue to be kept in ignorance. The spread of knowledge and consciousness about rights may easily carry with it increased contestation over the continued domination of the Drukpa elite.

What the outcome will be depends a lot upon how wisely the elite handle its mandate of power. The current re-emphasis on symbolic practices that cast local citizens as inferior beings suggests that it may possibly end with the revitalisation of previous rebellions – simply because the Bhutanese peasants are unlikely to accept their continued position of poverty and inferiority any less than were the Nepalese. In such a situation it is quite possible that India will intervene for

[76] E Hobsbawm and T Ranger, *The Invention of Tradition* (Cambridge, Cambridge University Press, 1983) 10.

humanitarian reasons. In this sense, the idea of 'oneness' generated by hierarchy and inequality is arguably the most significant long-term threat to Bhutanese sovereignty.

VIII. CONCLUSION

Prior to my field research, the Bhutanese case seemed an obvious choice for a study that exemplified how local governance could have a positive effect on local empowerment, even in a monarchy. The success story of Bhutan, hailed by the United Nations and, with them, many donors at the time of the research, is supported by the way in which the institutionalisation of local governance is rigorously implemented. This is rooted in a logic of governmentality that aims to increase the economic well-being of the locals by localising governance, and by making it more inclusive, transparent and accountable.

What was promoted in Bhutan was, however, a radically different way of rationalising social order; one that eschewed liberal governmentality. Social order has been rationalised in terms of hierarchy through a form of governance inspired by Confucian understandings of social order. Such an order is regulated by the norms of filial piety and a common understanding and knowing of one's place in the structure of social relations. These processes tend to promote a 'perverse effect' of empowerment by promoting a hierarchic relationship between the governors and the local citizens, as well as between the local elite and the marginalised groups.

8

Towards a Maldivian Nation-State: The Constitutions of 1932 and 1968

SHAMSUL FALAAH*

INTRODUCTION

RELATIVELY LITTLE HAS been written on the constitutional development of the Maldives.[1] This chapter explores the historical and political underpinnings of the constitutional foundings that shaped the Maldives as a modern nation-state. I argue that, of the seven constitutions the Maldives adopted between 1932 and 2008, the Constitutions of 1932 and 1968 are foundational. This chapter qualitatively identifies the main driving forces, principles, ideals and aspirations involved in the constitution-making processes and analyses the contributions and impact of the two founding constitutions. The remainder of the chapter is divided into five parts. Part I provides a historical backdrop of Maldivian constitutionalism while Part II examines the Constitution of 1932. Part III looks briefly at the 1953 republican Constitution and Part IV explores the Constitution of 1968, the second republican constitution. Part V discusses the legacy of the two founding Constitutions of 1932 and 1968, before concluding.

* The author gratefully acknowledges the support of the Academy of the Dhivehi Language, especially Ashraf Ali and Rafia Abdul Qadir of the Academy, for kindly providing pertinent research materials and the extremely helpful discussions with and information from Azeeza Afeef.

[1] Until 21 January 1969, the Maldives was known as 'The Maldive Islands'. Ministry of External Affairs, 'Proclamation' (21 January 1969).

I. HISTORICAL BACKDROP

A. Maldives: Origins and a Brief History

The Maldives is a group of 1,190 islands scattered in the Indian Ocean to the southwest of India and Sri Lanka. Early settlers were the *Dheyvis* from Kalibanga in India[2] and genetically Maldivians have a close connection with the people of mainland South Asia.[3] Later, the *Redi* and the *Kunibee* who were of the same origin arrived from India, and the Aryans settled in the Maldives during the sixth to seventh centuries, introducing Hinduism to the islands.[4] Not long after the Aryans arrived, the first kingdom was established in the Maldives.[5]

In the early period, Maldivians worshipped nature and objects such as the sun, moon and stars.[6] They were led by a *Sawamia*, who was not only a religious but a political leader as well.[7] During the third-century BCE, Buddhism was introduced to the Maldives[8] and remained the religion of the Maldivians until they embraced Islam in 1153 AD. After their conversion to Islam, the places of worship built during the Buddhist era were either destroyed[9] or transformed into mosques,[10] except in cases where pre-Islamic traditions existed.[11] The Maldives was a self-governing state for over 1,000 years before the Portuguese gained control of the islands in 1558 and occupied them for some 15 years.

[2] Naseema Mohamed suggests that these settlers came to the Maldives before the reign of Emperor Asoka of India in 269–232 BC. N Mohamed, 'Note on the Early History of the Maldives' (2005) 70 *Archipel* 7, 7 (hereinafter 'Mohamed, 'Note on the Early History''). The current inhabitants of the Maldives are of the same Aryan stock as the Sinhalese 'with an admixture of African, Arab and Indonesian blood'. Y Maumoon, *A General Overview of the Dhivehi Language* (Malé, National Centre for Linguistic and Historical Research, 2002) 11.

[3] J Pijpe et al, 'Indian Ocean Crossroads: Human Genetic Origin and Population Structure in the Maldives' (2013) 151 *American Journal of Physical Anthropology* 58.

[4] AA Shihabuddine, *Kitab Fi Athaari Meedhoo El-Qadimiyyeh* (Dhoondeyri Don Maniku tr, no date) 1650–87. There is evidence that Hinduism was also practised from the 8th or 9th centuries. See A Skjølsvold, *Archaeological Test-Excavations on the Maldive Islands*, vol 2 (The Kon-Tiki Museum Occasional Papers, Tiki Museum, 1991). See also R-Frias Xavier, *The Maldive Islanders: A Study of the Popular Culture of an Ancient Ocean Kingdom* (Barcelona, Nova Ethnographia Indica, 1999); C Maloney, *People of the Maldive Islands* (London, Sangam Books, 1980).

[5] Mohamed, 'Note on the Early History', (n 2) 9.

[6] ibid, 7.

[7] Shihabuddine, *Kitab Fi Athaari*, (n 4).

[8] For a detailed study on the pre-Islamic archaeology of the Maldives see A Forbes, 'The Pre-Islamic Archaeology of the Maldive Islands' (1987) 76 *Bulletin de l'École française d'Extrême-Orient* 281.

[9] See HCP Bell, *The Maldive Islands: An Account of the Physical Features, Climate, History, Inhabitants, Productions, and Trade* (Asian Educational Services, 2004) 204 [hereinafter 'Bell, *The Maldive Islands*']. See also FP de Laval, *The Voyage of Francois Pyrard of Laval to the East Indies, the Maldives, the Moluccas and Brazil*, vol 1 (New York, Cambridge University Press, 2010, Albert Gray tr, 1611) 448.

[10] According to Andrew Forbes, 'Buddhist shrines were adapted for Islamic use, however, and traces of former Buddhist usage or architectural style may still be found in a number of mosques both ruined and extant.' A Forbes, 'The Mosque in the Maldive Islands: A Preliminary Historical Survey' (1983) 26 *Archipel* 43, 48.

[11] H Al Suood, *The Maldivian Legal System* (Malé, Maldives Law Institute, 2014) 7.

Later, when the Dutch took control of Sri Lanka in 1645, the Maldives agreed to become a protected state of the Dutch who demanded an annual tribute. This tributary relationship was also assumed by Britain when the British took over Ceylon in 1796. At this time, the Maldives enjoyed the de facto protection of the Rulers of the Island of Ceylon,[12] a relationship that was formalised in 1887, through an 'enforced letter',[13] which historians have referred to as an 'Agreement'.[14] In this letter – which the British drafted and addressed to the Governor and Commander-in-Chief of the Island of Ceylon, Arthur Hamilton Gordon – the Sultan acknowledged the 'authority of the Sovereign of Great Britain as represented by the Government of Ceylon' over the Maldives. The Sultan also agreed not 'to enter into any negotiations or treaty regarding them [the islands of the Maldives] with any Foreign State except through the Ruler of Ceylon' and renounced 'any intention of doing so'. The Sultan further stated that he was 'desirous of being formally installed in the office of Sultan by the Government of Ceylon' and requested the Governor to confirm his Sultanate and to do so when installing his successors. The Sultan concluded by indicating his willingness to 'enter into any more formal agreement'.[15] Governor Gordon, replying on behalf of the British Crown, confirmed the Sultan in his office and promised to grant confirmation to his successors. He also assured the Sultan that the Queen would 'protect and defend the Maldive Islands from all foreign enemies whatsoever', and would abstain from interfering in the internal affairs, framing, and administration of the laws of the Maldives.[16] The letter concluded that it was unnecessary to enter into a formal agreement since the concessions were already made by that letter. It was these two correspondences that formed the 'Agreement'.[17]

[12] See Colonial Office, 'Maldive Islands: Correspondence Regarding the Agreement of 1887' (The National Archives 1887).

[13] Abdul Hakeem Hussain Manik claims that the Sultan rejected the British Government's request to enter into an agreement – a request provoked by the family rivalry to that of the Rannaban'deyri (who is in charge of the administration of the state). The second time, the British Government came with an agreement written in Arabic which the Sultan again declined. The third time they approached with a letter written in English (a language which the Sultan could neither speak, nor write, nor read). This time, when the Sultan refused to sign the letter, the British Government's delegation went back to their naval ship and threatened action by aiming its weaponry at Malé. Ultimately, the Sultan signed the letter under coercion by threat of force. See AHH Maniku, *Boduhulhuge Thaareekh* [History of Large Arson] (Malé, Novelty Printers and Publishers, 1998). It should be noted that by the 20th century, in a situation where consent was procured by coercion of a state by the threat or use of force, coercion of a representative of a state would be regarded as voidable or void. Based on this, I argue that this agreement is prima facie void or voidable. However, given the affirmation of the agreement by the Maldives for over eight decades and with its entering into force with new addendums of the agreement, the agreement can also be argued to be valid. See O Dörr and K Schmalenbach (eds), *Vienna Convention on the Law of Treaties: A Commentary* (Berlin, Springer, 2012) 857–98.

[14] See Bell, *The Maldive Islands*, (n 9).

[15] Colonial Office, 'Maldive Islands: Correspondence Regarding the Agreement of 1887' (CO 882/19, The National Archives 1887) vol Eastern No 172.

[16] ibid.

[17] The agreement consists of these two correspondences between the Sultan of the Maldives and the British Government in Ceylon, which means there is no one single document which forms the

One possible reason why the Sultan agreed to this 'protection' was the intense political rivalry between the members of royal families (who were also politicians) – in particular the rivalry between the Athireege and Kakaage families[18] – in the Maldives' highly-stratified class system.[19] Since the pre-Islamic period,[20] 'caste-groups'[21] or 'status-groups'[22] facilitated the rulers in protecting their monarch.[23] When one family became influential on the monarch, the other families would often seek the help of foreign powers to take over powerful positions in government.

At this time, Britain was also entering into protection agreements with several other states: Brunei (1888); the Malay States (1896); Kuwait (1899); and the Trucial States (1892). Given the way the British Government had forced the Sultan to enter into an agreement and the agreements made with other states thereafter, it is evident that the British intended to dominate the region, even by force if necessary. I thus argue that it was not only because of the rivalry between the dominant families coupled with the tensions with the Borah merchants that the Maldives entered into this Agreement.

With this Agreement, the Maldives formally became a British Protected State[24] under the 'authority' of the British Governor in Ceylon. Based on the wording of the letters, and the practice of their implementation, this

agreement. In addition to this, the two countries entered into five additional agreements: in 1948, 1953, 1956, 1960, and 1965 respectively.

[18] See AHH Maniku, *Iyye* [Yesterday] (Malé, Novelty Printers and Publishers, 1997) 8–10; M Naseer, *Dhivehiraajjeyge Mizamaanuge Thaareekhugai Hin'gi Emme Muhimmu Dhe Haadhisaa* [Two Most Significant Incidents in the Present History of the Maldives] (Malé, Novelty Printers and Publishers, 2010) 199–238; M Nasheed, *Dhagan'du Dhahanaa* (Malé, Loamaafaanu Printers, 1995) 143–223. Dominant families during this time included the Athireege and Kakaakge families. Maldivian history suggests that, in addition to the solar and lunar dynasties, there were six dynasties: the Hilaalee; Utheemu; Humawi; Isdhoo; Dhiyamigili; and Huraa.

[19] For a detailed study on the social stratification in the ancient Maldives see L Kulikov, 'Traces of Castes and Other Social Strata in the Maldives: A Case Study of Social Stratification in a Diachronic Perspective (Ethnographic, Historic, and Linguistic Evidence)' (2014) 139 *Zeitschrift für Ethnologie* 199.

[20] See HA Maniku, 'Archaeology in Maldives: An Historical Survey' (Malé, South Asian Archaeological Congress, 1993) 39.

[21] See Maloney, *People of the Maldive Islands*, (n 4) 274.

[22] See E Kattner, 'The Social Structure of Maliku (Minicoy)' (1996) 10 *International Institute of Asian Studies* 19–20. See also P Berger et al (eds), 'Seven Men, Six Women: Names and the Socio-Cosmic Order of Maliku (Minicoy Island)' in *The Anthropology of Values: Essays in Honour of Georg Pfeffer* (London, Pearson, 2010).

[23] See A Shakir, *Vihivana Qarunugethereygai Dhviehiraajje* [Maldives in the Twentieth Century], vol 1 (Malé, Novelty Printers and Publishers, 2004) 52–56.

[24] Protectorates and Protected States are two different terms. Protectorates are protected territories in which the British established an internal administration because there is no organised internal government (in addition to the control over external affairs). In contrast, Protected States are where there is an organised internal government and control of external affairs is surrendered to the British. Moreover, the British Protectorates, Protected States and Protected Persons Order 1949/140 identifies the Maldives as a Protected State. Therefore, unlike in almost all other literature on the topic, the Maldives is referred to as a British Protectorate, this chapter uses the term Protected State. See British Protectorates, Protected States and Protected Persons Order-in-Council 1949/140.

Agreement formed a suzerain-vassal state relationship, rather than a colonial relationship between the UK and the Maldives. This is confirmed in Article 1 of the Agreement entered into between the two countries on 14 February 1960 – the 'Alport Agreement' – which states that the UK will safeguard and protect the 'composite sovereign and independent state of the Maldives Islands'. Further evidence for this position can be found in the following response by Lord Taylor to a question asked in the British Parliament:

> Britain never had these islands. They were the property of, and belong to, the people of the Maldives and the Government of the Maldive Islands. They were in the relationship of a protected State.[25]

This relationship was ceased by the Anglo-Maldivian Agreement of 1965 under which the Maldives became independent.

B. An Historical Overview of the Legal System

The Maldives has had a legal system for over two millennia.[26] Before the country embraced Islam in 1153 AD, Buddhism dominated and its legal system[27] was based on a customary law known as *fooruve rudin*. The King was supreme and the ruling system 'was guided by time honoured customs and traditions'[28] The legal system has always been influenced by religion. Since the twelfth century, Islamic law's influence on the legal system is significant. Today, the legal system is a mix of Islamic and common law.

In ancient times, the Maldivian Government was a customised version of the political system in Ceylon.[29] The King, who acted as military leader to protect the state from foreign aggression, was also responsible for tax collection, dispensing justice, and protecting religion.[30] Disputes were resolved in the royal court established under the King and which was presided over by the chief cleric.[31] In appeal cases, the King ordered his judges, lords and officers to settle appeals.[32] In important matters, the King consulted with the noble chiefs and the ministers although their advice was not binding on the King who had absolute power in all state affairs.[33]

[25] 'New Anglo-Maldivian Agreement (Hansard, 26 July 1965)' (26 July 1965) https://api.parliament.uk/historic-hansard/lords/1965/jul/26/new-anglo-maldivian-agreement.

[26] Suood, *The Maldivian Legal System*, (n 11) III.

[27] The Maldives was a Buddhist country before 1153 A.C. See C Maloney, 'The Maldives: New Stresses in an Old Nation' (1976) 16 *Asian Survey* 654, 654.

[28] Maniku, 'Archaeology in Maldives', (n 20).

[29] See also Maloney, 'The Maldives', (n 27) 1.

[30] In matters of religion, the King consulted with his clergy. Laval, *The Voyage of Francois Pyrard*, (n 9) vol 1, ch 14.

[31] ibid.

[32] ibid, vol 1, chs 14–15.

[33] Suood, *The Maldivian Legal System*, (n 11) 9.

Unlike the influence of colonial laws in the pre-Independence South Asian legal systems, especially in India and Ceylon, colonial influence on the Maldivian legal system was negligible. Even though the Maldivian-British affairs were conducted through the British Government's official who was also responsible for Ceylon, Ceylonese law was explicitly excluded in the Maldives.[34] Moreover, no foreign power, not even the British ever established a colonial bureaucracy.

Before the promulgation of its first Constitution in 1932, customary law coexisted with Islamic law, although attempts were made to sidestep customary law in favour of the Shariah, and to abolish customs and practices contrary to Shariah.[35] The Sultan ruled autocratically as both head of state and head of government. He ruled according to traditional custom and Islam which constituted a form of constitutional convention. Take, for example, the appointment of public officials and the conduct of state affairs. Though the Sultan had all the powers of government, he administered certain matters through 'knights' selected from among those close to the Sultan. These members constituted an advisory majlis which advised the Sultan on matters of state. On the advice of these majlis, the Sultan's powers were divided into five specific departments, each headed by a minister appointed by the Sultan. The administration of justice came under the jurisdiction of the *Fandiyaaru* (judge) who was responsible for justice and under whom a *Naibu* (deputy) was appointed for each atoll. The general public have no say in state affairs although male residents of the capital Malé were involved in important matters such as deciding on the succession or removal of the Sultan. As such, the islanders were not represented in politics.[36] By 1903, when Sultan Muhammad Shamsuddin III ascended to the throne, all legislative and executive powers lay in his hands. He appointed a Prime Minister and delegated executive powers to close aides and associates (known as *Bodun* or 'headmen'), elite members of influential families. It was a form of aristocracy in which nobles functioned as advisers and bureaucrats.

II. THE FIRST MALDIVES CONSTITUTION (1932)

A. The Quest for a Written Constitution and Driving Forces

The impetus for drafting the Maldives' first Constitution came from within and without although previous studies have focused solely on the internal

[34] 'Nothing in this Order shall extend to the Maldive Islands.' Constitution of Ceylon: Ceylon (State Council) Order in Council, art 2 (Sri Lanka, 1931).

[35] Council for Linguistic and Historical Research, *Dhivehi Thaareekh* [Maldivian History] (Malé, Council for Linguistic and Historical Research, 1981) 77–78 [hereafter 'Madivian History'].

[36] U Phadnis and ED Luithui, 'The Maldives Enter World Politics' (1981) 8 *Asian Affairs* 166, 168.

driving forces.[37] The key internal driving forces behind the Constitution were: (a) the ongoing political feuds between the elites from the dominant families; (b) the Prime Minister; and (c) the Sultan. The *Bodun* (leaders), as members of the advisory councils to the Sultan, played a key role in protecting the monarch, and exerted varying degrees of influence on him.[38] During the late 1920s, the Athireegey family were influential, especially since Prime Minister Abdul Majeed Rannaban'deyrikilegefaanu was married to the Sultan's sister. The Head of Customs, and the Maldives' Representative in Ceylon were also members of the Athireegey family.[39]

According to prominent Maldivian historian, Ahmed Shakir, the main reason for the tensions was that influential political figures felt that Prince Hassan Izzuddin – who was next in line to the throne – lacked the maturity, religiosity and morality to succeed to the throne.[40] The British Governor in Ceylon, Sir Herbert Stanley, was aware of the situation and informed the Sultan that Stanley's successor, the Acting Governor, Sir Bernard Henry Bourdillon, was planning to visit the Maldives and requested that the Sultan facilitate Bourdillon's mission.[41] Even though there is no explicit mention of constitution-making, Stanley's note stated that Bourdillon had spent ten years in Iraq on behalf of the British Government, that he was very familiar with Muslim customs and that he intended to discuss such matters with the Sultan, his ministers, and representatives of the people. One can surmise that the purpose of Bourdillon's visit was to discuss and propose a constitutional solution that would solve the impasse over the Sultan's succession.

Mohamed Amin – a politician and writer who was a member of the Athireege family – claimed that Bourdillon visited the Maldives 'upon the request of the leaders of the Maldives'[42] and that the wording of Stanley's message suggested that the British Government in Ceylon learnt of the situation in the Maldives

[37] MA Didi, *Dhivehiraajjeyge Qaanoon Asaaseege Hayaaiy* [The Life of the Constitution of the Maldivian Constitution] (Malé, Novelty Printers and Publishers, 1950); People's Majlis, *Dhivehiraajjeyge Qaanoonee Hayaaiy* [The Life of the Maldivian Law] (1981); Maniku, *Iyye*, (n 18); Suood, *The Maldivian Legal System*, (n 11); TW Hockly, *The Two Thousand Isles: A Short Account of the People, History and Customs of the Maldive Archipelago* (New Delhi, Asian Educational Services, 2003); Shakir, *Vihivana*, (n 23) vol 1; A Shakir, *Vihivana Qarunuge Thereygai Dhivehiraajje: Adhulu Insaafaai Qaanoonu Asaasee* [Maldives in the Twentieth Century: Justice and Constitution], vol 3 (Malé, Dhivehi Bahaai Thaareekhah Khidhumaiy Kuraa Qaumee Marukazu, 2006); and VH Coelho, '*Constitutional and Political Developments in the Maldives*' (1979) 28 *Foreign Affairs Reports* 134, 134–48.

[38] Shakir, *Vihivana*, (n 23) 52–56.

[39] ibid, 54–55. According to the census report of 1931, even though there is no caste system in the Maldives, unlike some of the neighbouring countries, there is a difference between 'Royalties', their near relatives and 'Didi' (generally the children of a union between a female member and a male member of the 3rd generation, of the Royal Family and a commoner) class and the rest. Department of Information and Broadcasting, 'The Report on the Census of the Maldive Islands 1931' (1931) 31.

[40] Shakir, *Vihivana*, (n 23) 54.

[41] People's Majlis (n 37) 17–18.

[42] Didi, *Dhivehiraajjeyge*, (n 37) 3–4.

through the elites from the dominant families and other aspirants for a constitution, and not the Sultan. Amin further argued that there was discontentment among some people against the Prime Minister,[43] be they influential political figures or the Sultan. Suood claims that the Sultan felt compelled to protect his throne from the powerful Prime Minister, who was in charge of the-day-to-day running of the state and who lived a 'corrupt and lavish lifestyle' and ruled autocratically.[44]

Whatever the political factionalism and intrigues, there was a need for all these actors to find a way to share power. With a constitution, the Sultan could protect his throne, while the elite figures could prevent the Crown Prince Hassan from succeeding to the throne. More importantly, these elite figures would have the opportunity to demand or establish a fair share of power through the separation of the powers to curtail the Prime Minister's power. The Prime Minister would also benefit from such as arrangement which ensured that the Sultan would not have untrammelled power. The idea of a having a written constitution was conceived by some of the elite figures to pressure the Sultan and the Prime Minister so that they had no choice but to agree in order to protect their status and power. At the same time, these elites were closely related by blood or marriage with the nobility and royalty[45] and this could be the main reason why the idea of having a constitution gained such momentum so quickly. Finally, the elites succeeded in convincing the Sultan to seek the guidance of the British Government in Ceylon[46] to support a constitution as quid pro quo for power-sharing and safeguarding the throne.

The other internal driving force was Maldivians who had either travelled abroad,[47] or who had been educated overseas.[48] These people had long advocated for such a change. However, prominent Maldivian historian Ahmed Shakir, argued that the arrival of these educated Maldivians had nothing to do with the movement for the Constitution[49] as he did not consider the global or geopolitical milieu in which these changes were taking place. In this regard, it is important to note that the Maldives' Constitution of 1932 was adopted during a wave of constitution-making after the First World War.[50] In Sri Lanka and Egypt, where many of the elites who supported a constitution were educated, there was a new epoch and a quest for the constitutionalising and codification of Islamic law.[51] The Maldives' proximity to Sri Lanka allowed these elites to

[43] ibid, 5.

[44] Suood, *The Maldivian Legal System*, (n 11) 19.

[45] See Hockly, *The Two Thousand Isles*, (n 37) 139.

[46] See Didi, *Dhivehiraajjeyge*, (n 37) 3–4.

[47] Hockly, *The Two Thousand Isles*, (n 37) 139.

[48] It is difficult to trace the exact educational qualifications of these elites. One thing that is known is that most of them were multilingual.

[49] Shakir, *Vihivana*, (n 23) 52–53.

[50] See J Elster, 'Forces and Mechanisms in the Constitution-Making Process' (1995) 45 *Duke Law Journal* 364, 368–69.

[51] ibid.

travel there quite often and to observe the latter's system. The elites who studied in Egypt must have known about or witnessed the Egyptian Revolution which called for liberty, independence and democracy. This meant that even though the ordinary citizens were unaware of the existence of written constitutions and laws, these elites would have heard about the making of the Donoughmore Constitution of 1931 in Ceylon and constitution-making in Egypt.[52]

The general public, however, had no role in the movement for the constitution or were unaware of the need for a written constitution or laws. This did not prevent the elites from falsely 'manufacturing' public demand for a constitution. During Bourdillon's visit, for example, four Maldivian citizens were asked irrelevant questions and their answers were intentionally mistranslated to Bourdillon. The first person was asked about his opinion on the form of government. When he answered, the translated version given to Bourdillon was that the citizen wanted a 'democratic government'. The second person was asked about the number of wives he had, while the third was asked of how to make a drumstick. The fourth was asked how to catch mackerel. Regardless of how irrelevant their answers were, Bourdillon was told that these citizens wanted the Maldives to have a democratic government.[53] The interpreter was the Maldives Representative in Ceylon – another member of the Athigeere family – and this suggests the Prime Minister's influence in pushing for a constitution.

In addition to these internal forces, three external drivers may be identified. The first is the influence of the wave of constitution-making in many countries after the First World War,[54] which reached the Maldives' shores when the country was politically volatile, and there was a quest for a written constitution. The second was the fact that movements advocating constitutionalism and constitution-making were current in Sri Lanka and Egypt. The third driving force was the British Government's involvement in the process, from urging the Sultan to have a written constitution to offering recommendations for a final draft.

B. The Constitution Drafting Process

Before Bourdillon's visit, the Sultan convened a special majlis and stated that Bourdillon wanted to discuss the appointment of his successor with the ministers.[55] The majlis was asked to prepare an official response to Bourdillon. The Sultan declared that the proposal for governing through a council of ministers would be beneficial and good for all, as this would make governance more

[52] The next section highlights the similarities between the Egyptian Constitution and the Maldivian Constitution, which suggests that the members of the Maldives' Constituent Assembly were inspired by the Egyptian Constitution.

[53] Shakir, *Vihivana*, (n 23) 56.

[54] See Elster, 'Forces and Mechanisms', (n 50) 368–69.

[55] Sultan's Memorandum to the Majlis.

transparent and divide responsibility between the various ministers rather than have the Sultan bear the entire burden of governance personally.[56]

On 5 March 1931, Bourdillon visited Malé[57] and after consulting with some people,[58] provided the Sultan with his written advice.[59] On 19 March 1931, the Sultan established a Constitutional Majlis (CM) by royal decree. It was comprised of 14 members[60] who were supposed to be the most competent by education and experience.[61] The CM was chaired by a President, assisted by a Vice President and a secretary.[62] A senior clerk[63] and four assistant clerks were also appointed together with a *Ban'deyri* (Sergeant-at-Arms).

The CM was broadly mandated not only to frame a constitution but also to enact the laws necessary for managing all state affairs since 'there are no particular laws that are enacted and decreed to manage the state affairs'.[64] The CM was thus given both the constitutional and general legislative powers. The main purpose of the whole process of constitution-making was thus to fill the void of a written constitutional and legal system. The CM's powers were not unfettered. There was a blanket limitation that laws should not be contrary to Islam, and foreign-related laws be consistent with the agreement between the Maldives and the British Government.[65] Additionally, the mandate required the CM to incorporate existing customs, recognise the economic status of the state, and be cognisant of easing the people to the extent possible.[66]

The CM convened on 22 March 1931 and began its deliberations by first establishing its rules of procedure and appointing two sub-committees. The first sub-committee was tasked with recording old local customs (as mandated by the Sultan) and the second with translating laws sent by the Maldivian Representative in Ceylon that were in the English language.[67]

[56] ibid.

[57] Mohamed Amin writes that Bourdillon's visit was upon the request of the leaders of the Maldives to facilitate in constitution-making. Didi, *Dhivehiraajjeyge*, (n 37) 3–4.

[58] Even though it is highly likely, it is not known whether this consultation involved any discussions with the Borah merchants.

[59] Didi, *Dhivehiraajjeyge*, (n 37) 4.

[60] It began first with 12 members. Later, on 19 February 1932, two additional members (the last two in the following list) were appointed to the CM. It is important to highlight that these members appointed by the Sultan belonged to the capital island, Malé, suggesting that there was no fair representation of members from the atolls throughout the country. The appointed members are: (1) Al-Amir Abdul Majeed Rannaban'deyrikiligefaanu, (2) Al-Amir Ali Kudarannaban'deyrik ilegefaanu, (3) Al-Amir Ahmed Dhoshimeynaa Kilegefaanu, (4) Al-Sheikh Hussain Salaahuddin, (5) Al-Nabil Galolhugey Mohamed Didi, (6) Al-Amir Mohamed Farid Didi, (7) Ibrahim Thutthu Manik of Noomaraa Ganduvaru, (8) Hussain Hilmi Didi, (9) Ibrahim Ali Didi, (10) Ahmed Kamil Didi, (11) Al-Sheikh Ibrahim Rushdi Al-Azhari, (12) Al-Sayyid Kalhuhuraagey Abdulla Dhoshi Seedhi, and (14) Al-Amir Mohamed Amin Didi.

[61] See Didi, *Dhivehiraajjeyge*, (n 37) 7.

[62] Adam Naseer Manik and Abdulla Ismail were appointed as Assistant Secretaries.

[63] Al-Sheikh Malim Moosa Maafaiy Kaleygefaanu was appointed as the Senior Secretary.

[64] 'Royal Decree on Appointment of Constitutional Majlis' (1931).

[65] The Agreement of 1887.

[66] 'Royal Decree on Appointment of Constitutional Majlis' (n 64).

[67] Didi, *Dhivehiraajjeyge*, (n 37) 9.

The first sub-committee made a compilation of unwritten conventions practised in the Maldives in governing and affairs of state although we do not know if the sub-committee travelled to the various islands to record customs practised across the country. Almost two months after its first session, and after the two sub-committees completed their tasks, the CM appointed a seven-member committee to draft the Constitution on 25 May 1931.[68] The first draft of the Constitution was completed in just over a fortnight, on 9 June 1931 and presented to the CM in a special session on 10 June 1931. At this session, the CM decided that the draft be sent to all the members after it was presented to the Sultan on 16 June 1931. The Sultan sent this draft to Graeme Thomson, who had just assumed his post as Ceylon's Governor in April 1931.[69] On 10 October 1931, the Governor forwarded his opinion on the draft, proposing certain amendments[70] which would protect British rights and powers under the 1887 Agreement and at the same time safeguard the Sultan's powers.[71] Given the influence of the elites and aspirants for a constitution, it was beneficial for the British to pledge allegiance to the Sultan and safeguard his throne so they could gain a foothold in the new political structure.

Only a few of Thomson's proposed amendments were accepted by the CM. According to Mohamed Amin, this was because the CM felt that the proposed form of government was inappropriate for the Maldives because it was too 'lowly' or egalitarian but this explanation is overly simplistic.[72] Thomson proposed a government run by a state council,[73] similar to that proposed for Ceylon by the Donoughmore Commission. That proposal had also been rejected in Ceylon.[74] I argue that there are three possible reasons why the CM rejected Thomson's proposals. First, is the general Maldivian distrust of the British whom they saw as opportunistic colonialists and meddlers.[75] Second, the proposed model of government would place state power in the hands of a few members of the State Council and possibly confer wide-ranging powers on the Sultan or the Prime Minister, which was unacceptable to the CM. Finally, the CM feared that, with this form of government, the British would have even more opportunities to interfere with the appointment of key government officials.

Despite the Maldives' request to the British Government to facilitate the constitution-making process, certain features of the resulting Constitution were

[68] This committee was comprised of the following seven members: (1) Al-Amir Ahmed Dhoshimeynaa Kilegefaanu, (2) Al-Sheikh Hussain Salaahuddin, (3) Al-Amir Mohamed Farid Didi, (4) Ahmed Kamil Didi, (5)Ibrahim Ali Did, (6) Al-Sheikh Ibrahim Rushi Al-Azahari, and (7) Hussain Ali Didi.

[69] See People's Majlis, (n 37) 28–31.

[70] ibid.

[71] ibid, 29–31.

[72] ibid, 15.

[73] Didi, *Dhivehiraajjeyge*, (n 37) 4.

[74] 'The Ceylon Report' (1929) 19 *The Round Table* 295, 295.

[75] See Council for Linguistic and Historical Research, *Maldivian History*, (n 35).

wholly proposed by the CM members. For example, the CM adopted the right to vote with restrictions based on gender and literacy qualifications.[76] Indeed, it may well be argued that the main actors in the drafting process were the same as those who pushed for a written constitution in the first place.

According to Mohamed Amin, the foundations of the Constitution were based on the Constitutions of the UK and Egypt.[77] There is no other explicit mention of the sources relied on by the CM. When speaking of the UK Constitution, Amin may well have been referring to documents provided by Bourdillon. However, as I have argued elsewhere, the fundamental rights and freedoms enshrined in the Constitution bear significant similarity to the Egyptian Constitution of 1930.[78] Moreover, clauses such as those of state religion and official language were likely to have been inspired by the Egyptian Constitution.[79] This claim is buttressed by the fact that some CM members were well-versed in Arabic and had experience of the Egyptian constitutional system. Given the resemblance to the articles of the Egyptian Constitutions of 1923 and 1930, we can safely assume that the laws relied on by the CM included these two Egyptian Constitutions.

The elites from the dominant families and the aspirants for a constitution played a far more dominant role than the Sultan and the Prime Minister in agitating for a constitution. The British Government also played a key role in supporting the idea of a constitution and providing proposals and advice on the draft. In this regard, no significant role for the Prime Minister was identified. Given the roles, responsibilities and separation of powers established under the Constitution and its subsequent fate, elites from the dominant families and the aspirants for a constitution framed the first Constitution in their own favour. Indeed, after the Constitution was ratified, they assumed key positions in Parliament and the cabinet. The interests of the Sultan and the Prime Minister appeared to have been given short shrift, and this may well have precipitated the Prime Minister's resignation as the chairman of the CM in the midst of the constitution-making process.

C. Ratification of the First Constitution

Before the Constitution was ratified, the Sultan appointed a Consultative Council to facilitate the transition of government to the new constitutional system.

[76] It is likely that this could be inspired by the Egyptian Constitution of 1930.

[77] Didi, *Dhivehiraajjeyge*, (n 37) 15.

[78] For a relevant further discussion see S Falaah, 'Islamic Constitutionalism in the Maldives: Islamness of the Maldivian Constitution and Laws' in CM Fombad et al (eds), *Constitutions of the Countries of the World* (Oxford, Oxford University Press, 2018).

[79] See Constitution of Egypt 1930, art 3. Article 3 of the Constitution of Afghanistan of 1931 also declared Islam as the state religion.

The Constitution was ratified in a special durbar (session)[80] on 22 December 1932 where the Sultan's speech from the throne was delivered. The Sultan highlighted the reasons behind the formation of the Constitution and proclaimed the appointments for the newly-established public offices. This was followed by the response of the people to the Royal Speech in which the people praised and thanked the Sultan for his acceptance and facilitation of a written constitution and affirmed their allegiance and obedience to the Sultan and the Constitution.

The 1932 Constitution consisted of 92 articles and its Preamble read:

> Beseeching the guidance of the Almighty, I, Sultan Mohamed Shamsuddin Iskandar, son of Sultan Ibrahim Nooraddin Iskandar, ruler of the Maldive Islands, – in order to promote Solidarity and govern with Justice and Fairness amongst all with Equality, and intending the Engagement and Participation of all in the conduct of state affairs and that they live with Liberty and Safety in the Maldive Islands, and to govern whereby all the Maldivians are bestowed with Peace and Harmony, and successive Sultans and our Posterity live with Tranquillity – do hereby confirm and ordain the following Constitution to be observed for governing the State.

This preambular dictum calls for the promotion of solidarity, equality, justice and fairness, engagement and participation in state affairs, liberty, safety, peace, harmony and tranquillity. While this Preamble espouses commonly-held constitutional principles, values, and goals, it was clearly a 'top-down' instrument, emanating as it did from the Sultan, and not an affirmation or declaration of the people.

III. MAIN FEATURES OF THE FIRST CONSTITUTION

A. Structure of the State and Separation of Powers

The Constitution declares the Maldives as a protected state of the UK but with the full sovereignty and independence in internal affairs.[81] This being so, it is interdicted from entering into any treaty or political relation with any state other than the UK.[82] The Constitution also proclaims the Maldives as an 'elective-hereditary monarchy', reminiscent of the Germanic 'confirmation monarchy'[83] (a hybrid of the hereditary and elective monarchy). While the Preamble lacks any mention of the power or sovereignty of the people, Article 23 of the Constitution states that 'all the powers are derived from the citizens' and are to be administered in accordance with the separation of powers among the

[80] The court or public reception held by the Sultan.
[81] ibid, art 1.
[82] ibid.
[83] See FJ Stahl, *The Doctrine of State and the Principles of State Law* (Aalten, WordBridge Publishing, 2009) 141–42.

branches of the government: the monarch; the Ministerial Majlis (cabinet); Legislative Majlis; and the People's Majlis.[84]

The government is held accountable through periodic elections. The Constitution also established horizontal accountability mechanisms in the form of checks and balances between the branches of the government. The monarch is the highest authority and head of state and is inviolable[85] although he may not act in any manner contrary to the Constitution.[86] This limitation, coupled with the separation of powers and limitations arising from the 1887 Maldives-British Agreement created a non-sovereign monarchy although some clauses stated that the monarch would reign as the sovereign and not as a ruler.[87] The monarch is elected by a special majlis (congress) comprising the Ministerial Majlis, Legislative Majlis, the nobles, scholars, and elites in Malé.[88] The monarch had the powers of ratifying and administering the law.[89] He was empowered to veto bills passed by the Legislative Majlis,[90] appoint and remove public officials,[91] and issue temporary orders in times of emergency.[92] The monarch could also summon the Ministerial Majlis and the Legislative Majlis for extraordinary meetings.[93] In addition to these powers, the monarch was the chief of the armed forces.[94]

A bi-cameral legislature comprising the Legislative Majlis and the People's Majlis was created. The Legislative Majlis had 28 members (of whom seven were nominated by the monarch, four elected from the four wards of the capital Malé, and 17 members elected by the People's Majlis), and the tenure of the Legislative Majlis was five years.[95]

The primary function of the Legislative Majlis was law-making, meaning that it is an ordinary legislature even though the Legislative Majlis is a party to the joint session that forms a special majlis to approve certain laws[96] and

[84] Constitution of the Maldives 1932, art 23.

[85] ibid, art 27. This article is contradictory to articles on constitutional supremacy, especially, Art 54(3).

[86] ibid, art 42.

[87] See V Bogdanor, 'The Monarchy and the Constitution' (1996) 49 *Parliamentary Affairs* 407, 407.

[88] Constitution of the Maldives 1932, art 26.

[89] ibid, art 28.

[90] ibid, art 29.

[91] ibid, art 46.

[92] ibid, art 47.

[93] ibid, art 34.

[94] ibid, art 48.

[95] ibid, art 56.

[96] Article 30 referred to the laws that may vary the value of the Maldivian currency; impose taxes on the people; damage the sea and land-based military order and system; impair the rights and possessions of the Sultan and citizens; promote discrimination among the foreigners in the territory of the Maldives; impair the rights and protection to the public servants; impair the protection and security of the people from attacks of the enemy; impair the armed forces and the volunteers; impair the trade, dwellings, harbours, shipping, and any unit and land of the armed forces; impair the administration of justice; entitle the right of land ownership to foreigners; and entitle the right of foreigners to trade in the islands other than Malé.

to exercise the constituent assembly function.[97] Legislative competence was limited to the extent that no law contrary with the Agreement of 1887 could be promulgated.[98]

The People's Majlis was made up of 47 elected members (four for each large atoll, and two for each remaining atoll, one member for Fuvamulak Island and one member for each ward of Malé),[99] and was elected once a year in elections that took place in Malé, the capital.[100] This meant that the islanders living in the atolls, who account for around 92.6 per cent of the total population,[101] had no opportunity to exercise their right to vote. In addition to the appointment of 17 members to the Legislative Majlis, the powers and responsibilities of the People's Majlis included the power to approve any Bill sent by the monarch to the Legislative Majlis for further consideration which failed to be approved by a two-thirds majority. A profound law can only be implemented after notifying the People's Majlis and being gazetted. The Constitution is silent on what it means by profound laws.[102] However, it implies that 'profound laws' is referring to the range of laws stated under Article 30.

The annual budget of the government must be presented to a joint session of the Legislative Majlis and the People's Majlis.[103] The People's Majlis is also a party to the joint session that exercises the constituent assembly function and approval of certain laws.[104]

The bi-cameral legislature resembled that found in Ceylon's 1931 Constitution (Donoughmore Constitution)[105] which provided for a Parliament of two chambers, with the Senate members having been appointed by the Governor-General.[106] In the Maldives, the seven members of the Legislative Majlis were appointed by the monarch. Other features, such as the monarch's power to return Bills to Legislative Majlis for reconsideration, were likely to have been inspired by the Donoughmore Constitution. The Ministerial Majlis is responsible for all state affairs. Its members are appointed by the monarch in consultation with the Prime Minister;[107] appointments must be made from within the members of the Legislative Majlis. The Prime Minister, who must likewise be a member of the Legislative Majlis, is appointed by the monarch

[97] ibid, art 92.
[98] ibid, art 24.
[99] ibid, art 59.
[100] However, according to Art 89, as a transitional arrangement, the first Legislative Majlis will be comprised of members appointed by the monarch for 5 years. The composition as stated above will be after the completion of the transitional Legislative Majlis. ibid, art 61.
[101] Department of Information and Broadcasting, (n 39) 1–6.
[102] Constitution of the Maldives 1932, art 38.
[103] ibid, art 78.
[104] ibid, art 92.
[105] See Constitution of Ceylon, pt III.
[106] ibid, art 8 (1).
[107] Constitution of the Maldives 1932, art 50.

in consultation with the members of the Legislative Majlis. The Constitution established 12 governmental departments, each headed by a minister.[108]

The monarch's power to appoint and remove the chiefs of the armed forces, the declaration of war and peace, and the determining of treaties,[109] granting honours and titles,[110] are to be exercised in consultation with the Ministerial Majlis, as in his administration of all other state affairs.[111] His power to appoint and remove ambassadors is exercised in consultation with the foreign minister.[112] Under the Constitution, the Ministerial Majlis is made accountable to the legislature; ministers are required to be answerable to the Legislative Majlis in matters relating to their ministerial portfolios,[113] and to the monarch's orders.[114] The Finance Minister must present the annual budget to a session with both the chambers.[115] Both the People's Majlis and the Legislative Majlis have the power to pass no-confidence motions against the Ministerial Majlis,[116] while the Legislative Majlis can pass no-confidence votes against individual ministers[117] and hold hearings on ministers' alleged offences and make determinations thereon with a two-thirds majority.[118] Hearings against a minister other than the Prime Minister must be conducted in a special majlis comprising the Prime Minister, the head of the judiciary, the Attorney-General, the Head Procurator, and four members of the Legislative Majlis. If a hearing is against the Prime Minister, the special majlis with a similar composition will replace the Prime Minister with two ministers. If a hearing is against the monarch, two male royals will be added to the committee.[119]

i. Sovereignty of the People

In the pre-constitutional Maldives, sovereignty was vested in the monarch, but with the enactment of this constitution, the principle of sovereignty of the people was constitutionalised. The Constitution provides that the source of all state powers[120] be based on the people's consent. This popular sovereignty clause

[108] The following are the established departments: Department of the Prime Minister; Department of Defence; Department of Justice; Department of Finance; Department of Home Affairs; Department of Foreign Affairs; Department of Education; Department of Commerce; Department of Health; Department of Public Works; Department of Endowments; and Department of Agriculture.
[109] Constitution of the Maldives 1932, art 48.
[110] ibid, art 45.
[111] ibid, art 49.
[112] ibid, art 50.
[113] ibid, art 67.
[114] ibid, art 68.
[115] ibid, art 76.
[116] ibid, art 72.
[117] ibid, art 73.
[118] ibid, art 74.
[119] ibid, art 75.
[120] ibid, 23.

prohibits the government from disregarding the people's will. The Constitution thus transformed and heightened the political status of the Maldivians from subjects to citizens, a unique and unprecedented move among South Asian constitutional orders.[121]

ii. Supremacy of the Constitution

The enactment of the Constitution also constituted the Maldives as a constitutional supremacy. Powers of the monarch must be exercised within constitutionally prescribed bounds,[122] and no law may contradict the Constitution.[123] The Constitution strengthened this principle by requiring that any amendment – by way of any alteration, addition or deletion, or by a law on any matter prescribed in Article 30 – be made by a joint session of a special majlis before the monarch comprised of the People's Majlis, Legislative Majlis, elites and scholars residing in Malé at that point of time.[124] This may be regarded as an entrenchment clause[125] – doubtlessly influenced by the Maldives' constitutional past[126] – that prevents the form of government established from being amended or altered by the monarch or Prime Minister alone. Furthermore, the monarch may be impeached for violating a constitutional principle.[127] The Constitution is silent on the courts' judicial power and jurisdiction to review laws and administrative actions.

iii. Bill of Rights

A Bill of Rights (BOR) was enshrined and incorporated into the Constitution in Articles 4 through 22. At the time of its enactment, this was considered a most progressive and exceptional move, and the Maldives was the first among South Asian states to incorporate such a wide-ranging list of rights in the

[121] Bangladesh adopted this principle in its first Constitution. See the Constitution of Bangladesh 1972, art 7. See also ch 4 on Bangladesh in this volume.

[122] Constitution of the Maldives 1932, art 42.

[123] ibid, art 92

[124] ibid, art 92.

[125] This is the first time in the constitutional history of South Asia that an entrenched clause was adopted in a constitution. Bangladesh adopted an eternity clause in 2011 in art 7B of its Constitution. For a general discussion on entrenched clauses, See R Albert, 'Constitutional Handcuffs' (2010) 42 *Arizona State Law Journal* 663. See also Mi Hein, 'Impeding Constitutional Amendments: Why Are Entrenchment Clauses Codified in Contemporary Constitutions?' (2019) 54 *Acta Polit* 196.

[126] Constitutional scholars argue that '[c]ountries' constitutional histories also have a strong influence on the content of their present constitutions. Constitutional provisions tend to favour some individuals' interests over others, so once an attribute is entrenched, it often exhibits a high degree of path dependence, as those who are benefited by a provision fight for its continued inclusion.' See T Ginsburg and A Simpser (eds), 'The Content of Authoritarian Constitutions' in *Constitutions in Authoritarian Regimes* (Cambridge, Cambridge University Press, 2013).

[127] Constitution of the Maldives 1932, art 54(3).

Constitution.[128] The BOR guaranteed the rights and freedoms that were later to be entrenched in the Universal Declaration of Human Rights in 1948.[129] Civil and political rights guaranteed in the Constitution include: equality before the law and in the enjoyment of civil and political rights;[130] right to security of the person and freedom from arbitrary arrest;[131] right to retain and instruct legal counsel;[132] no punishment without law and freedom from torture;[133] prohibition of forced exile and freedom of movement;[134] right to privacy (right to inviolability of the home);[135] right to privacy of communications and correspondence;[136] freedom of expression;[137] freedom of the press;[138] freedom of assembly;[139] freedom of association;[140] and the right to present petitions to higher public officials against injustice.[141] The Constitution provided for the following social-economic rights: the freedom of education;[142] the right to a pension;[143] the right to hold property; the prohibition of punishment by public seizure of property;[144] and the prohibition of imposing a burden either by money or labour.[145] In addition to these rights and freedoms, the Constitution imposed an obligation on citizens to learn to recite the Quran and read and write both Arabic and Thaana.[146]

The BOR articles resemble those of the Egyptian Constitution of 1932. Indeed, some of its articles are almost identical. The only differences pertain to matters peculiar to the Maldives. For example, the freedom of religion is not guaranteed in the Maldives because all Maldivians are Muslims. At the same time, the freedom to use any language in social, private, or commercial dealings or religious affairs in the press and public gatherings is not safeguarded. While the Egyptian Constitution obliges the state to provide compulsory primary education, the Maldivian Constitution obliges all Maldivians to be literate in Arabic and Dhivehi and to read the Quran. The right to travel abroad is guaranteed but

[128] None of the Ceylonese Constitutions before 1932 (Soulbury Constitution of 1923 and Donoughmore Constitution of 1931) incorporated a BOR.

[129] The Universal Declaration of Human Rights 1848 (UN General Assembly, 10 December 1948).

[130] Constitution of the Maldives 1932, art 4.

[131] ibid, art 5.

[132] ibid, art 83.

[133] ibid, art 6.

[134] ibid, art 7.

[135] ibid, art 8.

[136] ibid, art 11.

[137] ibid, art 12.

[138] ibid, art 13.

[139] ibid, art 16.

[140] ibid, art 17.

[141] ibid, art 21. It is not clear whether this includes the judicial review of statutes and administrative actions and whether petitions can also be made to the courts.

[142] This was guaranteed as a freedom, not as a right, which means the government has no responsibility in providing education. ibid, art 15.

[143] ibid, art 22.

[144] ibid, art 10.

[145] ibid, art 17.

[146] ibid, art 14. Thaana is the script used for the Dhivehi language.

Maldivians are prohibited from emigrating. Overall, except for the absence of prohibition of gender discrimination in certain articles of the Constitution and the procedures of its protection and justiciability, the first Maldives Constitution represents a remarkable step in democratic constitutionalism.

iv. Judicial Independence

Even in the pre-constitutional era, the Maldives' judiciary was independent from the executive.[147] They decided cases independently, and their decisions were respected.[148] This independence remained a cardinal feature in the 1932 Constitution which safeguards judicial independence through four separate articles: (a) judges are independent unless they contravene the law and no person shall interfere with the judicial proceedings; (b) the establishment and organisation of judicial bodies for the islands and the powers of the judges shall be determined by law; (c) the removal and transfer of judges shall be made in accordance with the law; and (d) trials of offences to which banishment or the death penalty applies shall be by a jury. The Constitution also restricts the monarch's role in making any laws concerning the judiciary.[149] The jury could have been inspired by the practice in Ceylon, one of the first countries in the colonial rule to establish a jury system.[150]

v. Status of Islam and Islamic Law

As mentioned earlier, the CM was mandated to exercise its constitution-making power within the bounds of the 'religion of Islam'.[151] The Constitution does not define the Maldivian state as an Islamic state. Even so, Islam and Islamic law occupy a central place in the Constitution. Every citizen is expected to be literate in Arabic and Dhivehi and to read the Quran.[152] In addition, the monarch and members of the Legislative Majlis[153] must be Muslim and followers of Sunni Islam, and persons who have not been convicted of an offence for which a *ḥadd*[154]

[147] See Laval, *The Voyage of Francois Pyrard*, (n 9) vol 1, ch 15.

[148] MI Luthufi, *Ibn Battuta Dhivehiraajjeygai* [Ibn Battuta in the Maldives], vol 32 (National Centre for Linguistic and Historical Research 1991) 245. See also MI Didi, *Christopherge Nazarugai Dhivehin* [Maldivian in the Eyes of Christopher] (National Centre for Linguistic and Historical Research 1996) 40, 69–70.

[149] Constitution of the Maldives 1932, art 44.

[150] See L Jayasuriya, 'The Evolution of Social Policy in Sri Lanka 1833-1970: The British Colonial Legacy' (2001) 46 *Journal of the Royal Asiatic Society of Sri Lanka* 1, 2.

[151] 'Royal Decree on Appointment of Constitutional Majlis' (n 64).

[152] Constitution of the Maldives 1932, art 14.

[153] ibid, art 56.

[154] In Islamic Shariah, offences carry fixed, mandatory punishments that are based on the Quran or the Sunnah. See R Peters, *Crime and Punishment in Islamic Law: Theory and Practice from the Sixteenth to the Twenty-First Century,* Themes in Islamic Law 2 (Cambridge, Cambridge University Press, 2005) 53–67.

is prescribed.[155] The monarch is obliged to profess and respect Islam,[156] and must be impeached if he is convicted of a *ḥadd* offence.[157]

vi. British-Maldives Relationship

The Constitution acknowledges the Maldives' status as a protected state of the UK, which has control over foreign affairs. No law may be made in contrary to the 1887 Maldives-British Agreement.[158] The Constitution nonetheless proclaims the monarch to be the head of the state,[159] thus removing any doubt arising from the British Government's relationship with the Maldives. The article on installing the Sultan gives no role for the British Government,[160] which is contrary to the 1887 Agreement.

B. The Life and Death of the First Constitution

Unfortunately, the Maldives' first Constitution was short-lived. This dramatic abrogation of constitutional rule may be attributed to several reasons.

First, the elites, cabinet ministers and the Sultan were divided, selective, and instrumentalist in their approach to the drafting of the Constitution. The elites and the cabinet ministers wanted a stronger executive branch and to have a symbolic Sultan while the Sultan wanted to remain the de facto ruler.

Second, the Maldivians were isolated from the rest of the world and lacked exposure to modern constitutional systems. As such, they had become accustomed to an unwritten form of laws[161] and could not imagine adhering to written laws and a system of government that constrained the Sultan's powers through its cabinet ministers. In addition, some age-old customs had been codified under the new laws while others were now prohibited. A total of 40 laws were enacted within a span of eight months which was impractical[162] and caused barriers in obeying the laws.[163] Some of the controversial laws enacted soon after the Constitution include the law on timber, the law on foreign businesses, the law on health[164] and the law on cargo ships[165] which affected the hearts of the people bitterly.[166] The law on timber required that timber was to be sold by

[155] Constitution of the Maldives 1932, art 25.
[156] ibid, art 26.
[157] ibid, art 54.
[158] ibid, art 24.
[159] ibid, art 27.
[160] ibid, art 26.
[161] Shakir, *Vihivana Qarunuge*, (n 37) 63.
[162] Maniku, *Iyye*, (n 18) 40–43.
[163] Shakir, *Vihivana Qarunuge*, (n 37) 63–64.
[164] Didi, *Dhivehiraajjeyge*, (n 37) 48.
[165] ibid, 54.
[166] ibid, 49.

the state ending the longstanding practice of free use of timber by the people. The law on foreign traders imposed several fines on people who had been trading in the Maldives for many years without such impediments. For this reason, on 15 July 1933, foreign traders protested by ceasing to trade,[167] which resulted in an unbearable situation for the people[168] who were in many ways 'in the pockets of the foreign merchants' without whose assistance the Maldivians were not able to import staple foods.[169] The Borah merchants again protested and closed their shops on 15 August 1933. Even though the reforms by the health Act are positive and useful, the people were not ready for a 'sudden "swallow"' of these reforms.[170] These 'far-reaching and irritating'[171] reforms irked the Maldivians even more.[172] During the law-making process, members from the islands held separate meetings to express their opinions on the Bills proposed.[173] This shows that the reforms were not reflective of the people's aspirations as a whole,[174] especially, the islanders.

To make it worse, the law-making and the government lacked consideration of transitional articles or arrangements. The people's discontent was caused not only because of the new laws, but because incompetent, inexperienced, and overenthusiastic young ministers fared poorly in managing government affairs.[175]

The third reason was political infighting and a lack of collaboration among the ministers.[176] The Constitution created discontinuities in the Maldives' constitutional traditions and proclaimed a totally new constitutional legal order. The Sultan found this change unacceptable especially since he had untrammelled power before the Constitution was drafted. Several Bills were sent back for reconsideration by the Sultan.[177] Moreover, the Sultan's ire was further stoked when he was forced to ratify the *al-Aḥkām al-'Āmma* (General Laws) after the amendment of the Constitution.[178] The lack of avenues for a healthy party system led to political in-fighting and factionalism.

[167] ibid, 68.

[168] ibid, 49. Tensions arose between the Maldivians and the Borah merchants causing the British Government in Ceylon to intervene. A British government officer was sent to seek reconciliations between the two. After several negotiations, the Borah merchants left the last meeting in protest. The government imposed 'martial law' rules, which lasted for three days. The public started protesting, which resulted in injury to some Borah merchants. See Shakir, *Vihivana*, (n 23) 917 & 488.

[169] Didi, *Dhivehiraajjeyge*, (n 37) 50–51.

[170] ibid, 49.

[171] Hockly, *The Two Thousand Isles*, (n 37) 161.

[172] Shakir, *Vihivana Qarunuge*, (n 37) 64.

[173] Didi, *Dhivehiraajjeyge*, (n 37) 91.

[174] ibid, 41–43. Instead of supporting the rights of the people, the members were self-seeking.

[175] He also writes that the members of the People's Majlis debated the proposed Bills. However, it was not soon before tensions arose among the members, either intentionally or inadvertently, due to the divergent opinions and principles advocated by the members. ibid, 43.

[176] ibid, 86.

[177] Shakir, *Vihivana Qarunuge*, (n 37) 65.

[178] See Didi, *Dhivehiraajjeyge*, (n 37) 145–50.

The Sultan, to a group of 30 people, expressed his discontentment against the *al-Aḥkām al-'Āmma*, claiming that the laws were contrary to the Constitution, and the gazetted rules by the departments had resulted in immense hardship for the people.[179] Further, he alleged that the departments did not run in accordance with the Constitution and revealed that he first discussed these concerns with his brother, former PM, and Ibrahim.[180] However, there was no avail or ease even after the People's Majlis was convened as per the Constitution.[181] Therefore, intending that he should not abstain from responding to these issues, the Sultan sought the help of the people to gather at a decided date.[182] The Sultan gave the assurance that he was willing to go through whatever circumstances that may befall on them holding the assembly. There was no recorded further direction given by the Sultan nor the specific procedures of holding the assembly, except the religious prayers planned before the assembly.[183]

On 9 November 1933, a mob (*havaru*), as discussed above, provoked by the Sultan,[184] gathered at Gulhakulhey Square and demanded the resignation and removal of all the cabinet ministers except Mohamed Amin, Hassan Farid Didi and Mohamed Farid Didi, and banish those ministers and other deputy ministers and a member of the People's Majlis (a total of 7), to other islands. Then the mob demanded a government run by six ministers (including the three ministers they supported and three additional ministers) to be appointed under and headed by the former Prime Minister, Abdul Majeed Rannabandeyrikiligefaanu. The Sultan refused to remove and banish any minister without due process, and also refused to surrender any minister to the mob. This response infuriated the mob who vandalised some of the ministers' residences. Then they demanded that the Constitution be given to them. The Sultan ordered the Prime Minister Mohamed Farid to give the Constitution to the mob who tore the Constitution into pieces.

Two ministers resigned while some ministers sought resignation and banishment, which was declined by the Sultan. At last, the Sultan declared that he believed that it was within the best interests of the security of the Maldives that the ministers do as the mob demanded. The disgraced ministers and other officials then boarded a ship to Ceylon to brief the acting Governor of the situation.

The Sultan resumed his autocratic rule and the Constitution went into a legal limbo. The People's Majlis was dissolved, the Legislative Majlis was ceased or stopped and a Majlis comprised of 68 members from residents of Malé was formed, and the three ministers continued to run the government.

[179] People's Majlis, (n 37) 112.
[180] ibid.
[181] ibid.
[182] ibid, 115.
[183] ibid.
[184] ibid, 108–16.

On 25 December 1933, a Council of Ministers comprised of 5 ministers was convened by the people at the Gulhakulhey Square.

This created a constitutional interregnum as the Constitution was not suspended and thus partially continued in operation until it was amended on 5 July 1934. In the meantime, Sultan Muhamed Shamsudeen Iskandar III was dethroned[185] for wilful interference in the administration and exiled to Fuvahmulah City while the founders of the 1932 Constitution were banished to Colombo. He was replaced by Hassan Nooradeen Iskandar, son of Sultan Musir-ud-din, the Maldivian monarch who concluded the 1887 Agreement with the British.

It is important to note that the main reasons responsible for discontentment against the Constitution or the failure of the system of governance by the Constitution implies that the short life of the Constitution was not solely due to the Constitution in itself, but other constitutional limits on the rights of the people and political infighting. That said, the Maldives' first Constitution introduced its people to the idea of constitutionalism, albeit enmeshed with age-old constitutional conventions. However, its short life belies its long-lived legacy in the impact and influence it exerted on subsequent constitutions, right up to the present day.

C. A Founding Constitution?

As I have argued elsewhere, the drafting of this Constitution represented a 'constitutional revolution' and became the 'birth certificate' of constitutionalism and fundamental rights and freedoms in the Maldives.[186] Bill of Rights, separation of powers among the branches of the government, the constitutional checks and balances and the role of the state organs and public offices were established through the making of a model modern constitution for the formation of a nation-state. Most significantly, features such as the Bill of Rights, the state's religion and language, the checks and balances principle of ministers being answerable and accountable to the Parliament, judicial independence, and limited government were legacies that persisted long after that constitution's demise.

Given the 'home grown' features and the authority it owes to local legal factors,[187] this was an autochthonous constitution.[188] Despite its short-life it

[185] He was dethroned on 07 October 1934. The dethroning motion was moved by Hassan Farid Didi.

[186] Falaah, 'Islamic Constitutionalism', (n 78).

[187] See PC Oliver, 'Autochthonous Constitutions', in R Grote, F Lachenmann and R Wolfrum (eds), *Max Planck Encyclopedia of Comparative Constitutional Law* (Oxford, Oxford University Press, 2015).

[188] It should be noted that this was the first autochthonous constitution in South Asia.

was a remarkable achievement for a small state like the Maldives to establish an autochthonous constitution a decade before her neighbours. For these reasons, this Constitution laid the foundations for the making of Maldives as a modern nation-state.

IV. CONSTITUTIONAL DEVELOPMENTS 1934–1968

A. From Monarchy to Republic

In June 1934, the 1932 Constitution was amended and reduced to 84 articles from its original 92, with a further reduction to 80 articles in 1937. In 1940, during the outbreak of World War II, the 1932 Constitution was suspended. A special majlis stated that the Constitution and General Articles had been annulled as they 'did not fit the Maldives situation'. On 23 April 1942, Sultan Hassan Nooradeen sent a new 17-article constitution to the majlis for approval, stating that he wanted 'a suitable constitution to exist in the Maldives'. This Constitution vested the powers of the state in the Sultan, the Foreign Minister and the People's Majlis (which by this time was a body of six appointed members and 27 elected members).

Sultan Hassan Nooradeen was forced to abdicate in 1943 and was succeeded by Sultan Abdul Majid Didi, who refused to accept the crown and left for Egypt. He nonetheless reigned nominally until his death 1952. In the meantime, the Maldives was ruled by a four-member committee known as the Valy Committee in consultation with the Sultan; it was chaired by Hassan Fareed. This second Constitution was amended in 1951 to reinstate the right to freedom from arbitrary arrest and banishment, and the freedom of expression, speech and association. It also established a 34-member People's Majlis with a term of five years. On 20 October 1951, the People's Majlis appointed Mohamed Amin as the acting monarch who ruled in consultation with the Sultan, until the Sultan died on 21 February 1952. During this period, Mohamed Amin became the strongest political figure in the country.

These events coincided with the wave of constitution-making that followed the breakup of the French and British empires.[189] The elites considered whether or not to transform the Maldives into a republic. On 15 April 1952,[190] through a public referendum, Maldivians favoured a republic system over the monarchy and decided that Mohamed Amin would be their first *Walī al-'Amr* (head of the community or ruler or authority). Sir Ivor Jennings offered technical expertise during the making of this Constitution.[191] According to Jennings, he drafted

[189] See Elster, 'Forces and Mechanisms', (n 50) 369.
[190] The referendum result was announced on 18 April 1952.
[191] Maniku, *Iyye*, (n 18) 31.

the Constitution at the request of the Maldivian Prime Minister.[192] However, whether his draft included the proposals or opinions of the members of the Constituent Assembly, or was based solely on his experience and recommendations remains unknown. Writing derisively about the lack of democratic features in Jennings' draft, Abdul Hakeem Hussain Manik argued that Jennings had no knowledge of the community for whom he drafted the Constitution.[193] This Constitution (ratified on 01 January 1953; effective immediately) transformed the country's long-standing system of monarchy to becoming a presidential republic.

B. Main Features of the 1953 Constitution

While the 1953 Constitution opens with the voice of the people, it was anything but democratic. The Bill of Rights and checks and balances which had characterised the 1932 Constitution had been removed. Instead, a semi-presidential system with a powerful *Walī al-'Amr* (head of state and head of government) was established. The legislature was bi-cameral with two chambers: the People's House and the Senate.[194] The 1953 Constitution nonetheless provided for universal suffrage enabling the people to vote directly for the *Walī al-'Amr*.

The First Republican Constitution provided the same surprise as the Constitution of 1932. The abolishment of the monarchy was something totally new for the populace. More importantly, a government ruled by Mohamed Amin, a member of the Athireege family was unacceptable to its rival, the Kakaage family and this led to political infighting. At this time, the government was facing an economic crises and a famine (known as the 'republican famine').[195] This, coupled with the widespread corruption in the government, the allegations against Amin of being a womaniser,[196] strict laws passed at this time, which provided for the death penalty and amputation proved unbearable to the people. This offered the royalists an opportunity to unseat the republican government in a revolution on 21 August 1953. Amin's Muthaqaddhim Party was abolished followed by the dissolution of the People's House.[197] Amin was himself arrested.[198]

[192] I Jennings, *The Approach to Self-Government* (Cambridge, Cambridge University Press, 2011) 47. See also 'The Maldives Joins the Commonwealth' (1982) 8 *Commonwealth Law Bulletin* 1548.

[193] Maniku, *Iyye*, (n 18) 31.

[194] Constitution of the Maldives 1953, art 17.

[195] Jennings also claims that the failure of this constitution was due to the rapid deterioration of the economic conditions. See Jennings, *The Approach to Self-Government*, (n 192) 47.

[196] It should be noted that during this period, revolutionary changes were brought about allowing women to participate in state affairs such as in the government and in Parliament.

[197] The People's House was dissolved on 22 August 1953.

[198] *Walī al-'Amr* was arrested on 31 August 1953.

This development ran counter to the trend of constitution-making where state powers were constrained and fundamental rights were protected through constitutions.[199] This was simply not the case in the Maldives where the powers of government were widened rather than narrowed, and rights and freedoms jeopardised rather than safeguarded. The *Walī al-'Amr*, had the power to appoint half the Senate's members[200] and could thus control the Senate. He could also convene, sustain, and dissolve the Majlis (the People's House and the Senate).[201] The Constitution also allowed the People's House to grant the power of the Prime Minister to the *Walī al-'Amr*,[202] and by virtue of this, make the *Walī al-'Amr* a member of the People's House.[203] The *Walī al-'Amr* also had the power to appoint the Prime Minister.[204]

V. THE SECOND REPUBLICAN CONSTITUTION: 1968–1998

A. Resurgence of Republicanism

The 1953 Republican Constitution was abolished on 5 January 1954,[205] and on 31 January 1954 a public referendum reinstated the monarchy. A new constitution was adopted on 7 March 1954 and this lasted until the birth of the Second Republican Constitution on 11 November 1968. Between 1954 and 1968, the relationship between the British and the Maldivian governments soured due to a revolt in three southern atolls that resulted in the creation of a short-lived breakaway state, called the United Suvadive Republic. The country also had several phases of economic and social developments. The tension between the British and the Maldives provided the momentum for a Maldivian movement of independence.[206] On 26 July 1965, the Maldives gained full independence from the British and its political system underwent several significant changes. Once again, the main driving forces behind the new Constitution were the political infighting between politicians hailing from families other than the traditionally influential elite, and the state of, and urge for, economic, social, and cultural developments.

[199] See B Goderis and M Versteeg, 'The Transnational Origins of Constitutions: Evidence from a New Global Data Set on Constitutional Rights, 1946-2006' (2013) 2013–010 CentER Discussion Paper, 1.

[200] Constitution of the Maldives 1953, art 25.

[201] ibid, art 22.

[202] ibid, art 16.

[203] In these instances, the *Walī al-'Amr* was allowed to take part in the discussions but was not allowed to vote. ibid, art 16(b).

[204] ibid, art 11.

[205] The result of this referendum was announced on 10 February 1954.

[206] During the negotiations between the two governments to resolve the revolt in the southern atolls, on 27 September 1963, the Prime Minister Ibrahim Nasir wrote to the Commonwealth Secretary, Duncan Sandys, requesting independence.

On 3 October 1967, members of the People's Majlis were told that there would be a discussion to seek their opinion on the most appropriate form of government for the Maldives. This request was based on the Cabinet's decision to seek the opinion of the People's Majlis. On 15 November 1967, 40 of the 44 People's Majlis members voted in favour of a republic, and on 15 March 1968, by public referendum, the Maldivians decided to reinstate republicanism.[207] In view of this, the People's Special Majlis (the constituent assembly under the bicameral legislature in the then Constitution) adopted a new Constitution on 15 July 1968.

B. Main Features of the Constitution of 1968

The 1968 Constitution was not entirely new. In fact, it reinstated the 1932 Constitution except for the fact that it was based on a presidential system rather than a constitutional monarchy. It re-established the Maldives as a republic with strong presidential powers although not as powerful as that under the Constitution of 1953. This was the first constitution after the Anglo-Maldivian Agreement of 1965, under which the Maldives achieved total independence. With the amendments, the structure of the state established by this Constitution – such as the presidential system with a bi-cameral Parliament – lasted until the Constitution of 2008, surviving four amendments. In its essence, this Constitution contains similar democratic features to those of the 1932 Constitution, except for the absence of the principle of judicial independence. These features have been sustained in Maldivian constitutionalism for more than half a century until today and must thus also be considered foundational. The Constitution had the following main features.

i. Structure of the State and Separation of Powers

The Constitution proclaimed the Republic of the Maldives to be a sovereign and independent country[208] with a presidential republican system[209] and some parliamentary features. However, the Maldives reverted to a semi-presidential system when the Constitution was amended in 1970 and this system lasted until the third amendment in 1975.[210] The doctrine of the separation of powers[211] was established in this Constitution. The executive branch was made up of the

[207] The result of this referendum was announced on 01 April 1968. Over 81% of the voters preferred a republican system.

[208] Constitution of the Republic of the Maldives 1968, art 2.

[209] ibid, art 3.

[210] There were three amendments to this Constitution: 23 April 1970 (effective as of 26 April 1970), 2 February 1972 (effective as of 01 August 1972), and 15 April 1975 (effective as of 21 April 1975).

[211] Constitution of the Republic of the Maldives 1968, art 23.

President and the Cabinet while the bicameral legislature comprised the People's Majlis and People's Special Majlis.[212] The People's Majlis had 54 members, with eight members appointed by the President; eight members elected by the residents of Malé; and two members elected for each atoll of the Maldives.[213] The People's Special Majlis was made up of cabinet ministers, members of the People's Majlis; 46 members elected from Malé and the atolls (eight members from Malé and two members from each atoll) and eight members appointed by the President.[214] The President was empowered to convene the People's Special Majlis.[215] The President is both head of state and head of the government and is in charge of the administration of justice, having the power to appoint judges.[216] The President had unlimited power in appointing ministers to the cabinet[217] although the ministers were accountable to the People's Majlis.[218] The Majlis also had the power to pass no-confidence votes and hear trials against the ministers and to impeach the President.[219]

ii. Sovereignty of the People, Constitutional Supremacy and Limited Government

The Constitution established the principle of popular sovereignty by stating that the source of all powers of state affairs are derived from the people.[220] This Constitution also entrenched the doctrines of limited government[221] and constitutional supremacy.[222] These doctrines are reiterated in Article 75(b) which states that it is an impeachable offence if the President violates or abolishes a constitutional principle.[223] At the same time, constitutional amendments require the approval of the majority of the People's Special Majlis.[224]

iii. Bill of Rights

The 1968 Constitution reinstated the Bill of Rights[225] that was missing in the First Republican Constitution. The rights embedded in the Constitution were

[212] ibid, art 88.
[213] ibid, art 66.
[214] ibid, art 88.
[215] ibid.
[216] ibid, art 90.
[217] ibid, art 54.
[218] ibid, art 57–58.
[219] ibid, art 60–61.
[220] ibid, art 23.
[221] ibid, art 40.
[222] ibid, art 91.
[223] The Constitution does not define a constitutional principle. For further impeachable offences and grounds see ibid, art 52.
[224] ibid, art 87.
[225] ibid, ss 5–22.

almost identical to those found in the 1932 Constitution. This Constitution also reinstated the people's right to elect the President after the presidential candidates are endorsed by a secret ballot of the People's Majlis.[226] This was the first-time universal suffrage was constitutionally guaranteed to both sexes. Another safeguard pertinent to the protection of fundamental rights and freedoms is the prohibition on law-making in limiting the rights of the people.[227] This safeguard was first enshrined in the Constitution of 1932.[228]

iv. Status of Islam and Islamic Law

With the exception of the Maldives' 1953 Constitution, Islam and Islamic law have been given constitutional prominence. Islam was proclaimed as the state religion[229] and every citizen is required to be literate in Arabic and Dhivehi and to read the Quran.[230] Moreover, the freedom of education,[231] freedom of assembly,[232] freedom of expression,[233] freedom from restraint and the right to no punishment without law,[234] are guaranteed so long as such guarantees do not conflict with Islamic law. Another feature introduced by this Constitution was the supreme authority given to the President in propagating the tenets of Islam.[235] This role, which was first given to the Justice (the chief judge who is the head of the judiciary) in the First Amendment to the Constitution of 1932,[236] has lasted until the present-day except in the Constitution of 1997. The Constitution also requires the President,[237] cabinet ministers,[238] and members of the two chambers of the legislature[239] to be Muslims and followers of Sunni Islam. The oaths of the President,[240] cabinet ministers,[241] and members of the People's Majlis[242] also require them to obey Islam. They must also be persons who have not been convicted of an offence for which a *ḥadd* is prescribed.

[226] The first time universal suffrage was guaranteed for both sexes in a Maldivian Constitution was in the Constitution of 1954 (Fourth Constitution). ibid, art 26.
[227] ibid, art 75 (b).
[228] Constitution of the Maldives 1932, art 30(3).
[229] Constitution of the Republic of the Maldives 1968, art 3.
[230] ibid, art 16.
[231] ibid, art 17.
[232] ibid, art 18.
[233] ibid, art 7.
[234] ibid, art 8.
[235] ibid, art 36.
[236] Constitution of the Maldives 1932 (as amended by the first amendment effective as of 5 July 1934), art 72).
[237] ibid, art 27(a).
[238] ibid, art 55(a).
[239] ibid, art 67(a).
[240] ibid, art 28.
[241] ibid, art 56.
[242] ibid, art 68.

VI. LEGACY OF THE CONSTITUTIONS OF 1932 AND 1968

As pointed out in Parts II and II, the contributions of the Constitutions of 1932 and 1968 have been seen throughout the Maldives' constitutional history. The following is a brief analysis of the impact of these two Constitutions on the current Constitution of 2008.

Structurally and substantively, the introductory articles and the chapter on the Bill of Rights bear similarities with the Constitutions of 1932 and 1968 though the later chapters of the 2008 Constitution are closer to those of the 1968 Constitution. While the 1968 Constitution has more structural similarities to the current Constitution than the 1932 version, the latter may be said to have had a bigger impact on shaping the 2008 Constitution insofar as its democratic features (such as the Bill of Rights and judicial independence) are concerned.

The articles on national and religious identity established in the 1932 Constitution have never been contested and have been adopted in all the constitutions of the Maldives. Despite the vacillation between the monarchic and republican systems, the articles of the constitutions before the 1968 Constitution are largely similar. The 1997 Constitution (commenced on 1 January 1998) explicitly espoused the principles of Islam, unitarianism, and democracy.[243] The concept of 'unitarianism' was extensively developed under the 2008 Constitution.

Despite the adoption of the Westminster model in South Asia – a move favoured by Jennings[244] – the presidential system has, in the case of the Maldives, always prevailed over the parliamentary system. This continues to be the case in the 2008 Constitution too. Direct elections, first introduced in the 1953 Constitution, were reinstated in the 1968 version. This feature was one of the most controversial and extensively debated during the framing of the 2008 Constitution. After a heated debate, it was incorporated into the Constitution.[245]

While the public favoured a presidential system over a parliamentary system, the 2008 Constitution has features of both.[246] In adopting certain features of the parliamentary form of government – such as executive accountability to the legislature – members of the Constituent Assembly ignored the outcome of the public referendum.

[243] Constitution of the Republic of Maldives 1997, art 1.

[244] See H Kumarasingham (ed), *Constitution Maker: Selected Writings of Sir Ivor Jennings* (Cambridge, Cambridge University Press, 2014). See also M Malagodi, '"The Oriental Jennings", An Archival Investigation into Sir Ivor Jennings' Constitutional Legacy in South Asia' (2014) 14(1) *Legal Information Management* 33–37.

[245] During the constitution-making process, both parliamentary and presidential forms of government were proposed and debated in the Constituent Assembly. In addition, a public referendum was held to decide on the form of government, which showed that the public favoured the presidential over the parliamentary form of government.

[246] The Supreme Court of the Maldives also stated that the current Constitution had a hybrid form of government comprised of features of both presidential and parliamentary systems. See *Ali Waheed and Dhivehi Qaumee Party v State (Attorney General's Office)* No. 2010/SC-C/26, 2010/SC-C/25 (SCMV 9 December 2010).

Judicial independence was first established in the 1932 Constitution, but its scope was curtailed in successive constitutions. Most importantly, the Constitution of 1968 lacked this feature, but this has since been restored in the 2008 Constitution.

The fusion of powers and weak separation of powers and safeguards to protect fundamental rights and freedoms under the 1997 Constitution were heavily criticised by the members of the People's Special Majlis (constituent assembly) during the drafting of the 2008 Constitution. This led to the establishment of a multi-party democracy and a separation of powers that placed significant control in the hands of the People's Majlis.[247]

VII. CONCLUSION

I have sought to explore the historical-political and theoretical bases of the Maldives constitutional foundings and argued that the Constitutions of 1932 and 1968 were foundational as they heralded new dawns in the country's constitutional and political history. The systems introduced in these two Constitutions not only provided the apparatus for governance, but also envisioned the social and economic transformation that the Maldives would later undergo. These two Constitutions resulted from the successful national reconciliations in two different eras of constitutionalism. The historical backdrop to the making of the 1932 and 1968 Constitutions underlines the fact that, to a large extent, these Constitutions embodied the political compromise reached between the influential Maldivian political factions. These compromises are manifested in the power-sharing mechanism in these Constitutions.

We have also seen that both internal and external driving forces operated behind the drafting of the 1932 Constitution, but the 1968 Constitution was driven only by internal forces. In case of the 1932 Constitution, the ongoing political feuds between the elite figures from the dominant families, the aspirants for a constitution, the Prime Minister and the Sultan were the primary driving forces, while the British Government and the wave of constitution-making elsewhere acted as external driving forces. In case of the 1968 Constitution, the main driving forces were the internal political conflicts and the evolving politics, with new politicians from families other than the traditionally influential elite families, and the urge for economic, social, and cultural developments.

This chapter has shown that these two Constitutions had both democratic and undemocratic features and were influenced by the nation's constitutional past and by other similar jurisdictions. In this regard, the role of the founding constitutions in shaping the later constitutions and serving the political and

[247] The current Constitution adopted a one chamber Parliament only, the People's Majlis, which comprises both the legislative and constituent assemblies.

constitutional crises is noteworthy. Most remarkably, the principles established under the 1932 Constitution were upheld even during the constitutional interregnum that lasted for around one-and-a-half years until an amendment reinstated a constitutional order. In essence, these two constitutions have inspired and remained influential for Maldivian constitutional politics for decades. After eight decades of the Constitution of 1932 and four decades of the Constitution of 1968, their legacies linger on in the 2008 Maldivian Constitution.

9

Afghanistan: An Aborted Beginning

EBRAHIM AFSAH

INTRODUCTION

A Constitutional Committee formed at the end of March 1963 met regularly over the next year and completed a draft constitution, which the king referred to a larger Constitutional Advisory Commission for discussion and public airing, and then convened a broadly representative constituent Loya Jirga on September 9, 1964, the anniversary of the 1931 Constitution. It was the first Loya Jirga to keep its proceedings in writing, and its 452 members (including six women) subjected the articles of the draft to lively debate for eleven full days, altering some of them. The Constitution was signed by Mohammad Zaher Shah on October 1, 1964.[1]

I. A CONTEXTUAL PROLEGOMENON

IN 1964, AFGHANISTAN appeared on the cusp of a great developmental stride towards modernity and prosperity. Strategically located between the two competing blocs of the Cold War, its leaders had managed the fine art of extracting massive amounts of aid and technical assistance from both sides. Fuelled not least by such 'overkill in foreign aid',[2] the social and political fabric of the country had undergone massive changes, fuelling increasingly tense, ideology-driven domestic and external politics. When this period came to an end in 1963, the country's monarch instigated a concerted effort to create a new, forward-looking but socially acceptable institutional framework in which competing interests could be pursued orderly and peacefully. The resulting 1964

[1] SA Arjomand, 'Constitutional Developments in Afghanistan: A Comparative and Historical Perspective' (2005) 53(4) *Drake Law Review* 943–963, 951; relying largely on L Dupree, *Afghanistan* (Princeton, NJ, Princeton University Press, 1980), 565–87 [hereinafter 'Dupree, *Afghanistan*'].

[2] Dupree, *Afghanistan*, ibid, 755.

Constitution was and continues to be hailed by knowledgeable commentators as 'the finest in the Muslim world'.[3] Prospects for the country appeared unusually good – but then everything unravelled.

To understand the particular role played by this Constitution in the hopeful, but ultimately aborted, journey towards modern state- and nationhood, it might be useful to first consider what a different cultural artefact can tell us about young states in ancient societies.[4] In 2011, an extraordinary exhibition entitled *Afghanistan: Crossroads of the Ancient World* toured the world, exposing enthusiastic global audiences for the first time to the incredibly rich historical legacy of a country most associated with death, destruction and religious nihilism.[5] This incredible collection of some 21,000 pieces of *Bactrian* gold artefacts were made between 2200 BCE and 200 AD in and around what is today Afghanistan. They were excavated in 1978 by Soviet archaeologists just before the country descended into its still-enduring orgy of violence and remained in the National Museum[6] in Kabul until 1988, when the impending Soviet withdrawal meant that the civil war might finally reach the cities. The objects were then placed in the vault of the Central Bank, by Ameruddin Askarzai, the Bank's official in charge of the country's foreign reserve and gold holdings.

When the Taliban overran the city in 1996 they forced him to open the vault and looted the reserves. Despite threats to his life, Askarzai managed to keep the archaeological treasures hidden from the intruders and then quick-wittedly destroyed the vault's lock by breaking the key in it, thus sealing the door and keeping the artefacts safe. He divulged his secret only in 2003 to the new transitional government, upon which the vault was cut open, the artefacts retrieved and eventually shown again.[7] The well-publicised destruction of the monumental Buddha statues in the Bamiyan Valley leaves little doubt as to what would have happened to these objects without Askarzai's heroic act. But given the ongoing violence, it is unfortunately again doubtful whether these objects will remain safe in Kabul. Currently, the US is seeking to extricate herself from her long

[3] ibid, 565. Note Arjomand's endorsement: 'With the hindsight of a quarter-century of constitution-making in the Middle East and four subsequent Afghan constitutions, I tend to concur with Louis Dupree's judgment.' Arjomand, 'Constitutional Developments' (n 1) 960.

[4] This idea is not mine, see inter alia N MacGregor, *A History of the World in 100 Objects* (London, Penguin /British Museum, 2012).

[5] FT Hiebert and P Cambon, *Afghanistan: Crossroads of the Ancient World* (London, British Museum Press, 2011).

[6] The creation of the museum itself – the country's first – was part of the first, ill-fated wave of institutional modernisation at the outset of King Amanullah's reign in 1919, as is the actual building where it has been located since 1931, the former Kabul Municipality, created under the country's first Constitution from 1923. See also Dupree, *Afghanistan*, (n 1) 452; NH Dupree, *An Historical Guide to Afghanistan*, revised and enlarged edition (Kabul, Afghan Air Authority & Afghan Tourist Organisation, 1977) 92–93.

[7] P Wonacott, 'The Keeper of the Keys and the Mystery of the Bactrian Gold. Afghan Banker Who Risked His Life to Save Treasure From the Taliban Finally Gets His Due', *Washington Post*, 12 Aug 2009) A1.

military engagement in that country by negotiating directly with the Taliban,[8] and similar fears to those that prompted the placement of the Bactrian gold in 1988 have resurfaced. Few trust the durability of the constitutional edifice that has been forged since the American invasion in 2001.[9]

The vault and the gold it held symbolise a general characteristic of modernity, one that is especially pronounced in the developing societies of the South; societies that underwent modernisation at an accelerated pace and with much greater outside interference.[10] Writing in the context of Germany's political disintegration in the 1930s, Ernst Bloch called this phenomenon 'the simultaneity of the non-simultaneous', namely the perplexing occurrence of technological progress, rationality and institutional innovation, with their simultaneous violent rejection and atavistic insistence on the superiority of arbitrary elements of tradition.[11] He writes about the persistence of a tradition that has not run its course, amidst the prevalence of modern elements that have not yet been digested, creating an individual and collective inability to either continue established old patterns, or adapt and generate new mores, resulting in a yearning for the security of an *imagined* past:

> Not all people exist in the same Now. They do so only externally, by virtue of the fact that they may all be seen today. But that does not mean that they are living at the same time with others. Rather, they carry earlier things with them, things which are intricately involved. One has one's time according to where one stands corporeally, above all in terms of classes. Times older than the present continue to effect older strata; here it is easy to return or dream one's way back to older times.[12]

The persistence of such a 'nonsynchronous heritage' defies our attempts to comprehend.[13] We find elements categorically belonging to different times and spaces, coexisting in the here and now. But the categories we created for better analysis in abstract, deliberately simplified models of a complex reality,[14] these categories usually rely on some linear narrative of conceptual evolution and

[8] The Editorial Board, 'End the War in Afghanistan. It is time to bring American soldiers back home,' *New York Times*, 3 Feb 2019, A20.

[9] D Zucchino, 'Afghans Glad Trump Stopped Taliban Talks, Even if They Doubt His Explanation,' *New York Times*, 9 Sep 2019, A4.

[10] A Matin-Asgari, *Both Eastern and Western: An Intellectual History of Iranian Modernity* (Cambridge, Cambridge University Press, 2018); E Afsah, 'Contested Universalities of International Law. Islam's Struggle with Modernity' (2008) 10 *Journal of the History of International Law* 259–307; and J Ellul, 'Islam and Modernity' (2003) 3(3) *Oikonomia* 24–36.

[11] E Bloch, *Heritage of Our Times* (New York, Polity Press, 1991); E Bloch, *Erbschaft dieser Zeit*, (Frankfurt a.M., Suhrkamp, 1985).

[12] E Bloch, 'Nonsynchronism and the Obligation to its Dialectics' (translated from the German by Mark Ritter) (1977) 11 *New German Critique* 22–38, 22.

[13] This is the term his translator Mark Ritter prefers, see footnote 12.

[14] On this problem, see more generally E Derman, *Models Behaving Badly, Why Confusing Illusion with Reality Can Lead to Disaster, on Wall Street and in Life* (Chichester, Wiley, 2011); JD Singer, *Models, Methods, and Progress in World Politics: A Peace Research Odyssey* (Boulder, Colorado, Westview Press, 1990).

gradual development.[15] According to Bloch, 'the concept of progress does not envisage "cultural spheres" where time is atavistically fixed in space. Instead of unilinearity, it requires a broad, elastic, entirely dynamic multiverse, an enduring, often convoluted counterpoint of the historical voices.'[16] Hobsbawm has described this idea as 'the multidimensionality of human beings in society'.[17] The resulting social strains cannot be easily mediated because the archaic and the modern sphere dynamically interact and remain structurally linked.[18] Bloch alerts us that these contextual constraints will affect the ability of individuals to function effectively in modern structures not yet fully assimilated:

> Certainly, a person who is simply awkward and who for that reason is not up to the demands of his position, is only personally unable to keep up. But what if there are other reasons why he does not fit into a very modern organization, such as the after-effects of peasant descent, what if he is an earlier type? In general, different years resound in the one that has just been recorded and prevails.[19]

Consequently, Conrad describes transitional nations as being engaged in a 'process of "limping behind" the nonsynchronous integration' of a state and society in which the old and the half-digested new coexist uneasily.[20] This creates considerable scope for violent conflict as modern governance institutions are created by constitutional fiat with reference to ill-understood foreign models, thus setting in motion a process of consolidation and contestation[21] that leads to hybrid forms often unrecognisable to those familiar with the original model: 'The changes which a law undergoes when introduced into or received by a different culture are of considerable significance in comparative law. The Middle East is an extensive laboratory for the study of the transplantation of law from

[15] One of the articles of faith of post-modern and 'critical' scholars is their deliberate distrust of such 'grand narratives'. It could be argued that much of that insistence is barking up the wrong tree, warning about the reification of abstract models, a danger well contained by the conventional skills of the trade. The result is the well-known scepticism against modelling as such, and in the process against rationality, the scientific method and the very notion of truth. These are debates far beyond the scope of this chapter, but for an intelligent and spirited defence of universal standards, model-making and neutral investigation, see JA Lindsay, 'A Principled Defense of the University,' *Areo Magazine*, 23 March 2018, available at: https://areomagazine.com/2018/03/23/a-principled-defense-of-the-university/.

[16] E Bloch, *Tübinger Einleitung in die Philosophie* (Frankfurt, Suhrkamp, 1977) 146.

[17] EJ Hobsbawm, 'Working-class Internationalism' (1988) 1 *Contributions to the History of Labour & Society* 3–16, 14.

[18] B Dietschy, *Gebrochene Gegenwart. Ernst Bloch, Ungleichzeitigkeit und das Geschichtsbild der Moderne* (Frankfurt a.M., Suhrkamp, 1988)187.

[19] Bloch, 'Nonsynchronism', (n 12) 22.

[20] B Conrad, *Zur Ungleichzeitigkeit in der Weltgesellschaft. Erkenntnistheoretische Kommentare zur Kriegsursachenforschung*, Arbeitspapier Nr. 1/2002, Universität Hamburg – IPW Forschungsstelle Kriege, Rüstung und Entwicklung (Hamburg, Universität Hamburg – IPW, 2002), available at: www.wiso.uni-hamburg.de/fachbereich-sowi/professuren/jakobeit/forschung/akuf/ archiv/arbeitspapiere/weltgesellschaft-conrad-2002.pdf, 18, relying on Norbert Elias.

[21] J Siegelberg, *Kapitalismus und Krieg. Eine Theorie des Krieges in der Weltgesellschaft* (Münster/Hamburg, Lit Verlag, 1994) 137.

one culture to another.'[22] The resulting hybrid forms can be successful adaptations to local conditions, or dysfunctional mutations.

II. INTRODUCTION: WHERE TO BEGIN?

As the *Bactrian* gold shows, Afghanistan has been settled and traversed for a very long time, but little formal governance was established until quite recently.[23] Geography always exerted a strong influence on the political organisation of the area, impeding centripetal forces and making administration difficult.[24] But as the rich archaeological heritage attests to, the imposing mountains 'never truly served as barriers to cultural, economic, or political penetration, but merely funnelled people and ideas along certain routes'.[25] Political organisation during much of that time has followed a recurring process of fusion and fission, as outsiders subdued local forces and established some degree of control, which usually quickly dissipated as the outsiders waned or moved on.

Central governance was rarely established, and rarer still formalised. Alliances formed and reformed with shifting interests[26] and customary patterns of behaviour successfully resisted codification and domestication.[27] In the modern period, Afghanistan has experienced seven constitutional compacts, none particularly enduring.[28] Contemporary constitutional lawyers often seem to follow the biblical adage that 'in the beginning was the Word',[29] by focussing

[22] But note that Hill limits himself to a formal comparison of legal texts rather than examining the actual operation of institutional transplants with which we are concerned here. E Hill, 'Comparative and Historical Study of Modern Middle Eastern Law' (1978) 26(2) *American Journal of Comparative Law* 279–304, 285–86.

[23] The pre-modern history is succinctly presented in G Moltmann, 'Die Verfassungsentwicklung Afghanistans von 1901 bis 1986,' (1986) 35 *Jahrbuch des Öffentlichen Rechts* 509–574, 516–519; Dupree, *An Historical Guide*, (n 6)19–66.

[24] BR Rubin, *The Fragmentation of Afghanistan: State Formation and Collapse in the International System*, 2nd edn (New Haven, Yale University Press, 2002) 19.

[25] Dupree, *Afghanistan*, (n 1) 2.

[26] F Christa, *Alliance Formation in Civil Wars* (Cambridge, Cambridge University Press, 2012). See also D Mukhopadhyay, *Warlords, Strongman Governors, and the State in Afghanistan* (New York, Cambridge University Press, 2014); M Kimberly, 'Warlordism in Comparative Perspective' (2006) 31(3) *International Security* 41–73; A Giustozzi, 'Respectable Warlords? The Transition from War of All against All to Peace Competition in Afghanistan' (London, London School of Economics, Crisis States Research Seminar, 23 Jan 2003).

[27] See here the interesting continuity presented by F Barth, *Afghanistan or Taliban* (Oslo, Pax Forlag, 2010); F Barth, *Political Leadership among Swat Pathans*, London School of Economics Monographs on Social Anthropology, No 19 (New York, The Athlone Press, 1959).

[28] These are the formally promulgated ones between 1923 and 2004, but do not include the political testament of Abdur Rahman from 1901, the draft prepared by the Rabbani mujahedeen government in 1993, nor the draft prepared by the Taliban for their Islamic Emirate.

[29] 'In the beginning was the Word, and the Word was with God, and the Word was God.' John 1:1, King James Version.

on *who* uttered *which* words for *what* purpose.[30] They seem to take for granted that the text marks the beginning and that (legal) reality is affected in important ways by the choice of these words.[31]

In this edited volume, we all seek to describe how things were formed, how the present and future relate to past constitutional choices. Constitution-making in this perspective is an on-going process where choices made at the outset are likely to channel and constrain later options.[32] In the context of an emerging nation-state, where the shape and ethos of the state remains in flux, the beginning is often portrayed as a dramatic, conscious turning point: from a troubled past towards a jointly-embraced future.

The literature describing 'constitutional moments' is premised on such an idealised image of a single-minded political community, which like the individual hero at the heart of many epic stories,[33] faces a moment of truth and opportunity, crosses a threshold, accepts challenges, shoulders burdens and begins a jointly-undertaken adventure in search of communal redemption.[34] Jointly, one leaves the known and tainted world behind, and embraces a yet unknown, enticing but tenuous future that dawns at a precise moment of constitutional reckoning.[35]

[30] For an erudite example, see A von Bogdandy, 'Comparative Constitutional Law: A Contested Domain: A Continental Perspective,' in M Rosenfeld and A Sajó (eds), *The Oxford Handbook of Comparative Constitutional Law* (Oxford, Oxford University Press, 2012) 25–37.

[31] The emphasis on words is linked to the prevailing notion of constitutionalism as essentially limited government, where pre-determined norms limit the arbitrariness of political power. Tushnet describes this as having 'a government of laws not men', but he is painfully aware of the inherent contradiction therein: 'rules of law constrain only when, and to the extent that, they are implemented by a group of people who share certain values – that is, the rule of law must be the rule of men'. Consequently, 'constitutionalism, though necessary, is impossible'. M Tushnet, 'Constitutionalism and Critical Legal Studies,' in AS Rosenbaum (ed) *Constitutionalism: The Philosophical Dimension* (New York, Greenwood Press, 1988) 150.

[32] This is obviously not a new idea, nor limited to constitutional law but any legal or institutional reform. For examples in other spheres, see inter alia Jürgen Beyer and Jan Wielgohs, 'On the Limits of Path Dependency. Approaches for Explaining Postsocialist Institution Building in Critical Response to David Stark' (2001) 15(2) *East European Politics and Societies* 356–388; Robert Cox, 'The Path Dependency of an Idea: Why Scandinavian Welfare States Remain Distinct' (2004) 38(2) *Social Policy & Administration* 204–219; and David Wilsford, 'Path Dependency, or Why History Makes it Difficult But Not Impossible to Reform Health Care Systems in a Big Way' (1994) 14(3) *Journal of Public Policy* 251–283.

[33] This metaphor is based on the 'monomyth' proposed by Joseph Campbell, which he summarised as follows: 'A hero ventures forth from the world of common day into a region of supernatural wonder: fabulous forces are there encountered and a decisive victory is won: the hero comes back from this mysterious adventure with the power to bestow boons on his fellow man.' J Campbell, *The Hero with a Thousand Faces* (Princeton, New Jersey, Princeton University Press, 1968) 30.

[34] Redemption obviously involves a long, perilous and difficult journey of political reconstruction, see inter alia McEvoy, Kieran and J Morison, 'Beyond the 'Constitutional Moment': Law, Transition, and Peacemaking in Northern Ireland' (2003) 26(4) *Fordham International Law Journal* 961–695.

[35] In constitutional law, the idea of a decisive moment is often associated with B Ackerman, *We the People* (Cambridge, Massachusetts, Belknap Press, 1998). Some have applied the same terminology to different phases of international life, for instance the creation of the United Nations. For an influential position in that vein, see A-M Slaughter and W Burke-White, 'An International Constitutional Moment' (2002) 43(1) *Harvard International Law Journal* 1–21.

That moment could be borne from the realisation that a community had 'hit the bottom' and previous ways of doing business had led to such an undeniable catastrophe that 'social forces for change of such intensity are mobilised that the "inner constitution" of [the political] economy transforms under their pressure'.[36] This image of constitution-writing as a team-building exercise, as a form of collective trauma-therapy is powerful: a new identity emerges from a 'lasting constitutional arrangement that results from specific, emotionally shared responses to shared fundamental political experiences'.[37]

Powerful as an idea, such tangible symbolic moments are exceedingly rare. The vast majority of known constitutions, including almost all post-independence ones, emerged from often anti-climactic circumstances.[38] Furthermore, one needs to guard against ascribing to the written word a quasi-magical capacity to change social reality, something well-recognised in international or European law,[39] but equally pertinent in post-conflict state-building.[40] Perhaps too much can be made of the content of a written compact meant to set a political community onto a new trajectory, because the all-important institutional design and ethos will necessarily come to bear *after* the text has been negotiated. The constitutional text will ideally reflect the political culture of those meant to organise their affairs according to its norms, but no text can contain the entirety of the customs, conventions and compromises that will be necessary to make it a living reality.[41]

Writing constitutional history, one should thus resist the temptation to ascribe too much to the written word, while ignoring the context and actors through which the text came to be. Still, any narrative needs to start somewhere.

[36] G Teubner, 'A Constitutional Moment? The Logics of 'Hitting the Bottom' in P Kjaer, G Teubner and A Febbrajo (eds), *Critical Theory and Legal Autopoiesis* (Oxford and Portland, Oregon, Hart Publishing, 2011) 3–42, 4.

[37] A Sajó, 'Constitution without the Constitutional Moment: A View from the New Member States' (2005) 3(2&3) *International Journal of Constitutional Law* 243–261, 243.

[38] Sajó names only 'the United States, nineteenth century Belgium, and, perhaps, postapartheid South Africa' as meeting these criteria. ibid.

[39] Like Sajó, Weiler notes this with respect to the ill-fated 'Treaty establishing a Constitution for Europe', see JHH Weiler, 'On the Power of the Word: Europe's Constitutional Iconography' (2005) 3 (2&3) *International Journal of Constitutional Law* 173–190.

[40] BR Rubin, '(Re)Building Afghanistan: The Folly of Stateless Democracy' (2004) *Current History* 165–170.

[41] These challenges are expertly laid out with respect to Afghanistan in ch 24 'The Constitutional Period Begins, 1963–?' and ch 25 'Problems and Prospects' in Dupree, *Afghanistan*, (n 1) 559–658 and 659–666. For a discussion of these same shortcomings in the wake of the 2004 Constitution, see E Afsah, 'Constitutionalism without Governance: International Standards in the Afghan Legal System,' in A Nollkaemper, C Ruyngaert and E Kristjansdottir (eds), *Importing International Law in Post-Conflict States: The Role of Domestic Courts* (The Hague, Intersentia, 2012) 125–151. The German constitutional court judge Ernst-Wolfgang Böckenförde famously described this predicament in his 1967 essay 'Die Entstehung des Staates als Vorgang der Säkularisation' as the 'dependency of the liberal constitutional state on conditions which it cannot create itself'. This essay was reprinted in E-W Böckenförde, *Der säkularisierte Staat: Sein Charakter, seine Rechtfertigung und seine Probleme im 21. Jahrhundert* (München, Carl Friedrich von Siemens Stiftung, 2007) 43–72.

The opening anecdote of the Bactrian gold alerted us to Afghanistan's rich cultural heritage, and the inevitable arbitrariness of choosing a single beginning. The vagaries of this area's history and the complexity of its human landscape make the task of selecting a foundational moment particularly daunting.

In this edited volume, we generally seek to describe how the *first* constitution in a given country was made, and to explain the factors and actors that left their mark on both text and subsequent legal practice. The focus on the *first* document rests on our hypothesis that the initial written constitution is a factor in the *founding of a modern nation-state*. We are therefore not interested in unearthing in quasi-archaeological fashion necessarily the *earliest* layer of the legal palimpsest. Rather, we believe that both the process and the product of constitution-making are an important element of *nation-building*, defined not in ethno-linguistic, but in *political* terms as

> … a process of collective identity formation with a view to legitimizing public power within a given territory. This is an essentially indigenous process which often not only projects a meaningful future but also draws on existing traditions, institutions, and customs, redefining them as national characteristics in order to support the nation's claim to sovereignty and uniqueness. A successful nation-building process produces a cultural projection of the nation containing a certain set of assumptions, values and beliefs which can function as the legitimizing foundation of a state structure.[42]

As will become apparent, of the many Constitutions existing in Afghanistan, only the one adopted in 1964 managed to distil such shared aspirations while leaving the areas of disagreement – particularly the role of Islam in the social enterprise – sufficiently obscure to permit coordination by suspending acrimony.

III. CONSTITUTIONALISM AND NATION-BUILDING

All nations are, in Anderson's celebrated phrase, 'imagined communities'.[43] They are *imagined* because even in the smallest of nations, people cannot know or interact with most of their fellow citizens, 'yet in the minds of each lives the image of their communion'. They are *communities* because irrespective of the reality of inequality or abuse, 'the nation is always conceived as a deep, horizontal comradeship'.[44] As Anderson notes critically, it is this manufactured, keenly embraced *illusion of brotherhood*, which accounts for the enduring power of the conceptional idea, including a perhaps lamentable willingness to kill and

[42] A von Bogdandy et al, 'State-Building, Nation-Building, and Constitutional Politics in Post-Conflict Situations: Conceptional Clarifications and an Appraisal of Different Approaches' (2005) 9 *Max Planck Yearbook of United Nations Law* 579–614, 586.

[43] BR Anderson, *Imagined Communities: Reflections on the Origin and Spread of Nationalism* (London, Verso, 1991).

[44] ibid, 6–7.

die for it. He further notes three paradoxes that make nationalism so difficult to define, namely:

(1) The objective modernity of nations to the eyes of historians vs. their subjective antiquity in the eyes of nationalists;
(2) The formal universality of nationality as a socio-cultural concept vs. the irremediable particularity of its concrete manifestation; and
(3) The political power of such nationalisms vs. their philosophical poverty and even incoherence.[45]

The very idea of the nation is therefore a quintessentially modern phenomenon, intimately tied to the need for *cohesion* in a bureaucratically organised state. Because modern states are both much more capable and also much more demanding in terms of loyalty, participation and submission, all rely on some community-building ideology,[46] usually nationalism.[47] The nation is portrayed in quasi-organic terms as something primordial, eternal and natural through a deliberately 'invented tradition'.[48] Nietzsche termed this a 'usable past', namely the carefully curated memory of certain historical experiences able to serve as joint markers of identity, and the equally careful suppression of memories of divisive events.[49]

Which of Afghanistan's various constitutional documents should be considered foundational is therefore not primarily a chronological question, but rather one of consequence. Among the many constitutional documents, adopted by various, often ideologically incompatible Afghan governments between 1923 and 2004, one stands out by virtue of the carefully orchestrated and broadly participatory process and its resulting inoffensive, yet forward-looking substantive content. The 1964 Constitution embodied a deliberate effort to use the constitutional process as a tool for nation- and state-building.

The chief challenge, then as now, there as elsewhere, is the creation of a nation-state from the plethora of alternative organising principles, be they ethnic, linguistic, religious or other. The persistence of alternative, pre-modern forms of social organisation is particularly pronounced in the ethnic and tribal mosaic of Afghanistan,[50] but by no means unique to it.[51] The task

[45] ibid.

[46] See further, R Hardin, 'The Crippled Epistemology of Extremism,' in A Breton et al (eds), *Political Extremism and Rationality* (Cambridge, Cambridge University Press, 2002) 3–22, 12–15; see also A Anter, *Max Weber's Theory of the Modern State: Origins, Structure and Significance* (London, Palgrave Macmillan, 2014).

[47] See also E Gellner, *Nationalism* (London, Weidenfeld & Nicolson, 1997).

[48] EJ Hobsbawm and T Ranger (eds), *The Invention of Tradition* (Cambridge, Cambridge University Press, 1983).

[49] R Utz, 'Nations, Nation-Building, and Cultural Intervention: A Social Science Perspective' (2005) 9 *Max Planck Yearbook of United Nations Law* 615–647.

[50] CJ Schetter, *Ethnizität und ethnische Konflikte in Afghanistan* (Berlin, Reimer, 2003).

[51] S Issacharoff, 'Constitutionalizing Democracy in Fractured Societies' (2004) 58(1) *Journal of International Affairs* 73–93.

facing this society since the nineteenth century has therefore been a fairly universal one:

> Afghanistan, like the rest of the Afro-Asian world (and parts of Latin America), is *attempting to create a nation-state out of hodgepodge of ethnic and linguistic groups.* A nation-state, in the modern sense, is not simply a piece of real estate enclosed by boundaries, but more a pattern of attitudes, a reciprocal, functioning set of rights and obligations between the government and the governed – with emphasis on the individual rather than the group. In non-literate societies, however, kinship replaces government and guarantees men and women born into a specific unit [a] functioning set of social, economic, and political rights and obligations.[52]

Dupree might have been right that it ought to be possible to define the nation-state in a non-literate environment differently from the corporate model developed in the West.[53] According to that model, perhaps best epitomised by the nation-building efforts of France and Prussia, local identities are deliberately and successively eradicated through the imposition of universal schooling, conscription and increasing dependency on state-provided services, all under the credible threat of physical coercion.[54] In this paradigmatic Western experience, universal literacy and some degree of peasant liberation were deliberate tools used by the central authority to both weaken local notables and to increase revenue.[55]

Such social engineering gradually transferred particularistic attachments to a larger collective identity, a process which required considerable institutional strength and material power. Where these do not exist, subtler approaches must be chosen and weaker collective sentiments are likely to result. In principle, as Dupree notes, the 'desire to retain group identity and, more important, sets of rights and obligations within the group are not in themselves a threat to the creation of a nation-state'.[56] He correctly notes that literacy in itself cannot resolve the underlying dilemma and that the often forceful attempts by non-western leaders to eradicate tribal prerogatives and attachments have invariably failed, for few if any central governments have been physically able to '*replace* the delicate network of rights and obligations which make group survival possible'.[57]

[52] Dupree, *Afghanistan*, (n 1) 659, emphasis added.

[53] On the reception of the Weberian state, possible alternatives and the challenge of transposition, see L Pritchett and M Woolcock, 'Solutions When the Solution is the Problem: Arraying the Disarray in Development' (2004) 32(2) *World Development* 191–212; F Fukuyama, *State-Building. Governance and World Order in the Twenty-First Century* (London, Profile Books, 2005); and F Fukuyama, 'Why There Is No Science of Public Administration' (2004) 58(1) *Journal of International Affairs* 189–201.

[54] The process is well described by E Weber, *Peasants into Frenchmen. The Modernization of Rural France, 1870–1914* (Redwood, California, Stanford University Press, 1976).

[55] F Fukuyama, *The Origins of Political Order. From Prehuman Times to the French Revolution* (London, Profile Books, 2012) 433, described with respect to Denmark in D Landes, *The Wealth and Poverty of Nations. Why Some Are So Rich and Some Are So Poor* (London, Little, Brown and Company, 1998) 238–242.

[56] Dupree, *Afghanistan*, (n 1) 659.

[57] ibid, emphasis in the original.

Consequently, Afghan constitutional history is the story of the shifting relationship between a centre perennially *in statu nascendi* and competing power centres. In particular, it is the story of the highly idiosyncratic role played by formal law in a complex normative and political landscape.

IV. LOCATING THE 1964 CONSTITUTION

For much of Afghanistan's history, neither its borders, population or name were clearly defined.[58] Central government was unknown until 1747, when following the collapse of yet another Persian empire, a returning commander, Ahmad Shah Durrani, had himself declared King by a tribal gathering.[59] The year 1747 is a convenient one. It is easy to remember and it nicely places Afghan national history in a decidedly non-colonial frame. This explains perhaps why most Afghan historians and legal scholars[60] treat it as the beginning of the Afghan state; something 'followed sheeplike by western scholars' (as I once also did).[61] But Dupree's critique is apt. A personalised leadership endorsed by a council of tribal elders lacks the permanence and institutionalisation necessary to speak of statehood in anything resembling the modern sense of the word:

> I disagree [with the choice of 1747 as the beginning of the Afghan state], for, until 1880, the process of alternating fusion and fission dominated the political scene. By political fusion and fission, I mean the following pattern of events: A charismatic leader arises in a tribal society and, by military power, intrigue, and judiciously arranged marriages, unites several tribes into a confederation, which spreads as far as its accumulated power permits, creating an *empire*, not a *nation-state*. With (sometimes before) the death of the emperor, fission occurs, and the great empire once again segments into a multiplicity of tribal kingdoms. Later, another charismatic leader arrives and the process is repeated.[62]

[58] For a discussion, especially of the variety of the human and physical landscape and the various names under which the area has been known throughout history, see the introductions to Dupree, *Afghanistan*, (n 1) xvii–xx; HK Kakar, *Government and Society in Afghanistan: The Reign of Amir 'Abd al-Rahman Khan*, vol 5, Modern Middle East Series (Austin, University of Texas Press, 1979) xv–2; and S Wheeler, 'The Ameer Abdur Rahman' in SH Jeyes (ed), *Public Men of To-Day* (London, Bliss, Sands and Foster, 1895) 20–23. Still during the debates of the 1963 draft, there was considerable debate whether non-Pashtos should be considered Afghans. While the Constitution used Afghan to refer to all citizens of the country, most of the population identified the word with the Pashto ethnic group. See Dupree, *Afghanistan*, (n 1) 578. Since then, the term has lost its exclusive connotation with that ethnic group and since the late 1990s it is no longer disputed that the minorities are fully-fledged Afghans. See further CJ Schetter, 'Die Territorialisierung nationaler und ethnischer Vorstellungen in Afghanistan' (2003) 44(1) *Orient* 75.

[59] A fuller description of the instrument can be found in SQ Reshtia, 'La Loya Jerga' (1988) 7 *Central Asian Survey* 5–20, 6.

[60] R Bachardoust, *Afghanistan – droit constitutionnel, histoire, régimes politiques et relations diplomatiques depuis 1747* (Paris, L'Harmattan, 2003), 19; MH Kamali, *Law in Afghanistan: A Study of the Constitutions, Matrimonial Law and the Judiciary* (Leiden, Brill, 1985).

[61] Dupree, *Afghanistan*, (n 1) xix; and E Afsah and AH Guhr, 'Afghanistan: Building a State to Keep the Peace' (2005) 9 *Max Planck Yearbook of United Nations Law* 373–456, 389.

[62] ibid, xix, emphasis in the original.

For most of its history, the area was fought over by local (Persian and Indian) imperialists, before fratricidal wars and the intrusion of European imperialists (British and Russian) characterised its politics in the nineteenth century. This characteristic ebb and flow of fusion and fission stopped for the first time after the Second Anglo-Afghan War with the reign of Amir Abdur Rahman Khan (1880–1901), which marks the beginning of *modern* Afghanistan.[63]

Abdur Rahman came to power with British help and used that support to create a centralised military force strong enough to compel obedience for the first time. Where previous rulers had reigned as *primus inter pares* over a tribal empire, he established a process of 'internal imperialism' and conscious, if still rudimentary, nation-building through the creation of formalised institutions.[64] As someone with 'a special liking for statesmen with dictatorial tendencies', the Amir admired Prusso-German autocracy and had little appreciation for the parliamentary aspects of British constitutionalism.[65] It is therefore not surprising that no formal constitution was adopted during his reign. Shrewd but illiterate, with an acute sense of politics and the realities of power, he nevertheless left behind a political testament containing his constitutional vision for the state.[66] Furthermore, he showed considerable interest in legal reform and his autocratic but effective system of governance was sufficiently formalised to be describable in the language of contemporary constitutional law,[67] and it created a civil administration whose basic form endures to the present day.[68]

The Amir was effective for the same reason that his constitutional legacy is of limited utility to subsequent scholars of Afghan constitutional law. For the first and only time in Afghan history, he controlled a sufficiently strong central army that could ruthlessly compel obedience to central orders, not least regarding taxation and conscription.[69] This physical coercive power allowed him to suppress existing local autonomies and establish central governmental authority over tribal matters. He made no effort to institutionalise these arrangements, which quickly disintegrated once his son Habibullah[70] lost this central coercive

[63] See the contemporary biography by Wheeler, 'The Ameer Abdur Rahman', (n 58). For a modern assessment, see MH Kakar, *A Political and Diplomatic History of Afghanistan 1863–1901* (Leiden, Brill, 2006), ch 1 – 'The Reign of Amir 'Abd al-Rahman Khan'.

[64] Dupree, *Afghanistan*, (n 1) 419.

[65] 'To him the British Parliament was like a Kabul public bath, where everybody talks and no one is listened to.' See Kakar, *A Political and Diplomatic History*, (n 63) 13.

[66] The Amir left an autobiography intended as his political testament for his successors. It was compiled by his State Secretary (Mir Munshi). See SM Khan (ed), *The Life of Abdur Rahman, Amir of Afghanistan*, vol 1 (London: John Murray, 1900).

[67] As done for instance by his State Secretary. See SM Khan, *The Constitution and Laws of Afghanistan* (London, John Murray, 1900).

[68] R McChesney, 'The Economic Reforms of Amir Abdur Rahman Khan' (1968) 21(3) *Afghanistan* 11–34.

[69] See chs IV and V in Kakar, *Government and Society*, (n 58).

[70] Habibullah Khan (1872–1919) succeeded his father upon the latter's death in October 1901 and reigned till his death in 1919.

capacity. While successful, the edifice he built relied primarily on 'brute force and violence, instruments unavailable to modern-day peace builders', consequently his constitutional legacy is of limited interest to students of contemporary Afghan affairs.[71]

The Amir, however, was farsighted about the limited ability of any central government to overcome deep-seated cultural patterns. In his political testament, he stressed the difficulties of effecting lasting social change. In a much-quoted and woefully ignored passage, he cautions patience and moderation:

> My sons and successors should not try to introduce new reforms of any kind in such a hurry as to set the people against their ruler, and they must bear in mind that in establishing a constitutional government, introducing more lenient laws, and modelling education upon the system of Western universities, they must adopt all these gradually as the people become accustomed to the idea of modern innovations, so that they will not abuse the privileges and reforms given to them.[72]

The Amir's grandson, King Amanullah (1892–1960), initiated the Third Anglo-Afghan War, as a result of which Afghanistan won the freedom to conduct its foreign affairs independently through the 1919 Treaty of Rawalpindi. This date continues to be celebrated as Afghanistan's Independence Day, making the treaty another contender as a foundational document. Where his grandfather relied on Islamic legitimacy and military coercion to establish personal rule, Amanullah was influenced by modernist ideas and began an ambitious process of social engineering from above. It began a cycle that came to be repeated often throughout the twentieth century, namely an urban elite trying to remake Afghan society in its own image with imported ideas, but over-estimating the state's institutional capacity to overcome conservative, eventually violent rural opposition.[73] His was the first of many subsequent nation-building efforts by executive fiat, all of which invariably used statutory and constitutional means of unrealistic scope and ambition.[74]

V. TORTUOUS TRANSPLANTS AND RELIGIOUS RESISTANCE

Amir Abdur Rahman and his son Habibullah had been content to establish central authority in a relatively limited sense, exercising control only over urban areas and limiting excursions into the countryside to the repression of revolts,

[71] D Mukhopadhyay, *Warlords as Bureaucrats: The Afghan Experience* (Washington DC, Carnegie Endowment for International Peace, 2009), available at: https://carnegieendowment.org/files/warlords_as_ bureaucrats.pdf, 5.

[72] Sultan M Khan, *The Life of Abdur Rahman, Amir of Afghanistan*, vol 2 (London, John Murray, 1900) 190; V Gregorian, *The Emergence of Modern Afghanistan* (Santa Monica, Calif., Stanford University Press, 1969) 132–35.

[73] Dupree, *Afghanistan*, (n 1) 450–453.

[74] See chs 1 and 2 in Rubin, *The Fragmentation of Afghanistan*, (n 24).

leaving rural areas largely autonomous.[75] When he ascended to the throne and buoyed by his relatively successful conduct of the negotiations ending the war with the British, Amanullah set himself a political programme very much at odds with that of his predecessors. He embarked upon an ambitious legal reform project, culminating in a constitution approved by a carefully-chosen group of elders in 1923.[76] This document had been written with personal input from him and some Turkish and French advice, and it represented an extremely far-reaching effort to redefine the relationship between state and society.

The extremely violent reactions to it resembled traditionalist backlashes to similar efforts elsewhere in the Muslim world and concerned similar points of contention:[77] the role of Islam and especially the Hanafi *madhab* (Art 2), legal equality of non-Muslims (Arts 8 & 16), religious freedom (Art 2), the introduction of an independent judiciary (Arts 50–57), and universal state education (Arts 14–15). Many Afghan authors tend to lionise Amanullah[78] and his chief adviser Mahmud Tarzi,[79] and compare him favourably with other strong-willed Muslim reformers in Iran and Turkey.[80] Unlike them, however, Amanullah did not possess sufficient military might to enforce his modernist vision.[81] First he had to rescind important elements of his reform agenda and eventually to abdicate and flee the country in the face of a concerted tribal revolt and opposition by the clergy.[82]

[75] Barfield compares this approach to a Swiss cheese, in the sense that leaders 'do not assume uniformity across the country or their control of it'. See T Barfield, *Afghanistan: A Cultural and Political History* (Princeton, New Jersey, Princeton University Press, 2010) 67–70.

[76] 'The Constitution of the Preeminent Government of Afghanistan [Niẓāmnāmah-'i asāsī-'i dawlat-i 'illīyah-'i Afghānistān],' Kabul, Government Printing Office, 10 April 1923, available at: www.wdl.org/en/item/15007/.

[77] Compare this, for instance, with the Iranian constitutional revolution where exactly the same points of contention led conservative clergy to oppose the initial version. See SA Arjomand, 'The Ulama's traditionalist opposition to parliamentarianism: 1907–1909' (1981) 17(2) *Middle Eastern Studies* 174–190; see also Arjomand, 'Constitutional Developments', (n 1).

[78] 'Amir Amanullah Khan had cherished the ambition to see Afghanistan ranked as a Modern Civilised State, Constitutionalism was a part his scheme of modernization. He was conscious of backwardness of his people. He wished to bring them at par with the civilized people. He felt that not only economic development and education but political consciousness was also necessary to keep pace with the modern world.' See NM Chishti, *Constitutional Development in Afghanistan* (Peshawar and Karachi, Royal Book Company and University of Peshawar, 1998) 21.

[79] For a good account of his influential role, see V Gregorian, 'Mahmud Tarzi and Saraj-ol-Akhbar: Ideology of Nationalism and Modernization in Afghanistan' (1967) 21(3) *Middle East Journal* 345–368.

[80] 'Amanullah can be seen as the first reformer and progressive leader of Afghanistan, to be mentioned in one breath with Atatürk of Turkey or Reza Shah of Iran. His legacy is the establishment of the basic legal structure, the promulgation of individual freedoms and the foundations for Afghanistan's move towards the rule of law.' See MH Saboory, 'The Progress of Constitutionalism in Afghanistan,' in N Yassari (ed), *The Sharī'a in the Constitutions of Afghanistan, Iran, and Egypt* (Hamburg, Mohr Siebeck, 2005) 5–22, 7.

[81] 'If Tarzi, the thinker, and Amanullah, the activist, could have pooled their intellectual resources – backed by a loyal, Turkish-trained army – Afghanistan might today be farther along the road of modernization, instead of just beginning.' See Dupree, *Afghanistan*, (n 1) 457.

[82] For a comprehensive account, see LB Poullada, *Reform and Rebellion in Afghanistan, 1919–1929* (Ithaca, NY and London, Cornell University Press, 1973).

The 1923 Constitution, attractive in its liberal ethos and rational machinery of government, is little more than a literary document. It reflected a very narrow spectrum of opinion, did not leave much institutional trace and, most crucially, did not contribute to nation-building in the political sense outlined above. Given its extremely narrow social base, this Constitution can serve as an example of the transmigration of literary ideas among elite intellectuals.[83] But given its extremely limited, tortuous effect, it does not appear useful to speak here, at least not yet, of an instance of constitutional borrowing, let alone transplantation.[84]

The violent opposition to the 1923 Constitution arose from the material interests of rural tribal leaders and traditionalist clergy, expressed in terms of an incompatibility with Islamic mores. In this rhetorical stance, the anti-modernist opposition rejected the view that law was a technological innovation like any other, to be emulated by virtue of efficiency or convenience. Instead, they echoed what some comparative lawyers have termed the 'mirror theory of law' namely 'that law is the mirror of some set of forces (social, political, economic, whatever) external to the law'.[85] The legal system is deemed to reflect the spirit of the community it regulates, because 'each society reveals through its law the innermost secrets of the manner in which it holds men together'.[86]

The violent resistance to the package of legal reforms of which the 1923 Constitution was an integral part, illustrates the debate about the conditions under which the borrowing of legal ideas can take place. Alan Watson argued that legal transplants have been 'the most fertile source of development' within legal systems,[87] primarily because transplantation is 'socially easy' as 'the recipient system does not require any real knowledge of the social, economic, geographic and political context of the origin and growth of the original rule'.[88] Consequently, he saw the task of comparative law as investigating how different legal systems interact through such voluntary transplantation.[89] In other words, the enterprise of comparative law is about looking for *similarities* between distinct jurisdictions.

[83] On that aspect, see inter alia F Ahmed, *Afghanistan Rising: Islamic Law and Statecraft between the Ottoman and British Empires* (Cambridge, Mass., Harvard University Press, 2017); Matin-Asgari, *Both Eastern and Western*, (n 10); and M Boroujerdi, *Iranian Intellectuals and the West: The Tormented Triumph of Nativism* (Syracuse, NY, Syracuse University Press, 1996).

[84] For a good theoretical overview of the debate, see V Perju, 'Constitutional Transplants, Borrowing, and Migrations' in Mi Rosenfeld and A Sajó (eds) *The Oxford Handbook of Comparative Constitutional Law* (Oxford, Oxford University Press, 2012) 1304–1327.

[85] W Ewald, 'Comparative Jurisprudence (II): The Logic of Legal Transplants' (1995) 43(4) *American Journal of Comparative Law* 489–510, 491.

[86] RM Unger, *Law in Modern Society* (New York, Simon & Schuster, 1976) 47.

[87] He makes the argument with respect to western private law, but the argument applies likewise to public law, see Perju, 'Constitutional Transplants', (n 84) 1313.

[88] A Watson, 'Legal Transplants and Law Reform' (1976) 92 *Law Quarterly Review* 79–84, 81.

[89] Perju, 'Constitutional Transplants', (n 84) 1309.

Because the focus is on *rules* as 'bare propositional statements', not dependent on social connections, historical context or habits of thought, such differences are deemed to not pose an obstacle to the transferability of rules from one jurisdiction to another.[90] Pierre Legrand vehemently opposes this view: 'Anyone who takes the view that "the law" or "the rules of the law" travel across jurisdictions must have in mind that law is a somewhat autonomous entity unencumbered by historical, epistemological, or cultural baggage. Indeed, how could law travel if it was not segregated from society?'[91] It is significant that Legrand already regards legal transplants impossible within the western world, and this presumably precludes non-western states from receiving western constitutional ideas.[92] For him, *deliberate* cultural *differences* preclude legal borrowing already within relatively familiar western cultures:

> In enacting a rule for the reasons they do and in the way they do, as a product of the way they think, with the hopes they have, in enacting a particular rule (and not others), the French, for example, are not just doing *that*: they are also doing something typically French and are thus alluding to a modality of legal experience that is intrinsically theirs. In this sense, because it communicates the French sensibility to law, the rule can serve as a focus of inquiry into legal Frenchness and into Frenchness *tout court*. It cannot be regarded only as a rule in terms of a bare propositional statement. There is more to ruleness than a series of inscribed words which is to say that a rule is not identical to the inscribed words.[93]

Many of the claims concerning the transplantability of private rules apply likewise to the migration of constitutional ideas.[94] There is ample evidence of borrowing – both explicit and implicit in style, wording, methodology and interpretation[95] – but there is likewise an enormous degree of resistance against such transfers, with law seen clearly not merely as a collection of rules but the embodiment of a group's distinctiveness, perhaps even its soul *tout court*. In the western world, much of that resistance has been discussed in the context of the recently fraying European integration project.[96]

It is, however, in the Islamic world where the notion of constitutional transplantation has had a longer and more greatly contested history. Whether imposed

[90] A Watson, *Legal Transplants: An Approach to Comparative Law*, 2nd edn (Atlanta, University of Georgia Press, 1993) 96–97.

[91] P Legrand, 'The Impossibility of Legal Transplants' (1997) 4 *Maastricht Journal of European and Comparative Law* 111–124, 114.

[92] ibid, 113.

[93] ibid, 115.

[94] Perju, 'Constitutional Transplants', (n 84) 1313.

[95] See the literature mentioned in Perju, 'Constitutional Transplants', (n 84), particularly S Choudhry, *The Migration of Constitutional Ideas* (Cambridge, Cambridge University Press, 2006). See also the symposium entitled 'Constitutional Borrowing' in the (2003) 1 *International Journal of Constitutional Law* 177–324.

[96] Z Körtvélyesi and B Majtényi, 'Game of Values: The Threat of Exclusive Constitutional Identity, the EU and Hungary' (2017) 18(7) *German Law Journal* 1721–1744.

as a legacy of colonialism or voluntarily introduced by domestic reformers as in Afghanistan in 1923, Turkey from the Tanzimat to the Republic (1839–1923), or in Iran (1905–1911), the borrowing occurred voluntarily, that is not imposed in a colonial relationship of coercion. Those borrowing in the South did so because they admired and sought to emulate the efficiency, prestige and power of those in the North.[97] But the openly conceded admission of southern inferiority that justified and necessitated the borrowing, engendered religious resistance and an insistence on indigenous cultural autonomy. These critics argued that imported western norms were culturally alien and religiously objectionable.[98]

The 1923 Constitution floundered because it reflected the ideological vision of an extremely narrow demographic strata (ultimately only the King himself). It could therefore neither tap into societal self-perceptions, nor claim existing traditions of dispute-settlement or governance. That these elements could not be substituted through brute force by a central, modern army prematurely doomed the Constitution. Had a more careful, more accommodating approach been chosen, coupled with a stronger emphasis on the creation of credible political and coercive institutions, the tribal, clerical and societal backlash could perhaps have been avoided. In such a counter-factual narrative, 1923 could well have been Afghanistan's 'constitutional moment'.[99]

Still, the nature of the opposition to it suggests a wider and enduring resistance to the arrival of modernity throughout the Muslim world. Without referring directly to the Afghan reform effort, Hallaq rejects various legal reform efforts as indicative of a self-imposed 'ontological imperialism'. According to him, such lack of self-respect is the more startling given the comprehensiveness, adequacy and better suitability of Islamic law and forms of governance.[100] Echoing here much of Afghan traditionalist critique to imposed legal change from above, Hallaq laments the 'terminological distortion' behind even basic and supposedly general terms like 'law' or 'reform'. In his view, such discourse is:

> … articulating various political and ideological positions that inherently assume the Shari'a to be deficient and in need of correction and modernizing revision. 'Reform' thus insinuates a transition, on the one level, from the pre-modern to the modern, and on the other, from the uncivilized to civilized. It is framed by a notion of universalist

[97] It should be noted that during this volatile and exciting period of reform, Afghanistan was an active participant in the wider Muslim discourse on adapting to modernity. The period is well explored in Ahmed, *Afghanistan Rising*, (n 83).

[98] This is by no means merely a historical position, see HA Hamoudi, 'Dream Palaces of Law: Western Constructions of the Muslim Legal World' (2009) 32(2) *Hastings International and Comparative Law Review* 803–814; J Waardenburg, 'Islam as a Vehicle of Protest' in E Gellner (ed), *Islamic Dilemmas: Reformers, Nationalists, and Industrialization: The Southern Shore of the Mediterranean* (Berlin, Walter de Gruyter, 1985) 22–48.

[99] Dupree explicitly outlines such a counter-factual in his description of the failed efforts of the Great Afghan reformer Mahmoud Tarzi. Dupree, *Afghanistan*, (n 1) 457.

[100] Referring to E Lévinas and WB Hallaq, *Shari'a: Theory, Practice, Transformations* (Cambridge, Cambridge University Press, 2009) 4.

> historicism in which the history of the Other merges into the major and defining currents of the European (read: universal) civilizational march.[101]

He thus considers the very description of Islamic law as 'law' – not to mention the attempt to draft a constitution – as misguided, for that would:

> … project, if not superimpose, on the legal culture of Islam notions saturated with the conceptional specificity of nation-state law, a punitive law that, when compared to Islam's jural forms, *lacks* (note the reversal) the same determinant moral imperative.[102]

It is unclear how seriously Hallaq means this. Self-consciously labouring to re-establish the 'dignity' of Islamic law, it is not clear whether his celebration of an alternative form of governance in early Islam constitutes a rejection of the modern nation-state or a lament for a path not taken.[103] At the very least, he seems to reject the need to introduce into a traditional, tribal society, something as quintessentially modern and western as a written constitution:

> To view the new Muslims as desert dwellers who, before embarking on their conquests, lived an impoverished life of nomadism and tribalism can only lead to a theory in which all Muslim cultural forms, including legal institutions, were borrowings from the high imperial cultures of north, especially that of Byzantium. Such a view would comport with the now widespread perception of Muslims as backward, always in need of assimilating 'western' culture and values so as to keep pace with modernity and progress.[104]

Whatever position one would take on the question of the necessity of a western constitution, it is undeniable that all Muslim societies did eventually adopt one,[105] hereby clearly following a well-established global pattern.[106] What is more debatable is the extent to which the imported concepts (or the 'rules' to use Watson's term) are simply propositional statements whose implementation

[101] ibid, 3–4.

[102] ibid, 2–3.

[103] Recently, he has explored this lamentation further without offering a practical solution, see WB Hallaq, *The Impossible State: Islam, Politics, and Modernity's Moral Predicament* (New York, Columbia University Press, 2012).

[104] WB Hallaq, *The Origins and Evolution of Islamic Law* (Cambridge, Cambridge University Press, 2005) 26.

[105] Saudi Arabia and Taliban Afghanistan are often named as the staunchest holdouts, but the former did in fact adopt a 'basic law', while the latter did at least embark upon drafting a constitution. On the former, see AD Marar, 'Saudi Arabia: The Duality of the Legal System and the Challenge of Adapting Law to Market Economies' (2004) 19(1) *Arab Law Quarterly* 91–124; E van Eijk, 'Sharia and National law in Saudi Arabia,' in J Michiel Otto (ed), *Sharia Incorporated. A Comparative Overview of the Legal Systems of Twelve Muslim Countries in Past and Present* (Leiden, Leiden University Press, 2010) 139–180; FE Vogel, *Islamic Law and the Legal System of Saudí* (The Hague, Brill, 2000). On the latter, see M Mashal, 'What Do the Taliban Want in Afghanistan? A Lost Constitution Offers Clues,' *New York Times*, 28 Jun 2019, A10.

[106] 'Over the past two centuries, we have moved from a situation where almost no country had a written constitution to one where almost every country has one.' See DS Lutz, *Principles of Constitutional Design* (Cambridge, Cambridge University Press, 2006) 4.

do not depend on intimate knowledge of the context whence these ideas came. Legrand's rejection of the impossibility of legal transplants does not appear to be consistent with the global movement, if not convergence of constitutional ideas.[107] But his insistence 'that the meaning invested into the rule is itself culture-specific' is germane to our present investigation, because:

> … the propositional statement as it finds itself technically integrated into another legal order, is understood differently by the host culture and is, therefore, invested with a culture-specific meaning at variance with the earlier one (not least because the very understanding of the notion of 'rule' may differ). Accordingly, a crucial element of the ruleness of the rule – its meaning – does not survive the journey from one legal system to another.

Indeed, as subsequent practice in Afghanistan and elsewhere has made abundantly clear, transplanted constitutional ideas rarely operate as in their original environment. In fact, they rarely take root at all. So, while the comparative study of such ideas begins with the constitutional text, it is evident that this will not be sufficient. Constitutional concepts are interrelated and intimately connected to wider cultural norms and methodological approaches. In the peculiar context of Asia and Africa, one is thus dealing with the phenomenon of 'constitutions without constitutionalism'.[108]

VI. CONSTITUTIONS AS TOOLS FOR CONSOLIDATION AND COORDINATION

If the 1923 Constitution was an attempt to effect modernist social change from above, it failed spectacularly in the face of tribal and religious opposition and led to the King's downfall and a period of civil war.[109] Once the royal family re-established control, a new Constitution was promulgated in 1931 'to create at least a semblance of stability inside Afghanistan'.[110] The consolidation of royal power by Nadir Shah (1883–1933) explicitly renounced most of the legal reforms instigated under Amanullah and sought to return the country to mainstream Hanafi fiqh. The 1931 Constitution thus *looked* modern and employed western language and form, but its ethos was a deliberate renunciation of participatory government, legal equality and individual rights. In this respect,

[107] Perju, 'Constitutional Transplants', (n 84) 1325–26; R Dixon and EA Posner, 'The Limits of Constitutional Convergence' (2011) 11(2) *Chicago Journal of International Law* 399–423.

[108] HWO Okoth-Ogendo, 'Constitutions without Constitutionalism: Reflections on an African Political Paradox,' in D Greenberg et al (eds), *Constitutionalism and Democracy: Transitions in the Contemporary World* (Oxford, Oxford University Press, 1993) 65.

[109] For an insightful and sympathetic account, see F Ahmed, 'In the Name of a Law: Islamic Legal Modernism and the Making of Afghanistan's 1923 Constitution' (2016) 48 *International Journal of Middle East Studies* 655–677.

[110] Dupree, *Afghanistan*, (n 1) 461.

the ensuing 'illusion of popular participation without proper enforcement provisions'[111] might appear at first glance a paradox, resembling similar insincere covenants in much of the Muslim world.[112] Brown has explained the apparent contradiction of such 'constitutions in a non-constitutional world'[113] with the perceived power-generating aspect of a written constitution.[114] Rulers clearly believe that a written constitution could be useful to consolidate power, however insincere the commitment to rights, consultation and division of power contained therein.

Like many of its successors, the 1931 Constitution was not a very impressive document. It was logically inconsistent and reflected in this methodological discrepancy, the evident disinterest of power holders to actually abide by its provisions. Dupree offers a succinct summary of its structure and content, which needs no restatement beyond his correct summary assessment:

> The 1931 Constitution embodied a hodgepodge of unworkable elements. Extracted from the Turkish, Iranian, and French constitutions and the 1923 Constitution of Amanullah, plus many aspects of the Hanafi *Shari'a* of Sunni Islam and local custom (*'adat*), several of these last contradictory to the *Shari'a*. Many of the Constitution's 110 articles and 16 parts seemed to have been borrowed at random from the various sources.[115]

What is interesting for the comparativist and practitioner is the resulting plurality of applicable laws and the perplexing multitude of incompatible organising principles for state and society; something that continues to bedevil Afghanistan's reconstruction effort.[116] This Constitution sought to retain executive power in the hands of the royal family, but conceded key demands of an amorphous opposition. Economically, the Constitution followed then-current fashions and enshrined a semi-socialist system, yet simultaneously claimed to protect private property and free enterprise, while in reality a communal subsistence economy prevailed. To acquiesce the most vocal opposition group, the state conceded the judiciary back to the clergy, but without clarifying the applicable law.

[111] ibid, 464.

[112] See more generally, KA El Fadl, 'The Centrality of Shari'ah to Government and Constitutionalism in Islam,' in R Grote and T Röder (eds), *Constitution-Making in Islamic Countries: Between Upheaval and Continuity* (New York, Oxford University Press, 2012) 35–62; and SA Arjomand, 'The Kingdom of Jurists: Constitutionalism and the Legal Order in Iran,' in Grote and Röder, ibid, 147–170.

[113] NJ Brown, *Constitutions in a Nonconstitutional World: Arab Basic Laws and the Prospects for Accountable Government* (Albany, State University of New York Press, 2002).

[114] D Law and W-C Chang, 'Chinese Constitutionalism: An Oxymoron?,' in G Jacobsohn and M Schor (eds), *Comparative Constitutional Theory* (London, Edward Elgar, 2018) 476–514; J deLisle, 'States of Exception in an Exceptional State: Emergency Powers Law in China,' in V Vridar Ramraj and AK Thiruvengadam (eds), *Emergency Powers in Asia. Exploring the Limits of Legality* (Cambridge, Cambridge University Press, 2010) 342–392.

[115] Dupree, *Afghanistan*, (n 1) 464.

[116] See inter alia G Swenson, 'Why US Efforts to Promote the Rule of Law in Afghanistan Failed,' (2017) 42(1) *International Security* 114–151.

Consequently, judges had to administer several distinct and incompatible sources of law: Hanafi fiqh; royal decrees (*farman*); laws passed by the legislative, usually prepared by ministries (*qanun*); ministerial decrees (*ta'limat namah*) and administrative guidance (*rahnamay-e edari*); as well as the Constitution itself (*qanun assasi*).[117]

The ensuing legal and political landscape is difficult to penetrate and riddled with inefficiency and paralysis. Anticipating the many frustrations of today's development practitioners trying to make sense of the extreme discrepancy between form and a confounding legal reality,[118] contemporary commentators were scathing in their assessment of this constitutional setting. Compared with the lofty aspirations promulgated a decade earlier, the 1931 Constitution did not seem to 'do much'.[119] However, such a harsh assessment fails to do justice to the concrete role played by a constitutional document in Afghanistan's peculiar social arrangements.

Dupree's highly critical stance of its internal inconsistencies and illusory stipulations might actually point to the source of its *hidden strength*, which accounted for its surprising longevity. He notes acerbically that this document 'only partially suited the Afghan character and social system, which can be generally described as tribal, authoritarian, patrilineal, and patriarchal'.[120] Given the violent backlash against the previous Constitution, the 1931 text extensively accommodated Islam and the clergy. This obviously calls into doubt the effectiveness of many of the rights and organisational mandates contained therein, but as Pasarlay notes, this might perhaps have been a virtue rather than a vice:

> Seen from the paradigm of coordination theory, however, the 1931 Constitution was far more effective than the one that preceded it precisely because it identified key stakeholders who needed to be at the negotiation table; it deferred on many of the controversial questions that the first Constitution had tried to answer; and because the government was careful not to exercise any of its latent powers in a way that would offended (*sic*) powerful stakeholders. The 1931 Constitution was actually closer to the social and political realities of Afghan society than the 1923 Constitution.[121]

Pasarlay relies on the theory proposed by Russel Hardin that sees constitutions as 'coordination devices' which powerful actors *voluntarily* choose to abide by.[122] Consequently, the compact should neither be evaluated by its normative

[117] Dupree, *Afghanistan*, (n 1) 471.

[118] See inter alia M Schoiswohl, 'The New Afghanistan Constitution and International Law: A Love-Hate Affair' (2006) 4 *International Journal of Constitutional Law* 664–676.

[119] DN Wilber, *Afghanistan: Its People, Its Society, Its Culture*, 2nd edn (New Haven, Yale University Press, 1962) 145–149.

[120] Dupree, *Afghanistan*, (n 1) 464.

[121] S Pasarlay, *Making the 2004 Constitution of Afghanistan: A History and Analysis through the Lens of Coordination and Deferral Theory*, PhD Dissertation, University of Washington (Seattle, 2016), 77.

[122] ibid, 2–3.

content nor its methodological stringency, but solely on its *effectiveness in coordinating politics*, ie channelling the competing interests of powerful actors.[123] Unlike most commentators, Pasarlay comes to a fairly positive evaluation of the 1931 Constitution, *because* of and not in spite of its many internal contradictions, the prominent role attributed to Islam, and its paralysing distribution of organisational mandates. Precisely because it resolved and precluded little, this arrangement kept all major stakeholders on board and allowed the royal family to maintain its position by neutralising the various competitors, all of whom found a version of their preferred social vision reflected in the Constitution.

Given its longevity and relative success in coordinating diverse social actors for more than three decades – longer than any other constitutional arrangement in Afghanistan to date – the 1931 Constitution could credibly lay claim to be this country's foundational document, were it not for the drastic social changes that occurred in the 1950–1960s and which irredeemably removed the basis for its acceptability. To integrate the new actors and movements brought about by these social changes and the turmoil that accompanied them, King Zahir Shah instigated the process leading to the drafting of the 1964 Constitution. Like its predecessor, the aim of this Constitution was to consolidate state power and to place executive authority on a firmer footing, which took into account these dramatically new social realities. These changes necessitated the creation of a constitutional framework fit for nation-building, thus justifying the enduring importance of the 1964 Constitution as Afghanistan's foundational document.

VII. CONTESTATION AND CONSTITUTIONAL COMPROMISE

The constitutional document that coincided and contributed to the founding of the modern nation-state, however rudimentary, could not have been either the 1923 or the 1931 constitutions. The first was an overly-ambitious vision imposed on a recalcitrant rural population by an urban elite in charge of an exceedingly weak state. The second, recognising that weakness, effectively abandoned social engineering and left an atavistic and fragmented society to its own devices by recognising two long-standing ideological paradigms: traditional Islam and tribal power.

Once the 1931 Constitution was adopted and royal power consolidated, came the 'avuncular period' (1933–1953), which saw the gradual rise of modern, state-provided education, the creation of a small but growing state bureaucracy offering employment opportunities for the newly-trained, and the beginning of

[123] R Hardin, 'Why a Constitution?,' in DJ Galligan and M Versteeg (eds), *Social and Political Foundation of Constitutions* (Cambridge, Cambridge University Press, 2013) 51–72, 61; see also R Hardin, *Liberalism, Constitutionalism and Democracy* (Oxford, Oxford University Press, 1999).

modern, often state-supported manufacturing and cash-crop agriculture. With these socio-economic changes, new political movements emerged: 'liberals' and 'nationalists', and later communists and Islamists. While tribal and religious interests remained powerful, political parties emerged among the newly-created urban intelligentsia that began to dispute the direction of *national* policy based on fundamental *ideological* disagreements.[124]

To be sure, as elsewhere in the developing world, ethnic and tribal affiliation remain powerful to this day and often lurk behind ostensible ideological affiliations.[125] But it was only when political parties entered the scene that real ideological differences were formulated for the first time. Only when national institutions became operational and worth fighting over, did the *idea* of national politics centred around a national Parliament emerge. It is easy to overstate the demographic impact of these changes, as the vast majority of Afghans continued to live very local and isolated lives dominated by tribal affiliation and the dictates of religion and custom. Still, modernity had arrived and irrevocably altered the social make-up of society and its politics. This in turn required a renegotiation of the constitutional order.

After Nadir Shah was assassinated in 1933, his son Mohammad Zahir Shah (1914–2007) became King, but did not rule until much later. For the next 20 years, his three paternal uncles carried out the affairs of the state until 1953, a period during which the external environment dramatically transformed.[126] Aid rents offered generously by the competing geostrategic blocs allowed the Afghan state to drastically expand its internal transformative ambition, while externally the bi-polar competition and the unsettled border issue with newly-independent Pakistan made ordinary Afghans aware of its national existence for the first time. The King's cousin and son-in-law Daoud Khan reflected these new ideological currents, vigorously and divisively pursuing them during his premiership from 1953 to 1963.[127]

[124] These changes are ably summarised in Pasarlay, *Making the 2004 Constitution of Afghanistan*, (n 121) 82–87. It is interesting to note that political parties were envisaged in the political structure laid down in the 1964 Constitution but did not exist yet. Dupree saw this as perhaps the key reason the political system collapsed, see his Epilogue in Dupree, *Afghanistan* (n 1) 664. Once political parties did belatedly emerge from the student politics of the 1960s, their role was disastrous, see T Ruttig, 'Islamists, Leftists – and a Void in the Center: Afghanistan's Political Parties and Where They Come from 1902-2006', Konrad-Adenauer-Stiftung e.V., Berlin und Kabul (2006), available at: www.kas.de/c/document_library/, 4–6.

[125] This became perhaps most visible in the ethnic schism within the communist movement with its mortally antagonistic Parcham and Khalq wings, which were essentially just different designations for the respective Tajik and Pashto groups. For a brief discussion, see inter alia *Background Paper: Afghanistan: Political Parties and Insurgent Groups 1978–2001*, Australian Government: Migration Review Tribunal, Canberra (2014), available at: www.ecoi.net/en/file/local/1154721/1226_1369733568_ ppigl.pdf, 8–10.

[126] For a succinct account of this period, see Dupree, *Afghanistan*, (n 1) 477–498.

[127] Dupree offers here a comprehensive, perhaps overly sympathetic account, see ibid, 499–558. On both periods see also Rubin, *The Fragmentation of Afghanistan*, (n 24); A Rasanayagam, *Afghanistan: A Modern History – Monarchy, Despotism or Democracy? The Problems of Governance in the Muslim Tradition* (London, IB Tauris, 2005).

During this period, intense superpower competition offered many opportunities for the Afghan state to extract financial and technical assistance from both sides, leading to an unusually strong international presence in the country. Large economic and social transformations were underway, fuelling the political movements and parties that had begun to develop in the decades since 1931. When Daoud Khan stepped down in 1963 over the economic disruptions caused by his aggressive stance towards Pakistan over their disputed border ('Pashtunistan'), King Zahir Shah appointed the technocrat Minister of Mines and Industries Dr Mohammad Yousuf as Prime Minister. Where previously the Afghan state had always been the personal responsibility of the ruler and his family, the King now intended to separate the royal family from the affairs of state[128] and to institutionalise government, politics and administrative services in formal, predictable, socially stable and legitimate ways.

The principal means chosen for this task was the drafting of a new constitution. It is this document, promulgated in 1964, which can justly lay claim to be Afghanistan's foundational Constitution. This claim rests on three distinct considerations: First, it was necessitated by and reflected socio-economic changes which irreversibly pushed Afghanistan from its pre-modern, tribal existence into a modern age characterised by an awareness of and necessity for national politics. Second, both process and substance explicitly acknowledged the deep ideological and social divisions in Afghan society; divisions that were created or exacerbated by structural changes of modernity, including urbanisation, expansion of education and pressures towards secularisation. Third, the Constitution coincided with a period of relative social stability, economic growth and institutional development characterised by moderate politics and reasonable accommodation of all groups.

This period came to a sharp end with Daoud Khan's coup on 17 July 1973, who deposed his cousin the King (who was away in Italy seeking medical treatment) and turned Afghanistan into a left-leaning republic. The coup was cataclysmic. Not only did it set off wave after wave of ideological radicalisation, it led to the disintegration of much of the state administration, civil war, mass displacement, economic collapse and societal regression. The left-leaning republic was swept away in a communist coup in 1978, followed by an internal communist counter-coup and an invited Soviet intervention from 1979 to 1988, an internationalised civil war that continued until 1992, followed by an even more intense period of fighting between different warlords until 1996, when the Taliban imposed their draconian rule. It was only in 2001 that the Taliban were toppled from power through international intervention. Each one of these successive regimes introduced their own constitutional document, accompanied by administrative purges, social dislocations and legal revisions. When the

[128] This became the famous Article 24 which forbade members of the royal family – and thus Daoud Khan – to play any part in politics.

internationally supported negotiations for a transitional government convened in November 2001 in Bonn, they quickly settled on the 1964 Constitution as the only consensual and workable basis for the way ahead.[129]

The 1964 Constitution is a remarkable document. Its content has been described by the knowledgeable Louis Dupree as 'the finest in the Muslim world' at the time,[130] a sentiment repeated by others – with far less justification – with respect to the 2004 Constitution that incorporated large parts of it.[131] What made this document so special was the single-minded conviction – primarily on the part of the King – that socio-political conditions in the country had so dramatically changed that merely amending the existing constitutional framework would not be sufficient.

VIII. PROCESS AND SUBSTANCE

As outlined above, the previous two Constitutions had been elite products with extremely little input from and impact on wider sections of a population normatively at odds with that elite. Unlike the first Constitution, which sought to transform society according to a certain image of modernity, and unlike the second Constitution, which contended itself with a certain Potemkin-like unreality that abandoned any pretext of actually seeking to regulate societal affairs and factional politics, it was now felt that a genuine basis for the *res publica* had to be found: effective, workable and acceptable to all. It is this aspiration and the broadly legitimate process that was put into motion to bring it about that merit its designation as a foundational document in the creation of the Afghan nation, understood in the political sense outlined above.

When his cousin stepped down as Prime Minister, King Zahir Shah realised that the internal and external changes of the past three decades required a fundamental reorganisation of the state to accommodate the new political movements that had sprung up alongside the tribes and clergy. Given the large aid payments Afghanistan had benefited from in the past, the state was much stronger than it had ever been since the time of the 'Iron Amir' Abdur Rahman Khan, who ruled from 1880 to 1901. While one should not overstate the coercive ability of this still fragile state apparatus, the constitutional process indicated

[129] Section II(1), 'Agreement on Provisional Arrangements in Afghanistan Pending the Re-establishment of Permanent Government Institutions (Bonn Agreement),' S/2001/1154, New York, United Nations, 5 December 2001, available at: www.un.org/News/dh/latest/afghan/afghan-agree.htm. For the details of the negotiations and the justification of this choice, see Afsah and Guhr, 'Afghanistan', (n 61) 413 et seq.

[130] Dupree, *Afghanistan*, (n 1) 565.

[131] Feldman, for instance, praised it as a model for Islamic democracy, being 'pervasively Islamic' yet 'thoroughly democratic'. See N Feldman, 'A New Democracy, Enshrined in Faith,' *New York Times*, 13 Nov 2003, A31. There are very good reasons, both logically at the time and certainly empirically with the benefit of hindsight, to doubt the wisdom of this assessment.

that the credible threat of physical subjugation did have a moderating influence on tribal and clerical representatives, leading to a remarkable willingness to compromise:

> The writers of the 1964 Afghan Constitution used Islam as a weapon against the traditionalists. The implacable attitude of former Prime Minister Sardar Mohammad Daoud toward the conservative religious leaders helped to smother potential opposition from these quarters during the constitutional *jirgah*. Prime Minister Daoud had not hesitated to use his military base of power to smash any opposition, secular or religious, to his modernization plans. Religious leaders at the *Loya Jirgah* remembered this, and for the most part limited their comments to technical points. They often made long, involved, clarifying statements, sometimes surprisingly objective in the modernist sense.[132]

Except for the years under Abdur Rahman Khan, whatever political structure existed relied on tribal loyalties and customary laws, which in turn depended on personal charisma and communal acceptance. At the 'national' level, this mirrored the traditional power structure at various levels of (Pashto) tribal organisation.[133] In this traditional concept of political authority, it was the tribe that possessed 'sovereign' power to both regulate and adjudicate disputes. At each hierarchical level of tribal organisation, a leader or *khan* was entitled to exercise 'executive' power, but only subject to the acceptance of the collective and its customary law.[134]

Some have, rather anachronistically, described these arrangements as proto-democratic, emphasising the Afghan predilection for equality and autonomy. It is certainly possible to see the *jirga* as a rudimentary form of parliamentary representation, and throughout the subsequent Afghan constitutional history the precedent of the *loya jirga* has served a powerful legitimising and stabilising role. But these positive attributes cannot obscure the fact that all Afghan states have been exceedingly weak in executive power, in particular their ability to collect revenue. It is not necessary to restate here the precise contours of Afghan dynastic succession,[135] but we must note that virtually all Afghan states, from the first recognisably modern one under Abdur Rahman Khan to the present Ghani Government, have relied on subsidies provided by external powers.[136]

[132] Dupree, *Afghanistan*, (n 1) 579.

[133] Described well in Barth, *Political Leadership*, (n 27); and Moltmann, 'Die Verfassungsentwicklung Afghanistans', (n 23) 515.

[134] Similar arrangements existed in many places and the Pashto system of political organisation has been likened for instance to that of the ancient Germanic tribes. See J Schwager, *Die Entwicklung Afghanistans als Staat und seine zwischenstaatlichen Beziehungen* (Liepzig, 1932) 22ff.

[135] For a comprehensive overview of the process of state-formation, see Rubin, *The Fragmentation of Afghanistan*, (n 24) 45ff.

[136] This extreme dependency on foreign financial support is acknowledged in the clear-eyed lessons-learned report by the US Inspector General under the apt heading 'Spending Too Much, Too Fast' JF Sopko, *Stabilization: Lessons from the US Experience in Afghanistan* (Washington, DC, Special Inspector General for Afghanistan Reconstruction, 2018) 56–58. There is little indication that this dependency will abate soon: 'Donors, led by the United States, currently provide some

This aid-dependent rentier state had little interest in engaging in the difficult process of forging a common national identity through the creation of institutions, such as universal basic education, a conscript army, a joint civil service able to collect revenue, etc. As Rubin notes, all Afghan states have followed the same rentier pattern:

> Abdul Rahman Khan used these coercive resources to establish the basic state structures that endured until the fall of Najibullah in 1992: a Pashtun ruler using external resources to reign over an ethnically heterogeneous society while manipulating that social segmentation to weaken society's resistance.[137]

King Zahir Shah resumed power in 1963 while benefitting from a relatively high degree of popular legitimacy and generally low expectations about the delivery of services etc. The constitutional process he immediately set in motion was meant to both bolster his legitimacy, as well as create a better organisational foundation for the functioning of the central government. The process was well managed, avoided centrifugal backlashes, and did result in a much-improved logical structure for running the state machinery. This cannot be said about the 1923 Constitution nor that of 1931. What thus set the 1964 Constitution apart is the procedural legitimacy it achieved and the lack of popular, especially rural opposition it engendered.

One of the reasons it was successful in this regard is its relative lack of ambition in terms of social engineering and nation-building. The lack of a nation corresponding to a modern political entity is fairly common and it is questionable whether ambitious nation-building efforts along the prototypical French model are possible in the weak institutional environments typically encountered in the developing world. In the Afghan context, a strong national identity ultimately came about not through the state's deliberate social engineering, but paradoxically through the collapse of that state and the common experience of exile and resistance.[138] To be sure, this national identity came to coexist with equally strong ethnic affiliations, but despite continued strong inter-ethnic antagonisms, the *idea* of Afghanistan and the desirability of belonging to its community is no longer questioned by any significant group or individual. Ironically, it has been the common experience of conflict and displacement – both strongly driven by

$8.5 billion a year in on-budget grants to the Afghan government and in off-budget spending for reconstruction. These financial inflows account for about 75% of the country's public expenditures for security, education, law enforcement, health, and other development functions. The United States alone provides more than $4 billion a year for reconstruction efforts in Afghanistan – not including the costs of U.S. military operations there.' JF Sopko, *46th Quarterly Report to the United States Congress* (Washington, DC, Special Inspector General for Afghanistan Reconstruction, 30 January 2020), available at: www.sigar.mil/pdf/quarterlyreports/2020-01-30qr.pdf.

[137] Rubin, *The Fragmentation of Afghanistan*, (n 24) 19.

[138] The eventual creation of an Afghan national consciousness through the shared experience of displacement, exile and war is well told by CJ Schetter, 'Der Afghanistankrieg – Die Ethnisierung eines Konflikts' (2002) 33(1/2) *Internationales Asienforum* 15.

ethnic rivalries – that has achieved what generations of idealistic intellectuals and social engineers failed to achieve: the existence of the Afghan state is no longer questioned by anyone.[139]

Where prior to the onset of violent conflict in 1978, most Afghans perceived of themselves primarily in terms of kinship only very loosely tied to territory, the dual impact of foreign invasion and political fragmentation created for the first time a truly *national* identity.[140] Before the conflict, neither the Afghan state nor membership in the nation meant much to a geographically sequestered and ethnically diverse population.[141] This changed through the common experience of exile and military struggle, giving tangible meaning to the idea of the nation as a group sharing a common fate, a '*communauté de destin*'.[142]

This development has had major tangible benefits. There are, for instance, virtually zero incidences of secession or receptiveness to outside irredentist overtures despite continuing extreme antagonism between ethnically-organised armed groups. This is a remarkable state of affairs for anyone familiar with ethnic conflict elsewhere.[143] Contrary to what most observers continue to claim, Afghanistan is therefore *not* in need of nation-building, because a very strong sense of national identity has already come into existence.[144] What it still needs to establish is a political culture of institutionalised collaboration and peaceful disagreement:

> The fundamental need in Afghanistan is not nation building, as is so often said … Afghanistan is a nation, though disputes over how to govern and share power in that nation are acute. What Afghanistan needs above all is assistance in building a state.[145]

Such assistance has been forthcoming in unprecedented levels since the September 2001 terrorist attacks led to the American ultimatum to the Taliban Government to hand over the perpetrators it had been sheltering. The Taliban's refusal to do so led to the American invasion of the country, legally justified with reference to self-defence. As this claim was widely accepted by the international community, the invasion led to a broadly legitimate and supported international assistance effort. The initial basis for these efforts was the 1964

[139] '… le pouvoir central n'est pas remis en question'. O Roy, 'De la stabilité de l'État en Afghanistan' (2004) 59(5/6) *Annales Histoire, Sciences Sociales* 1183–1202, 1202.

[140] Schetter, 'Der Afghanistankrieg', (n 138).

[141] Rubin, *The Fragmentation of Afghanistan*, (n 24) 22.

[142] Bachardoust, *Afghanistan*, (n 60) 21.

[143] S Tang, 'The Security Dilemma and Ethnic Conflict: Toward a Dynamic and Integrative Theory of Ethnic Conflict' (2011) 37 *Review of International Studies* 511–536; SM Saideman and RW Ayres, 'Determining the Causes of Irredentism' (2000) 62(4) *Journal of Politics* 1126–1144; D Carment and P James, 'Internal Constraints and Interstate Ethnic Conflict: Toward a Crisis-Based Assessment of Irredentism' (1995) 39(1) *Journal of Conflict Resolution* 82–109.

[144] Roy, 'De la stabilité de l'État en Afghanistan', (n 139) 1202.

[145] BR Rubin, 'Statement to Implementation Group,' 2002, available at: www.unama-afg.org/docs/; Rubin, '(Re)Building Afghanistan', (n 40).

Constitution, correctly identified as the one document in the palimpsest of Afghan law both substantially sound and broadly legitimate. Forming the basis for the interim and transitional governments, it likewise served as the model for both the substance and the procedure of the 2004 Constitution. Both of these documents suffer from considerable shortcomings and internal contradictions, not least with respect to the ill-understood concept of the separation of powers and, as in virtually all other Muslim nations, differences about the appropriate role of religion and especially Islamic law in public life. Nevertheless, either document could have served as an adequate basis for a reasonably effective and representative state, were it not for lack of other crucial ingredients, most notably an inchoate political culture and a dysfunctional civil service.

IX. CONCLUSION

The 1964 Constitution plays an awkward role in this context. The conventional wisdom – much appreciated and propagated by Afghans themselves – holds that a reasonably efficient, generally benevolent state existed prior to the onset of violent conflict. During that romanticised 'golden age' in the decade from 1963 to 1973, relations between different societal groups were constructive, state and economic capacity was steadily rising, and the overall trajectory looked promising. To be sure, this idealised picture is heavily influenced by the terrible events that followed and more than a little rosy tint of nostalgia is discernible. The state was very weak, human capital was exceedingly feeble, with literacy hovering around 5 per cent, and other indicators of human and economic development equally abysmal. Still, in 1972, Louis Dupree, perhaps the most knowledgeable scholar of that country, could end his magisterial book by stating with confidence:

> Afghanistan's problems and prospects are not unique in the Afro-Asian world, but, so far, its actions toward problem solving have been more sensible and less bloody than most. On whatever social, economic, political, or cultural scale one wishes to use, the Afghans have made as much, if not more, progress (however defined) as any other developing nation.[146]

While he candidly acknowledged persisting problems, especially the utterly dispiriting and irresponsible nature of Afghan politics,[147] Dupree notes approvingly that a *vision* for the future existed. A vision, to be sure, which remained to be implemented against the odds, but a vision nonetheless and one that was broadly shared by elites and public alike. This vision had been laid down in

[146] Dupree, *Afghanistan*, (n 1) 663.
[147] Dupree described parliamentary politics of the time as a 'charade' comparable to a (bad) Hollywood thriller, (n 1) 664.

a foundational document carefully set in motion by the King. It was skilfully drafted and, perhaps even more importantly, legitimised through an elaborate, extensive and culturally appropriate process.[148]

Both its substantive quality and its procedural legitimacy separated it from the documents that came before and after it, and it came to embody genuinely popular aspirations during a rare hopeful period in Afghanistan's history. In hindsight, the King and the Constitution he had initiated became symbols for a 'golden' period when Afghans still acted 'more sensibly and less bloody than most'. But signs of trouble were already evident at that time. This was not unexpected, given the inherent challenges for a society being propelled into modernity. Dupree thus wrote accurately if ominously in 1972, just a year before the constitutional monarchy was swept away in a coup:

> The Constitution has become a cultural document, expressing the ideals of society and establishing the mechanics for achieving these ideals. In addition, the fate of the Constitution relates to the fate and fortunes of King Mohammed Zahir Shah. If anything should happen to him, the whole course of political development could be drastically changed. The King serves as a symbol to his people until constitutional ideals can be transformed into realities – until the nation-state ceases to be an abstraction.[149]

In hindsight, the 1964 Constitution proved quite inadequate as a blueprint for the 'mechanics' of governance, which had less to do with its substantive content, both normative and operational, than with inadequate administrative capacity and political culture. Before its descent into fratricide, radicalisation and mass displacement, Afghanistan under the constitutional monarchy appeared like a *normal* country and her odds for success did not look too bad. Like other southern nations, the country seemed to tread along a clearly-defined developmental path. The actual circumstances that accounted for Afghanistan's enduring descent into chaos are highly contingent, linked to unique geo-political and local conditions unlikely to be repeated elsewhere. Still, the persistent failure of constitutional transplants to take root and serve as an effective basis for governance in much of the southern world seems to indicate that a more organic and comprehensive approach to constitution-making is required:

> Constitutions can flourish and succeed only if they are firmly planted in the cultural soil from which they gain legitimacy. Thus, growing constitutions embodies the not so novel idea that constitutions and laws should reflect and be derived from the cultural norms in which they must endure. Constitutions that are not firmly grounded in the cultural mores of the society in which they operate are destined to fail, become irrelevant, or be shaped and adapted to meet the needs of the culture and society in which

[148] The process is described in detail in Dupree, ibid, 565–87.
[149] ibid, 663.

> they are situated. Indeed, most postcolonial constitutions in Sub-Saharan Africa have largely succumbed to irrelevance and debacle.[150]

Ruth Gordon continues to explain the failure of post-colonial constitutional transplants due to their reliance on foreign concepts with little or no connection to the cultural landscape they are meant to govern. She contrasts this with the experience of Somaliland, where without external assistance a constitutional compact was created based on the culture, knowledge and experiences of the people themselves, concerning issues that truly mattered to them.[151] The same could have been said about the process that led to the 1964 Afghan constitution, which likewise did not rely much on external technical advice and did broadly incorporate local sentiments. The very high esteem with which Afghans to this day hold that Constitution and the monarch who instigated it reflects this local anchoring.

The 1964 Constitution thus became the cherished symbol for three things: an era many remembered as stable and prosperous; ideological and ethnic unity; and international esteem for what was then (and in many respects, still is) considered one of the most progressive, technically sophisticated constitutional documents in the Muslim world. Both its high technical quality and, especially, its symbolic value as the repository of positive communal memories ensured that it would form the natural basis for the 2004 Constitution, conceived after a similarly inclusive consultation and drafting process. The failure to create a constitutional government, or any type of effective government after both 1964 and 2004 seems to point to a darker truth not fully acknowledged by most comparative constitutional scholars: neither the process nor the substance of a constitutional settlement might matter as much as it is often assumed. What seems to have doomed the enterprise was the failure to patiently build the mundane institutional underpinnings of modern government rather than settle the higher order normative disputes that arose. After all, constitutionalism presupposes the existence of a modicum of governance.[152]

[150] R Gordon, 'Growing Constitutions' (1999) 1(3) *University of Pennsylvania Journal of Constitutional Law* 528–582, 530–531.

[151] ibid, 532 & 582. See also S Chesterman, *You, the People: The United Nations, Transitional Administration, and State-Building* (Oxford, Oxford University Press, 2004).

[152] Rubin, '(Re)Building Afghanistan', (n 40); Afsah, 'Constitutionalism without Governance', (n 41).

Index

www.ingramcontent.com/pod-product-compliance
Ingram Content Group UK Ltd.
Pitfield, Milton Keynes, MK11 3LW, UK
UKHW020249290926
15470UKWH00002B/817

9 781509 930258